NATIVE AMERICAN GENEALOGICAL SOURCEBOOK

Genealogy Sourcebook Series

African American Genealogical Sourcebook

First edition

Asian American Genealogical Sourcebook

First edition

Hispanic American Genealogical Sourcebook

First edition

Native American Genealogical Sourcebook

First edition

NATIVE AMERICAN GENEALOGICAL SOURCEBOOK

edited by
Paula K. Byers

An International Thomson Publishing Company

NEW YORK • LONDON • BONN • BOSTON • DETROIT • MADRID
MELBOURNE • MEXICO CITY • PARIS • SINGAPORE • TOKYO
TORONTO • WASHINGTON • ALBANY NY • BELMONT CA • CINCINNATI OH

Staff

Editor: Paula K. Byers
Managing Editor: Neil E. Walker
Contributing Editor: Charles B. Montney
Associate Editors: Brian Escamilla, Christopher M. McKenzie, Geri J. Speace
Permissions Associate: Maria L. Franklin

Production Manager: Mary Beth Trimper

Product Design Manager: Cindy Baldwin
Art Director: Pamela Galbreath

Manager of Data Entry Services: Benita Spight
Data Entry Supervisor: Rhonda A. Willis
Data Entry Coordinator: Gwendolyn Tucker
Senior Data Entry Associate: Civie Ann Green

Systems and Programming Supervisor: Theresa A. Rocklin
Programmer: Charles Beaumont

This book is printed on acid-free paper that meets the minimum requirements of American National Standard for Information Sciences—Permanence Paper for Printed Library Materials, ANSI Z39.48-1984. ♾™

ISBN 0-8103-9229-1
Printed in the United States of America

I(T)P Gale Research Inc., an International Thomson Publishing Company.
ITP logo is a trademark under license.

Library of Congress Cataloging-in-Publication Data

Native American genealogical sourcebook / edited by Paula K. Byers.
p. cm.
Includes bibliographical references and indexes.
ISBN 0-8103-9229-1
1. Indians of North America—Genealogy—Handbooks, manuals, etc.
2. Indians of North America—Genealogy—Directories. 3. North America--Genealogy--Research--Handbooks, manuals, etc. I. Byers, Paula K. (Paula Kay), 1954-
E98.G44N37 1995
929'.1'08997--dc20 95-36734

10 9 8 7 6 5 4 3 2 1

Native American Genealogical Sourcebook Advisory Board

Table of Contents

List of Figures

Records Specific to Native Americans - Addendum

Introduction to *Native American Genealogical Sourcebook*

Native American Genealogical Sourcebook is the fourth volume to be published in the *Genealogy Sourcebook Series (GSS)*. This series is designed to be a first-stop guide to researching the genealogy of any person with a(n) Native, Asian, African, or Hispanic American heritage.

Native American Genealogical Sourcebook is a convenient guide which includes all the information required to begin genealogical research. Part I consists of informative essays prepared by Mary Lynn Sharpe, George J. Nixon, and Jimmy B. Parker - all experts in the field of Native American genealogy. Combining historical data and practical genealogical advice, the essays reveal the steps that must be taken to ensure a successful search for information. The essays cover:

- The basic migration patterns of Native Americans in the United States and historical events which impacted their lives.
- Traditions and customs which, when described and explained, will ensure that the information discovered will be interpreted correctly.
- Basic genealogical records, an explanation of the data they contain, and their pertinence to the research of Native Americans.
- Genealogical records particular to Native Americans — their location and what information they provide with an addendum specifically detailing records pertaining to the Five Civilized Tribes.
- Concrete examples of what may be found in a genealogical record to help in applying the information to ancestral research.

In addition, a bibliography is provided at the end of each essay as a guide to further information.

Part II lists information resources which can provide just thc help needed to overcome obstacles in your research. Hundreds of national, regional, state, and foreign organizations and media are listed including:

- libraries and archives
- genealogical societies
- museums
- newsletters
- databases
- microfilm/microfiche
- periodicals
- guides and directories

These entries were carefully selected from a comprehensive database compiled by Gale Research Inc. Additionally, new information was compiled or updated from telephone research, questionnaires, and key secondary sources to ensure the comprehensiveness and accuracy of the information found in this section of the sourcebook.

Part III provides three indexes. The Author, and Title and Organization indexes will allow you to quickly find sources of information listed in Part II. The Subject index allows you to pinpoint information provided in the essays in Part I concerning a specific topic.

Concept and Scope

While the large scope of the subject area precludes answering every question that may arise, this sourcebook will serve to get you started, showing you where and how any further information you may need can be found.

The basics of genealogical research have been included regardless of ethnic background because depending on how many generations have passed since the lifetime of the ancestor being researched, the basic records can apply to all. The more recently in time the object of your research lived, the more likely this will be true. Libraries, archives, organizations, and media which have a broad focus, non-specific to Native Americans, are included for the same reason. The experts or material found therein will be able to offer direction to those Native American genealogical groups, archives, and materials which are available locally. Knowing these basic avenues will also allow you to converse and exchange information with or ask questions of other genealogists or family researchers.

Also included herein are organizations/media specifically concerned with Native Americans. The farther back your ancestor lived in time, the more imperative information unique to this group becomes.

In order to get the maximum benefit from the information provided in this volume, it is highly recommended that you read the **User's Guide** which directly follows this introduction.

Acknowledgements

Our thanks for the use of the material detailing mission records:

Carriker, Robert C. and Eleanor R. Carriker. From *Guide to the Microfilm Edition of the Pacific Northwest Tribes Missions Collection of the Oregon Province Archives of the Society of Jesus.* Scholarly Resources Inc., 1987. © Copyright 1987 by Scholarly Resources Inc. Reprinted by permission of Scholarly Resources Inc.

We would also like to express our appreciation to the Advisory Board members, Mary G. Butler Hilliard, Jimmy B. Parker, and Patricia Smith (*White Buffalo Woman*), for their advice and recommendations concerning the production of this volume.

Suggestions and Comments are Welcome

We see the *GSS* as an ongoing series, constantly reflecting advancements and changes in the field of genealogical research. As such, we appreciate any suggestions or information you may provide. Further, if we listed an organization or database which is not very helpful or neglected a publication or archive which you consider essential, do not hesitate to let us know about it. All questions, suggestions, and comments may be sent to:

Genealogy Sourcebook Series
Gale Research Inc.
General Biography/Genealogy
835 Penobscot Building
Detroit, MI 48226-4094
Phone: (313)961-2242
Fax: (313)961-6741
Toll-free: (800)347-GALE

User's Guide

Native American Genealogical Sourcebook consists of three parts: essays on genealogical research; a directory of libraries and archives, private and public organizations, print resources, and other media which aid one in applying the information provided in the essays; and a section of indexes listing the authors, titles and organizations, and subjects covered herein.

Part I. Conducting Genealogical Research

This section consists of three chapters of essays. At the end of each chapter is a bibliography of sources which were either mentioned in the essay or enhance the information provided within that chapter.

Background Material - Things to Know Before You Begin

Historical Overview. Information on the migration of Native Americans in United States - how, why, and to what extent it occurred. Describes the policies and laws of the various governments with which Native Americans interacted. The addendum at the end of this chapter provides a timeline which highlights historical events in the fifteenth through the nineteenth centuries that impact genealogical research of this group.

Possible Problems in Interpreting Data. Discussion of the confusion caused by lack of knowledge about naming customs of Native Americans, tribal location and affiliation, enrollment status, family customs and the meanings of various terms of kinship, and other things which might cause one to misinterpret data.

Basic Genealogical Research Methods and Their Application to Native Americans

Getting Started. Explains how a family researcher or genealogist finds information and records the data so that it is easily and quickly accessed when needed and the methodology is campatible to that used by other researchers, encouraging the sharing of information. Discusses the various forms used for recording information. Emphasizes the importance of citing the source of that information.

Basic Genealogical Sources. Lists the basic records genealogists seek when conducting research and specifically states how important each is in the conduction of Native American research.

Secondary Sources. Defines secondary sources (specifically newspapers, periodicals, newsletters, and bibliographies) and their relevance to family researchers.

Repositories. Explains the importance of several types of repositories. Lists those holding collections important to Native Americans.

Case History. Traces a specific Native American family through various genealogical records. Shows how and what information can be located in certain documents.

Records Specific to Native Americans

Historical Background. Provides a brief summary of the institutions created by the U.S. government to deal with Native Americans.

Records. Describes records created specifically for Native Americans - the reason for their creation, what information was listed, where the records may be located, etc. The addendum at the end of this chapter details records that are available which pertain to the Five Civilized Tribes.

Records Custodians. Outlines the broad range of respositories, organizations, private individuals, churches, etc. which might house genealogical collections concerning Native Americans.

Secondary Sources. Discusses published Native American genealogies, histories, and biographies. Emphasizes the usefulness of publications of local historical and genealogical societies.

Part II. Directory of Genealogical Information

This section consists of four chapters providing information on organizations or media which may prove helpful in conducting genealogical research (**for information as to how to read each entry, *see* the section "Reading an Entry" which appears after the description of "Other Media" and precedes the description of Part III**):

Libraries and Archives

This chapter lists federal, state, local, university, and foreign libraries or archives which hold sources valuable to genealogical researchers. Entries are arranged alphabetically by the state where they are located and subarranged alphabetically by name within each state. All fifty states, plus the District of Columbia, are included. Libraries and archives whose name implies a national or regional focus can be found listed in the "National and Regional" section which precedes the listings by state. However, it should be kept in mind that many of the libraries and archives listed by state may also have a national or regional focus. Any archive or library particularly helpful to Native American research located in a country outside the United States is listed at the end of the states.

Private and Public Organizations

This chapter lists national, regional, state, and local genealogical societies, museums, and other groups which may provide instruction, materials, or referrals. Entries are arranged alphabetically by the state where they are located and subarranged alphabetically by name within each state. All fifty states, plus the District of Columbia, are included. Organizations whose name implies a national or regional focus can be found listed in the "National and Regional" section which precedes the listings by state. However, it should be kept in mind that many of the organizations listed by state may also have a national or regional focus. Any organization helpful to Native American research located in a country outside the United States is listed at the end of the states.

Print Resources

This chapter lists periodicals, books, atlases, newspapers, and other print material which may help further your research. Again, listings are arranged alphabetically by state, however they are listed not under the state where they are published but under the state which their content covers. For example, *Ottawa and Chippewa Indians of Michigan, 1855-1868*, though published in Maryland, would be listed under Michigan. Any sources covering several states or various regional areas appear under the "National and Regional" section which precedes the state listings. Foreign sources are listed at the end of the section.

Other Media

This chapter covers electronic, video, microfilm, or microfiche sources. Entries are arranged alphabetically by product title.

Reading an Entry

Entries in *Libraries and Archives* and *Private and Public Organizations*. A brief description of the individual components of the fictitious entry shown at the bottom of the next page follows. Each numbered item in the entry is explained in the descriptive paragraph bearing the same number.

[1] **Name of Organization or Library/Archive.** Name of parent organization, society, library, archive or agency that is supportive of genealogical research. *See* item 22 (**AKA**) for those organizations which may be known by two or more distinct names.

[2] **Address.** The permanent address of the library, archive, organization.

[3] **Phone**. Phone, fax, and/or toll-free number(s) of addressee.

[4] **Contact.** Contact person or an officer of the organization, library, or archive listed.

[5] **Staff.** Number of employees.

[6] **Description.** Purpose of organization.

[7] **Founded.** Date archive, organization, or library was founded.

[8] **Subjects.** Subject area(s) covered by the library or archive.

[9] **Members.** Membership of the organization.

[10] **Special collections.** Any special manuscripts, files,

materials held by the library or archive.

11 **Regional groups.** Number of regional groups affiliated with the organization.

12 **State groups.** Number of state groups affiliated with the organization.

13 **Local groups.** Number of local groups affiliated with the organization.

14 **Holdings.** Number of volumes or archival materials held by the library or archive.

15 **Subscriptions.** Number of serials and magazines subscribed to by the library or archive.

16 **Services.** Whether library or archive offers interlibrary loan, copying, or any other services to its patrons.

17 **Computerized services.** Electronic services the library or archive offers - Internet access, on-line searches, etc.

18 **Telecommunication services.** Electronic mail address of the organization.

19 **Special catalogs.** Specialized catalogs that the library or archive has available for patrons' use concerning a specific topic or format.

20 **Special indexes.** Specialized index that the library orarchive has available for patrons' use concerning a specific topic or format.

21 **Affiliated with.** Name of any organization with which listee is affiliated.

22 **Also known as.** Any other names by which the library, archive, or organization may be known.

23 **Formerly.** Any name by which the library, archives, or organization used to be known.

24 **Remarks.** Additional information on the library, archive, or organization which might be useful.

25 **Publications.** Name of publication produced by the library, archive, or organization.

Entries in *Print Resources* and *Other Media*. A brief description of the individual components of the fictitious entry shown on the next page follows. Each numbered item is explained in the descriptive paragraph bearing the same number.

26 **Name of Product.** Name of publication, database, video, or microfiche which provides genealogical information. *See* item 60 (**AKA**) for media which may be known by two or more names.

---

1 **Norton Genealogical and Biographical Society**
2 101 Oath Street
New York, NY 10013

3 Phone: (123)123-4567
4 Willard Q. Tohn, Exec. Dir.

5 **Staff:** 11. 6 **Description:** To discover, procure, and perpetuate information and items relating to genealogy, geography, and local history. Maintains research library of 65,000 sources including manuscripts and microforms; publishes compiled data and source material for genealogists and historians. 7 **Founded:** 1869. 8 **Subjects:** Ancestry of Africans, Hispanics, Asians, and Native Americans. 9 **Members:** 1400. 10 **Special Collections:** Gorton Historical Collection on localities surrounding Gorton, NH. 11 **Regional Groups:** 8. 12 **State Groups:** 50. 13 **Local Groups:** 225. 14 **Holdings:** 17,000 volumes and manuscripts. 15 **Subscriptions:** 240 serials. 16 **Services:** Interlibrary loan. 17 **Computerized Services:** Internet access; OPAC. 18 **Telecommunications services:** Electronic mail address, jonesc@cmu.edux. 19 **Special Catalogs:** Union List of Serials for Maryland. 20 **Special Indexes:** Indexes, guides, and bulletins to the proprietary collection. 21 **Affiliated with:** National Association for History. 22 **Also known as:** American Institute for Southern Genealogy. 23 **Formerly:** U.S. Genealogical Institute (1986). 24 **Remarks:** Subscription includes an surname locating service. 25 **Publications:** *Newsletter*, semiannual; *Norton Genealogical and Biographical Record (NYG&B)*, quarterly; offers list of publications.

[27] **Address.** The permanent address of the publisher or vendor which produces or distributes the publication, database, video, or microfiche product. Phone. Phone, fax, and/or toll free-number(s) of addressee.

[28] **Phone.** Phone, fax, and/or toll-free number(s) of addressee.

[29] **Contact.** Author, editor, or contact person for the product listed.

[30] **Subtitle.** Subtitle of print source.

[31] **Covers.** Subject material covered in the print source.

[32] **Publication includes.** Type of information included in the print source.

[33] **Description.** General information describing the source.

[34] **Languages.** Indicates the different language versions of the medium available.

[35] **Type.** Indicates the product type - digest, bibliography, microfiche, CD-Rom, etc.

[36] **Entries include.** Describes the information each entry in the print source includes.

[37] **First Published.** Date the print source was first published.

[38] **Arrangement.** How the material in the print source is arranged.

[39] **Indexes.** Whether, and what type of, indexes appear in the print source.

[40] **Pages.** Number of pages in the print source.

[41] **Subjects.** Subjects covered in the print source or other medium.

[42] **Audience.** Intended readership of the print source.

---

[26] ***A Guide to Research in Brighton, Iowa***

[27] 246 MacElroy Avenue
Suite 246A
Des Moines, IA 36692

[28] Phone: (456)789-1233
Fax: (222)898-7897

[29] Sarah Day-Byner, Author

[30] **Subtitle:** *A Guide to Resources in Your Area.* [31] **Covers:** 200 organizations concerned with genealogy. [32] **Publication includes:** List of newspapers published since 1890. [33] **Description:** To list and decribe organizations which provide resources necessary to conduct genealogical research. [34] **Languages:** Korean, English. [35] **Type:** Directory. [36] **Entries include:** Organization name, address and phone number. [37] **First published:** 1993. [38] **Arrangement:** Classified alphabetically by organization name. [39] **Indexes:** State, subject. [40] **Pages:** 50. [41] **Subjects:** Vital statistics from the tri-state area of Indiana, Ohio, and Kentucky. [42] **Audience:** Genealogists and historians. [43] **Frequency:** Biannual, March. [44] **Indexed:** Biannually in *Genealogy Resource Index (GRI).* [45] **Publication Date:** March 1993. [46] **Circulation:** 17,000. [47] **Price:** $14.95, plus $2.50 shipping; payment with order. [48] **Subscription:** $22.95/yr. [49] **Send orders to:** Acme Publications, Box 22, Dayton, OH 45426. [50] **U.S. Distributor:** Genealogical Publications Co., P.O. Box 97, 204 Malvern St., Phoenix, NM 44238. [51] **ISBN:** 0-8103-7126-3. [52] **ISSN:** 0197-562X. [53] **Geographic coverage:** Northwestern U.S. [54] **Timespan:** Most recent two years. [55] **Updating:** Quarterly. [56] **Also includes:** Glossary, list of special collections. [57] **Online availability:** DIALOG Information Services (file 266). [58] **Also on line as part of:** Genealogical and Historial Abstracts. [59] **Alternate electronic formats:** CD-ROM, General History Index. [60] **Also known as:** *Directory of Regional Facts.* [61] **Former titles:** *Directory of Local History* (1972). [62] **Former database name:** Genealogy Line. [63] **Remarks:** Subscription includes a surname locating service.

43 **Frequency.** How often the print source is published.

44 **Indexed.** If and how often the print source is indexed.

45 **Publication date.** Date current edition of product was published.

46 **Circulation.** Number of subscribers to print source.

47 **Price.** Price of source.

48 **Subscription.** Cost of periodical subscription.

49 **Send orders to.** Address to send print source orders to if different from main address.

50 **U.S. distributor.** U.S. distributors of any publications produced by foreign countries.

51 **ISBN.** ISBN of the print product.

52 **ISSN.** ISSN of the print product.

53 **Geographic coverage.** Describes areas covered by the material in the medium cited.

54 **Timespan.** The timespan covered in the medium.

55 **Updating.** How often the medium is updated.

56 **Also includes.** Additional information included in the print source.

57 **Online availability.** Lists electronic formats from other producers allowing access to the product.

58 **Also online as part of.** Lists electronic formats which include this product as part of their larger database.

59 **Alternate electronic formats.** Availability of the product in electronic formats produced by the same publisher.

60 **Also known as.** Other names by which the product is known.

61 **Former titles.** Former name(s) by which the print source was known.

62 **Former database name.** Former name(s) by which the database was known.

63 **Remarks.** Additional information on the product which might be useful.

Part III. Indexes

This section consists of author, title and organization, and subject indexes which provide the page number(s) wherein the information cited can be located.

Author Index

All appearances of a specific author or editor cited in the "Print Resources" and "Other Media" sections of Part II are listed and the page number(s) on which this information appears are provided.

Title and Organization Index

All appearances of a specific title or organization name cited in Part II are cited and the page number(s) on which the information appears are provided.

Subject Index

Page number(s) wherein a specific topic, term, or location is discussed in the essays located in Part I are cited.

Part I
Conducting Genealogical Research

**Background Material —
Things to Know before You Begin**

**Basic Genealogical Research Methods
& Their Application to Native Americans**

Records Specific to Native Americans

Background Material—Things to Know Before You Begin

Mary Lynn Sharpe

Mary Lynn Sharpe, A.G., is a professional genealogist accredited in Native American research. A free-lance writer, she also serves as a specialist in the Family History Department of the Genealogical Society of Utah in Salt Lake City.

Historical Overview

The history of North American Indians is a broad topic not easily covered in one book, much less in one chapter. Many approaches of study are possible. However, the focus here will be on genealogical research—the process of searching written records to trace a family back over the generations.

Since no tribe in pre-Columbian times had an alphabet or a written language, there are no early written records kept by the tribes. However, alternatives to written records do exist. Each tribe had an oral tradition which told of their beginnings as humans or as a society. These myths of origin were important in the religious expression of the tribe. Some tribes used pictographs to record important events and time counts on cliff or cave walls or animal hides. For example, the Kiowa and Sioux made a winter count, describing the year's events with pictographs on buffalo hides. Seasonal counts were common especially with the Plains tribes. In addition to significant events, the number of individuals (but not their names) in a tribe were noted as were, sometimes, the number of horses owned. Some eastern tribes used *wampum* belts (introduced by European traders as a form of currency) as a mnemonic to record important events. Different colored shell beads were used to convey specific messages: red or black meant war; white meant peace. While each of these records tell about the history and culture of a tribe, they are less useful in determining genealogical data: names, dates, and places.

For that reason, this historical overview concentrates on the time period after the arrival of the Europeans in the New World. If this section is less about Native American history and more about the policies of the European and American institutions that surrounded and intruded upon the activities of Native Americans in North America, it is because it was these institutions which began creating written records about Native Americans. This section gives a brief overview of the historical periods when records with genealogical information were kept. The bibliography at the end of the chapter has suggestions for further study.

Major Culture Areas in 1500

It is generally accepted by historians that the original natives of America drifted into the Western hemisphere from Asia across a land bridge where the Bering Strait now separates Alaska and Siberia. These immigrants multiplied and spread from Alaska through South America. Their gradual adaption to new environments eventually established the cultures of the historic tribes met by European explorers. Population estimates vary, but there may have been as many as seventy-two million Native Americans in the Western hemisphere by 1492. By the time Europeans arrived in the Americas, they had divided into hundreds of tribes with different cultures. Nearly 300 different languages were used by over seven million people living north of the Rio Grande by 1500.

In this chapter, *tribe* (the ambiguity of which is discussed in the section ''Possible Problems in Interpreting Data'') is used generically for convenience, not to generalize about the various Native American cultures and societies. These societies varied from wandering bands to complex nations composed of families grouped into clans. In a few more populous nations, the clans were part of a larger subdivision called a *moiety*. Within each moiety the clans were ranked by custom and prestige. The most important clans made up the military, political, and religious leadership of the nation.

It is not practical to provide histories of each tribe herein. However, it is possible to classify the tribes into

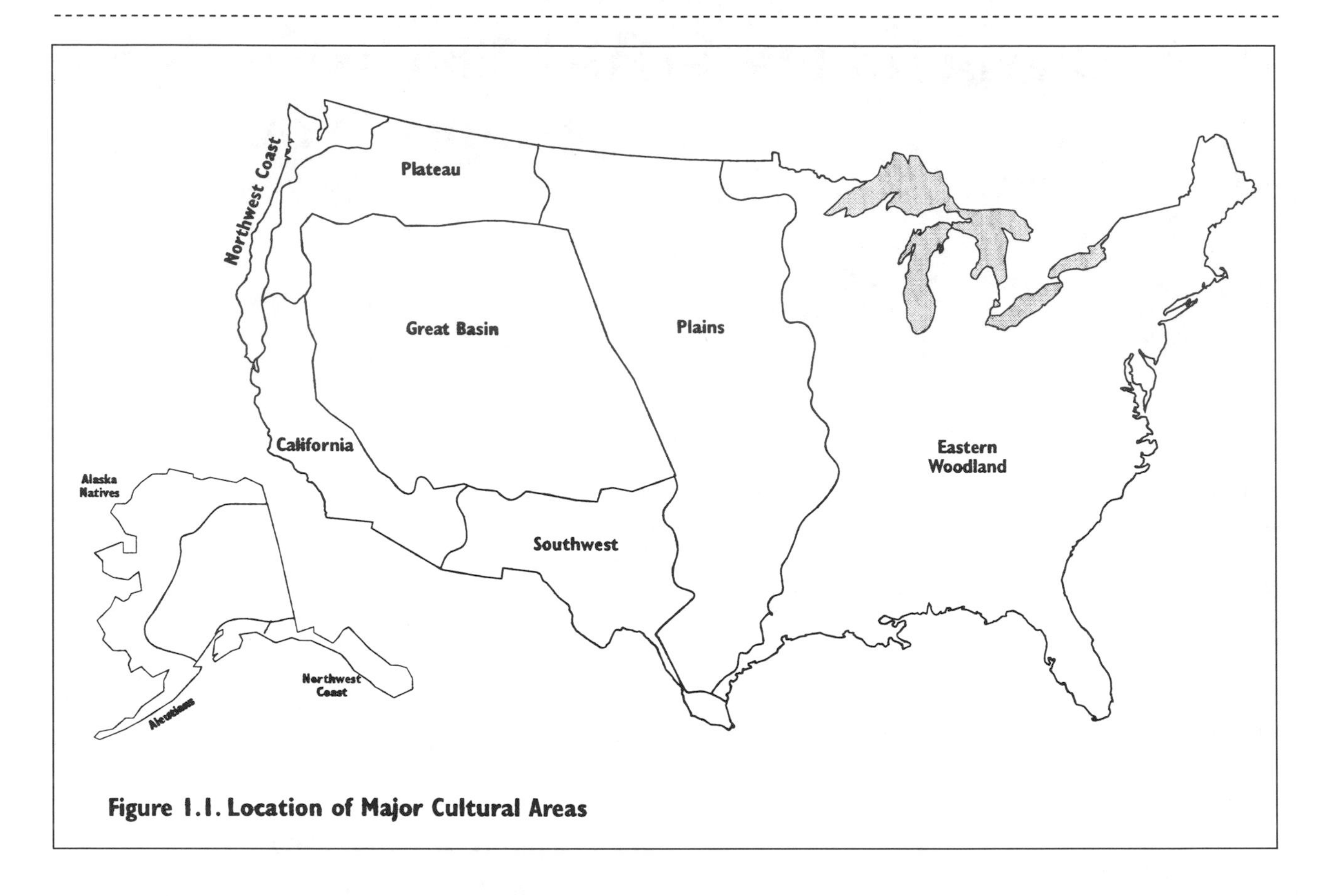

Figure 1.1. Location of Major Cultural Areas

major culture groups based on their daily and seasonal life, language, family and kinship systems, and economic structure. (See Figure 1.1.) The background of the culture groups illustrates the diversity of North American Indians and establishes the basis for understanding their later history.

Eastern Woodland. This area ranged from the St. Lawrence River and the Great Lakes to the Gulf of Mexico and from the Atlantic coast to the Mississippi River. The principal language families were Algonquin, Iroquoian, Muskhogean, and Siouan.

The tribes who spoke the Algonquin languages were in two groups. The northern group, which included the Abenaki, Penobscot, and Chippewa, ranged from the north shore of the Great Lakes eastward into Maine. Because of the cold climate they practiced no agriculture, sustaining life by hunting, fishing, and gathering roots. Tribes were nomadic with no permanent villages. Descent was patrilineal, reckoned through the father's family.

The southern group, living where the climate was warmer, supplemented their hunter-gatherer economy by farming semi-permanent village sites. Some of the tribes had matrilineal social systems. The entire group established a complex political organization arranged in confederations for mutual defense.

The Iroquois tribes lived year round in permanent villages enclosed by log palisades and were concentrated in the southern border area of Canada and northern New York. Their economy was based on agriculture with some hunting and gathering. They also traded with other tribes. Their society was matrilineal, family continuity and clan affiliation were determined through women. Each nation was governed by a council of *sachems* or headmen chosen by the female heads of clans. There was a strong warrior tradition and the tribes were noted for the confederations they established for mutual defense. The largest tribes in this language family, the Seneca, Cayuga, Oneida, Onondaga, and Mohawk, were organized into the League of the Five Nations. (In 1713, after the Tuscaroras moved north, it became the League of the Six Nations.)

The Muskhogean tribes lived in an area which ranged from the southern Atlantic Coast to the lower Mississippi valley and from Tennessee to the Gulf of Mexico. Although the Cherokee spoke an Iroquoian language, their customs were similar to their Muskhogean neighbors: the Creek, Choctaw, Chickasaw, and Natchez. All of these tribes had a complex culture rooted in the mound-building societies of the past. Their economy was based on agriculture along with some hunting, gathering, and trade. They had a complex political and social organization based on matrilineal families organized into clans and moieties. They also formed strong confederacies for mutual defense.

By 1500, the Siouian-speaking woodland tribes had been pushed from the Ohio River valley into the Mississippi and Missouri River valleys by the expansion of the Algonquin and Iroquois tribes. Their economy changed as they moved closer to the Great Plains with tribes closest to the plains abandoning agriculture for the buffalo hunt. Social organization also changed in response to the changing economy, so that nomadic patrilineal, patrilocal tribes replaced the agrarian matrilineal, matrilocal structure in the East. The tribes were loosely affiliated to a council of chiefs chosen from towns or bands of hunters. Annual religious festivals tied the villages and bands together.

Great Plains. The great plains were primarily grasslands extending south from Canada to the Rio Grande and west from the hundredth meridian to the Rocky Mountains. The Osage, Missouri, Kansa, Otoe, Omaha, Iowa, and Ponca, all Siouan-speaking, lived in the Missouri river basin; the Mandan and Hidatsa lived in the north in palisade villages which became trade centers; and the Caddoan-speaking Pawnee were in the west in Nebraska. By 1500, the Teton Sioux, Cheyenne, and Arapaho were just beginning to drift onto the plains to pursue the huge herds of buffalo that populated the area. The Comanche, Kiowa, Blackfeet, and Crow lived at the western border of the plains, entering the area for the annual buffalo hunt, then returning home.

Before they had horses, game was pursued on foot and personal belongings were carried on a *travois* (animal skins laced between two poles with one end pulled by a person and the other end dragging on the ground). The reintroduction of the horse into the New World revolutionized life on the plains by 1700. Over thirty tribes entered the plains and forged a hybrid culture which centered around the horse and buffalo. Although no common language was spoken, they devised sign language so that different tribes and bands could communicate. As the plains culture developed, descent reckoning and marriage rules became more flexible. For instance, women became important in processing buffalo and polygyny became common.

Great Basin. The Great Basin tribes ranged across Utah and Nevada from the Rocky Mountains to the Sierra Nevada. Speaking a common language, these nomads traveled on foot in small bands via a seasonal wandering route. The bands were small family groups of extended family members numbering approximately twenty-five to thirty people. Although the scarcity of food discouraged social association, several family groups sometimes wintered together in a village. The changing composition of the winter villages created interrelationships among different families across a large region.

Plateau. This area covers the interior of the northwest United States between the Rocky Mountains and the Cascades. When white men reached the area, the natives lived in small semipermanent fishing camps along major water routes. Although there was little tribal identity, there were bonds of ethnic sameness and a common language existed even though each settlement was autonomous. By the early eighteenth century the horse had reached the upper Columbia River basin and the Nez Perce, Cayuse, and Yakima tribes built up large herds.

California. There was a diverse native population in California—at least 105 distinct tribes with dialects of six different languages. Tribal groups were established in permanent locations by 1600, each group inhabiting its own land defined by specific recognized boundaries. In the mild climate, the tribes needed only simple dress and shelter. Because of food surpluses and ease of getting food, no agriculture was practiced. The tribes had a rich and varied ceremonial life, yet their political organization consisted of simple, extended family units with a headman. Due to the absence of a complex political system and material culture, despite the dense population and abundant food supply, early whites who encountered California Native Americans wrongly concluded they were more primitive than other tribes.

Southwest. The Southwest culture area included all of present Arizona, part of New Mexico, southeast Utah, southwest Colorado, and west Texas. The varied topography included mountains, low deserts, and high plateaus. The climate was generally arid so water was precious. There were three groups of tribes in this area: Pueblo, Riparian, and Intruder.

The Pueblo, Hopi, and Zuni tribes all descended from prehistoric Anasazi farmers. They used irrigation to cultivate corn, their major crop, and lived in politically autonomous towns where religion was the primary integrating force.

The Riparian tribes lived southwest of the Pueblo people along the Salt, Gila, San Pedro, Santa Cruz, and Colorado rivers. The Pima, Papago, and Sobiapuris in the east spoke Uto-Aztecan languages, while in the west, the Yuman-speaking Yavapais, Maricopa, Mohave, and Yuma lived in towns later called *rancherías*. All of these societies were primarily agricultural with some hunting and gathering. They irrigated water from nearby streams to raise corn.

The Intruder group, consisting of two large parties of Athapaskan-speaking raiders, had moved into the area by

1500. The Apache peoples were scattered in bands: the Jicarilla, Kiowa, Lipan, Chiricahua, Mescalero, and San Carlos. The Navajo became more sedentary, adopting weaving and farming from the Pueblo culture.

Pacific Northwest. The native peoples of the Pacific Northwest lived in the coastal areas between the mountains and the sea from the Prince William Sound to what is now northern California. In this mild climate, food was so abundant that no agriculture was practiced. This group had a complex social and religious system with a distinct class structure. One unique custom was the ''potlatch,'' a celebration of an important event where the host gained prestige by giving away his wealth. There was a rich religious life with elaborate, dramatic rituals, ceremonies, and dances. The Tongass, Niska, Gitskan, and Haisla and other tribes lived in the colder northern region. The southern tribes, including the Coos and the Chasta Costa, shared some traits with the California tribes, whereas the Snoqualmie, Puyallup, and other tribes on the eastern border of the region traded with their neighbors in the Plateau culture.

Alaska Natives. Alaska was inhabited by people of very different cultures: Indians and Meso-Indians. By 1000 A.D., the Alaskan Meso-Indians had become what we would recognize today as the Eskimos and Aleuts. As the most recent immigrants from Asia to the New World, they shared a common language and physical characteristics similar to that of their Asian ancestors.

The Eskimo lived in small isolated family groups on the Alaska mainland, while those who lived in coastal areas hunted seal, walrus, and whale. Those who lived inland hunted caribou and other game. Some hunted both land and sea game in different seasons.

The Aleuts lived on the Aleutian chain of islands off the coast of Alaska. They shared a common language and ancestry with the Eskimo, although their culture was similar in some ways to the Northwest Coast Native Americans. They hunted sea animals like the Eskimo, but salmon and birds were their primary source of food.

The Alaska Indians, including the Haida and Tlingit tribes who lived along the coast and on offshore islands, were an extension of cultures found in the Pacific Northwest. The Athapascans lived in the interior where the Yukon climate meant long, snowy winters and short summers. They lived in hunting bands in semi-permanent villages, relying on snowshoes and dog sleds or, when streams thawed, canoes for transportation.

European Colonization

European exploration in North America began as early as 1001 A.D. when Norsemen landed on the coast of Newfoundland and increased in the late fifteenth century, beginning with the voyages of Columbus. A few permanent settlements were established in the sixteenth century. Settlement continued through the seventeenth century and increased in the eighteenth century.

The Europeans who explored and settled the New World had a similar goal although they came from different countries: to increase national and personal wealth through trade. The national prestige of their country of origin was elevated as colonies were established in the New World. As Native Americans were encountered, converting the ''heathen'' and spreading Christianity became another goal.

The strategies for colonizing were determined by the natural resources discovered in each area explored. The effects of colonization varied, depending on the country's overall ambitions in the New World and the differing cultures that were encountered.

Spain. Mainland North American Indians met Europeans for the first time in the sixteenth century when Spanish explorer Ponce de León landed on the coast of Florida in 1513. St. Augustine, established in 1565, became the first permanent European settlement.

Spain was the first European power to establish guidelines for dealing with the native inhabitants. Pope Clement VI urged Charles V, the Spanish king, to ''compel and with all zeal cause the barbarian nations to come to the knowledge of God . . . not only by edicts of admonitions, but also by forces and arms, if needful, in order that their souls may partake of the Heavenly Kingdom'' (O'Brien 1989, 38). This papal message, called the *requerimiento* or requirement, was delivered to the tribes as they were conquered and forced into virtual slavery. Only for Native Americans who proved themselves ''civilized'' by adopting the Christian religion and the language and customs of the Spanish was freedom considered.

The Crown established the *encomienda* system in 1512 which satisfied everyone except Native Americans. Male Native Americans could work for a portion of a year, either farming or helping to construct buildings, in return for acceptance in society. This arrangement reassured the clergy that the natives would be converted. The *encomenderos*, who were conquistadors and officials, were pleased with the cheap labor the encomienda system provided for industry or the construction of public works. The encomenderos paid the Crown a head tax on each Native American. Native Americans who gained civilized status were known as *indios capaces*. The missions and the military posts as well as the farmers, ranchers, and miners who formed settlements, all needed the Native Americans and viewed them as a resource. As such, the Spanish did not usually expel them from their lands.

In 1521 the Spaniards conquered the Aztecs and the colony of New Spain was established in modern Mexico.

From there, the Spanish moved north into the Southwest and California. Juan de Oñate established San Juan de Yunque, now the San Juan Pueblo, in New Mexico in 1598. Moving north into Texas prior to the 1700s, Spain had established a string of missions, presidios or forts, and rancherías from Baja California to San Francisco by 1776. All of these settlements were part of Mexico when it became an independent nation in 1821. In 1848, after the Mexican War with the United States, most of the territory was ceded to the United States with the remaining territories in the southwest obtained as a result of the Gadsden Purchase (1853).

France. The French established trading settlements at Sable Island, Nova Scotia, in 1598; Tadoussac, Quebec in 1601; Port Royal, Nova Scotia in 1605; and Quebec in 1608. France also claimed lands along the St. Lawrence Valley, the Great Lakes, and the valleys of the Ohio and Missouri Rivers. In addition, Robert Cavelier, Sieur de la Salle, had navigated the Mississippi River by 1682 and claimed its upper valley and the upper Missouri valley for his native country. By the eighteenth century, France also held land along the lower Mississippi.

The French government intended to establish balanced colonies with a variety of enterprises. However, the quick profit of fur trade deemed it the most successful and primary enterprise. The French capitalized on the existing Native American trade network in the Northeast. The Huron acted as middlemen in this network. By the late 1500s, the fur trade dominated the network and transformed the economy. The French traders, in the course of their ventures, learned hunting, trapping, and survival skills from the natives. In the process they also learned native languages and, at times, intermarried.

Unlike the Spanish, the French did not need large tracts of land or a captive labor force in their promotion of the fur trade. However, even though the French recognized tribal sovereignty and land rights in most cases, the end result of their intrusion into the New World, like the Spanish, was not favorable to the natives. The French brought European diseases which reduced the native population. The Native Americans lost their self-sufficiency as they became dependent on trade goods. The fur trade affected tribes even if they were not directly involved as overtrapping and hunting depleted the wildlife. Tribes that wanted to continue the native way of life were forced to migrate further west. This strained relations with neighbors and increased inter-tribal warfare.

Converting the heathen and teaching them French culture became the responsibility of missions run by Catholic clergy. The Recollects, Jesuits, Sulpicians, and Capuchins were the largest French religious orders in New France. The Recollects established missions in the St. Lawrence valley in 1615. The Jesuits, who became the leaders among the missions, began arriving at about the same time. In some areas, the missionaries wanted to contain migratory congregations for more effective teaching. They established settlements called "reductions," where their scattered converts were brought to live together. This new living arrangement sometimes had the unhappy effect of increasing the natives' exposure to diseases. The Jesuits and other missionaries often lived among the more sedentary tribes such as the Huron.

After 1763, the British expelled the French from all of North America but Canada. However, France controlled the Louisiana Territory from 1800 as a result of treaties with Spain and sold it to the United States in 1803.

Holland. Dutch territory in North America included most of what is now New York and Pennsylvania. Their initial interest was in the fur trade, so they did not appropriate large tracts of land when they established trading posts and villages. Although, converting the natives to Christianity was not a major objective, the Dutch Reformed Church did minister among the tribes. To establish the credibility of their claims to other European countries, the Dutch carefully negotiated each land transaction with the Native Americans.

Relations deteriorated in the 1630s when the Dutch began to need more land for other uses. Overtrapping had seriously depleted the wildlife resources, limiting the fur trade, and English settlements were moving closer. To protect their holdings in North America, the Dutch decided to expand settlement. They established agricultural colonies under a *patroon* system. This was a feudal system where a colonial landlord or patroon collected rents from tenant farmers. Each patroon received the title to a land grant in return for purchasing the land from the Native Americans and settling tenant farmers on it. In 1664, the Dutch were driven from North America by the English.

Russia. The Russian *promyshlenniki* or fur traders established claims in the Pacific Northwest in the mid-1700s. The Russian crown did not regulate the trade, except to require a tribute payment and encourage the establishment of Russian Orthodox missions among the natives. The early promyshlenniki often exploited the natives, obtaining native labor and furs through force or extortion.

Permanent Russian settlements were established beginning in 1784. Treatment of the natives improved with the development of large fur trading companies. Russian Orthodox missionaries began teaching the natives in the Aleutian Islands and on Kodiak Island in 1794. Missionary efforts increased among the Aleut in 1824 and were expanded among the Eskimo and Alaska Native American tribes in the interior. Although the Russians sold Alaska to the United States in 1867, Russian Orthodox missionaries continued working in local churches, schools, and missions with six mission schools still in existence as late as 1900.

England. John Cabot sailed on the first English voyage to North America in 1497. In 1585 an English colony was established at Roanoke, Virginia. The Jamestown colony was established in Virginia in 1607. Most of the English who settled in North America were farmers who came for land, although some of the early English immigrants came to participate in the fur trade.

Since the English Crown did not set guidelines for acquiring title to land in North America, each colony developed its own policy regarding land acquisition from and trade with Native Americans. The history of the mainland English colonies in the seventeenth century was summed up as "the expansion of White settlement onto native lands and the peaceful or forceful transfer of ownership of those lands from Red to White hands" (Berkhofer 1973, 129).

Successful farming depended on the English obtaining exclusive rights to large tracts of land. Even if the tribe's lands were not taken over immediately, white encroachment destroyed their subsistence of hunting and collecting native plants. Over time, this forced the tribes in the areas where the English settled to do one of three things: they could resist white settlement by force, convert to white customs, or move further west and risk the hostilities of the tribes who already lived there.

As English settlement expanded, so did England's legal jurisdiction. There were three categories of legal status for Native Americans under colonial law. First, any Native American who lived away from his tribe as a slave, servant, or free person was subject to the same laws applied to any other colonist in the same station. Secondly, members of independent tribes were considered foreigners, although they were tried in English courts if they broke English law. Finally, some tribes were already subject to the Crown, due to conquest or trade agreements. While these tribes were under colonial protection and subject to English law, their settlements were not integrated into colonial society.

Converting the Native Americans to Christianity and white civilization was usually left to the Protestant missionaries who began coming to America in the seventeenth century. The Puritans, however, who settled in New England, had their own methods of converting the natives. They viewed the seasonal migrations of the Native American tribes as a sign of disorganization and established "Praying Towns" as safe havens for converted Native Americans who wished to live like the colonists. At one time, there were fourteen of these colonies around Massachusetts Bay and seven more in central Massachusetts.

As game and land became scarce with continued English expansion onto Native American lands, relations deteriorated culiminating in wars between the English and the natives at various times throughout the colonies. Many were killed on both sides, but the flood of immigrants continued. Increasingly, the colonists, who once thought the Native Americans ripe for conversion, began to see them as savages who should be exterminated.

Colonial Wars

France and England competed for control of trade and territory in North America. The native tribes, often involved in the conflicts, became pawns in a series of wars which began in the late seventeenth century in Europe and continued in North America. The conflicts in North America, known collectively as the French and Indian Wars, lasted many years. In fact, the fight between France and the Virginia Colony for control of the Ohio River valley in 1754 was the fourth war in sixty years. The wars ended in 1763 when France ceded Canada and all other French lands east of the Mississippi River to England. At that time, France ceded New Orleans and all claims to land west of the Mississippi River to Spain. (France briefly regained control of the territory from 1800 to 1803.)

The Proclamation of 1763, which ended the war, established the Appalachian Mountains as the eastern boundary of an Indian Territory, setting the precedent of separate lands for Native Americans. The Proclamation decreed that Native Americans were entitled to occupy their lands and anyone who had settled on land not ceded by Native Americans was to leave. All future land deals were to be between the British Crown and tribal representatives.

The Crown established the Imperial Department of Indian Affairs to regulate trade, maintain peace at trading posts, and prevent unlawful entry onto Native American lands. Two superintendencies were created: one for the northern colonies and one for the southern colonies. The superintendents were ambassadors who observed events, negotiated treaties, and tried to keep peace between frontier settlers and Native Americans. They regulated interaction between Crown subjects and the tribes, but had no involvement in the internal affairs of the tribes. The Crown and its American colonies related to the tribes as though they were sovereign nations.

Tribes were again involved in colonial conflicts during the American Revolution. Many sided with the British—especially the Iroquois and Muskogee confederacies. The colonists created their own Commission on Indian Affairs to try to keep Native Americans out of the conflict. A message from the Continental Congress to the Six Nations of the Iroquois read, "This is a family quarrel between us and Old England. . . . We desire you to remain at home, and not join on either side, but keep the hatchet buried deep'' (McNickle 1978, 49). Tribes allied with both sides suffered heavy losses. By the end of the war, the Iroquois lands had been ravaged and many Iroquois who had been loyal to the Crown emigrated to Canada, although reservations were established in western New York for those who opted to remain.

The Native American Policy of the United States

As discussed above, during European colonization in North America, Native American lands became territories of various countries—each of which tried to convert Native Americans into loyal subjects by replacing native cultures with those of the Europeans. The tribes who lived on the outer edges of the continent were most affected by European intrusion. However, while some European influences were carried inland along trade routes, for the most part, the tribes in the continental interior escaped the brunt of European encroachment.

When Britain's American colonies gained their independence and became the United States, they continued to acquire territories. (See Figure 1.2.) In 1790, Spain ceded the territories in the Pacific Northwest. With the Louisiana Purchase (1803), the interior continent west of the Mississippi from New Orleans to Canada was acquired. At the end of the War of 1812, the Red River Valley in what is now Minnesota was ceded by Britain. The border between Canada and the United States was later established at 49th parallel increasing U.S. border lands. In 1819 Spain ceded Florida. Texas was annexed by the United States in 1845, causing a war with Mexico which ended in the Mexican Cession of 1848 (discussed above). The United States acquired the remaining Southwest in the Gadsden Purchase in 1853. Alaska was purchased in 1867 from Russia. The United States ultimately reached from east to west across the North American continent. As new territories were added, more native tribes came under federal domain. The new nation took a turn at subjugating and transforming the tribes.

U.S. Native American policy was modeled after the British Crown's with the Continental Congress establishing three regional departments to administer Native American affairs in 1775. From 1781 through 1789, under the Articles of Confederation, the federal government regulated the native's affairs and trade. This practice continued after the Constitution was adopted.

Two immediate problems concerning Native Americans confronted the new nation. Spain and England still held territories in North America, representing a threat to the United States. The first objective of U.S. Native

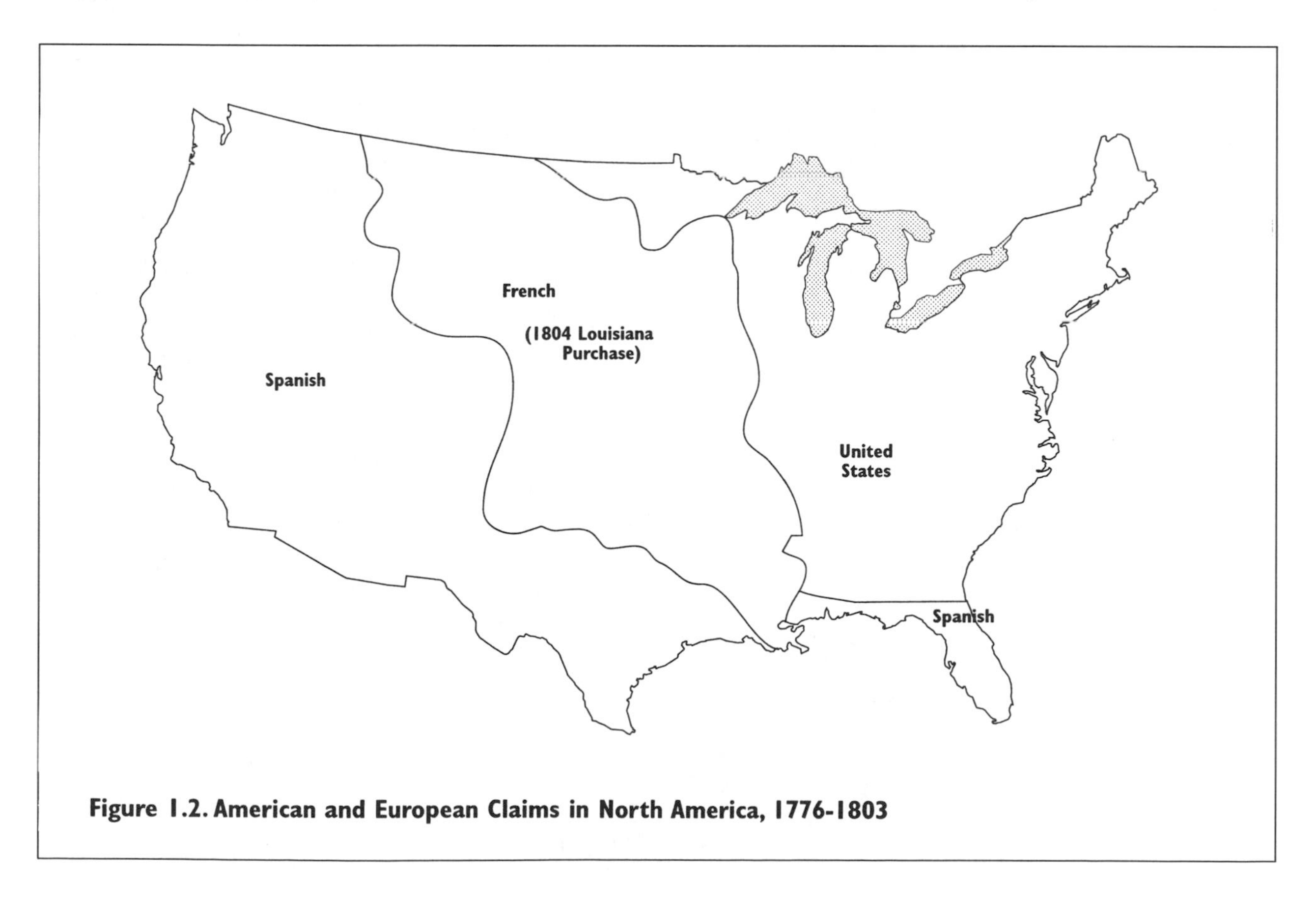

Figure 1.2. American and European Claims in North America, 1776-1803

American policy was to prevent the native tribes from forming alliances with England and Spain. The continued growth of the United States generated the second dilemma. The government, in obtaining more western lands, had to decide who to deal with among the Native American tribes who impeded progress. The fighting of the Revolutionary War had temporarily eased pressure on the frontier. Once the Revolution ended, however, migration west was renewed.

The Treaty of Paris, which ended the Revolution in 1783, established the Mississippi River as the western border of the United States. The Northwest Ordinance, passed in 1787, defined the territory of the Old Northwest (modern Ohio, Illinois, Indiana, Michigan, Wisconsin, and part of Minnesota) and established a procedure for admitting new states into the Union.

The Northwest Ordinance was not intended to safeguard Native American homelands. Rather, it legalized taking them away. Article three established the basis for the federal reservation system, stating: "The utmost good faith shall always be observed towards the Native Americans; their land and their property, rights and liberty shall never be invaded or disturbed, unless in just and lawful wars authorized by Congress, but laws founded in justice and humanity shall from time to time be made, for preventing wrongs being done to them, and or preserving peace and friendship with them" (Prucha 1975, 52).

Four Trade and Intercourse Acts were passed between 1790 and 1799 to regulate trade and land deals with Native Americans. These acts licensed traders and established government trading houses or "factories" to sell American goods to Native Americans on credit. They also provided for the appointments of Indian agents. The factory system lasted until 1822, when the Office of Indian Trade was abolished along with the trading houses. Independent traders were licensed after that time.

In 1824 the Secretary of War created the Office of Indian Affairs, later called the Bureau of Indian Affairs, within the War Department to take over the responsibilities of the Office of Indian Trade. This arrangement was formally recognized by an act of Congress in 1832. In 1849 the Bureau of Indian Affairs came under the jurisdiction of the Department of the Interior.

Removal. The basis for the removal policy was established as early as the seventeenth century when Praying Towns were founded for the Christian Indians in New England. A few reservations were already established by colonial governments in the seventeenth and eighteenth centuries: the Mashpee Reservation in Cape Cod, 1660; the Pequot Reservation in Massachusetts, 1683; and the Fall River Reservation, also in Massachusetts, 1709. In 1676, the Sulpicians established the Caughnawaga reservation for the Mohawks in Quebec. These early reservations were more to separate the tribes from other Native Americans than to segregate them from whites. The removal of the Stockbridge tribe from Massachusetts to New York, and later to Wisconsin, was typical of a later strategy to relocate tribes in the west.

Early leaders of the United States acknowledged that Native American land rights should be recognized. Henry Knox, the Secretary of War under George Washington, suggested that land should not be taken from tribes without their consent except in war or with just cause. Thomas Jefferson felt the federal government should help the Native Americans transform their economy from hunting to farming. The Native Americans would need less land if they had an agrarian economy. Their surplus land could be ceded to the government, which would then open it up to white settlers. Jefferson also proposed exchanging with Native Americans their lands in the east for lands west of the Mississippi.

The removal from the Old Northwest began after the Revolution when the native tribes resisted white encroachment in the territory. There were various wars including Little Turtle's War (1790–1795) and Tecumseh's Rebellion (1809–1811). After the United States' War of 1812 with England, the issue of settlement was moot. The tribes in the Old Northwest, particularly those which had sided with England, were viewed more than ever as obstacles to expansion. The Kickapoos, Shawnees, Delawares, Miami, and Ottawa migrated from the Great Lakes, across the Mississippi River, to land in modern Missouri. By 1825, when the Erie Canal was completed, the Sac and Fox, Winnebago, Sioux, and Potawatomi had been removed to west of the Mississippi. The Chippewa moved up into northern Wisconsin.

Cherokee emigration from the Old Southwest (the present-day Southeast, east of the Mississippi River) began as a trickle in 1794 with the expulsion of The Bowl, a Cherokee leader. His band crossed the Mississippi River and settled on the St. Francis River in what later became Arkansas Territory. The Bowl and some of his people moved to the northern frontier of Mexico circa 1819 at the invitation of the Spanish government to discourage Americans from encroaching in Texas.

Several other groups of Cherokee voluntarily emigrated to Indian Territory in the early 1800s. Under the terms of an 1817 treaty, more than 700 enrolled and over 1000 actually removed to Indian Territory. In 1828 some of the Cherokee who had already migrated once agreed to move further west.

The United States concluded several treaties with tribes from the Old Northwest and Old Southwest between 1815 and 1820. These treaties assigned land in Indian Territory to tribes willing to migrate.

Most removals resulted from the Indian Removal Act of 1830, which provided for exchanging Native American lands for lands west of the Mississippi River. (A separate Indian country to be located west of the Mississippi River between the Red and Missouri Rivers was proposed in Congress as early as 1825; a change from the ''west of the Appalachians'' proposed in 1763.) By the time the Removal Act was passed, settlers were already moving into the Mississippi Valley into areas where tribes had been relocated. Establishing a distant territory for Native Americans was proposed as a solution to avoid further uprooting—a colonization zone withdrawn from settlement. The Act declared, ''. . . That it shall and may be lawful for the President of the United States to cause so much of any territory belonging to the United States, west of the river Mississippi, not included in any state or organized territory, and to which the Indian title has been extinguished, as he may judge necessary, to be divided into a suitable number of districts, for the reception of such tribes or nations of Indians as may choose to exchange the lands where they now reside, and remove them . . .'' (Prucha 1975, 52). Over 100,000 Native Americans moved west of the Mississippi River during the first half of the nineteenth century.

The Removal Act initiated an era of increased control of Native Americans by the federal government. Prior to its enactment, the laws relating to Native Americans were primarily to fulfill treaties. There were laws which created a bureaucracy for administering Native American affairs, but none of them invited the kind of regimentation the Removal Act allowed.

President Andrew Jackson employed the Indian Removal Act to remove the remaining tribes from the Old Southwest whose lands had already been reduced. The Cherokee were concentrated in eastern Tennessee, northwestern Georgia, and eastern Alabama; the Creeks in western Georgia and Alabama; the Choctaw in southern Mississippi and southwestern Alabama; and the Chickasaw in northern Mississippi and northwestern Alabama. After 1819 the Seminole were in Florida. Each of these tribes existed as separate nations, surrounded by the states, but exempt from state laws.

The tribes had attempted to adapt to the white culture by converting to a civilization such as Thomas Jefferson had proposed. However, before they could assimilate, gold was discovered on Cherokee land in 1829. In response, Georgia, Mississippi, and Alabama all passed laws to get the tribes out by allowing for state confiscation of their tribal lands.

The legality of this action was challenged in the Supreme Court. Chief Justice John Marshall studied the treaty process from colonial times and offered opinions in landmark decisions. His decision in *Cherokee Nation v. Georgia* in 1831 recognized the legality of the Cherokee claim to the land. However, while the constitution allows foreign nations to sue a state, the Court had to decide whether the Cherokee Nation qualified as a foreign nation before it could rule on the land claim. Marshall ruled that the Cherokee Nation consisted of domestic dependent nations. ''It may well be doubted whether those tribes which reside within the acknowledged boundaries of the United States can, with strict accuracy, be denominated foreign nations. They may, more correctly, perhaps, be denominated domestic dependant nations. . . . They and their country are considered by foreign lands as well as by ourselves, as being so completely under the sovereignty and dominion of the United States that any attempt to acquire their lands, or to form a political connection with them, would be considered by all as an invasion of our territory'' (O'Brien 1989, 57). This ruling formalized the guardianship relationship of tribes with the U.S. federal government and became the basis of Native American policy.

In *Worcester v. Georgia* (1832), Marshall further defined the protectorate relationship of the tribes with the federal government. Although the federal government was the guardian of the tribes, this did not diminish their sovereignty as distinct, independent, political communities. Under this ruling, the Cherokee Nation was not subject to the laws of the states.

Unfortunately, the executive branch of government felt no obligation to uphold the Court's decision and the removal process continued. The Mississippi Choctaws left first, followed by the Cherokee, Muskogees, Chickasaw, Creeks, and Seminoles.

Between 1835 and 1838 voluntary emigration continued on a limited basis. However, most of the Cherokee lingered in the east, refusing to believe they would have to give up their land. They were later rounded up by federal troops and forcibly removed in a series of expeditions which collectively have become known as the Trail of Tears.

As a result of removal, the Choctaws lost 6,000 people to illnesses suffered during the trek and after resettlement, about fifteen percent of their population. Although the Chickasaw removal was more peaceful, there were heavy casualties; the Creeks and Seminoles suffered almost fifty percent mortality. For the Creeks these losses occurred mostly after removal due to disease and poor living conditions. The Seminole losses were created during their war against the United States (1835–1842) which resulted in their being forced to move.

As the United States continued to grow, portions of Indian Territory yielded to the pressures of white western migration. (See Figure 1.3 for a view of Indian Territory in 1834.) Lands were taken when the transcontinental

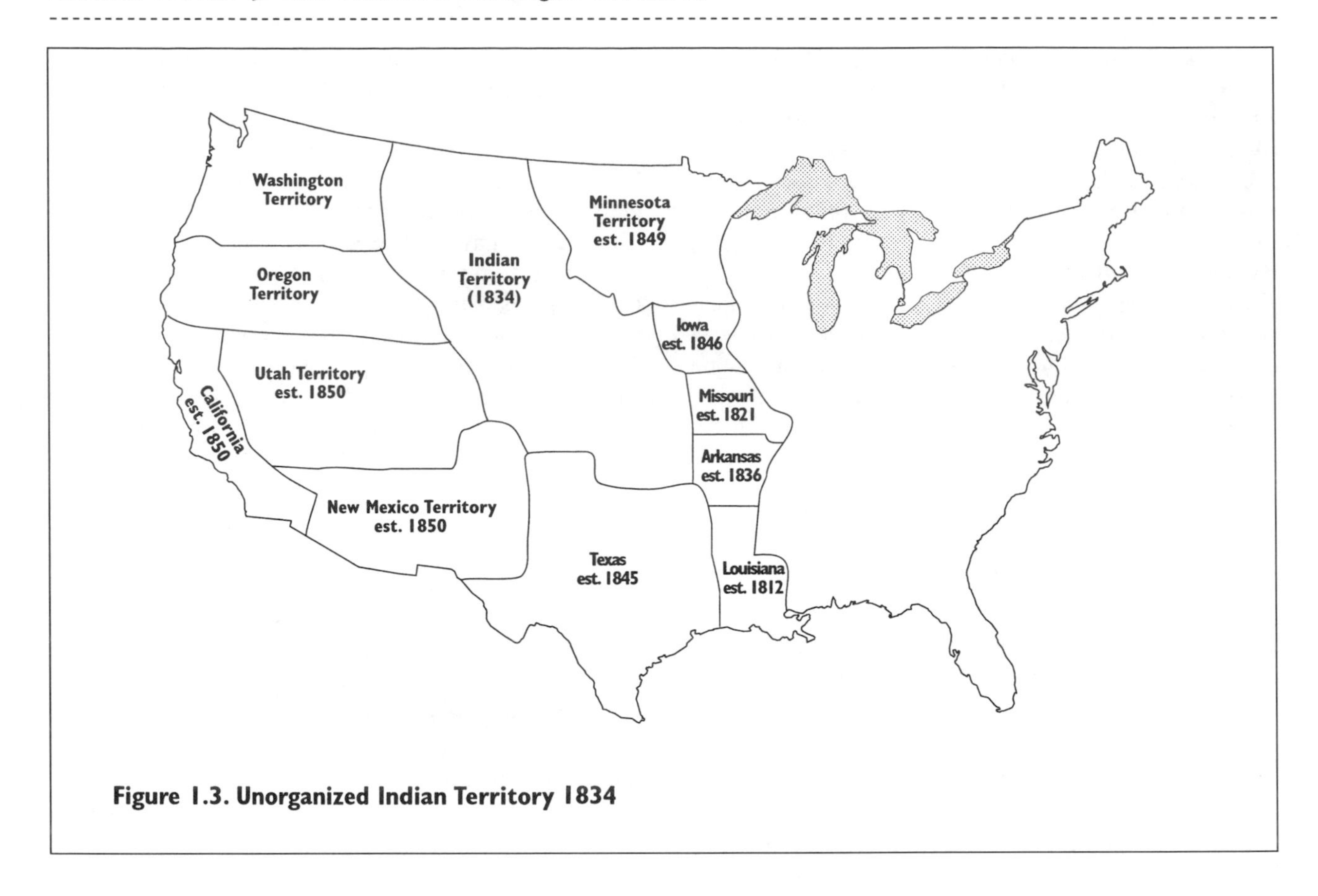

Figure 1.3. Unorganized Indian Territory 1834

railroad was constructed. The Kansas and Nebraska Territories were carved out of Indian Territory in 1854 and opened for homesteading in 1862. After Kansas became a state, tribes native to that area were relocated to lands confiscated from tribes already in Indian Territory.

Reservation. The reservation policy was aligned with the removal policy. The main objective of removal was to obtain Native Americans lands for white settlement. In the reservation era, this concept was refined. Instead of removing the tribes to one large Indian territory, tribes were confined to specific areas with specific boundaries.

As the United States expanded, the federal government built forts on the frontier. First came the soldiers; settlers soon followed. In the nineteenth century, the native tribes resisted the settlers. Many Indian wars (among which were the Plains Wars) were subdued by the army and treaties were negotiated which usually resulted in the tribe(s) ceding part or all of their lands and accepting a reservation in exchange.

The reservation was supposed to be the center for tribal management and reformation. On the reservations, Native Americans could be taught Anglo American customs and transformed from hunters to farmers. The reality for some of the tribes was more like receiving a prison sentence. Many tribes endured great poverty and deprivation because their native economies had been destroyed.

Result of removal and reservation policies. The outcome of the policies was the massive redistribution and concentration of Native Americans which left few tribes east of the Mississippi after 1850. Often, relocations split tribes into two or more groups on different reservations in different areas of the country. For example, the Cheyenne were settled in both Montana and Oklahoma. As a result of various Cherokee migrations and divisions, there were groups of Cherokee in North Carolina, Oklahoma, Arkansas, and Texas. More than one tribe could be relocated to a single reservation, such as the Wind River Reservation in Wyoming, which has both Shoshoni and Arapaho.

During the 1850s, fifty-three reservation treaties were negotiated with the tribes. At one time, Native Americans had been promised the land from the Mississippi river to the Rocky Mountains as Indian Territory, but from 1853 to 1857 the federal government obtained 174 million acres from that region. Tribes in Arkansas, Iowa, and Missouri moved west to Kansas, Nebraska and Oklahoma.

After 1885 there was little resistance from the tribes. They had been defeated by the unstoppable westward migration of white settlers, the extinction of the buffalo, disease, new technology (particularly the transcontinental railroad), and the emerging U.S. Native American policy of unilateral federal action.

By 1890 Indian Territory contained twenty-one separate reservations run by eight agencies. Each agency had at least two tribes under its jurisdiction and some oversaw more than five different tribes.

Assimilation and Allotment. The Congressional Peace Commission, appointed to end the Plains Wars, cited, in 1867, government failure to honor treaties and white demands for more land as causes of the wars. Their conclusion was that it was no longer possible to imagine a future for Native Americans out of the mainstream of society. Federal strategy was altered from negotiating with the tribes as sovereigns to attempting to assimilate them into mainstream white culture. Because one hundred fifty years of contact had not diminished tribal identity, the assimilation was accomplished through legislation.

In 1871, Congress ended the treaty process with a rider to an appropriation act which confirmed that no Indian nation or tribe in the United States would be recognized as an independent entity with whom the United States would have to sign treaties. Previous treaties would be upheld, but there would be no more negotiation. The United States, alone, would legislate Native American policy.

Between 1880 to 1910 the Supreme Court reinforced assimilation policies. In the *United States v. Kagama* decision (1886), the tribes were recognized as separate peoples, but because of the treaties signed, they were "wards" of the United States. The court ruled that while the United States was bound by the treaties to protect the tribes, it could define what form that protection would take (i.e., assimilation, for the tribes' own good). In *Lone Wolf v. Hitchcock* (1903), the precedent of absolute Congressional authority over Native American affairs was established.

The bureaucrats and well-meaning reformers who developed and implemented the assimilation process did not allow for cultural variety. The idea was to erase Indianness of any kind. From 1875 to 1885, further concentration policies were implemented to escalate the process: tribes from different reservations were consolidated into a common reduced reservation administered by a single agency, and the assigned reservation area was reduced to improve surveillance and reduce administrative costs. Both forms of concentration had another significant consequence. As the tribes were concentrated onto smaller reservations, the vacated lands could be opened up for settlement.

To achieve further assimilation and Native American self-sufficiency, it was decided that their land holdings (held in common by the tribe) would be individualized and reduced—allotment in severalty. The General Allotment Act (1887), also known as the Dawes Act, made possible the achievement of this goal by authorizing the U.S. president to request a survey of each reservation to facilitate the preparation of tribal rolls. (For a detailed analysis of records created as a result of this Act in regard to the Cherokees, Choctaws, Chickasaws, Creeks, and Seminoles, see "Records Specific to Native Americans—Addendum.") After a reservation was surveyed, the lands were divided into allotments, 160 acres to each family head, eighty acres to a single person aged eighteen years or older, forty acres to single persons under age eighteen. The title to each allotment would be held in trust by the U.S. government for twenty-five years until the owner had proven competency.

Surplus lands after the allotment were appraised and sold to the federal government to become public lands. Proceeds from the sale of the surplus lands were to be held in trust by the federal government and dispensed for Native American benefit.

The immediate goal of allotment was to teach farming techniques and instill the values of individualism and private property ownership in Native Americans. The long range goal was to end federal obligation to Native Americans and assimilate them as citizens.

Non-Native Americans shared in allotment by being included in tribal rolls through marriage, adoption, or proven claim of Native American or freedmen descent. After the Civil War, slaves owned by members of the Five Civilized Tribes, the Creeks, Chickasaws, Seminoles, Choctaws, and Cherokees, were included in tribal membership and thus, became eligible for allotments.

There were restrictions on the sale of the allotments, but leasing agreements were often used to circumvent the policy. Leasing allotments to non-Native Americans was originally prohibited, but was later justified as a means for Native Americans to earn income while learning from white role models. Only farming land was supposed to be allotted, but agents sometimes allotted grazing, timber, and mining lands in order to open up more surplus lands. In some cases, the lessee paid a pittance while stripping the allotment of its resources.

In addition, protective clauses in the law were not upheld. Land speculators could purchase inheritance rights or secure guardianship of Native American children who were heirs as tribal heirship customs were superseded by state and local laws. In some states, if a Native American did not make progress in farming his land, he was taxed. Federal and state governments granted rights of way through allotted lands to railroad and telegraph companies. Cases of bribery and graft were not uncommon among government and corporate officials.

The 1906 Burke Act allowed the sale of allotments by those unable to develop their own land. In some cases, an individual wanting to acquire allotted land forced government administrators to issue competency certificates to Native Americans who had been unwilling to apply for them in order to remove trust restrictions. This enabled the individual to take advantage of the allotee and acquire the desired property cheaply.

While the allotment policy was in effect between 1887 and 1934, the reservations and nations of the sixty-seven tribes in Indian territory were liquidated. The lands of the Kickapoos and Potawatamis in Kansas, the Sioux in Nebraska and the Dakotas, the Northern Cheyenne and Arapaho in Wyoming, the Gras Ventres and Blackfeet in Montana, the Jicarilla Apaches in New Mexico, and the Mohaves in the lower Colorado River region were allotted in their entirety.

Two thirds of all the lands held by all the tribes in 1887 had been allotted by the time the act was repealed in 1934. Overall, more than one hundred reservations were allotted and the tribes lost eighty percent of their lands or an estimated ninety million acres.

The Sisseton in South Dakota were among the first tribes to be allotted. When the land was surveyed in 1892, the tribe held 918,000 acres. When the land was allotted, 2,000 tribe members were given allotments from 300,000 acres. The remaining acres were sold as surplus and opened for homesteading.

By 1901 roughly 35,000 acres, originally allotted to tribal members, was still owned by Native Americans. The trust status removed, two thirds of that land was sold. Eighty thousand acres of land were distributed to heirs in diminishing parcels. And still, the Sisseton were not assimilated into white culture. After they spent the proceeds from the sale of their lands, many became homeless. Especially since the population of the tribe had increased during this period to 3,000 and none of the surplus lands had been held in trust for descendants of the original owners.

Overall, allotment benefitted white settlers most. Native Americans did not receive their final landed birthright. Further, the Dawes Act ended the power of tribal governments on allotted reservations. The government interacted directly with individual Native Americans rather than through tribal spokesmen.

As tribal governments became less important, the Bureau of Indian Affairs became more involved in daily lives of Native Americans. The Bureau established many schools for native children during this time period. The schools were a means of assimilating the next generation. In 1887 there were more than 14,000 students enrolled in 227 Native American schools.

In 1924 Congress conferred citizenship to all Native Americans born within the territorial United States. This was partly in appreciation for voluntary Native American service in World War I, but it was also a continuation of the U.S. government's desire for the assimilation of Native Americans.

In 1926 the government authorized the Meriam Institute for Government Research, a privately endowed foundation, to study the social and economic condition of Native Americans in the United States. Their study concluded that conditions were deplorable and the Bureau of Indian Affairs (and the allotment policy) had failed to meet the needs of Native Americans in the United States. There was widespread malnutrition, suffering, and dissatisfaction among Native Americans in regard to their exclusion from managing their own affairs. The remedial actions proposed included ending allotment. The report recommended that while federal programs should seek to advance economic position and foster social adjustment, Native Americans should be allowed to live within the dominant civilization without being obliterated by it. The Meriam report signaled a shift in policy based on the philosophy that any help given to Native Americans should develop and build on their values and customs, rather than destroying them.

The findings of the Meriam Commission coincided with the philosophy developed in response to the Great Depression, that government resources were obligated to provide for the minimum needs of citizens. When Franklin D. Roosevelt was elected President of the United States in 1933, he appointed John Collier as the Commissioner of Indian Affairs. The emphasis of the Collier administration was tribal restoration, reorganization, and intertribal cooperation. It resulted, in 1934, in the Indian Reorganization or Wheeler-Howard Act which, in effect, extended the New Deal to Native Americans.

The Indian Reorganization Act ended the allotment process, returned unsold allotted lands to the tribes, and provided for the purchase of new lands. It also encouraged tribal constitutions, courts, and businesses and instituted loans and building funds to increase educational opportunities for Native Americans, emphasizing reservation day schools instead of boarding schools. The act also promoted the hiring of Native Americans by the Bureau of Indian Affairs which encouraged Native American involvement in management and policy making at both national and tribal levels. In addition, it extended the Native American trust status and granted Native Americans religious freedom.

The Johnson-O'Malley Act, passed the same year, authorized federal contracts with states or private agencies to provide social, educational, medical, and agricultural services to help raise Native American standards of living.

Despite the progressive nature of Collier's administration, the federal government still maintained unilateral power over Native American affairs. Bureau of Indian Affairs agents continued to administer many Native American programs. Moreover, federal attention was diverted from tribal affairs at the onset of World War II. After the war, federal Native American policy reverted to a renewed emphasis on assimilation.

In 1946 the Indian Claims Commission was established to hear suits regarding Native American lands illegally taken by the United States. The commission could mandate repayment for these lands. It could also rule in favor of compensation for unfair land negotiations, and restitution for misuse of tribal trust funds, the loss of hunting and fishing rights, and the appropriation of mineral, timber, and water rights. (It is important to realize, however, that illegally taken lands were not given back.) Restitution for the land was based on its the value at the time it was taken. Part of the agenda for the Indian Claims Commission was to clear the slate of tribal claims in preparation for ending federal obligation to the tribes.

Termination. The late, post-war, 1940s ushered in an era of great industrial and urban expansion in the United States. Once again, the federal government was pressed to find land and natural resources to meet the demands of population growth. Once again, they looked to Native American lands as part of the solution. Some in Congress demanded that the trusteeship of the Bureau of Indian Affairs be dismantled.

Senator Arthur V. Watkins of Utah led the termination movement in Congress. Watkins, chairman of the Senate Committee on Indian Affairs during Dwight D. Eisenhower's presidential administration, was convinced that Native Americans could not hope to maintain an identity separate from mainstream American life. He attacked Roosevelt's misdirected social experiments which had perpetuated the illusion of a future for Native Americans as Native Americans.

Congress began devising the termination policy in the 1950s. The Termination Resolution, passed in 1953, called for Native American equality under the law and the eventual termination of federal supervision of several allotted lands. Native American lands were once again accessible to appropriation and tribal autonomy attacked.

The same year, Public Law 280 transferred jurisdiction for civil and criminal law in regard to Native Americans in each state to California, Minnesota, Nebraska, Oregon, and Wisconsin, respectively. It further authorized all other states in which reservations were located to assume similar jurisdiction. Now the laws of an individual state applied to reservations located within its borders. In addition, that state could tax Native American lands.

The concurrent Resolution 118 of the eighty-third Congress urged that Native Americans be freed from federal supervision and control as soon as possible. It directed the Secretary of the Interior to review existing laws and treaties and recommend amendments and nullifications to release the United States from its obligations to the tribes.

The termination policy was implemented by Congress in 1954 when it authorized the United States to terminate its supervision of two major tribes: the Menominee in Wisconsin and the Klamath in Oregon.

Congress enacted a series of laws to diminish Native Americans' status as a special group. The Bureau of Indian Affairs transferred the responsibilities for education to individual states and those for health care to the Department of Health, Education, and Welfare.

The federal government offered economic incentives to promote assimilation and encourage urbanization training. The Voluntary Relocation Program (later called the Employment Assistance Program) was created in 1952. Native American families willing to relocate from rural allotments and reservations to urban centers were provided with free vocational training and assistance with housing and employment. By 1960 35,000 had relocated (although thirty percent later returned).

The government's termination policy ended in the 1960s. It failed primarily because the states did not want to pay for services previously provided by the federal government.

Current policy. Today Native American tribes are classified by the federal government as being recognized by a state; federally recognized; terminated; or unrecognized. Over 502 tribes are currently recognized by the federal government. They have a trust status with the federal government which provides assistance with health care, education, and economic development. There are twenty-six other tribes recognized by states, mostly in the East. Terminated tribes have ended their political relationship with the federal government and receive none of the benefits granted to tribes still recognized. (The federal government had determined that these tribes were most able to administer themselves. Of course, many of these tribes owned lands rich in natural resources; removal of government restrictions meant that the resources were available to the general population.) Unrecognized tribes never made a treaty with the United States. As with terminated tribes, they own no tribal lands and have no political relationship with the United States. In a few unique cases, a tribe has membership of different statuses. For example, full-blooded members of the Ute tribe remain wards of the government, a federally recognized tribe, while the half- and mixed bloods agreed to take their share of tribal assets proportional to their numbers and are now terminated.

Summary. U.S. Native American policy evolved through many stages and suffered various reversals over the years and it continues to evolve. During each of the policy periods described in this chapter, records were created which contain genealogical information. Later chapters will discuss these records in detail.

Possible Problems in Interpreting Data

Many American families claim to have heard from various relatives over the years that somewhere back on the family tree there is an Native American ancestor. At some point a family member may decide to verify the legend through genealogical research. Another may begin researching Native American ancestry because of the desire to establish membership in a tribe and prove eligibility for benefits. Others may have discovered Native American ancestry in the course of researching their family tree. There are probably as many reasons for tracing a family history as there are families to trace. No matter the reason for researching Native American ancestry, the basic research process is the same.

Genealogy is the study of the history of families. It entails searching records to document ancestry and descent. Who were my people? Where and when did they live? What records will tell me about their lives? These questions stimulate genealogical research.

To begin answering them in regard to Native American ancestors, some background research must be conducted. First, the tribe with which your ancestor was affiliated must be determined. Then, a study of the history of that tribe should be conducted to learn where the tribe lived, its pattern of migration, the groups with which it interacted, and the records that were created in response to its existence. Studying the customs of the tribe will help in interpreting these records. Thorough background research can save considerable time and trouble in locating and understanding records containing information about an ancestor.

Determining Tribal Affiliation.

Knowing that you might have a Native American ancestor somewhere in your family is not much help, but often that is the only information people have when they begin to search for Native American ancestry. If this is your situation, basic genealogical research as discussed in this volume's "Basic Genealogical Research Methods . . ." should be conducted in an effort to acquire some solid data which can be used to acquire information on the Native American ancestry.

Identifying the Native American ancestor(s) and the name of the tribe narrows the search considerably. Placing an ancestor in a specific place at a specific time helps even more. Comparing that information to what is learned about the movements of the tribe will help to determine which records should be searched.

To determine the tribal affiliation of an ancestor, discover the places he or she lived (particularly the place of birth) and find out which tribes were in the area during the ancestor's life. Local histories can provide specific information about an area. Tribal histories or statewide histories of Native American tribes such as *A Guide to the Indian Tribes of Oklahoma* (Wright) can also be helpful. *The Indian Tribes of North America* (Swanton) and *Handbook of Indians North of Mexico* (Hodge) list the names of North American tribes and give a brief history of each. Both list variant spellings and names for a specific tribe and are cross-referenced by state to help determine which tribes were located in a particular area.

As you search for the name of your ancestor's tribe, you may find the tribal names confusing. Even the meaning of the word "tribe" may be ambiguous. While anthropologists today use the word to describe a social group of numerous families, clans, or generations combined with their dependents, slaves, or adopted strangers, the term has not always had that meaning. English explorers in the New World used the term "nation," which at the time indicated a heathen race as well as the area where they lived. The term "tribe" did not come into general use until the 1900s. The concept was forced on Native Americans by white societies as interaction between the two groups increased.

John R. Swanton, an ethnologist, complained that even among well known tribes in the eastern United States, the word was not applied uniformly. For example, the Creeks were called a tribe when they were actually a confederation of several tribes. In parts of California, western Oregon, and Washington, the words tribe and town were used interchangeably. The Powhatan "tribe" encompassed more than thirty separate tribes which had been loosely allied since before the settlement of Virginia.

Often tribes were known by more than one name. The tribal name could be a designation the members had been known by for centuries—many tribes have a collective term for themselves in their own language which means "the people." Or the name of the tribe could be derived from something they were called by other tribes, traders, missionaries, or explorers.

For example, the name Apache probably came from ápachu (enemy), the Zuni name for the Navajo who were called Apaches de Nabaju by the Spaniards. The Apache called themselves Inde or Nde. The Comanche called them Tá-ashi, which meant "turned up," referring to the toes of their moccasins while the Cheyenne called the Apache Xa-hë-ta-ñó, for "those who tie their hair back." The Hopi called them Tasámewé or "bastards" (Swanton 1952, 1984, 327–328).

Tribal Location

The variations of tribal name and the ambiguity of the terminology used to describe a tribe add to the difficulty of determining exact tribal location. Most tribes were migratory. Even the most sedentary tribes moved more often than groups in white cultures. As white settlement in North America increased, the native population was often forced to relocate. As noted above, almost every tribe was removed, relocated, dispersed, concentrated, or forced to migrate at least once after contact with Europeans or Americans.

Enrollment Status

Was the ancestor enrolled with a tribe? As the white population in North America increased, European nations and, later, the United States, made various treaties and agreements with the tribes. As this interaction occurred, tribal membership began to be qualified and described. By the end of the nineteenth century, the individual tribes were the final authority in setting membership criteria, although Congress could change the requirements set by the tribe. For example, in 1931 Congress restricted Eastern Cherokee membership to those of no less than 1/16 Cherokee blood.

In 1934 the Wheeler-Howard Act defined three categories of people: persons of Native American descent who were members of a recognized tribe under federal jurisdiction; all persons who were descendants of such members who on June 1, 1934, were residing within the boundaries of an Indian reservation; and all other persons who were at least fifty percent Indian blood.

The act encouraged Native Americans to enroll in a tribe and tribes to compile membership rolls after defining membership criteria which might be based on blood quantum, lineage, enrollment or allotment status, residence, or some combination of these. Not everyone who was eligible enrolled. The pride in one's Indianness has increased dramatically since the 1960s and 1970s. Prior to that time, many were reluctant to admit their Native American blood. Others, distrusting the U.S. government, avoided interaction with federal organizations even if it meant they did not receive treaty payments with the rest of the tribe. If your ancestor was not enrolled or recorded with the tribe, perhaps a sibling was.

Naming Customs

Naming customs vary between tribes with most Native Americans having several names over their lifetime. A person's birth name was often changed at puberty. A new name might be given after some unusual event or to bestow war honors. To further complicate matters, in many Native American languages, names were interchangeable between genders.

Many tribes adopted new naming customs as they interacted with the white population. After the 1800s, the government sometimes imposed naming customs on the tribes. Some Indian agents thought a surname was needed for census lists. Accordingly a surname was invented. Sometimes an English nickname became the family's surname. A Native American name from one family might be used as the surname for an extended family.

In addition, when a Native American converted to Christianity or enrolled in school, he was given a new name. In Luther Standing Bear's autobiography, *My People the Sioux*, he explains how his name was changed. Standing Bear's father was named Spotted Horse at birth because *his* father had captured many spotted horses from neighboring tribes. When Spotted Horse was old enough to go on the warpath, he earned the name Standing Bear for bravery in a battle with the Pawnee. Because Standing Bear had killed many enemies, he named his first son Plenty Kill. When Plenty Kill was sent to the Carlisle School in Pennsylvania, all the new students were lined up, boys on one side, girls on the other. A school official then had each one come up to the blackboard and choose a new name from a list of names. Plenty Kill could not read, so he pointed to a name at random (Luther) from the boys' list. He kept Standing Bear, his father's name, as his surname (Standing Bear 1975, 1–5, 137).

Many federal officials and tribal advocates foresaw that an allotment system, where tribal lands would become individually owned, was inevitable. Such a system would result in litigation over land, inheritances, and titles. To ease the legal process, they favored changing Native American names to make their naming system compatible with the American system based on the father's surname.

After the Dawes Commission began compiling enrollment records in the 1890s, the Bureau of Indian Affairs tried to standardize names. In 1902 guidelines were established. It was preferred that the Native American name of the father became the family surname (rather than a translation of the name) unless it was too long or clumsy. A long name could be shortened by an official familiar with the Native American's language without losing its identity. If a translation of a name was necessary or had already become generally accepted, that translated name was to be written as one word.

Studying the naming customs of your ancestor's tribe is a vital part of your background research. Knowing when and why an ancestor's name might have been changed will help to find him or her in different records at various stages of life.

Native American Family Customs and Kinship Terminology

Just as the set up of a family varied between tribes, so did the kinship terminology used by each tribe.

Marriage customs were varied, but most tribes practiced exogamy which meant that the bride and the groom had to be from different clans. Both monogamy and polygamy were practiced as well, depending on the tribe. The form of polygamy practiced was most commonly polygyny, where a man had more than one wife. In such cases the man might marry sisters and maintain one household.

Polyandry, where a wife had more than one husband, was uncommon. It was sometimes practiced in harsh climates like the Arctic or the Great Basin (a region between the Wasatch and Sierra Nevada Mountains), where the economic burden of supporting a wife and family was too difficult for one man.

Multiple marriages were common because of high mortality rates due to disease, death in childbirth, and warfare. Generally, agricultural tribes were mother-centered or matrilineal. The hunter-gatherer tribes were usually patrilineal or father-centered. If the social system was matrilocal it meant a couple lived with the wife's family after marriage.

Studying the kinship systems for an ancestor's tribe will help in accurately interpreting relationships listed in records. For example, in a matrilineal matrilocal society, the husband's role was to sire children. Any children born to the couple were considered part of the mother's clan and lived in her household. Heirship was reckoned through the mother. Often, the mother's brothers reared her male children. The father was busy bringing up his sister's sons. In this society the terms for father and uncle (mother's brother) might be interchangeable. In some tribes, general terms might be interchangeable between generations. The same term might be used for both the grandfather and grandson, depending on the context and who was speaking.

Bibliography

Adair, James. *History of the American Indians*. London, 1775. Reprint. Johnson City, TN: Wautauga Press, 1930; New York: Promontory Press, 1974? 508p. Includes bibliographic references and index.

Berkhofer, Robert F. *Salvation and the Savage: An Analysis of Protestant Missions and American Indian Response, 1787–1862*. Lexington: University of Kentucky Press, 1965. Reprint. Athenaeum, New York, 1976; Greenwood Press, Westport, CT, 1977. 186p. Other title: *Protestant Missions and American Indian Response, 1787–1862*. Includes index and bibliography.

Berkhofer, Robert F. *The White Man's Indian*. Images of the American Indian from Columbus to the present. First edition. New York: Knopf, 1978. Reprint. Vintage Books, New York, 1979. 261p. Includes bibliographic references and index.

Cohen, Felix. *Handbook of Federal Indian Law, with Reference Tables and Index*. Washington, D.C.: U.S. Government Printing Office, 1942. Reprint, with added foreword, biography, "bibliography of Felix S. Cohen," "tribal index of materials on Indian law," and bibliography. University of New Mexico Press, Albuquerque, 1971.

Driver, Harold E. *Indians of North America*. Chicago: University of Chicago Press, 1961. 667p. Includes bibliography.

Fixico, Donald L. *Termination and Relocation: Federal Indian Policy, 1945–1960*. Albuquerque: University of New Mexico Press, 1986. 268p. Includes index and bibliography.

Foreman, Grant. *Indian Removal*. The emigration of the Five Civilized Tribes of Indians. First edition. Norman: University of Oklahoma Press, 1932. 415p. Includes bibliography.

Freeman, John F. *A Guide to Manuscripts Relating to the American Indian in the Library of the American Philosophical Society*. Memoirs of the American Philosophical Society; v. 65. Philadelphia: American Philosophical Society, 1966. 491p. Includes bibliography.

Gibson, Arrell Morgan. *The American Indian: Prehistory to Present*. Lexington, MA: D.C. Heath & Co., 1980. 618p. Includes bibliographies and index.

Goodman, James M. *The Navajo Atlas*. Environments, resources, people, and history of Dine Bikeyah. Norman: University of Oklahoma Press, 1982. 109p. Includes index and bibliography.

Graymont, Barbara. "New York State Indian Policy after the Revolution." In *New York History*, vol. 57 (October 1976), pp. 438–474.

Hagan, William T. *American Indians*. Third edition. The Chicago history of American civilization. Chicago: University of Chicago Press, 1993. 239p. Includes bibliographic references and index.

Hagan, William T. "Full Blood, Mixed Blood, Generic, and Ersatz: The Problem of Indian Identity." In *Arizona and the West*, no. 27 (Winter 1985), pp. 309–326.

Hodge, Frederick Webb. *Handbook of American Indians North of Mexico*. Two volumes. Bulletin (Smithsonian Institution. Bureau of American Ethnology); 30. Washington, D.C.: 1907–1910. Reprint. New York, 1959; Rowman and Littlefield, Totawa, NJ, 1975. Vol. 1: A-M, vol. 2: N-Z. Includes bibliography.

Hoover, Herbert T. *The Sioux: A Critical Bibliography*. Bibliographical series (Newberry Library Center for the History of the American Indian). Bloomington: Indiana University Press, for the Newberry Library, 1979. 78p. Includes bibliography and index.

Jackson, Curtis E., and Marcia J. Galli. *A History of the Bureau of Indian Affairs and Its Activities Among the Indians*. San Francisco: R & E Research Associates, 1977. 162p. Includes bibliography.

Jacobs, Wilbur R. *Dispossessing the American Indian: Indians and Whites on the Colonial Frontier*. New York: Charles Scribner's Sons, 1972. 240p. Includes bibliographic references.

Jennings, Francis. *The Invasion of America: Indians, Colonialism, and the Cant of Conquest*. Chapel Hill: University of North Carolina Press, for the Institute of Early American History and Culture, 1975. 369p. Includes index and bibliography.

Jennings, Jesse D. *Prehistory of North America*. Second edition. New York: McGraw Hill, 1974. 436p. Includes bibliography.

Johnson, Kenneth W. "Sovereignty, Citizenship, and the Indian." In *Arizona Law Review*, vol. 15 (1973), pp. 973–1003.

Josephy, Alvin M. *The Indian Heritage of America*. Revised edition. American Heritage Library. Boston: Houghton Mifflin Co., 1991. 416p. Includes bibliographic references and index.

Kappler, Charles J. *Indian Affairs: Laws and Treaties*. Six volumes. Washington, D.C.: U.S. Government Printing Office, 1903. Other title: *Kappler's Indian Affairs*. Also known as the Kappler report. Includes indexes.

Kelsay, Laura E., comp. *Cartographic Records of the Bureau of Indian Affairs*. United States National Archives and Records Service Special List; no. 13. Washington, D.C.: National Archives and Records Service, General Services Administration, 1977. 187p. Other title: *List of Cartographic Records of the Bureau of Indian Affairs*.

McDonnell, Janet A. *The Dispossession of the American Indian, 1887–1934*. Bloomington: Indiana University Press, 1991. 163p. Includes bibliographic references and indexes.

McNickle, D'Arcy. "Indian and European: Indian—White Relations from Discovery to 1887." In *Annals of the American Academy of Political and Social Science*, May 1957, pp. 1–11.

McNickle, D'Arcy. *Native American Tribalism: Indian Survivals and Renewals*. New York: Oxford University Press, for the Institute of Race Relations, London, 1973. Reprinted with new introduction, 1993. 190p. Other title: *The Indian Tribes of the United States*. Includes bibliographic references and index.

McReynolds, Edwin C. *The Seminoles*. Civilization of the American Indian Series, vol. 47. Norman: University of Oklahoma Press, 1957. 397p. Includes bibliography.

Margon, Arthur. "Indians and Immigrants: A Comparison of Groups New to the City." In *The Journal of Ethnic Studies*, vol. IV (Winter 1977), pp.17–28.

Marquis, Arnold. *A Guide to America's Indians: Ceremonials, Reservations, and Museums*. Norman: University of Oklahoma Press, 1974. 267p. Includes bibliography.

Nabokov, Peter. *Native American Testimony: A Chronicle of Indian-White Relations from Prophecy to the Present, 1492–1992*. New York: Viking Penguin, 1991. 474p. Includes bibliographic references and index.

O'Brien, Sharon. *American Indian Tribal Governments*. First edition. The Civilization of the American Indian Series, vol. 192. Norman: University of Oklahoma Press, 1989. 349p. Includes bibliography and index.

Otis, D.S. *The Dawes Act and the Allotment of Indian Land*. The Civilization of the American Indian Series, vol. 123. Norman: University of Oklahoma Press, 1973. 206p. Includes bibliographic references.

Parkman, Francis. *The Jesuits in North America in the Seventeenth Century*. France and England in North America, part second. Boston: Little, Brown & Co., 1909. 586p. Includes index.

Prucha, Francis Paul. *American Indian Policy in the Formative Years: The Indian Trade and Intercourse Acts, 1790–1834*. Cambridge: Harvard University Press, 1962; Lincoln: University of Nebraska Press, 1970. 303p. Includes bibliographic notes.

Prucha, Francis Paul. *Documents of United States Indian Policy*. Lincoln: University of Nebraska Press, 1975. 278p. Includes bibliography and index.

Prucha, Francis Paul. *The Great Father: The United States Government and the American Indians*. Two volumes. Lincoln: University of Nebraska Press, 1984. 1302p. Includes bibliography and index.

Purdue, Theda. "Cherokee Women and the Trail of Tears." In *Journal of Women's History*, no. 1 (1989), pp. 4–30.

Riddick, John F. *A Guide to Indian Manuscripts: Materials from Europe and North America*. Reference Guides to Archival and Manuscript Sources in World History, no. 2. Westport, CT: Greenwood Press, 1993.

Ronda, James P. and James Axtell. *Indian Missions: A Critical Bibliography*. Bibliographical series (Newberry Library Center for the History of the American Indian). Bloomington: Indiana University Press, for the Newberry Library, 1978. 85p. Includes index.

Schmeckebier, Laurence F. *The Office of Indian Affairs; Its History, Activities, and Organization*. Service monographs of the United States government; no. 48. Baltimore: Johns Hopkins Press, 1927. Reprint. AMS Press, New York, 1972. 591p. Includes bibliography.

Sheehan, Bernard W. *The Seeds of Extinction: Jeffersonian Philanthropy and the American Indian*. Chapel Hill: University of North Carolina Press, for the Institute of Early American History and Culture at Williamsburg, Virginia, 1973. 301p. Includes bibliography.

Simpson, Lesley B. *The Encomienda in New Spain: Forced Native Labor in the Spanish Colonies, 1492–1550*. The beginning of Spanish Mexico. Revised and enlarged edition. Berkeley: University of California Press, 1929. Reprint, 1950. 257p. Includes bibliography.

Spindel, Donna. *Introductory Guide to Indian-Related Records (to 1876) in the North Carolina State Archives*. Raleigh: North Carolina Division of Archives and History, 1977.

Standing Bear, Luther. *My People, the Sioux*. Lincoln: University of Nebraska Press, 1975. 288p.

Sturtevant, William C. *Handbook of North American Indians*. Twenty volumes. Washington, D.C.: Smithsonian Institution, 1978–. Includes bibliographies and indexes.

Sugden, John. "Early Pan-Indianism: Tecumseh's Tour of the Indian Country, 1811–1812." In *American Indian Quarterly*, no. 10 (Fall 1986), pp. 273–304.

Svoboda, Joseph G. *Guide to American Indian Resource Materials in Great Plains Repositories*. Lincoln: University of Nebraska Center for Great Plains Studies, 1983.

Swanton, John R. *Indian Tribes of North America*. Classics of Smithsonian anthropology. Originally published as the Bureau of American Ethnology Bulletin #145, reprint edition 1969. Reprint (fourth edition). Washington D.C.: Smithsonian Institution Press, 1984. 726p. Includes bibliography and index.

Thornton, Russell. *American Indian Holocaust and Survival: A Population History Since 1492*. The Civilization of the American Indian Series, vol. 186. Norman: University of Oklahoma Press, 1987. 292p. Includes bibliography and index.

Thornton, Russell. *The Cherokees: A Population History*. Indians of the Southeast. Lincoln: University of Nebraska Press, 1990. 237p. Includes bibliographic references and index.

Thwaites, Reuben Gold. *The Jesuit Relations and Allied Documents*. Travels and explorations of the Jesuit missionaries in New France, 1610–1791; the original French, Latin, and Italian texts, with English translations and notes. Seventy-three vols. Cleveland: Burrows Brothers Company, 1896–1901. Includes index: vols. 72 (A-I) and 73 (J-Z).

Utley, Robert M. *The Indian Frontier of the American West, 1846–1890*. First edition. Albuquerque: University of New Mexico Press, 1984. 325p. Includes bibliography and index.

Utley, Robert M. *The Last Days of the Sioux Nation*. New Haven: Yale University Press, 1963. 314p. Includes bibliography.

Waldman, Carl and Molly Braun. *Atlas of the North American Indian*. New York: Facts on File, 1985. 276p. Includes bibliography and index.

Wilkinson, Charles F. and Eric R. Biggs. ''Evolution of the Termination Policy.'' In *American Indian Law Review*, vol. 5:1 (1977), pp. 139–184.

Wright, Muriel H. *A Guide to the Indian Tribes of Oklahoma*. Civilization of the American Indian Series, vol. 33. Norman: University of Oklahoma Press, 1951. 300p. Includes bibliography.

Woodward, Grace. *The Cherokees*. Civilization of the American Indian Series, vol. 65. Norman: University of Oklahoma Press, 1963. Seventh printing, 1982. 359p. Includes bibliography and index.

Background Material—Addendum

George J. Nixon

A brief biography of the author is provided in the chapter "Basic Genealogical Research Methods and their Application to Native Americans."

Native Americans: Timeline of Events

The Fifteenth and Sixteenth Centuries

1570 (1490?). Two dates are given for the founding of the League of the Six Nations. Its democratic system of government is the most liberal in the world at this time. This group first included the Mohawk, Oneida, Seneca, Cayuga, and Onondaga. The Tuscarora were admitted later, under patronage of the Oneida.

1584. Indians living off the coast of North Carolina meet a party of English colonists who land on Roanoke Island. During the years 1585–1586, the colonists either blend with the Indian population, or are lost. There is nothing further known of them.

1585. Several Indian villages are burned to the ground in Sir Richard Grenville's Virginia settlement. Men, women, and children are killed. Many are sold into slavery.

1587. Indians living off the coast of North Carolina meet still another party of colonizers under their governor, John White. White leaves the colonists to sail home. When he returns three years later, they are not to be found. This group of colonists becomes known as the "Lost Colony," and only the Indians knew what became of them. It is possible that the natives integrated the newcomers into their community.

The Seventeenth Century

The seventeenth century began with the aggressive entry of Europeans into the North American continent. They were greeted amicably by the Indians who provided them with much aid, without which their survival would have been questionable. Conflict arose when the Indians discovered the motives of the invaders: taking the natives' land. Dissension arose among the Indians themselves, when treacherous individuals chose to befriend the Europeans, receiving nothing in return. War erupted in full with the efforts of Philip (Metacomet) to drive the invaders from the land in 1675–1676. This effort was defeated, in large part due to the treachery of individual Indians, as well as the superior arms of the British. The rebellion of the Pueblos took place in this century, with early victories for the Pueblos, and, ultimately, defeat at the hands of the Spanish in consort with some Pueblos. The Tarahumars rebelled again and again, finally being forced to flee to the mountains. Rebellion flared all over Indian country, wherever Europeans settled, and the pattern was generally the same: hospitality repaid by slavery and intimidation, and finally, conquest.

1609. Indian sovereignty takes on international significance when the English Crown rcaffirms by law the "sovereignty of Indian nations."

A Mohawk longhouse is invaded by French explorer Samuel de Champlain, who attacks the Indians with muskets. Many Mohawks are killed.

1615. An Oneida village is attacked by Champlain. The Indians drive him off.

1619. The Indians sign a treaty of trade and friendship with two Dutch traders at Tawagonshi in New York. This is believed to have been the first treaty between Europeans and Indians.

1622. The Pawhattan Confederacy attacks the Jamestown settlements, destroying plantations and killing the settlers. They are led by Opechancanough, a Susquehannock chief.

1623. The tribes of Massachusetts plan an uprising against the English. Massasoit, Wampanoag chief, informs Miles Standish of the plan. Standish declares war on the tribes of Massachusetts. The Indians had objected to the taking of their land by the English, the destruction of their crops, and the forced labor exacted by the English.

1624. The Iroquois make a treaty with the French.

1626. The Shinnecock Indians accept $24.00 worth of trinkets from the Dutch on May 6, and the Dutch believe they have purchased Manhattan Island. Purchase of land, however, was unknown to the Indians, who believed they had merely permitted the foreigners to use the land.

1629. The Pueblos see the establishment of missions, and dissension begins to grow among the people. Some wish to accept the missions; others do not. The Pueblos resist efforts to place them in feudal bondage.

1633. The Hopi continue to resist the imposition of Catholicism. The Zuni kill the missionaries living among them.

A smallpox epidemic rages among the Pequot Indians, who had welcomed the Pilgrims.

1637. The eastern tribes are subjected to genocide by the Dutch and English. Many Pequot are massacred; some are sold into slavery. The Indians had resisted incursions into their land and destruction of their economy by Europeans.

1641. The Raritan Nation, in an effort to regain its land, attacks Staten Island, New York.

1642. The Shinnecock are massacred by Dutch settlers in New York. The attack is headed by Dutch governor Kieft and Sergen Rudolf with their soldiers. The date of this massacre, February 25, has gone down in the annals of history as the most brutal massacre in America.

1644. Indians of Massachusetts Bay Colony are forbidden to come into town or into the houses of the English on Sunday, unless it is to attend public meetings.

1649. Dissension among the tribes erupts in armed conflict over support to the European invaders. The Iroquois put 1,000 men into the field, in battle against the Hurons, who support the French. The battle takes place near the shore of Ontario's Georgian Bay. Many Hurons are killed, as are two French Jesuit missionaries.

1655. The Hopi are subjected to discipline by Father de Guerra, who punishes the Hopi, Juan and Cuna, for "an act of idolatry." Cuna is beaten to unconsciousness, beaten again inside the church, and then doused with turpentine and set afire. Despite the torture, the Hopi's struggle to maintain their religious and cultural independence continues.

1656. The Yuchi Indians in Virginia defeat the English.

Indian reservations are planned by the United Colonies, meeting in Virginia. The native people are unaware of this decision, but their fate is sealed as plans are made to contain them in restricted areas.

1661. The Pequot War erupts in Rhode Island against the English and their allies, the Narragansetts and Mohegans.

Chief Massasoit of the Wampanoags dies. He ceded nearly all of the tribe's land to the Europeans without authorization from the tribe.

The Franciscan priests issue a decree prohibiting the Pueblos from practicing their religion. Kivas (traditional Pueblo ceremonial structures) are raided, masks are removed, and ceremonial equipment is destroyed.

Indians in Virginia are required to wear plaques when visiting British settlements.

1662. Smallpox wipes out thousands of Iroquois and Susquehannahs.

Alexander, the son of Massassoit, friend of the Pilgrims, is arrested and subjected to interrogation by the British. Chief Metacom (or "King Philip," as he was known to the English) who is also Massassoit's son, is questioned and intimidated as well.

1664. Several Canadian tribes sign a treaty of friendship with the English.

1670. The Zuni people rebel against religious oppression by the missionaries.

1671. Metacom is again subjected to interrogation by the British. They ask whether he is preparing an uprising.

1672. On October 7, White Mountain Apache raid Hawikum, largest of the Zuni Pueblos, in an attempt to rid the Pueblos of missionary control. They kill the friar, Pedro de Abila y Ayala.

1675. A group of young Wampanoag enter Swansea, Massachusetts, to protest the grazing of cattle on their land, which is destroying their crops. They shoot cattle and settlers abandon their homes for several days.

The Wampanoag, led by Metacom, organize to rid themselves of white rule. On June 24, Metacom leads an attack against the English in the southern part of New England. The war begins in earnest. The Wampanoag attack and burn the settlements of Rehoboth, Taunton, Dartmouth, and Middleburough. Fighting continues until August. Northfield and Deerfield are attacked in September. On September 28, Northampton is burned. On October 5, the Indians attempt to remove the whites from their land and Springfield is burned. The English strike back in December, attacking the villages of the Narragansetts and burning to death 600 non-combatants.

1676. War of the Wampanoag, which is joined by other tribes, continues under the leadership of Metacom. Indians attack the following Massachusetts towns: Sudbury, Groton, Medfield, Lancaster, Marlborough, Andover, Woburn, Billerica, Chelmsford, Braintree, Weymouth, and Scituate.

In August, Metacom is captured and executed.

1680. Pueblos revolt against Spanish slavery and religious persecution. Land is reclaimed by the Indians. A battle takes place in the streets of Santa Fe, and the Spanish begin a mass exodus from Pueblo country, leaving New Mexico to the Pueblo people.

1682. The Delaware Indians agree to treaty talks with William Penn.

1686. The Delawares consummate a treaty with Penn.

1687. Iroquoian fishing parties are attacked and captured by the French on the St. Lawrence River.

1688. An army of 1,200 Iroquois men invade the island of Montreal. They seek to revenge French cruelty to the Indians.

1689. The Iroquois attack Lachine, Quebec, after the French invade their longhouse. They keep the French under siege for two months.

1692. The Pueblos are reconquered by the Spanish.

1696. The Pueblos are finally defeated, and subjected to Spanish law.

Onondaga, an Indian town in New York, and its stores of corn are destroyed by Frontenac (Louis de Buade). Oneida Castle in New York is also destroyed by the French.

The Eighteenth Century

During the eighteenth century the Indians were continually pushed further west. White settlers took more and more Indian land. The treaty era began in earnest between the U.S. government and Indian nations. During this century the government began officially the forcible removal of Indian tribes. In 1786 the U.S. Confederated Congress established two departments which dealt with Indians: The Northern Department with jurisdiction north of the Ohio River and west of the Hudson River in New York; and the Southern District, which covered the areas south of the Ohio River.

In 1787 the Northwest Ordinance was proclaimed, laying the basis for settlement of whites beyond the Allegheny Mountains, and the formulation of early Indian policy.

When the War Department was created by Congress in 1789, Indian affairs remained a function of the Secretary of War. In 1790 Congress passed an act for the regulation of trade with the Indians.

During this century, particularly towards its end, people began to recognize that the Indians were a critical element in the development of the new United States.

Treaties continued to be made with the Indian nations until the end of the nineteenth century, by which time the government acknowledged the sovereign status of the tribes. A new era of Indian economy began, with the horse becoming a major factor in the native economy, particularly among the tribes of the High Plains.

1700. The Ottawa tribe makes a treaty with the French in Montreal.

A treaty is proposed at Santa Fe, but is rejected by the Pueblo's traditional leaders when the Spanish government refuses to restrict the activities of the missionaries. The Hopi, who oppose the treaty, destroy Awatovi and kill the Christianized Indians. Governor Cubero moves to punish the Hopi, but is not successful.

The Cherokee Indians have the use of firearms.

1703. The Indians learn that bounties have been offered in Massachusetts for Indian scalps at the rate of $60.00 per scalp.

Apalachee Indians of Florida are attacked by white settlers and their Indian allies. Their towns are burned.

The Five Nations Indians become British subjects, but they have no knowledge of this new international alignment, brought about through the Treaty of Utrecht, which ceded Arcadia, Newfoundland, and the Hudson Bay territory to England. Nor were they consulted about their enforced allegiance to the British Crown.

1706. The Navajo people are subjected to repeated raids by the Spanish. The Navajo resist and are successful.

The Hopi defeat a Spanish force in present day New Mexico/Arizona.

1712. The Tuscarora migrate from the southeast coast to New York state due to the wars over slavery.

1722. The Tuscarora Indians are admitted to the Iroquois Confederacy, becoming the sixth nation in the League of the Iroquois.

The Abnaki are attacked by an English expeditionary force, located around the French mission at Norridgewock. The Indians are defeated.

1723. Indian students are at this time attending the College of William and Mary in considerable numbers. A building is erected for their use, the Brafferton.

1729. The Nachez Indians are attacked by the French.

1730. Seven Cherokee chiefs and headmen embark on an international mission of negotiations with the British Court at London. They enter into an alliance known as "The Articles of Agreement" with the Lords Commissioners. Negotiations had started at Nequassee (now known as Georgia).

1737. The Penn treaty with the Delawares is finally consummated. The treaty stipulates that there will be no forced removal of the Delawares.

1738. Nearly half of the Cherokee tribe in Georgia is destroyed by smallpox, brought by white slave traders through Charleston, South Carolina, to Georgia.

1746. The Huron leader Orontony moves against the French. Huron villages are destroyed.

1751. The Pima Indians, under leader Oacpicagigua, organize a rebellion against the Spaniards and the missionaries in November. The Spanish governor responds by installing a special garrison of soldiers.

1758. The Lenape and Unami are placed on a reservation set up by the state of New Jersey. It is called Brotherton, and is comprised of 1,600 acres of the Indians' own land.

1759. Alaskan natives are killed by members of the Russian expedition led by Pushkareff. There are raids into Alaska for slaves.

A Delaware prophet calls for a holy war against the whites, recommending that only traditional weapons be used.

1763. The War of the Ottawas begins, led by Pontiac. The Indians successfully attack Detroit and several other English forts.

Lord Jeffrey Amherst, the British commander, distributes smallpox-infected blankets to the Indians starting a widespread epidemic.

The ''Paxton Boys,'' a mob from Paxton, Pennsylvania, destroy a settlement of Christian Indians at Lancaster, Pennsylvania.

1765–1766. Two treaties are made between the Canadian Indians and the British Crown. These treaties recognize the equal sovereignty of the British Crown and Iroquois, but also establish that the British have the right to make laws for the Indians. The treaties are known historically as the ''Two Row Treaty,'' and the ''Silver Calumet Treaty.''

1768. The Six Nations are forced to surrender all lands between the Ohio and the Tennessee Rivers to the English, but the Iroquois ceded land to which they had no right.

1769. Pontiac is assassinated.

The land of the Indians of San Diego is visited by Spanish missionaries and soldiers. They welcome the visitors, only to learn very quickly that they have now become forced laborers and slaves.

1775. A group of Cherokee Indians migrates to Arkansas.

1777. Chief Dragging Canoe and the Cherokees are forced to sign treaties ceding large tracts of their land.

1778. On September 17, the Delaware sign a treaty with the newly established U.S. government. Statehood for the Delaware tribe is promised, with a seat in Congress. For unknown reasons, this promise was never fulfilled. However, this treaty was the first between the United States and an Indian Nation.

1779. Many of the Iroquois continue to fight against U.S. troops.

1780. The Hopi and Zuni Indians are ravaged by smallpox.

1782. Christian Delawares are massacred at Gnanenhutten, Ohio.

The Yuma Indians revolt, wiping out the missions, and destroying all vestiges of Spanish oppression.

1785. The Cherokee, Catawba, Creek, Chickasaw, Choctaw, and other tribes are forced to sign the Treaty of Hopewell, ceding millions of acres of land in Kentucky, Tennessee, North Carolina, and other areas to the Americans.

A campaign of extermination is fully launched against the Apache. Alcohol is introduced to demoralize them.

1789. Delaware Indians migrate in small groups to Missouri.

1790. Indians of the Northwest Ohio Territory are attacked by 400 armed men, known as the ''Miami Expedition,'' commanded by Colonel John Hardin. Hardin's troops are ignominiously defeated, and the armed force retreats.

1791. Villages of the Wea Tribe are destroyed by U.S. troops.

Little Turtle, a Miami war leader, attacks the forces of General Arthur St. Clair, governor of the Northwest Territory.

1794. The Oneida, Tuscarora, and Stockbridge Tribes sign a treaty with the United States, providing that the federal government make education available to them.

The Pickering Treaty is signed between the Seneca and the United States.

Under pressure, more Cherokee Indians migrate to the Arkansas-Texas area. Cherokee Indians who fought with the English during the American Revolution now surrender, probably the last of the English forces to do so.

A treaty is signed at Greenville by the Potawatomi, the Kickapoo, and the commonwealth of Massachusetts. Large tracts of land are ceded to the state.

The Nineteenth Century

Every year of the nineteenth century was significant for Native American history. The century was marked by war with the Indians, and attempts to negate their title to their land.

1802. The Osage Indians move from Missouri into Oklahoma.

1803. The Kaskaskia Indians cede their Illinois land to the U.S. government.

1804. The Sac and Fox Indians are confronted with a treaty which is illegally signed by unauthorized persons, and the Indians lose fifty million acres of land.

1805. The Creek Tribe's title to land in the South is extinguished under duress.

1807. Joseph Brant, Mohawk leader, dies on November 24.

1809. The Delaware, Potawatomi, and other tribes are forced to cede three million acres of their land for $7,000 including land in Wisconsin, Indiana, Illinois, and portions of Ohio and Michigan.

1810. Tecumseh, a Shawnee leader, repudiates the fraudulent land purchases made in 1809, at a meeting between the Indians and General Benjamin Harrison's treaty commission.

1811. At the Battle of Tippecanoe, Tecumseh's brother Tenskwatawa, the Prophet, leads a premature attack on the Americans, led by General Harrison, and is defeated.

The Apache rebel again, following the unsuccessful settlement policy of the U.S. government.

1814. General Andrew Jackson demands and receives 23 million acres of Creek land, which is nearly all of the state of Alabama and a fifth of the state of Georgia.

1815. The first of many treaties and agreements is signed with the Sioux. Treaties are also signed with the Iowa and the Potawatomi.

1816. A treaty is made with the Winnebago.

1817. The Delaware cede all their remaining land.

1818. The Quapaw Indians cede all their remaining lands. Reservation land is set aside for them, a mere fraction of their original holdings. A treaty is made with the Osage, giving them parcels of land which have already been ceded to Cherokee who migrated into Arkansas. The treaty with the Tamaroa is made, ceding all their lands in Illinois, and providing for their removal. A treaty of land cession is signed with the Peoria Indians.

The Seminole Indians begin to war against the United States.

1819. The Kickapoo cede their land to the United States.

1820. The state of Maine is created from the commonwealth of Massachusetts. A total of 395,000 acres of land which had been set aside for the Passamaquaody Indians are sold off and the proceeds from the sale placed in the state treasury.

1823. The Seminole Indians sign a treaty establishing a reservation.

1824. The Quapaw are forced to cede their land and remove to the Oklahoma Territory.

The Iowa Indians cede all their land to the state of Missouri.

The Indians of the United States come under the jurisdiction of another governmental agency, the Bureau of Indian Affairs (BIA), established under the War Department.

1825. The first treaty with the Cheyenne is signed.

The Osage and Kansa Indians cede all their land in exchange for two small reservations.

1829. The Delaware Indians, with the final cession of their land in Ohio, remove to the Oklahoma Territory.

1830. The Western Cherokee exchange their land in Arkansas for land in the Oklahoma Territory.

The U.S. Indian Removal Act is passed by Congress. Eastern Indian tribes are faced with removal. President Jackson's signature implements the ''voluntary'' exchange of eastern Indian lands for territory west of the Mississippi River.

1831. The Choctaw people are removed to the Oklahoma Territory. The Seneca Indians cede some of their land.

The Black HawkWar begins.

1832. The BlackHawk War is over, the Indians having been driven through the forests directly into the Bad Axe Massacre on August 3.

After a long period of negotiation with the U.S. government, the Cherokee Nation finally comes before the Supreme Court. Chief Justice John Marshall, in *Worcester v. Georgia*, decides that the Cherokee Nation is sovereign, with rights to the soil of their homeland and not subject to state or federal forces. President Andrew Jackson ignores the decision of the Supreme Court in a historic mockery of democratic justice, and the removal process continues.

The appointment of a Commissioner of Indian Affairs, who is to report to the Secretary of War, is authorized by Congress.

1833. The Chippewa, Ottawa, and Potawatomi Indians cede 300,000 acres of their land. They are to be removed.

1835. The Comanche Indians make a treaty with the United States, ceding all their Louisiana land. They move to the Brazos River area.

The Seminole people receive an ultimatum: remove or be removed by force. Agent Thompson, with his civilian army on its way to force Seminole removal, is ambushed at the Battle of the Great Wahoo Swamp.

Congress enacts the ''Reorganization Act,'' empowering the army to quarantine Indians in order to expedite their ''civilizing'' process.

The notorious ''New Echota Treaty,'' is signed by the Ridge Group, which represents only a small fraction of the Cherokee Nation.

1836. The Creek Indians are forcibly removed to Oklahoma.

Congress ratifies the New Echota Treaty despite protests of the Cherokee National Council. Dissension over the false treaty arises throughout the United States. Depredations continue against the Cherokee in Georgia and they are forced to remove.

1837. The Kiowa and Apache Indians make a treaty with the United States.

1838. The Cherokee Indians are marched by force to the Oklahoma Territory over the Trail of Tears.

1840. The Winnebago are removed to Oklahoma. Most of them return that same year to their own lands, violating instructions to the contrary.

Eastern Cherokee who remain in North Carolina are given a small reservation in that state.

1846. The Kaskaskia Indians cede to the United States two million acres. They are allowed only a small reservation.

1849. Gold is discovered in California.

The Treaty of Guadalupe Hidalgo is signed between the United States and Mexico.

Control of the Bureau of Indian Affairs is transferred from the War Department to the Department of the Interior.

1851. Plains Indian tribes sign the Treaty of Fort Laramie, making land cessions and permitting roads to be built through their land.

1852. A treaty is signed by the Mescalero and Chiricahua Apache Indians at Santa Fe.

1854. The Oto Tribe cedes its Nebraska land to the United States.

Washington State tribes cede two-thirds of their land at the Treaty of Medicine Creek, reserving certain lands and the right to hunt and fish in perpetuity.

1859. Kansa Indians cede one-half of their reservation to the United States. The Caddo tribes on the Texas Brazos River move to Oklahoma near the Washita River.

1861. The Cheyenne and Arapaho make a treaty ceding their lands in Kansas, Wyoming, Nebraska, and Colorado, with the exception of the triangular reservation located near the Big Sandy Creek on the Purgatoire River in southeastern Colorado.

The Apache, at a meeting held during a truce with the United States, are taken prisoner. Cochise, chief of the Chiricahua, escapes.

1862. Cochise and Mangas Coloradas, Mimbreño Apache chief, declare war against the United States.

1863. The Wallowa cede their land in the Treaty of Lapwai.

The Utes sign a treaty in which they are given a reservation in Colorado, in exchange for most of their land.

Mangas Coloradas is captured under a flag of truce and then shot.

The Navajo are imprisoned. More than one-half of the tribe dies during four years of captivity.

The Nez Perce are forced onto reservations.

1867. The U.S. government and the Cheyenne, Arapaho, Kiowa, and Comanche sign the Medicine Lodge Treaty which provides for land cessions and removal to Oklahoma.

The natives of Alaska are unaware that the United States and Russia have signed a treaty in which the United States has purchased the territory of Alaska. The treaty provides that citizenship (and implicitly, land title) be withheld from the "uncivilized tribes." This issue results in a massive land claim by Americans due to their government's failure to negotiate with the natives instead of with Russia, a foreign power.

1868. The Sioux sign a new Fort Laramie treaty in which the railroads will be permitted to go through their territory. Red Cloud signs the treaty, and is denounced as a traitor.

The imprisoned Navajo are permitted to return to their land.

1869. The Kiowa Indians enter their Oklahoma reservation.

The Utes make a treaty with Kit Carson, a representative of the U.S. government.

1870. The Modoc War starts in Oregon.

1871. The United States, through an enabling act of Congress, ends the treaty-making process with the tribes.

1872. Two thousand non-combatant Modoc Indians are given lands in Oregon for a reservation. The remaining Modoc Indians are removed to Oklahoma.

1873. The Kansa Tribe sells all of its remaining reservation land, and removes to Oklahoma.

The Ute Indians cede a portion of their Colorado land.

1874. President Ulysses S. Grant creates the Pyramid Lake Reservation in Nevada with an executive order.

The Ute Indians cede a strip of land seventy by one hundred miles in the San Juan mining area of Colorado.

The Apache Tribes, and generally all Arizona tribes, are moved from the War Department's jurisdiction to that of the Bureau of Indian Affairs. President Grant orders the removal of the Apache from the Verde Reservation to the San Carlos Reservation.

1875. The Ponca Tribe is removed to Oklahoma from Nebraska.

1877. Sitting Bull, leader of the Hunkpapa Sioux, takes his people to Canada.

Chief Joseph starts to lead his tribe, the Nez Perce, to Canada but is caught before reaching his destination. He and his surviving people are sent to Oklahoma.

1878. The southern Ute people cede eighteen million acres of their land.

The Carlisle Indian School is established in Pennsylvania. It is a boarding school designed to instill the work ethnic into Indian children.

1881. Sitting Bull returns from Canada and is killed by reservation guards.

1883. The Kickapoo are removed from Mexico to Oklahoma.

1884. The Alaskan Organic Act is passed, and the United States promises "title to Alaskan Native Lands" to the natives of Alaska.

1885. The Nez Perce are allowed to return from Oklahoma to the Colville Reservation in the state of Washington.

1887. The Dawes Act is passed, making Indian land available to others, and generally destroying the Indian economy and culture. The act provides that allotments of land be made to heads of families and individuals.

1889. The Cheyenne-Arapaho tribe loses 3.5 million acres of its land when the United States sells it to others.

1891. Lands of the Kickapoo in Oklahoma are ceded and allotted.

1893. The Cheyenne Outlet is opened to homesteaders.

The Dawes Commission is established to prepare rolls of the names of Indian families living on reservations to enable the allotment of land owned in common by the tribe into single-family plots. Many Indians, through fraud, are excluded from the rolls.

The United States extinguishes all tribal titles in the Oklahoma, prior to granting statehood.

1894. Congress acts to allow the Apache prisoners in Florida to return west with their families to Fort Sill, Oklahoma.

Basic Genealogical Research Methods and their Application to Native Americans

George J. Nixon

A professional genealogist since 1976, George J. Nixon studied history at the University of California, Los Angeles, and served in the U.S. Navy. His areas of research include the United States and Canada, specializing in and lecturing on Native American genealogy. In addition to his practice as a self-employed genealogist and author, Mr. Nixon serves in the identification of missing heirs for a major probate research firm.

Getting Started

Good charting and record keeping techniques are an absolute requirement for the amateur, as well as the professional, genealogist. Simply put, without adequate record keeping technique, you will find yourself floundering in a sea of paper without a compass to guide you.

Charting and Record Keeping Forms

There are numerous record keeping forms available to the genealogist ranging in format from the very simple to the elaborate and complicated, however, any record keeping system needs to include the following forms:

Family Group Sheet. A genealogical form designed to show information about the family unit, it includes information about the husband, wife, and children.

Lineage or Pedigree Chart. A form used in genealogical research to illustrate graphically the direct ancestors of the principal subject, it provides a synopsis of the information contained on the family group sheets.

Research Calendar or Log. A form (see Figure 2.1) used to record the sources searched and the results of each search. It contains the name of the principal subject of research; date of the search; name of the library, repository, or archive where search was made; library call number; description and general condition of the source; research objective; comments about research findings; and document number.

Document Extract Form. A form used to record information which cannot be photocopied. Many records are in such poor condition that photocopying or other handling is not allowed. This form contains the same information found on the research calendar in addition to an extract of all pertinent information found in the original document. The form is numbered as if it was an original document.

Among the numerous forms utilized by Native American agents in their record keeping were census, probate and heirship, school records, welfare, health, vital records, annuity/payroll, and family register forms. Modified versions of these forms can be incorporated into your own record keeping system. As such, they become document extract forms and should be numbered as you would any original document in your research file. (See Figures 2.4 through 2.10 for examples of modified forms.)

Correspondence Log. Form containing information about correspondence relating to research: date, to whom, response, results, etc.

Research Source Checklist. A simple checklist of sources to be searched. Categories of sources are: family records, vital statistics, compiled sources, public sources, and private sources.

All of these forms are important to the genealogist and are designed to enable the researcher to quickly determine what research has been completed and to plan the course of future research.

The Native American Family Group Sheet

Most genealogical forms in use today allow for the notation of information about an individual or a family unit. These forms, however, do not allow for easy recording of information about an individual or family of Native American descent.

Tracing the ancestry of an individual with Native American origins requires knowledge of such things as the "roll number" (number assigned to a person on a

Research Calendar

Page _____ of _____

Subject:

Researcher: | **File No.:**

Library or Repository / Call Number	Description of Source	Indexed / Condition	Search Objective	Time Period Searched	Comments	Document Number

Figure 2.1. Research Calendar. Accommodates recording of information about sources searched and results found.

tribal roll) or "allotment number" (number assigned to a person wishing to be included in allotments of Native American lands) and, perhaps most important, his or her Indian name.

Information on the Native American family group sheet (see Figure 2.2, parts 1 and 2) should include the following: husband's and wife's English and Indian names, English translations of the Indian names, tribe, degree of blood, roll or allotment number, date and place of birth, date and place of baptism, date and place of marriage, how married, date and place of death, date and place of burial, father's and mother's English and Indian names, English translation of Indian names, father's and mother's tribe and degree of blood, roll or allotment numbers, information about other marriages of the husband and/or wife, and information concerning plural marriages of the husband. An additional page for information about children should be included.

Home Sources

Every household contains a papertrail: photographs of grandparents or great-grandparents, diaries, scrapbooks, and correspondence between relatives. These items may have been kept for remembrance of ancestors long deceased. That dusty old shoebox in the closet often holds the solution to many a genealogical puzzle. Insurance policies, military discharge papers, and medical records may have been retained in the expectation that they would be needed for some purpose in the future. Stuck away, long forgotten, they become valuable sources of information to the genealogist. All of these documents and treasures provide some type of information about the ancestor: perhaps only a place of former residence; or a reference to Aunt Maud, whom you had forgotten about. Perhaps scrawled on the reverse of that old photograph is a date and name of the photographic studio with the local address. The return address on an old envelope can provide you with a clue about the location of a relative about whom you have only heard through conversations of your parents.

Photographs can provide clues to your Native American heritage, but keep in mind that appearances can be deceiving and certain physical characteristics are only clues, not proof, of ethnicity.

Interviewing a family member. Oral history has always been important in Native American culture. The legends and histories of many tribes have been preserved through oral history.

The personal interview of a family member can enrich your family history tremendously. In a successful interview, parents and other relatives provide a great deal of information which might otherwise be lost.

The interviewer needs to first determine who should be interviewed. This person should be old enough to have lived through historically significant events, but young enough to remember them well.

One source suggests:

> It is best not to interview your own parents. A child may have an excellent relationship with his mother and father, but the child is still their child. . . . Parents can never be completely candid with their children, and often it's much easier for them to talk to a less emotionally-involved [interviewer. . . . The purpose of an oral history is to find out the meaningful events in a person's life, not to rehash old family feuds. (Epstein and Mendelsohn 1978, p. 14)

It is a good idea to prepare for the interview by first gathering some background information. The subject's full English name and, if available, the Indian name and translation; the tribe; date and place of birth; places where the subject lived as a child; marriage information; names of siblings and children; military service; occupation; interests; and hobbies.

For examples of subjects to cover in an interview, see Figure 2.3.

For the novice, a good example of an interview can be found by consulting the Duke University Oral History Collection. This collection, supported by Doris Duke, was an effort to record Native American oral histories. The collection is quite large and covers a wide range of topics. This collection, of course, is also an excellent source of genealogical information. (See "Private Collections" in the "Records Specific to Native Americans" chapter for more information.) For instance, an interview with Grandma Benally, a Navajo woman, was conducted on May 4, 1968, at Canyon del Muerto, Canyon de Chelly, Arizona. An interpreter was employed to assist with the interview which is seventeen pages in length and covers a myriad of topics. In response to a suggestion that she tell about her maternal grandmother, she replied:

> Well, my maternal grandmother's name was Nah-dli-yani-bah. And my grandmother's name was Nah-dli-yani-bah. And my maternal grandfather was named Dineh-tlohl. And that was the name of my old maternal grandfather. And my mother was named Tah-dee-zbah. Any my father was named Tlizi-lani. He didn't have a name, they just called him Tlizi-lani, or Many Goats. And his name was Tlizi-lani, that was my father, and that's how it is. And my paternal grandmother was named Yinil-bah, and that was my paternal grandmother. And her husband was Ton-tsoni clan and that was the father of my father, and his name was Tah-tsoni-hadil-chahli. And so that's how it is, and that's all there is to that. Do you want me to tell about the other part, too? And this is where it ends. My maternal grandmother was born at Tseh-bi-ghaa-ho-dzani (Hole in the Rock, or Hole through the Rock). And she was born there in the corner of the rocks there, or a cove. And this is just what I have heard, I wasn't present at her birth. Then, when she was born, she was given a name; and the name was Yi-dah-ni-bah. And that's what she was called. And so she was born there. And her paternal grandparents, I don't know

Family Group Sheet: Native American.

Page of

Husband's English Name:					
Indian Name:					
EnglishTranslation:					
Tribe:		Degree of Blood:		Roll No./Allotment No:	
Date of Birth:		Place:			
Date of Bapt:		Place:			
Date of Marriage:		Place:			
How Married:					
Date of Death:		Place:			
Date of Burial:		Place:			
Father's English Name:					
Indian Name:					
English Translation:					
Tribe:		Degree of Blood:		Roll No./Allotment No.	
Mother's English Name:					
Indian Name:					
English Translation:					
Tribe:		Degree of Blood:		Roll No./Allotment No:	
Other wives:	1)				
Plural Marriages:	2)				
	3)				
	4)				
Wife's English Name:					
Indian name:					
English Translation:					
Tribe:		Degree of Blood:		Roll No./Allotment No:	
Date of Birth:		Place:			
Date of Bapt:		Place:			
Date of Death:		Place:			
Date of Burial:		Place:			
Father's English Name:					
Indian Name:					
English Translation:					
Tribe:		Degree of Blood:		Roll No./Allotment No:	
Mother's English Name:					
Indian Name:					
English Translation:					
Tribe:		Degree of Blood:		Roll No./Allotment No:	
Other Husbands:	1)				
	2)				
	3)				
	4)				

Figure 2.2. Native American Family Group Sheet (Part 1). Accommodates information about the husband and wife as gathered from agency records and other sources.

FAMILY GROUP SHEET: NATIVE AMERICAN. **PAGE OF**

Husband:						
Wife:						
No.	Sex	English Name:				
		Indian Name:				
		English Translation:				
		Tribe:		Degree of Blood:		Roll No/Allotment No:
		Date of Birth:		Place:		
		Date of Bapt:		Place:		
		Date of Death:		Place:		
		Date of Burial:		Place:		
No.	Sex	Englixh Name:				
		Indian Name:				
		English Translation:				
		Tribe:		Degree of Blood:		Roll No/Allotment No:
		Date of Birth:		Place:		
		Date of Bapt:		Place:		
		Date of Death:		Place:		
		Date of Burial:		Place:		
No.	Sex	Englixh Name:				
		Indian Name:				
		English Translation:				
		Tribe:		Degree of Blood:		Roll No/Allotment No:
		Date of Birth:		Place:		
		Date of Bapt:		Place:		
		Date of Death:		Place:		
		Date of Burial:		Place:		
No.	Sex	Englixh Name:				
		Indian Name:				
		English Translation:				
		Tribe:		Degree of Blood:		Roll No/Allotment No:
		Date of Birth:		Place:		
		Date of Bapt:		Place:		
		Date of Death:		Place:		
		Date of Burial:		Place:		
No.	Sex	Englixh Name:				
		Indian Name:				
		English Translation:				
		Tribe:		Degree of Blood:		Roll No/Allotment No:
		Date of Birth:		Place:		
		Date of Bapt:		Place:		
		Date of Death:		Place:		
		Date of Burial:		Place:		

Figure 2.2 continued. Native American Family Group Sheet (Part 2). Accommodates information about the children as gathered from agency records and other sources.

Suggested Outline for Interview

1. Where and when born
2. Names and descriptions of paternal and maternal grandparents and great-grandparents: interests, physical traits, occupations
3. The Reservation
   A. Conditions of life: typical day—how spent
   B. Description of the home, siblings, holidays
   C. Description of the town, agency, school
4. Stories and traditions

Suggested Outline for Family History

1. Childhood
   A. Memories of parents and/or grandparents, great-grandparents: physical characteristics, occupations
   B. Siblings: names, characteristics
   C. Other relatives remembered
   D. Education: elementary school, teachers, classmates
   E. Remembrances of family vacations, illnesses, reunions, position in neighborhood
   F. Religious background: church, religion in home, holidays
   G. Chores at home, responsibilities
2. Young Adulthood
   A. Adolescence: changes in ideas, physical looks, friends
   B. High school: teachers, grades, dating, awards
   C. Jobs during school, summer, camp experiences
   D. Hobbies and interests: differences between then and now, athletics, political ideas
   E. College and graduate (or professional) school, if any. Events at school: jobs, friends, awards
3. Military Service
4. Career Choice
   A. Where worked and why. Job conditions
   B. Impressions of co-workers, superiors; promotions; travel assignments; accomplishments; professional organizations and affiliations; salaries
5. Dating and Marriage
   A. How young people met
   B. Where met spouse
   C. Parents' reactions
   D. Spouse: physical characteristics, education, occupation
   E. Description of the wedding. Decision where to live. Early years of marriage: anecdotes, basic survival

Figure 2.3

6. Family Life
   A. Children: names, when born, physical and psychological characteristics, interests
   B. Attitudes about childraising: differences from own upbringing, changes with later children, problems
   C. Family vacations, religious upbringing, illnesses, traditions, family cures, family expressions
7. Travel
   A. First trip away from hometown: where, why, how different from hometown, attitude towards hometown on return
   B. Travel to other cities and countries: impressions—negative and positive, anecdotes.
8. Later Life
   A. Happy events and pleasant memories
   B. Problems: illnesses, deaths, traumatic experiences
   C. Political events: wars, the Depression, memories of presidents, political rallies, national and local events, changes in society, changes in technology
   D. Philosophy of life (what has been of outstanding importance): family, job, politics, religion, friends. Advice to grandchildren

Figure 2.3 continued

who they were or what they were, but they gave her the name. Her father and her paternal grandparents gave her the name. And I don't recall the name of her paternal grandmother. And her father they called Host-i-tsini. And that was the father of my maternal grandmother. And her paternal grandmother, I don't remember her name. And the father of my maternal grandmother, they called him Hosti-i-tanni. And we were born for the same clan, he was also born of the Tlizi-lani clan. And that's who they called Tsini. And that was my maternal grandmother's father. And her mother was named Bizhil-bah. And this was the mother of my maternal grandmother. And the man that was her father was called Tse-yini-neh-i. And this was the father of my grandmother on mother's side. My father was named Tse-hini-neh-i, this is what my grandmother used to say. And they had land down in the canyon, and that's where they gave birth to their children. And then from here on things are not known. This is the way that things are told. And my maternal grandmother must have come from a large family—they were seven girls, and they have all scattered about, and there are still some that are still living. And that her mother had seven girls, and so they were one family. And those were girls, there were five boys, the brothers of my maternal grandmother. Maybe they are counted in there also. And they were my maternal grandfathers . . . and there was one who was the older brother of my maternal grandmother and his name was Tlaii (Lefty), and there was another one named Nahl-das, and there was a man that wasn't named properly, they called him Bil-nahachi, and that was the uncle of my grandmother on her mother's side. And these were the older folks then. And there was one called Ba-ah-lili. And these were the brothers of my maternal grandmother. And so that's how it is, and that on my grandmother's side. And on my mother's side, do you want me to continue on with that? My mother's name was Tah-de-zbah. And they called her Tah-dez-bah. And her mothers, the mother of my mother, which was another mother, or an aunt of my mother. And they were as one. And her father was my maternal grandfather, that was her father. The one that I said they named Asdsah-hush-keh. And there was one named Asdsah-ahl-tsi-hi; and they were of one also. And the . . . my mother's father's mother was named Asdsah-hush-keh, and she had sisters, and from there on it is not known again. It wasn't just recently, but it was a long time ago that they died. And the stories are just told about them. . . . (Benally 1968)

Basic Genealogical Sources

Agency Census Records

There are four basic census forms used by government agencies to record information about Native American families residing on reservations.

Agency Census Form—1885–1910. This form was used between 1885 and 1910. Information includes name of tribe, reservation, census number, Indian name, English name, sex, relationship, and age.

Agency Census Form—1911–1928. Information includes name of tribe, reservation, present census number, previous census number, Indian name, English name, sex, relationship, and date of birth (see Figure 2.4). By including present and previous census numbers, it is easier to trace an individual through the censuses (this is important if the name has changed). Notice the "age" column is now "date of birth," although until 1929, in most cases, only the year of birth was listed.

Agency Census Form—1929. The form (see Figure 2.5) includes name of tribe, reservation, present census number, previous census number, Indian name, English name, allotment or annuity number, sex, date of birth, degree of blood, marital condition, relationship to head of family.

The agent was given specific instructions as to the completion of this form. Names were to be listed alphabetically and in a specific order: head of family, wife, then children in order of their ages. A family was defined as: (a) both parents and the unmarried children living with them. In the case of plural wives, the oldest wife with her unmarried children was listed first and the others in order of their ages; (b) either parent and the unmarried children, if the other parent was deceased or permanently residing elsewhere; (c) a single person over eighteen years of age, not living with any relatives.

Agency Census Form—1930 and after. This form (see Figure 2.6) includes name of tribe, name of reservation, census number, surname, given name, sex, age at last birthday, tribe, degree of blood, marital status, relation to head of family, whether living at jurisdiction where enrolled, whether living at another jurisdiction, address if living elsewhere, whether a ward of the government, allotment or annuity number.

After 1932, year of birth was recorded in the age column and the last census role number was typewritten in the relationship column. In 1938 a new column, "last census roll number," was added. Forms were discontinued in 1940. (See the "Records Specific to Native Americans" chapter for additional information.)

Federal Census Records

Perhaps the two most important federal censuses for Native Americans were those conducted in 1900 and 1910 that included "Indian Population" schedule sheets. (Native Americans who had assimulated were enumerated with the general population of the U.S.) These two censuses provide important information about the individual's English and Indian names, tribal affiliation, tribal affiliation of parents, degree of Native American and white blood, degree of Native American and white blood of parents, education, and land allotments.

Enumeration of Native Americans in the federal census prior 1880 can present an identification problem to researchers. It is not unusual to encounter an Native American family enumerated as "Mulatto" or "Black." This is quite common in the states of Alabama, Georgia, Tennessee, North Carolina, South Carolina, Louisiana, and Mississippi. By 1880 such instances are less common, but the researcher should keep the possibility of misidentification in mind. In addition, the odds as to whether the census taker would choose to enumerate Native American groups in his area varied greatly.

There is a special 1880 enumeration of Native Americans who were residing on reservations close to military forts. It was conducted in the states of Oregon, Washington, and California.

Federal censuses after 1910 did not offer separate Indian schedules.

State Census Records

The interim censuses of Michigan, Minnesota, Wisconsin, Kansas, Iowa, Nebraska, North Dakota, South Dakota, and Montana can be very useful to the researcher. In those states where reservations are located, the interim census often includes an enumeration of the reservation(s). Even if a family is living off the reservation, the designation of "Indian" is still given.

As in the case of federal censuses, the researcher needs to keep in mind that a Native American family may be listed as "Mulatto" or "Black" on an interim census.

Probate and Heirship Records

Affidavit as to Lawful Heirs. Information includes state, county, name of decedent, name of tribe and reservation, allotment number, locality and description of land owned by the decedent, date of death, age, marital status, and the names of any heirs (see Figure 2.7).

Report of Heirship. A very important record, this is a four page form and contains the following information: name of agency, date, name of decedent, name of tribe, allotment number, annuity number, voucher number, state of residence at time of death, date of death, age, location of property or real estate, description of land allotment owned by decedent, description of personal property, names of children of decedent's children, names of parents of decedent, brothers and sisters of decedent, names of children of deceased brothers and sisters, names of other lineal descendants of decedent, names of grandparents of decedent, names of collateral relatives, and the names of individuals determined to be heirs of the decedent (see Figure 2.8).

Data for Heirship Finding. Information includes name of allottee, age, date of death, allotment number, annuity

INDIAN CENSUS ROLL

Census of the .... *Indians of* .... *Agency,* ....
on ...., *19*....., *taken by* ...., ...
(Name) (Official Title)

NUMBER.		INDIAN NAME	ENGLISH NAME	Relation-ship	DATE OF BIRTH	Sex
Last	Present					

File Number:	Repository:		Call Number:
Description of source:			
Indexed:	Condition:	Time Period:	Date:
Search Objective:			
			Document No:

Figure 2.4. Agency Census Roll Form (1911-1928) modified into a Document Extract Form for record keeping purposes.

INDIAN CENSUS ROLL

Page ....

Census of the .... tribe of the .... reservation of the ....

jurisdiction, as of ...., 19....., taken by ...., Superintendent.

CENSUS NUMBER.		NAME			Allotment Annuity Identification Number	Sex	Date of Birth			Degree of blood	Marital condition	Relationship to head of family
			English									
Present	Past	Indian	Surname	Given			Mo.	Day	Year			

File Number:	Repository:		Call Number:
Description of source:			
Indexed:	Condition:	Time Period:	Date:
Search Objective:			
			Document No:

Figure 2.5. Agency Census Roll Form (1929) modified into a Document Extraction Form for record keeping purposes.

INDIAN CENSUS ROLL

Census of the ....reservation of the ....Jurisdiction, as of .... 19....., taken by .... Superintendent.

Number	Name		Sex	Age at Last Birthday	Tribe	Degree of Blood	Marital Status
	Surname	Given					
1	2	3	4	5	6	7	8

Relation to Head of Family	Residence					Ward	Allotment, Annuity, and Identification Number
	At Jurisdiction Where Enrolled	At Another Jurisdiction	Elsewhere				
	Yes or No	Name	Post Office	County	State	Yes or No	
9	10	11	12	13	14	15	16

File Number:	Repository:		Call Number:
Description of source:			
Indexed:	Condition:	Time Period:	Date:
Search Objective:			
			Document No:

Figure 2.6. Agency Census Roll Form (1930-) modified into a Document Extraction Form for record keeping purposes.

AFFIDAVIT AS TO LAWFUL HEIRS.

INHERITED INDIAN LANDS.

State of ....}
County of ....}

.... and ....

of lawful age, each first being duly sworn, say:

That the affiants were well acquainted with ....

Deceased, who was the identical Indian of the .... Tribe of Indians residing on the .... Reservation, to whom a trust or other patent containing restrictions upon alienation was issued for h............ allotment, No. ...., for the following described land situate in the County of ...., State of ...., to wit:

....

....

....

Affiants further say that they are well acquainted with the family of the said ...., deceased allottee; that .... died on or about the ....day of ...., 190........, at the age of .... years, ...married and with .... issue, leaving as h............ sole heirs at law the following-named persons:*

....

....

....

Affiants further say that they are each well acquainted with the grantors who acknowledged a deed bearing date ...., 190........., conveying the above described land to ....; that the said persons are the identical persons by name hereinbefore mentioned as the sole heirs of the deceased allottee.

Affiants further say that the said allottee did not reside upon h.......... homestead or allotment, nor cultivate the land sold during h.......... lifetime and immediately preceding h.......... death.

Affiants further say that they are each residents of .... County, State of ...., and have been for over .... last past, and are members of the .... Tribe of Indians.

witnesses:

....

....

Subscribed in my presence and sworn to before me this .... day of ...., 190.........

....

Notary Public.

My commission expires ...., 190.........

*Here state every material fact necessary to show descent of the allotment of the deceased allottee under the laws applicable. The names and ages of all the heirs of the allottee should be given, and also the relationship of each heir to the allottee. If any of such heirs have since died, the date of death should be stated, and the names and ages of his or her heirs should be given, with relationship, etc.

File Number:	Repository:		Call Number:
Description of source:			
Indexed:	Condition:	Time Period:	Date:
Search Objective:			
			Document No:

Figure 2.7. Affidavit As To Lawful Heirs Form modified into a Document Extract Form.

Page 1 of 4

REPORT OF HEIRSHIP.

.... AGENCY,

.... 19..............

Decedent..,Tribe...

Allotment No. ...., Annuity Roll No. .... (last on which paid), Voucher No. ...., ... Qr.,.................... (Year.)

State of domicile at time of death ...., Date of death..

Age ...., Location of real property, State of...

ESTATE, so far as known, under Government control. (If inherited property is not partitioned, describe all and give proportion. If heirs have not been determined, describe property in which decedent had an apparent interest.)

REAL PROPERTY. (Original and inherited. Describe original on first line.)

Allotment		Description of Land, Date of Trust Patent, Act Under Which Allotted.	Heirs Found by Department.	
No.	Name of allottee.		Date.	Serial No.

PERSONAL PROPERTY.

Amount	Source	Where Deposited

File Number:	Repository:		Call Number:
Description of source:			
Indexed:	Condition:	Time Period:	Date:
Search Objective:			
			Document No:

Figure 2.8. Report of Heirship (page 1 of 4) modified into a Document Extract Form.

CHILDREN OF DECEASED CHILDREN. Page 2 of 4

Names of Grandchildren	Sex and Age	Names of Both Parents, How Married--Indian Custom or Ceremony. (If one is white, so state.)	If Grandchild is dead, Give Date.

PARENTS OF DECEDENT. (If either is white, or of a different tribe, so state.)

Names	Allotment		Marriage		If Either is Dead, Give Date	Tribe
	No.	Date.	Date.	Indian Custom or Ceremony		

BROTHERS AND SISTERS.

Name	Brother or Sister	Age	Name of common Parent if Not of Whole Blood.	If Brother or Sister is Dead, Give Date.

File Number:	Repository:		Call Number:
Description of source:			
Indexed:	Condition:	Time Period:	Date:
Search Objective:			
			Document No:

Figure 2.8 continued. Report of Heirship (page 2 of 4).

ISSUE OF DECEASED BROTHERS OR SISTERS.

Page 3 of 4

Name of Nephew or Niece.	Sex and Age.	Names of Parents, and How Married.	If Child is Dead, Give Date.

OTHER LINEAL DESCENDANTS OF DECEDENT. (Identify persons named by allotment number, or by number on annuity roll on which last paid, describing voucher. Designate parents and grandparents through which heir inherits by letters *f, m, gf, gm, ggf, ggm,* etc.)

Name of Descendant Who Survived Decedent. (If dead, give date; and give family surviving on extra sheets.)	Age.	Names of Parents and Grandparents of Descendant.

GRANDPARENTS OF DECEDENT. (If any are white, so state.)

Names of Father's and Mother's Parents.	Married.		Tribe	If Dead, Give Date
	Date	Indian custom or Ceremony.		
Paternal gf,				
Paternal gm,				
Maternal gf,				
Maternal gm,				

COLLATERAL RELATIVES. (Give line of descent from common ancestor of decedent; give names and designate parents and grandparents of heir in line from common ancestor by letters *f, m, gf, gm, ggf, ggm,* etc. Identify by allotment No. or by number on annuity roll on which last paid.)

Names of Nearest Relatives Who survived Decedent.	If Dead, Give Date; and Use Extra Sheets for Surviving Family.	How Related to Decedent--Degree.	Ancestry in Line from Common Ancestor.

File Number:	Repository:		Call Number:
Description of source:			
Indexed:	Condition:	Time Period:	Date:
Search Objective:			
			Document No:

Figure 2.8 continued. Report of Heirship (page 3 of 4).

ADDITIONAL INFORMATION:.. Page 4 of 4.

....

....

....

....

....

CONFLICT between the official record and the testimony. (If any, give description; if no conflict, say "none.")

....

....

....

....

....

I HEREBY CERTIFY that I have made a careful investigation as to the relatives of the decedent; that my report is correct and substantiated by official records and by the testimony taken at a hearing held on ...., day of ...., 19........., under the provisions of the act of June 25, 1910 (36 Stats., 355), and that it appears that at time of the hearing the heirs of the decedent, ..., and the descent of the estate are as follows:

Heir or Devisee. (Designate which.)	Relationship to Decedent.	Description of Property. (Give amount of personal property.)	Proportion Taken by Descent, Distribution, or Devise.

....

(Official designation.)

File Number:	Repository:		Call Number:
Description of source:			
Indexed:	Condition:	Time Period:	Date:
Search Objective:			
			Document No:

Figure 2.8 continued. Report of Heirship (page 4 of 4).

roll number, voucher number, description of land, date of patent (title, deed), act under which allotment was made, father's name and allotment number, mother's name and allotment number, spouse's name and allotment number, probable heirs and addresses (see Figure 2.9).

Departmental Findings Determining the Heirs of Deceased Indians. Information includes name of decedent, agency, allotment number, date of patent, act under which allotment was made, file number, date of death, date of decision, description of allotment, names of heirs.

Inherited Interests in Estates. Information includes names of heirs, share, names of estates.

Index and Heirship Card—Enrollee. Information includes head of biological family and relation to decedent, head of economical household (household wherein enrollee actually resides) and relation to decedent, allotment number, account number, date of death, probate number, district of residence and address, sex, date of birth, tribe, degree of blood, marital status, name of father and allotment number, name of mother and allotment number, name of spouse and allotment number, names of heirs, remarks. (See the ''Records Specific to Native Americans'' chapter for additional information on Native American wills and heirship matters.)

Vital Records

After the turn of the century, births and deaths were reported by the Bureau of Indian Affairs official in the form of an annual report. In some states, duplicate birth, death, and marriage records were filed with the county and state vital records departments as well. The primary source for these records, prior to about 1920, is the agency having jurisdiction over the reservation. Among the northwestern tribes, Catholic Church records are an excellent source of vital records.

Individual History Card. Information includes tribe, sex, census or allotment number, English name, Indian name, date of birth, date of death, English translation of Indian name, name of father and mother, date of death of father and mother, census or allotment number of father and mother, names of paternal and maternal grandparents, date of death of paternal and maternal grandparents, census or allotment number of paternal and maternal grandparents, names of brothers and sisters, census or allotment numbers of brothers and sisters, names of half-brothers and half-sisters, census or allotment numbers of half-brothers and half-sisters, names of paternal uncles and aunts, census or allotment numbers of paternal uncles and aunts, names of maternal uncles and aunts, census or allotment numbers of maternal uncles and aunts (see Figure 2.10). These can be found at the local regional branch of the National Archives.

Birth Report. Information includes date, name, sex, degree of blood, tribe, date and place of birth, name of mother, remarks.

Annual Report of Births. Information includes state, reservation, agency or jurisdiction, beginning and ending date of report, census roll number, surname, given name, date of birth, whether born alive or stillborn, sex, tribe, degree of Native American blood of father, degree of Native American blood of mother, degree of Native American blood of child, whether a resident at jurisdiction where enrolled, residence if at another jurisdiction.

Annual Report of Deaths. Information includes state, reservation, agency or jurisdiction, beginning and ending dates of report, number on last census roll, surname, given name, date of death, age at death, sex, tribe, degree of blood, whether a resident at jurisdiction where enrolled, residence if at another jurisdiction. All of these records can be found at the regional archives. (See the ''Records Specific to Native Americans'' chapter for more information on vital records.)

School Records

School records normally provide the student's name, residence, name of parent(s) or legal guardian, and age. Often the previous school attended is also given. School records specific to Native Americans include:

School Census Card. Information includes name of child; degree of Native American blood; sex; name, tribe, and degree of Native American blood of father and mother; county; name of head of family; school district; address; school name; health condition of child (poor, fair, moderate, good or excellent); tribe of child; date of birth; grade; date of index card; remarks; name and title of transcribing official.

Permanent School Census Card (a). Information includes student's name; degree of Native American blood; account number; name, tribe, and address of father and mother; year attended school; name of school attended; date of attendance; reason for late attendance; grade; number of miles to public school; whether living with parents or guardian; date of birth; authority (source of information) for date of birth; nature of defect if any; whether employed.

Permanent School Census Card (b). Information includes student's name, degree of Native American blood, date and place of birth, authority for date of birth, tribe, sex, address, name of father and mother, names of paternal grandparents, name of maternal grandfather, names of maternal grandparents, degree of Native American blood of grandparents, tribe of grandparents, roll numbers of parents and grandparents.

DATA FOR HEIRSHIP FINDING

Allottee .... Age ....

Date of death ....

Allotment No. .... Annuity No. .... Vou. .... Qr. ....

Description of land ....

....

Date of Patent ....

Act under which allotted ....

Father's name .... Allotment No. ....

Mother's name .... Allotment No. ....

Spouse's name .... Allotment No. ....

PROBABLE HEIRS	ADDRESS

File Number:	Repository:		Call Number:
Description of source:			
Indexed:	Condition:	Time Period:	Date:
Search Objective:			
			Document No:

Figure 2.9. Data For Heirship Finding modified into a Document Extract Form.

INDIVIDUAL HISTORY CARD.

(Formerly Allottee Family History Card.)

Tribe........................ Sex.............. Census or Allotment No. ....

English name........................ Born.......................... Died..........................

Indian name........................ English Translation of Indian name ....

	DIED	Census or Allotment No.*
Father		
Father's Father		
Father's Mother		
Mother		
Mother's father		
Mother's mother		

Brothers and Half-Brothers	Census or Allotment No.	Uncles, Father's Side	Census or Allotment No.
Died			
Died			
Died			
Died		Uncles, Mother's Side	
Died			
Died			
Died			
Sisters and Half-Sisters			
		Aunts, Father's Side	
Died			
Died			
Died		Aunts, Mother's Side	
Died			
Died			

File Number:	Repository:		Call Number:
Description of source:			
Indexed:	Condition:	Time Period:	Date:
Search Objective:			
			Document No:

Figure 2.10. Individual History Card modified into a Document Extract Form.

Application for Admission to Boarding School. Information includes name of applicant; date; agency; tribe; degree of Native American blood; birthplace; home address; whether home is located on reservation; distance to public school; schools previously attended; dates of attendance; grades completed; reasons for leaving previously-attended schools; name and relationship of person with whom the applicant lives; number of brothers and sisters; number of persons living in home; number of rooms in home; language spoken in home; other names by which the applicant is known; full name of father and mother; whether parents are living; home post office of parents; agency where enrolled; tribe of parents; roll number of parents; degree of Native American blood of parents; education of parents; acres of land owned; income of property; by whom employed; social security number; roll number of grandparents, if parents not on roll; religious preference.

Application for Admission to Non-Reservation School and Test of Eligibility (a). Information includes name and location of Native American school, state, name of applicant, date of birth, age, sex, post office address, tribe, degree of blood, distance from public school, length of term, number of grades in public school, number of teachers, reason for not attending public school, record of attendance (primary, elementary, junior high school, senior high school), reason for application to non-reservation school, preference of courses, previous industrial experience, previous training in music, previous experience in athletics, religious preference.

Application for Enrollment in a Non-Reservation School (b)—a variation of *a*. Information includes English and Indian name of student; name of parents; tribe; reservation; degree of Native American blood; whether either parent is white and, if so, which; whether either parent is allotted and, if so, on what reservation; age of student; name of reservation school attended; date of attendance; whether ever dismissed and, if so, why; physician's certificate of health; endorsement of agent or superintendent.

See the "Records Specific to Native Americans" chapter for more information.

Welfare Records

Department of Public Welfare, Report on Application for General Relief. Information includes first, last, and middle name; address; household number; date of application; date investigation completed; whether employable; family status (single, divorced, widowed, married, separated, or deserted); maiden and married name if applicant is female; variant spellings of surname; information about residence and citizenship; information about residence during past two years; name of landlord; names and vital information about members of household.

General Assistance Record. Information includes family name, variations of family name, address, date, names and vital information about members of household, tribe, family status, maiden name if female, date and place of marriage, wife's previous marriage, husband's previous marriage, children's relatives not in household, religious affiliation, information about military service.

Annuity Payroll Records

Information includes name of tribe, annuity payroll number, name, age, sex, per capita amount, amount paid, mark or signature, signatures of witnesses, date, and remarks.

Cemetery Records/Tombstone Inscriptions

Cemeteries provide valuable information to the researcher. Headstones provide information about dates of birth and death, and often provide clues to other family members who may be buried nearby.

The researcher should not overlook sexton's records, which provide information about the purchaser of the plot, the person who is interred, and dates of interment.

Before visiting a cemetery on a reservation or tribal property, the researcher should obtain permission from tribal officials. Local genealogy societies often maintain gravesite listings. Checking with a local genealogy and/or historical society can often save a trip. The tribe may also maintain cemetery records.

If there is an Native American and non-Native American intermarriage, the family may be buried in a cemetery off the reservation.

Native American Church Records

The records of Native American churches are not part of tribal or government agency records. For this reason, researchers need to direct their attention towards church historical departments and archives.

Reservation churches of the past were, for the most part, of the "mission" type and their records were usually held in regional church repositories. While many of the original missions have long since vanished, their records may be found in the regional or national headquarters of the parent churches.

The Chancery Office of the Catholic Archdiocese in Seattle, Washington, maintains historical church records for the Native American churches within its jurisdiction. Names from church records have been entered into an "Indian Register" which also provides the volume and page number where the original information may be found.

Several of the Catholic Church records of the northwest region have been microfilmed and are available at many libraries.

The Pacific Northwest Tribes Missions Collection of the Oregon Province Archives of the Society of Jesus

The microfilm edition of the Pacific Northwest Tribes Missions Collection of the Oregon Province Archives brings together 30,000 manuscript pages prepared by Jesuit missionaries in the nineteenth and early twentieth centuries.

The records, as well as the history of the missions, are well described in the *Guide to the Microfilm Edition of the Pacific Northwest Tribes Missions Collections of the Oregon Province Archives of the Society of Jesus* (Karriker).

Listed here are the records of those missions that have baptismal, marriage, and death/burial records. Several of the missions retained copies of government census rolls and records of the Native American schools within their jurisdictions.

St. Mary's Mission, Montana: St. Mary's Mission baptismal record, ''Index to Baptisms at St. Mary's Mission Bitter Root Valley, 1866–1904; ''St. Mary's Mission marriage record, ''Liber Matrimoniorum,'' 1866–1894; St. Mary's Mission death record ''Liber Mortuorum,'' 1866–1893; St. Mary's Mission school attendance records, 1919–1940; quarterly school reports for St. Mary's Mission on government forms, 1941–1945; St. Mary's Mission School reports, attendance, 1950–1954; St. Mary's Mission Parish census book, 1948–49; St. Mary's Mission Parish census of late 1940s and 1950s.

St. Ignatius Mission, Montana: Fifty-five marriage certificates of Indians at St. Ignatius, 1901–1907; List of Jesuits buried at St. Ignatius Mission (to 1924); plus a list of those who died at St. Ignatius Mission (to 1942); St. Ignatius Mission Book of Baptisms, 1841–1854; Book of Marriages, 1844–1854; and Book of Deaths, 1844–1854 in twenty-seven handwritten pages. Also a summary of the baptismal records, 1852–1854; St. Ignatius Mission Book of Baptisms, ''Liber Baptismorum, 1854–1873,'' in Latin; also a translation of first twelve entries in baptismal register; St. Ignatius Mission Book of Deaths, ''Liber Defunctorum in Missions S. Ignatii, Wash. Territ,'' 1852–1873, in Latin; also a summary of the number of marriages celebrated at St. Ignatius Mission, 1856–1879; St. Ignatius Mission Book of Marriages, ''Matrimonia,'' 1856–1873, in Latin; Matrimonial Records of the Mission, 1898–1913, in Latin; St. Ignatius Mission Book of Sick Calls, April 26, 1914–February 14, 1853; Flathead Reservation school census of Indian children (only the last quarterly reports for the dates 1916–1923, 1926, and 1928–1930); also a summary statement of St. Ignatius mission school for 1878–1891; ''Attendance at St. Ignatius Mission School(s) from 1888—from reports preserved to September 1895;'' ''Record of St. Ignatius Mission School,'' for the Boys Department in the 1890s; Indian Census at St. Ignatius, no date, in two notebooks; Census Roll for Indians on Flathead Reservation, 1941 and 1948–1949; Census of Our Lady of Sorrows Church at Cusick, Washington, undated, unsigned.

St. Joseph's Mission, Idaho: A List of Catholics who have died near St. Joseph's Mission, Slickpoo, Nez Perce Co., Idaho, 1872–1903; notebook listing those who died near mission, alphabetically by baptismal name; St. Joseph's Mission Register of Deaths, 1906–1919; Record of Baptisms at St. Joseph's Mission, by family name; St. Joseph's Mission Register Vol. 1, 1867–1893, Liber Matrimonium, Baptism, Confirmations (also First Communions, 1913–1916); Census of Indians, June 3, 1912.

St. Paul's Mission, Washington: St. Paul Baptism Register, ''Register Baptizatorum'' covering August 1847 to December 1851. There are entries of 1839 and 1840 copied from another register; also scattered entries from 1869–1870.

St. Francis Regis Mission, Washington: St. Francis Regis Mission at Colville, ''Baptismal Register and Liber Mortuorum,'' St. Francis Regis Mission; baptismal register is 1867–1872, death register is for 1873–1917; St. Francis Regis Mission at Colville ''St. Regis Mission . . . Baptismal Record, 1867–1887;'' Immaculate Conception Church, Colville, ''Book of Baptismal and Marriage records, 1864–1888; St. Paul Mission and St. Francis Regis Mission marriage records, 1848–1879; St. Francis Regis Mission at Colville, record book of baptisms, deaths, marriages, 1870–1893; St. Francis Regis Mission at Colville burial record book, 1853–1887; St. Francis Regis Mission at Colville, baptismal and marriage record, 1852–1866, in Latin; quarterly Indian school reports for St. Francis Regis Mission at Colville, 1893, 1894, 1900, 1901, 1902; Indian Census of Colville Reservation, June 30, 1917, revised June 30, 1918; Census Spokane Indians of Colville Agency as of June 30, 1927; ''Census of Indians living in the Colville Reservation completed in the year 1923;'' Census of Colville Reservation, 1937.

St. Peters Mission, Montana: ''Quarterly Report of St. Peter's Industrial School,'' covering 1892–1893. Contains student names, addresses, and dates of attendance.

Holy Family Mission, Montana: Census 1923 Blackfeet Agency, June 30, 1923 (carbon copy); ''Reports of Holy Family Indian School,'' register of pupils at Holy Family, 1893–1914; quarterly school reports for Holy Family Mission School, 1911–1933 (except 1926).

St. Paul's Mission, Montana: Typed and handwritten Indian Census of 1939; another census, undated; Indian school reports, December 30, 1890, and December 30, 1891; quarterly school reports for 1928, 1929, 1934, and 1935.

St. Francis Xavier Mission, Montana: Book of ''Names of the Crow Indians,'' with English equivalents; Census of the Crow Tribe, 1902–1903; Catholic census book for Big Horn Valley, 1907 (includes Pryor, 1909, and Black Lodge).

Sacred Heart Mission, Idaho: Record Book of DeSmet Industrial School; quarterly school reports for Sacred Heart Mission School, 1886–1894, not inclusive; Sacred Heart Mission Baptismal Records, 1842–1914; Sacred Heart Mission Marriage Records, 1843–1914; Sacred Heart Mission Burial Records, 1844–1914; Sacred Heart Mission Church record book, 1914–1936 (contains burial, baptismal, and First Communion rolls); Coeur d'Alene Indian census, including school children, by family name, completed in November 1918 and updated in 1920s (index); ''Quarterly Boarding School Report,'' or ''Report of Attendance,'' 1911–1923; ''Report of Attendance'' at Sacred Heart (De Smet) Mission school, 1927–1937; Census of Coeur d'Alene Indian families in 1878–1879; ''1937 Census of Coeur d'Alene Indian Reservation of Northern Idaho Agency, Lapwai, Idaho,'' as of January 1, 1937; Sacred Heart Mission, ''First Holy Communions and Confirmations,'' 1892–1931 at De Smet; Record De Smet Industrial School lists of school attendees and tribe affiliation.

Other Church Records

"Catholic Church Records of the Pacific Northwest." A companion group of records to those described above, this collection includes early church registers in the present states of Washington and Oregon, and includes St. Louis Register, Volume I and II, (1845–1900); Gervais Register, (1875–1893); Brooks Register, (1893–1909); St. Paul, Oregon, (1839–1898); Grand Ronde Register, I and II, (1860–1898); St. Michael the Archangel Parish, Grand Ronde Indian Reservation, Grande Ronde, Oregon; St. Patrick's Parish, Muddy Valley, Oregon.

Hudson's Bay Company Archives: Records of the Hudson's Bay Company, which are housed in provincial archives throughout Canada and in university libraries throughout the United States, are a major source of Native American historical and genealogical records.

Employed by the Hudson's Bay Company, traders traveled along the West Coast region establishing Forts Colville, Nez Perce, and Boise among or near Native American tribes. Native American men and their wives were employed at these forts and at the farms of Hudson Bay Company employees. Many of the Hudson Bay Company men intermarried with Native American women. After the Treaty of 1846, setting the boundary between the United States and Canada, these forts were gradually phased out.

Records of marriages, baptisms, and funerals performed by the company's clergy were preserved under the auspices of the Church of England and are contained in the collection of the Hudson's Bay Company. See Figure 2.11 for a description of the records of the Red River Settlement with their classification reference. The original register is preserved in the Synod Office of the Winnipeg Anglican Church of Canada.

Among the records of the Hudson's Bay Company is a large collection of diaries and journals of its agents and employees. These journals provide insight and valuable historical information about Native Americans.

Military Records

Records Relating to Confederate Military Service. There are muster rolls for various Native American organizations raised by the Confederate government, in addition to other rolls for white organizations that served in the Indian territory.

Most of the relevant information has been abstracted onto cards by the Adjutant General's Office, which had custody of the records. These records include a file for each individual who served in a specific organization or unit. There are also caption and record-of-event cards, which contain information about the activities of each unit as a whole.

Military service records reproduced by the National Archives and Records Administration include *Compiled Service Records of Confederate Soldiers Who Served in Organizations Raised Directly by the Confederate Government,* and *Compiled Service Records of Confederate General and Staff Officers and Nonregimental Enlisted Men.* Both include records of the Cherokee, Chickasaw, Choctaw, Creek, Osage, and Seminole organizations, and the latter group includes files for such staff officers as Brigadier Generals Stand Watie, Douglas H. Cooper, and Albert Pike. Individual files in both collections include original papers in addition to abstracts on cards. Most of the information pertains to the administrative aspects of an officer's career, including appointments, resignations, and recommendations for promotion.

Records Relating to Regular and Volunteer Army Organizations. There is a large volume of material pertaining to military service performed by Native Americans as scouts, guides, and soldiers in regular and volunteer Army organizations, beginning with Will Shorey's corps of Cherokee scouts in 1800. Also available are records of the Cherokee, Choctaw, and Creek organizations that fought in the War of 1812 and in the first Seminole War of 1817–1818; Menominee and Potawatomi in the Black Hawk War; friendly Creek Indians in the Creek War;

Red River Settlement

Series I Reel No.	Classification Reference H.B.C. Archives	Brief Description	Dates	Approx. No. Frames
4M4	E. 4/1a	Register of Baptisms	1820-1841	117
4M5	E. 4/1a	Register of Baptisms	1820-1841	98
4M5	E. 4/1b	Register of Marriages and Burials	1820-1841	79
4M5	E. 4/2	Register of Baptisms, Marriages, and Burials	1841-1851	122
4M5	E. 5/1	Census Returns	1827	15
4M5	E. 5/2	Census Returns	1828	16
4M5	E. 5/3	Census Returns	1829	20
4M6	E. 5/4	Census Returns	1830	22
4M6	E. 5/5	Census Returns	1831	25
4M6	E. 5/6	Census Returns	1832	30
4M6	E. 5/7	Census Returns	1833	38
4M6	E. 5/8	Census Returns	1835	34
4M6	E. 5/9	Census Returns	1838	50
4M6	E. 5/10	Census Returns	1840	43
4M6	E. 5/11	Census Returns	1843	43

Figure 2.II. Red River Settlement Records.

Pueblo who accompanied the Navajo expedition of 1849; and the first, second, and third Indian Home Guard Regiments who fought for the Union Army in the Civil War.

Before the Civil War, Native Americans who served with the army were either enlisted in volunteer organizations or hired in civilian capacities by army officers in the field. An act of July 18, 1866 (14 Stat. 332), authorized the president to enlist and employ up to 1,000 Native American scouts; after this date Native American scouts served as part of the regular establishment. Native American service in infantry and cavalry regiments, authorized by General Order 28, Headquarters of the Army, Adjutant General's Office, dated March 9, 1891, was tried experimentally for several years.

Enlistment papers generally were prepared for each soldier who enlisted in the regular army. In completing an enlistment paper, the enlistee indicated by his signature or mark his willingness to perform military service for a specified period. Usually, the papers also included information about the enlistee's age, place of birth, physical attributes, marital status, occupation, as well as date and place of enlistment. Enlistment papers for Native Americans were, for the most part, maintained separately in a single series, 1866–1914, although some are dispersed among series pertaining largely to non-Native Americans.

The information from each enlistment paper was abstracted and entered into registers, which also contain information about service performed after enlistment, including the date of and reason for termination of service. Enlistment registers for Native Americans also were maintained separately.

Muster Rolls. Muster rolls were lists of soldiers present or accounted for in a particular unit, in most cases a company. They were also prepared at the regimental level to indicate field and staff officers. Muster rolls were submitted on forms supplied by the Adjutant General's Office and covered two-month periods.

Muster rolls provide the name, rank, enlistment data, and wage of each individual. Frequently, space was allowed on the rolls for comments about the state of discipline, military instruction, military appearance, arms, accoutrements, and clothing of the unit as a whole. The "record of events" section, when properly completed, gave a brief account of the unit's activities over the two-month period. Muster rolls for organizations of Indian Scouts for the period from 1866 to 1912 are filed together at the National Archives and include rolls for units from Arizona, California, Montana, Nebraska, North Dakota, Oklahoma, Oregon, South Dakota, Texas, Utah, Washington, and Wyoming.

Naturalization Records

In 1924 Native Americans were collectively naturalized and granted United States citizenship. Thus, there are no naturalization records such as might be found for an individual immigrating from a foreign country.

Genealogy Newspaper Columns

Many tribal newspapers include some form of genealogy column or section devoted to genealogical queries. If the tribal newspaper that you are interested in does not provide such a column, a letter to the editor, making your query, will suffice, especially if the paper is located in a small town.

Other Types of Records

Voter lists. These records are public information. Voter lists usually contain the individual's full name, residence, and date of birth. In the case of a naturalized citizen, the date and place of naturalization and the court is given.

City directories. If the family resided in a large metropolis, city directories can be a valuable tool in determining when an individual first arrived in the city, the name of his spouse and other family members residing at the same address. In the case of a death of the husband, the widow is usually listed as "widow of. . . ."

The sudden absence of an individual in a city directory does not necessarily indicate a death. It may mean that the family removed to another place.

Local histories. Local histories, or county histories, are a great source of genealogical information. County histories published in the late 1880s and early 1900s usually include biographical information about early county residents and their families. Depending upon the publisher, these biographies can be very brief or very extensive.

Often a county gazetteer will include a directory of local merchants and farmers.

Employment records. Employment records can provide the individual's full name, date and place of birth, next of kin, education, and job experience, as well as the name and address of previous employers.

"Who's Who" publications. "Who's Who" publications provide capsule biographies of individuals who have attained notoriety through some achievement in his/her profession or contribution to society. There are such publications for almost every profession, region, and ethnic group.

Social Security records. When any individual applies for a social security card (Form SS-5), his/her full name, residence, date and place of birth, and present employer are given. This information is only available for deceased persons and can be acquired under the Freedom of Information Act. Information may be requested from the Social Security Administration in Baltimore.

Secondary Sources

Secondary sources are usually abstracts or copies of original records compiled by an individual or group to allow easy access. These secondary sources will, in turn, lead you to the original records.

An example of a secondary source is ''Catholic Church Records of the Pacific Northwest.'' The compilers extracted information from microfilms of the original registers. In this instance, the compilers had thc luxury of comparing the microfilm with the original document when there was any question of content. The result is a very valuable source with a minimum of errors. When there was a question that could not be resolved, the compilers clearly indicate the problem. Unfortunately, there is a great deal of material published that simply perpetuates errors in interpretation. Seek out the original document or manuscript if you feel there is any discrepancy.

Native American Newspapers, Periodicals, and Newsletters

These are always a good source of information. Most tribes publish either a newspaper or newsletter on a regular basis which provides information about local events, tribal politics, and vital statistics.

Bibliographies

Bibliographies provide an excellent source of titles and publications by and about Native Americans. Any public or university library will have a selection of bibliographies among its holdings.

Guide to American Indian Documents In the Congressional Serial Set: 1817–1899 (Johnson), *Native Americans: An Annotated Bibliography* (Hoxie and Markowitz), and *A Bibliography of Contemporary North American Indians* (Hodge) are among the most useful.

Repositories

The record groups discussed in this text are all available, in some form, in a library or repository. Repositories, simply put, are the warehouses of our national documents.

When you have completed your basic groundwork, exhausted all the information resources in your immediate vicinity, you may find the need to seek information that can only be obtained from records kept in some repository outside of your geographic area.

Perhaps you need to look at tribal rolls for your tribe, but they are not available in your area. The nearest regional branch of the National Archives, for example, might be in Seattle, Washington. You can plan a visit to the Record Center, or perhaps engage the services of a professional researcher to do the research for you. Sometimes it is not convenient to make a visit to a distant repository, in which case you might consider the latter choice.

In any case, you should prepare a detailed plan of your intended research and clarify your objective(s). You may want to contact the archive to determine what records the repository has that will aid your research. Inquire about any copyright or usage restrictions that the repository might enforce. Most libraries and repositories have a brief listing of their rules and restrictions. Usually they are minimal and are intended to protect and preserve the materials placed in their care. Some private libraries may have more stringent rules. Some repositories allow only writing materials, a tablet, and a pencil in the research room. Restrictions as to the number of documents allowed per request may be enforced. Often, photocopying is not allowed, except if performed by a staff member, and then only at his or her convenience. While these restrictions may seem severe, they are enforced in order to preserve the collection. It is also prudent to double check the hours of operation and the exact location of the repository.

The National Archives

The National Archives and its Regional Branches provide, upon request, detailed descriptive pamphlets and booklets about their record holdings. Other major libraries have prepared inventories and research aids, explaining how to find and use the material you are seeking.

Keep in mind that the archival staff is there to assist you, as well as to maintain the collection. Never be embarrassed to ask a seemingly ''dumb'' question.

Family organizations

Organized by members of a specific family and persons having a surname in common, family organizations provide a means of collecting and organizing genealogical information based on this common factor.

Such organizations often provide a newsletter or publication about members and current research projects as well as information about annual family reunions and other gatherings (a good source of potential interview subjects).

Native American Genealogical Society Libraries

Many genealogy societies maintain Native American research groups and collections on Native American history and genealogy. If the society is limited to the local geographic area, available information may lean towards those tribes resident in the area. Larger societies may encompass the entire state or a region covering several states. Often their data is stored in a local library.

Libraries Holding Major Collections

The Henry Huntington Library, San Mateo, California. Among its holdings are the *Soliday Collection of Fort Nisqually Papers* of the Hudson's Bay Company and the *Puget Sound Agricultural Company* for 1833 to 1870. There are trade books, account books, journals, and letters. The trade and account books list names of Native American employees. The *Reader's Guide to the Huntington Library* provides information about the various materials housed in the library.

The Bancroft Library, Berkeley, California. Hubert Howe Bancroft devoted several volumes to native races. These volumes contain a great deal of Native American history for the period prior to 1883. Two excellent sources of information about holdings of the Bancroft Library are *Catalog of Printed Books in the Bancroft Library* and *A Guide to the Manuscript collections of the Bancroft Library*.

The Beinecke Rare Book and Manuscript Library, Yale University, New Haven, Connecticut. Consult *Catalogue of Western Americana Manuscripts in the Yale University Library* by Mary Withington. This catalog describes the contents of each collection, many of which contain articles of Native American history.

The Newberry Library, Center for the History of the American Indian, Chicago. Holds approximately 130,000 books, articles and manuscripts on Native American and American frontier history. Consult *Catalog of the Edward E. Ayer Collection of American Indians* in the Newberry Library.

State Historical Society of Wisconsin (S.H.S. of W.), Madison, Wisconsin. This society holds the Lyman Draper Manuscript Collection, a major collection of correspondence, interviews and material collected by Draper during his tenure as the society's director. This collection has been microfilmed and a guide to the collection has been published. It contains a gold mine of information about early explorers, Native American leaders, and frontiersmen.

Huntington Free Library, National Museum of the American Indian, Bronx, New York. Holdings include over 40,000 volumes on the archeology, ethnology, and history of the Native American.

The Library of Congress, Washington, D.C. Consult the *Guide to American Indian Doctoral Dissertations* and the *Inventory to the National Indian Collection of Indian Manuscripts*.

U.S. Department of the Interior Library, Washington, D.C. Contains material on Native Americans as well as on the other departments within the Department of the Interior. A valuable research tool is the *Bibliographical and Historical Index of American Indians* (1966).

Public Libraries

Public libraries, like genealogical societies, almost always maintain information about the Native American community in the local area. Public libraries in larger cities often maintain Native American interest groups. See the Bibliography at the end of this chapter for library guides.

Case History

Case Study Concerning the Mississippi Chippewa Indians of the White Earth Reservation, Minnesota

The case study that follows was compiled from available records pertaining to the Mississippi Chippewa Indians of the White Earth Reservation in Minnesota (see Figure 2.12). It will serve to show how research might be conducted and records might be examined. Descriptions of some of the records have already been given, but there are two groups of records that are unique to the Chippewa, and will not be found among records of other agencies: ''The Case Files and Indian Affidavits of the Linnen and Moorehead Investigations, 1909, in the Records of United States Attorneys and Marshals (Record Group 118)'' and ''Papers of Ransom Judd Powell.'' Similar records can be found at all of the regional branches of the National Archives.

The White Earth Agency

The White Earth Agency was the successor to the Chippewa Agency, which was established in 1851. The Chippewa Agency was responsible for the Native Americans in Minnesota known collectively as the Chippewa of the Mississippi, as distinguished from the Chippewa of Lake Superior at the La Pointe Agency. Some of its bands (smaller groups within some tribes), however, were not actually Chippewa of the Mississippi. In 1872 the agency was moved to the White Earth Reservation. In 1873 a

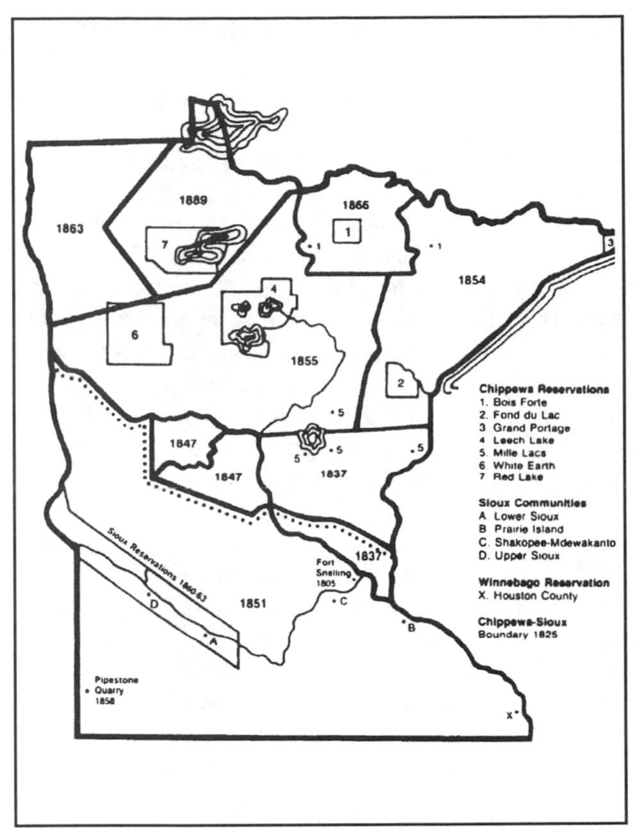

Figure 2.12. Location of White Earth Chippewa Reservation.

separate agency was established for the Red Lake Chippewa, and in 1874 an agency was established at Leech Lake for the Pillager and Lake Winnibigoshish Chippewa living in that area and the Chippewa of the Mississippi living at White Oak Point. The Chippewa Agency at White Earth then had charge of the other Chippewa of the Mississippi (including those who lived at Mille Lacs), the Otter Tail Pillagers, and the Pembina Chippewa. Beginning in 1878 the agency was called the White Earth Agency. In 1879 the Red Lake and Leech Lake Agencies were consolidated into the White Earth Agency.

In 1899 a separate agency was again established at Leech Lake for all the Leech Lake, Cass Lake, Lake Winnibigoshish, White Oak Point, and Red Lake Chippewa except those who had moved to the White Earth Reservation. The White Earth Agency was responsible for White Earth, Gull Lake, Removal and Nonremoval Mille Lac, Removal White Oak Point, Pembina, Removal Fond du Lac, Otter Tail, Removal Leech Lake, and Removal Cass and Winnibigoshish Chippewa. Most of these Native Americans lived on the White Earth Reservation. The term *removal* denotes Native Americans who had moved from ceded reservations to White Earth, mainly under the direction of the Chippewa Commission. In 1922 the White Earth Agency was abolished, and the Native Americans were assigned to the new Consolidated Chippewa Agency.

Records. The records of the agency, 1874–1922, include a general series of correspondence with some annuity rolls; affidavits; receipts; application forms of different types; lists; minutes; other records; letters received from the commissioner of Indian Affairs, with registers; general letters sent to the Commissioner of Indian Affairs and others; letters sent concerning land, heirships, and education; stubs of land certificates; applications for allotments; allotment schedules; records relating to investigations of allotments; logging and timber contracts; certificates of completion of timber contracts; annuity payment rolls; receipt rolls for goods issued to Indians; issue books; applications of Indians for lumber; medical reports; death certificates; police and court records; personnel and financial records; school reports; applications for enrollment in nonreservation schools; school census reports; attendance reports; and questionnaires concerning former pupils and school facilities. For the White Earth Boarding School there is correspondence, class schedules and study programs, a register of pupils, attendance books, and rosters of employees. There is also some correspondence, 1910–1914, of special agent John H. Hinton, who was appointed to investigate the fraudulent alienation of Native American allotments, as well as correspondence, docket books, and other records of examiners of inheritance for 1911–1921.

Chippewa Commission

Also with the records of the White Earth Agency are records of the Chippewa Commission, established in 1889 to negotiate with the Chippewa bands or tribes in Minnesota for the cession and relinquishment of all their reservations, except White Earth and Red Lake, and for the reduction of these reservations to the area actually needed by the Native Americans. An individual Native American could choose between receiving an allotment in severalty on the old reservation or moving to White Earth. The commission was to direct the removals and make the necessary allotments. It was also required to compile a census of the Native Americans. These Native Americans agreed to the cessions, but most of them decided to remain on their old land. In 1896 the commission was reduced to one member, and it was discontinued in 1900. The last commissioner transferred the commission's records to the White Earth Agency. These records include correspondence, enrollment records, proceedings in enrollment cases, census rolls, a register of the arrival of Native Americans at White Earth, a record of goods issued to Indians, allotment schedules, a tract-book, last wills and testaments of Native Americans, rosters of employees, and account books.

The Consolidated Chippewa Agency

The Consolidated Chippewa Agency was established in 1922 for Chippewa Indians living on various reservations in northern Minnesota previously assigned to the White Earth, Leech Lake, and Red Lake Agencies. The White Earth and Leech Lake Agencies were abolished. The Red Lake Agency continued to be responsible for the Red Lake Chippewa but not the Native Americans of the Nett Lake (Bois Fort Chippewa), Grand Portage, and Fond du Lac Reservations, who had been assigned to the Red Lake Agency only since 1920. (These three reservations had been consolidated under the Fond du Lac Agency in 1919; an agency for each had been broken off from the La Pointe Agency during the years 1906 to 1911.) In December 1954 the Consolidated Chippewa Agency and the Red Lake Agency were merged to form the Minnesota Agency. Red Lake was re-established as an independent unit in 1964, and the name Minnesota Agency was retained for the former Consolidated Chippewa Agency.

Records of the Consolidated Chippewa Agency. The records, 1889–1954, include many inherited from predecessors. The agency records include general correspondence, ledgers and accounts for individual Native Americans, census data, council proceedings of negotiations between Chippewa Indians and the United States in 1889, and records concerning births and deaths, heirship, tribal enrollment, unpaid annuities, tribal delegations, forestry, grazing, and land.

Identified as records from Leech Lake (1915–1931) are general correspondence, including letters received by the farmer in charge (an agency employee who acted as an agent, and sometimes taught the Native Americans agricultural techniques) at Leech Lake from 1922 to 1930, and accounts of individual Native Americans; a reservation census; land allotment files; timber sales records; a register of employees; and Leech Lake Hospital and Sanatorium correspondence.

Identified as records from White Earth (1892–1931) are general correspondence, including correspondence of the forest guard who was the agency field representative at Beaulieu from 1922 to 1926 and at White Earth from 1926 to 1929, and of the field clerks at White Earth and Mahnomen from 1930 to 1935. There is also school correspondence; records of accounts of individual Native Americans; stubs of certificates for land allotments; equity files for land claims; records of timber sales; and census, allotment, and annuity rolls.

For the Grand Portage School there are some records, 1913–1931, relating to activities of the teacher who also had general charge of the Grand Portage Reservation and for a time served as deputy special officer for liquor control.

Records of the Statistics Division, Indian Census Rolls and Supplements

These records, 1885–1940 (Records of the Bureau of Indian Affairs, Record Group 75), the result of an act of July 4, 1884 (23 Stat. 76, 98), required agents and superintendents to submit an annual census of the Native Americans in their charge. In practice, many did not comply every year, and some (for example, the Navajo agents and superintendents) did not comply for many years. The information given for an individual varies but usually includes English and/or Indian name, roll number, age or date of birth, sex, and relationship to head of family. Beginning in 1930 the rolls also give the degree of Native American blood, marital status, ward status, residence, and, sometimes, other information. During the 1930s complete new rolls were not prepared every year. For certain years (1935, 1936, 1938, and 1939) and most jurisdictions, there are only supplemental rolls of additions and deductions usually comprised of lists of births and deaths. For 1931 or 1932 there are often recapitulations of births and deaths since 1924. There are a few rolls dated later than 1940, but they were not required after that year. Most of the 1940 rolls are still held by the Bureau of Indian Affairs at their regional offices. They have not been turned over to the National Archives, so they have not been distributed to genealogical libraries. Therefore, those that are in genealogical libraries are not always complete. The census rolls are arranged alphabetically by name of agency or school and thereunder by year. For jurisdictions with more than one tribe or band there may be several rolls for each year. On the earlier rolls there often is no discernible order to the listing of families, but the later rolls are arranged alphabetically by surname of head of family. These census rolls have been reproduced as M595, and the accompanying descriptive pamphlet includes a tribal index, which also usually appears on the first screen of the roll. If the index is out of print, you will have to go to the National Archives to see the index and roll.

Records of the Bureau of the Census (Record Group 29).

The first decennial census that enumerated Native Americans as a separate race was taken in 1860. For this and the following census, however, only those living with the general population were counted. In 1880 an attempt was made to enumerate non-taxed Native Americans, which meant those living on reservations. A special schedule was prepared, but it was used only for a few reservations near military installations. There are schedules in the National Archives of the United States for those Native Americans in Washington Territory under the Yakima Agency near Fort Simcoe and the Tulalip Agency; the Hunkpapa, Miniconjou, and Oglala Sioux of the Standing Rock Agency near Fort Yates, Dakota Territory; and the various tribes of the Round Valley Reservation, California. The census was to include all Native Americans living on October 1, 1880. The schedule requested the name of the tribe, reservation, agency, and nearest post office; the number in the household and a description of the dwelling; and the Indian name (with an English translation) of each person in the family with his relationship to the head of the family, marital and tribal status, description, and information about occupation, health, education, ownership of property, and source of subsistence. Often the enumerator was unable to furnish all the data required, but in some cases, information was added about tribal customs or living conditions.

Most of the census schedules for 1890 were destroyed by fire, but the Census Bureau used a special schedule for Native Americans to prepare the *Report on Indians Taxed and Non-Taxed in the United States Except Alaska* (1894). Other special reports on Native Americans were published from information gathered in the 1910, 1930, 1950, and 1960 censuses. There is also information about Native Americans in the general population schedules for 1900 and later years, but only those for 1900, 1910, and 1920 are available for research because the Census Bureau requires seventy-two years to have passed before census returns are opened to the public. The population schedules through 1920 are available on microfilm through the National Archives and Records Administration. They may also be available through your local library, genealogical society, or LDS Family History Center.

Records of United States Attorneys and Marshals (Record Group 118)

U.S. attorneys investigate violations of federal criminal laws, present evidence to grand juries, prosecute federal criminal cases, and serve as the government's attorney in civil litigation in which the United States is involved or has an interest. U.S. Marshals execute and serve writs, processes, and orders and notify the Department of Justice of defiance of federal authority. Their records relate to many of the same cases and other matters as those of federal district courts. Most of their records are in the regional branches of the National Archives.

Most of the records concerning Native Americans are dispersed among records of the general population, but there are case files, correspondence, and Native American genealogies, 1910–1923, of the U.S. Attorney for the District of Minnesota, relating to an investigation of alleged land allotment frauds perpetrated against the Chippewa Indians of the White Earth Reservation (in the regional archive in Kansas City). (Regional Archives Microfilm Project No. 79-1. Case Files and Indian Affidavits of the Linnen and Moorehead Investigations. 1909.)

Papers of Ransom Judd Powell

The Ransom Judd Powell papers (undated and 1843, 1896–1938) in the Minnesota Historical Society's Division of Library and Archives relate to Powell's involvement with the Ojibwe (Chippewa) Indians of the White Earth (Minnesota) Reservation; first, as a member of a government commission established by Congress in 1913 to compile a roll of land allotments within the White Earth Reservation and determine the blood status of each allottee and second, as legal counsel to various lumber companies seeking title to Ojibwe lands and to various White Earth Reservation Native American lands. The collection includes Ojibwe genealogies, census records, transcripts of legal testimony, correspondence, notes, abstracts of legal title, deeds, and other papers.

In 1913 Powell was appointed to a commission established by Congress on June 30, 1913, to determine the genealogy of some 200 Ojibwe families living on the White Earth Reservation, in order to judge conclusively which families were mixed bloods and therefore, possessed the legal right to alienation (the right to sell land without government approval) over their reservation land allotments. The commission's work was carried out with the assistance of Dr. Albert E. Jenks of the anthropology department of the University of Minnesota, and Dr. Alex Hrdlicka of the Smithsonian Institution, an anthropologist specializing in the physical characteristics of Native Americans.

Correspondence and Related Papers, undated and 1896–1938, are arranged chronologically (on microfilm reels 1–4) and include information on the commission appointed to compile the roll of reservation Native Americans and their genealogies, the blood status of particular Native Americans, the claims of various Ojibwe Indians to allotments on the White Earth Reservation, and related matters. Much of the correspondence for the 1896–1921 period relates to legal cases involving Powell's various lumber company clients who generally were defendants in U.S. government suits seeking the return of timberlands to their Ojibwe sellers. The undated papers contain several completed genealogical questionnaires completed by White Earth residents.

Legal Case Files appear on microfilm reels 4–7. This series consists of case files relating to the blood status of various Ojibwe Indians (files 1–14), Native American estate claims (files 15–19), swamplands on the White Earth Reservation (file 20), and land titles and transfers (files 15–22). Files 1–14 contain transcripts of legal testimony; files 15–22 include correspondence and related materials; and files 23–24 are notes and correspondence. Each file is arranged chronologically.

There are also subject files (microfilm reels 8–9) consisting of Native American genealogies, "List of Hinton Full-Bloods (John H. Hinton was a special agent appointed to investigate the fraudulent alienation of Native American allotments) in Numerical Order," unidentified lists, "Anthropological Blanks, data gathered by Albert Ernest Jenks, University of Minnesota" (1915), undated Additional Allotment Schedule, and two copies of *Lists Showing the Degree of Indian Blood of Certain Persons Holding Land Upon the White Earth Indian Reservation in Minnesota and a List showing the Date of Death of Certain Persons Who Held Land Upon Such Reservation.*

There are several additional volumes (microfilm reels 9–15). One volume, undated and unidentified, contains columns of original allotment numbers and additional allotment numbers. Other volumes include an index to land allotments and roll numbers for 1906, an undated allotment record, undated plat book, undated index to volume six of the *Book of Indian Families,* undated *Book of Indian Families,* undated "Genealogies of Allottees," "Schedule of Allowances of Land Made to the White Earth Band of Chippewa Indians of Minnesota on the White Earth Indian Reservation in that State by the Chippewa Commission under the Provisions of the Act of Congress Approved January 14, 1889" (25 Stat. 642) and the Instructions of the Commissioner of Indian Affairs (1907), 1843 "Signers Pay Roll" (La Pointe, Wisconsin, annuity roll), undated "Allotments Reported for Suit" and related allotment lists, undated allotment list, four copies of the "Roll of the Chippewa Indians allotted Within the White Earth Reservation in the State of Minnesota, Prepared by the Commission appointed under the Act of June 30, A. D. 1913" (the content and/or the marginal notes vary from copy to copy), two undated "Plat Books, White Earth Indian Reservation," and an undated "Plat Book Townships 141–146" (vol. II).

The last series consists of five supplemental plats of White Earth Reservation land parcels.

Case Study: The Family of Pug-o-nay-ig-wabe and Ay-zhe-ne-caw-zood

The subject of this case study is the family of Pug-o-nay-cum-ig-wabe and Ay-zhe-ne-caw-zood, both full-blood Mississippi Chippewa Indians who, until their death, resided on the White Earth Reservation. Pug-o-nay-cum-ig-wabe was born about 1843 and Ay-zhe-ne-caw-zood was born about 1845 in Minnesota. There were at least seven children born to Pug-o-nay-cum-ig-wabe and Ay-zhe-ne-caw-zood.

The objective of this case study is to learn as much as possible about this family; both ancestors and descendants are sought.

White Earth Reservation is located in northwestern Minnesota in Mahnomen, Clearwater, and Becker counties. Native American communities within the reservation are White Earth, Pine Point/Ponsford, Naytahwaush, Rice Lake, Callaway, Elbow Lake, and Ebro. Ogema, Waubun, and Mohnomen are other cities within the reservation boundaries. The major cities outside the boundaries are Detroit Lakes, Park Rapids, and Bagley, with Bemidji sixty-nine miles to the northeast.

The Indian census rolls (1885–1940) provide general information about the family such as age, sex, and relationships. Generally, these census rolls are consecutive by year beginning in 1885. This provides a means to track a family year by year and easily determine births and deaths of family members. Keep in mind that an older child of marriageable age may appear in the census within his or her own household.

It is very important to be aware of the variance of spelling in Indian names. We know that Pug-o-nay-*cum*-ig-wabe and Pug-o-nay-*cumig*-wabe are the same person, because other family members are recognizable from one census to another. But there may be an instance when the individual appears with a family in one census year, but in the next census year he or she is listed singularly with a variation in the spelling of the name. One means, although not foolproof, of determining the correct identity is by noting what families precede and follow the family you are researching in each census roll. In the next census, you may find that although the census roll number has changed, the names just preceding and following your subject are the same as in the previous year indicating that this is the correct subject. If your subject is listed with both Indian and English names, confirming the identity is not so difficult.

The earliest census of the White Earth Agency in Minnesota was taken in 1885. However, there is an earlier "1883 Payroll" for the Mississippi Chippewa, which lists the family of Pug-o-nay-cum-ig-wabe which shows: Pug-o-nay-cum-ig-wabe, Husband, age 40; Ay-zhe-ne-caw-zood, Wife, age 38; O-bah-bah-musk-co-way-be-quay, Daughter, age 19; Naugh-ah-cum-ig-ish-kung, Daughter, age 13; E-quay-zance, Daughter, age 4; Kay-zhe-way-we-dung, Son, age 2.

The 1885 census, in comparison with the 1883 Payroll, shows a difference in the sex of Naugh-uh-cum-ig-ish-kung (see Figure 2.13).

Naugh-ah-musk-co-day-way-be-quay is listed as a "daughter" in 1883, but in 1885 this child is listed as a "son." The daughter E-quay-zance, age four years in 1883, does not appear in the 1885 census.

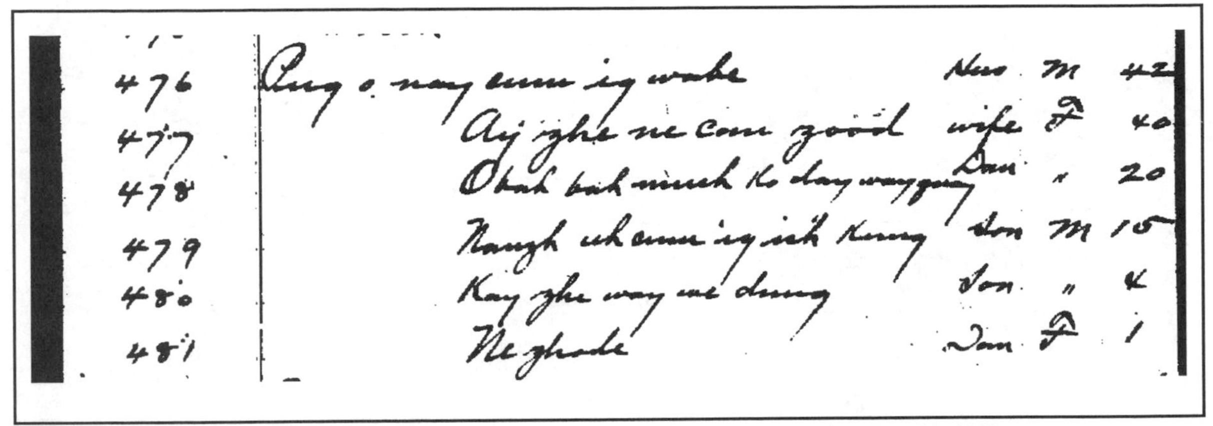

476	Pug o nay cum ig wabe	Head	M	42
477	Ay zhe ne cum zood	wife	F	40
478	O bah bah mush ko day way quay	Dau	"	20
479	Naugh uh cum ig ish kung	Son	M	15
480	Kay zhe way we dung	Son	"	4
481	Ne zhade	Dau	F	1

Figure 2.13. Census of Mississippi Chippewa Band of Indians on White Earth Reservation, June 30, 1885.

Pug-o-nay-cum-ig-wabe is enumerated as number 476. His wife and children are included as 477, 478, 479, 480, and 481. The children are: O-bah-bah-mush-ko-day-way-quay, a daughter, age 20; Naugh-uh-cum-ig-ish-kung, a son, age 15; Kay-zhe-way-we-dung, a son (it will be shown that this child was, in fact, a female), age 4; and Ne-zhade, a son, age 1.

The 1890 Census of the Mississippi Chippewa Indians of the White Earth Agency reveals that O-bah-bah-mush-ko-day-way-quay is no longer in the family and a child was born in 1886 (see Figure 2.14).

Notice that the census roll numbers for this family have changed. In later census rolls, both the present roll number and previous roll number are listed.

Pug-o-nay-cum-ig-wabe and his wife Ay-zhe-ne-*cah* zood are listed first, followed by their children: Kay-zhe-way-we-dung, Ne-zhade, Kay-bay-gah-bow-e-quay, and Naugh-*a*-cum-ig-ish-kung.

Again, note the variations in spelling. In many families, the use of an English name does not appear in the early census rolls. After 1900 it is more common to encounter both an Indian and English names, facilitating easier identification of the family. Also, in later years, the families usually appear in alphabetical order.

In 1895 the family included Pug-o-nay-cum-ig-wabe, Ay-zhe-ne-*kah*-zood, Kay-zhe-way-we-dung, Ne-*zhash, Kay*-Bay-gah-bow-e-quay, Charles, and Que-we-zaince (see Figure 2.15). Again, note the variance in spelling. In this census, we encounter the first occurrence of an English name associated with the family. Charles was born in 1890 and Que-we-zaince was born in 1888, but does not appear in the 1890 census.

By 1900, all seven of the children have been accounted for (see Figure 2.16). This is the first census wherein Kay-zhe-way-we-dung appears as a female.

In 1905 there is a drastic change in the family (see Figure 2.17). Only two children are at home, Charles and *Qua-wa*-zaince. Kay-zhe-way-we-dung appears in a separate household with a daughter just one month old.

Kay-zhe-we-way-we-dung is given the English name of Ida Ground. Her one month old daughter, born in May 1905, is Jane Ground.

The daughter, Jane Ground, does not appear in the 1910 census so it is assumed she died between 1905 and 1910.

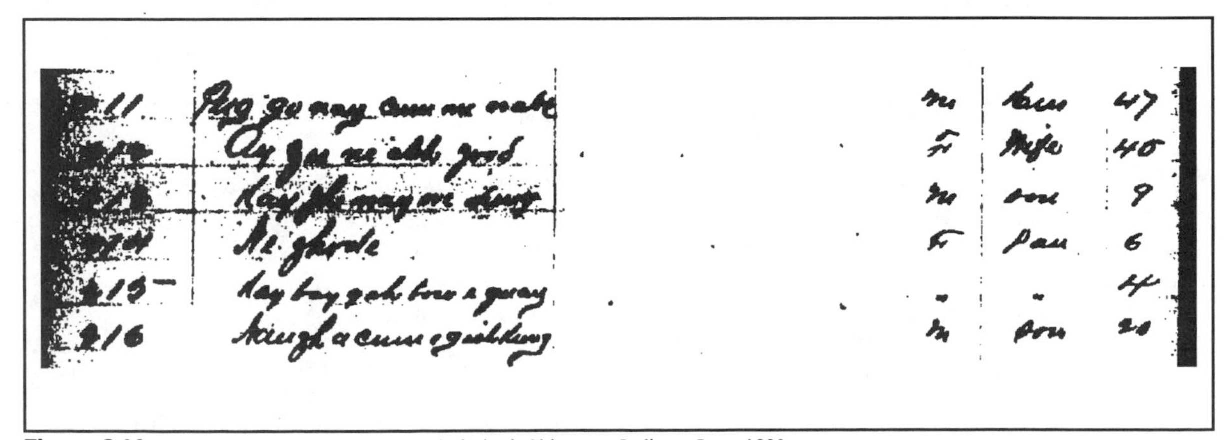

411	Pug o nay cum ig wabe	M	Head	47
[illegible]	Ay zhe ne cah zood	F	Wife	40
[illegible]	Kay zhe way we dung	M	Son	9
[illegible]	Ne zhade	F	Dau	6
415	Kay bay gah bow e quay	"	"	4
416	Naugh a cum ig ish kung	M	Son	20

Figure 2.14. Census of the White Earth Mississippi Chippewa Indians, June 1890.

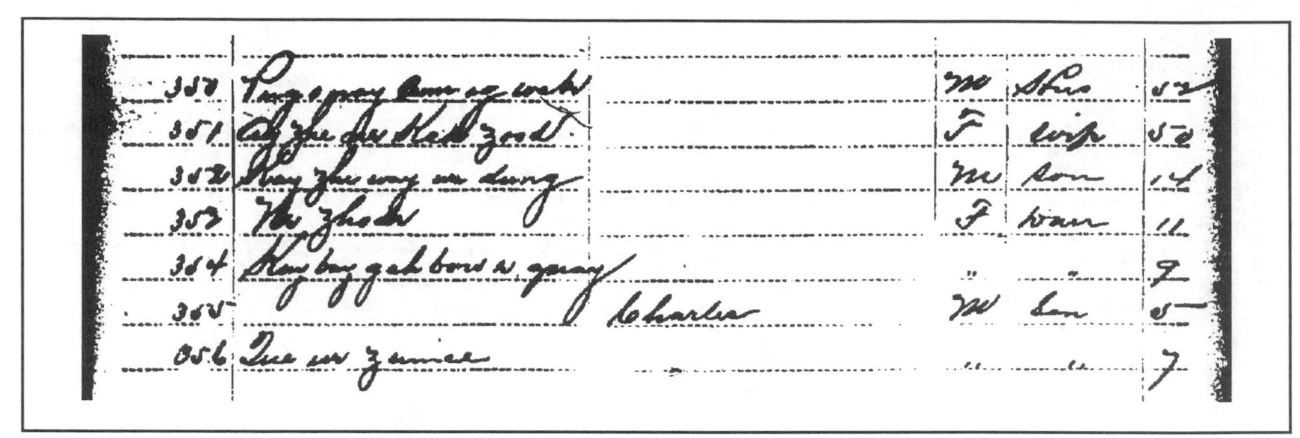

350	Pug e nay cum ig wab		M	Hus	52
351	Ay zhe ne kah zood		F	wife	52
352	Kay zhe way we dung		M	Son	14
353	Ne zhade		F	Dau	11
354	Day bay gah bow e quay		"	"	9
355		Charles	M	Son	5
356	Que we zaince		"	"	7

Figure 2.15. Census of the White Earth Mississippi Chippewa Indians, June 29, 1895.

408	Pug e nay cum ig wab		M	Hus	57
409	Ay zhe ne kah zood		F	wife	55
410	Day bay gah bow e quay		"	Dau	14
411		Charles	M	Son	10
412	Que we zaince		"		12
413	Kay zhe way we dung		F	Dau	19

Figure 2.16. Census of the White Earth Mississippi Chippewa Indians, June 1900.

478	Pug-o-nay-cum-ig-waib		M	husband	62
478	Ay-zhe-ne-cah-zood		F	wife	60
479		Charles	M	son	15
480	Que-we-zaince		"	"	17
481	Kay-zhe-way-we-dung	Ida Ground	F	mother	24
482		Jane "	F	dau	[illegible]

Figure 2.17. Census of the White Earth Mississippi Chippewa Indians, June 30, 1905.

The seven children of Pug-o-nay-cum-ig-wabe and Ay-zhe-ne-caw-zood have been identified as O-bah-bah-mush-ko-day-way-quay (Female), born ca. 1865; Naugh-uh-cum-ig-ish-kung (Male), born ca. 1870; Kay-zhe-way-we-dung (Female), born ca. 1881; Ne-zhade (Female), born ca. 1885; Day-bay-gah-bow-e-quay (Female), born ca. 1886; Que-we-zaince (Male), born ca. 1888; Charles (Male), born ca. 1890

In 1910, Pug-o-nay-cum-ig-wabe and Ay-zhe-ne-cah-zood are at home with no children in the household (see Figure 2.18). Kay-zhe-way-we-dung again appears with the English name of Ida Ground and now has a son named Eddie Jones.

The 1915 census again shows Pug-o-nay-*cumig*-wabe and Ay-zhe-ne-cah-zood with no children in their household. *Pay*-zhe-way-we-dung (another variation in spelling), or Ida Ground, is enumerated with her sons

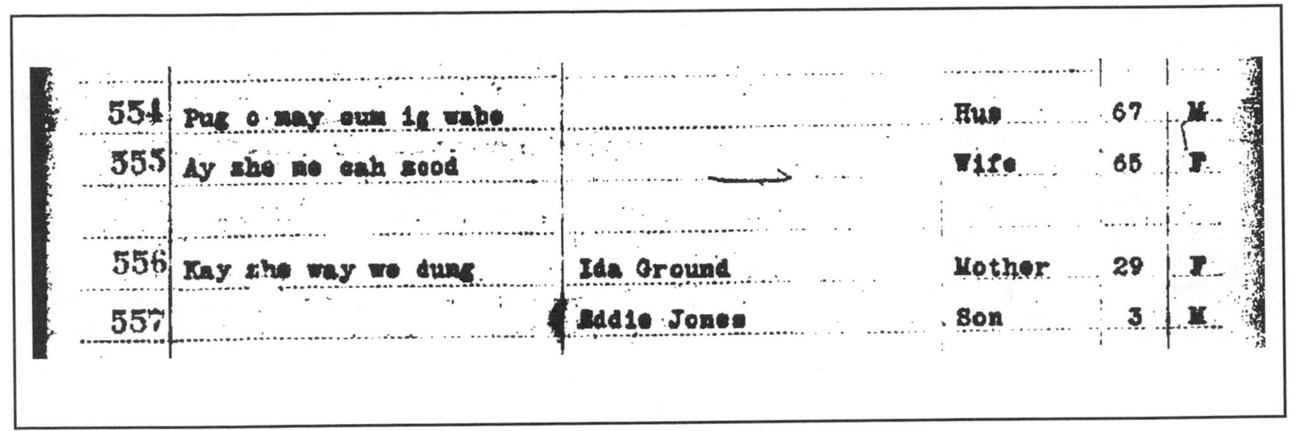

554	Pug o may cum ig wabe		Hus	67	M.
555	Ay zhe ne cah zood		Wife	65	F.
556	Kay zhe way we dung	Ida Ground	Mother	29	F.
557		Eddie Jones	Son	3	M.

Figure 2.18. Census of the White Earth Mississippi Chippewa Indians, June 1910.

Eddie, Thomas, and Charles Jones, in a separate household.

Special legislation for White Earth Reservation, the Clapp Rider of 1906, greatly reduced the restrictions on the transfer of Native American land so that timber interests and farmers would not have to wait the twenty-five years required under general allotment laws. The Clapp Rider provided that all adult ''mixed-bloods'' could take title to their allotments and sell their land if they wished. Adult ''full-bloods'' were also allowed to sell their land when the Secretary of the Interior believed that they were competent to handle their own affairs, a decision which was usually left to the discretion of the agent with testimonials offered on the Native American's behalf serving as evidence of competence. The legislation was interpreted as immediately passing title to the adult mixed-bloods.

The Clapp Rider triggered the rapid transference of land. Fraud and improper dealings were extensive, as subsequent investigations by Linnen and Moorehead (appointed by the BIA) would show.

Since full-bloods could not sell their land immediately, blood designation was important. (Lawsuits and court action depended on blood determination.) A roll taken in 1910 (the Hinton Roll) had shown 927 full-bloods. In 1913 Congress authorized that another roll be taken. An anthropologist, Alex Hrdlicka, came to White Earth to prepare the roll.

His report was filed as the 1920 Blood Roll. There are known and obvious errors in this roll but the federal government is now bound by it because of the federal acceptance of the roll in 1920.

The records that were generated by the Linnen and Moorehead investigations have been previously cited in the ''Records of the United States Attorneys and Marshals.'' It is to these records that we now turn in order to gather more information about the family of Pug-o-nay-cum-ig-wabe.

The following information was obtained from documents found in these records:

Affidavit of Ay-zhe-ne-cah-zood. July 21, 1909:

> That she is a full blood Native American of the Otter Tail Pillager band of Chippewa Indians belonging to and residing upon the White Earth Reservation in Minnesota, that her father's name was Day-dodge, and her mother's name was Way-show-aush-ko-gwan-nay-be-quay; that the names of her grandfather and grandmother on her father's side were Gwoy-dow-wee and unknown, and the name of her grandfather and grandmother on her mother's side were Ash-ke-buck-ke-cooshe-shay and O-min-quah-quod-oke; and that each of said persons was a full blood Indian:
>
> That this deponent was allotted the S ½ of NE ¼ sec 31 Twp 141 Range 37 #432 on said White Earth Reservation, and that on or about the __________ day of __________ __________ 190___ she sold said land to __________ __________.

Affidavit of Pug-go-nay-cunig-wabe and wife Ah-zhe-ne-caw-zood:

> Pug-o-nay-cumig-wabe and his wife Ah-zhe-ne-caw-zood, being first duly sworn, each for himself and not one for the other, testify on oath as follows:
>
> We had a son named Que-we-saince, who is now dead. He died in November, 1906, and was 19 years old at the time of his death. He was a full blood Indian of the Mississippi band of Chippewa Indians. Both my wife, herein named, and myself are full blood Indians.
>
> My wife's (Ah-zhee-ne-caw-zood) father's name was Day-dodge; her mother's name was Way-shah-wah-ko-gwab-wah-be-quay, both of whom were full bloods.
>
> My father [Pug-go-nay-cumig-wabe's father] was Way-nah-saung, my [Pug-go-nay-cumig-wabe] mother was O-ge-zhe-aush-e-quay, both of whom were full bloods.
>
> Our deceased Que-we-zaince, sold his original allotment, No. 1592 for ____________________ during the summer of 1908 to Schoeneberger, cashier of the First National Bank of Park Rapids, Minn., for, we think, $125.
>
> At the time our deceased son, Que-we-saince, made such sale of such tract of land he was then but 19 years old and a

> minor, and under the law, could not legally dispose of said land, and we, each of us, therefore do pray that said land be restored to the legal heirs, and your petitioners will forever so pray.

Affidavit of Bay-bah-dwung-gay-aush, Nay-che-wah-quah-ung, Wah-be-shesh, No-de-nah-quah-aun, and Po-go-nay-cumig-wabe, August 2, 1909:

> That they are personally acquainted with Charles Pug-o-nay-cumig-wabe, and that he is a full blood Indian of the Mississippi bands of Chippewa Indians belonging to and residing upon the White Earth Reservation in Minnesota, that his father's name is Pug-o-nay-cumig-wabe, and his mother's name is Ah-zhe-ne-cah-zood, that the names of his grandfather and grandmother on his father's side were Way-wa-sang, and O-ge-zhe-ah-she-quay, that the names of his grandfather and grandmother on his mother's side were Day-dodge and Way-shah-washk-ko-gwa-na-be-quay; that each of said persons was a full blood Indian.

Affidavit of Kay-bay-ga-ba-week or Kay-gah-way-we-dung (Ida Ground Jones), August 14, 1909:

> That she is a full blood Indian of the Otter Tail Pillager band of Chippewa Indians belonging to and residing upon the White Earth Reservation in Minnesota.
>
> That her father's name is Po-go-nay-cumig-wabe and her mother's name is Ah-zhe-ne-caw-zood. That the names of her grandfather and grandmother on her father's side were Way-wah-sung and O-ge-she-aush-a quay and the names of her grandfather and grandmother on her mother's side were Day-dodge and Way-sha-wauh-squo-gunn-nay-beek.

These documents have supplied the names of both the paternal and maternal grandparents and great-grandparents. Notice, again, the variance in the spelling of some of the names in the documents cited above.

In the affidavit of Ay-zhe-ne-cah-zood she is described as being a member of the ''Otter Tail Pillager Band of Chippewa Indians,'' as is Ida Ground Jones in her affidavit. This is perhaps a minor consideration since the Otter Tail Pillager Band were considered Chippewa, but when searching the agency rolls, it is important to be aware that a search of the census of the Otter Tail Pillager band of Chippewa may also be necessary when attempting to identify her parents and/or grandparents.

The death of Charles Pug-o-nay-cum-ig-wabe is said to have occurred in November 1909 when he was nineteen years old. Note that Charles was given his father's Indian name as his own surname. Charles is the only child to be identified in this manner.

Having defined the family of Pug-o-nay-cum-ig-wabe through the use of agency census rolls, we turn now to a unique group of records, the Ransom Judd Powell papers. It is among this group of papers that we will discover a great deal more about our subjects.

Among the papers of Ransom Judd Powell are two very important records. The first is the ''Anthropological Blank'' used by Albert Ernest Jenks to gather information which would be used to determine the ''blood status'' of certain members of the Mississippi Chippewa. The second group of records is the ''Book of Indian Families.'' There is an incomplete index to this book. Powell wrote an explanation of these records which appears at the beginning of the index:

> The above described book of Indian families grew out of an attempt on the part of the defendants in the famous White Earth litigation to ascertain the blood status of the Indians by tracing their genealogy.
>
> Commencing in 1912 more than three years were spent by the writer with a crew of Indians and interpreters, and the Indian genealogies are the result. The cost was approximately thirty thousand dollars and the value proved to be little or nothing, so far as the litigation was concerned.
>
> But as genealogies of hundreds of Native Americans, whose descendants are and will continue to be citizens of this and other states, the book is unique.
>
> Rolls of Indian bands and tribes have [been] made but this book traces relationships of all those listed therein.
>
> There are errors, and several families were never completed, for the writer had not the time to finish them nor to carefully edit the work. He planned to finish the collection and accompany the family records with notes and anecdotes derived from the writer's long and intimate association with these Indians, whose history he knows and whose language he speaks, but the labor is too great, and the compensation is entirely lacking, so the record is left as it is. Even so, this record should be carefully preserved for in the future there will be those who may find herein the proof of Indian ancestry so many have hitherto sought.
>
> Anyone wishing to avail himself of the information contained in this family book should first connect himself with some White Earth allottee. If the original allotment number is known, the name can be found from the judicial status roll on file in three places—the Office of the clerk of the U.S. Court for Minnesota, Sixth Div. at Fegus Falls; the Consolidated Indian Agency now at Cass Lake, Minnesota, and the office of the Secretary of the Interior in Washington, D.C.
>
> From the name, the family record can be traced through the index and the cross-references. (Notation made by the compiler of the record on May 29, 1933.)

The ''Anthropological Blanks'' were compiled by Albert Ernest Jenks, of the University of Minnesota. Data collected was to be used to determine the ''blood status'' of the certain members of the Mississippi Chippewa. The forms contain the following information: Indian name; tribe; band; age; residence; date; measurements of head, face, and nose; description of hair, eyes, and teeth; kinship; blood status; and remarks.

The Anthropological Blank of Ay-zhee-nee-kaw-zood is shown in Figure 2.19. The blank is dated October 26, 1915. Ay-zhee-nee-kaw-zood was then seventy years old. She resided in Pine Point. Her father was Day-dodge or Wah-say-ge-shig. Her mother was Way-zow-wash-ko-gwa-nay-be-quay. Her blood status was 1/64 white through her father. Under ''Remarks'' is the additional information that she was the ''mother of Mrs. Charles

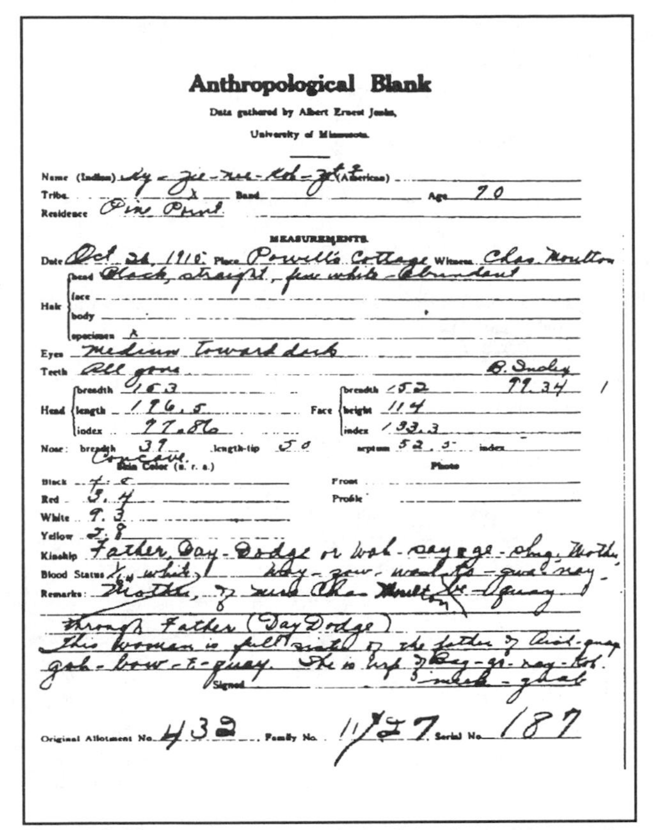

Anthropological Blank

Data gathered by Albert Ernest Jenks,
University of Minnesota.

Name (Indian) Ay-zhee-nee-kaw-zod (American)
Tribe   Band   Age 70
Residence Pine Point

MEASUREMENTS.

Date Oct. 26, 1910 Place Powell's Cottage Witness Chas. Moulton
Hair: head Black, straight, few white, abundant; face; body; specimen x
Eyes medium toward dark
Teeth All gone   B. Indey
Head: breadth 153; length 196.5; index 77.86
Face: breadth 152; height 114; index 133.3   77.34
Nose: breadth 37; length-tip 50; septum 52.5; index
Concave.
Skin Color (n. r. a.): Black 4.5; Red 3.4; White 9.3; Yellow 2.8
Photo: Front; Profile
Kinship Father, Day-Dodge or Wah-say-ge-shig. Mother
Blood Status 1/4 white
Remarks: through Father (Day Dodge). This woman is full sister of the father of Aish-quay-gah-bow-e-quay.
Signed
Original Allotment No. 432 Family No. 11/27 Serial No. 187

Figure 2.19. Anthropological Blank of Ay-zhee-nee-kaw-zood.

Moulton'' and ''the full sister of the father of Aish-quay-gah-bow-e-quay.''

At the bottom of the blank is the original allotment number, the family number, and the serial number. The allotment number and the family number provide the key to other records. Both of these numbers are used as references to the genealogies compiled by Ransom Judd Powell between 1912 and 1923.

The allotment number is very important to identification of your ancestor. Your subject may be recorded with only his or her Indian name, as in the case of Pug-e-nay-cum-ig-wabe. While the spelling of an Indian name can and will vary from one record to another, the allotment number seldom changes. A census roll number, as has been shown, can change yearly, but an allotment number will usually stay the same. If there is a change, or a correction, it will be noted clearly.

One method of locating someone among the many and varied documents found in the Ransom Judd Powell papers is to review the allotment registers, noting the original allotment number and the additional allotment number which precedes the name of the individual. By using these numbers, you can locate the pedigree chart. The original allotment number will be found in the upper right corner of the pedigree chart. When you have found the pedigree chart of your subject, check those which surround it for charts of possible brothers and sisters.

Bibliography

Additional information on these sources may be found in Part II.

Butler, Ruth Lapham. *A Checklist of Manuscripts in the Edward E. Ayer Collection.* Chicago: The Newberry Library, 1937. 295p.

Carpenter, Cecelia Svinth. *How to Research American Blood Lines.* A manual on Indian genealogical research. Meico Associates edition. South Prairie, WA: Meico Associates, 1984. 81p. Includes bibliography. Reprint. Heritage Quest, Orting, WA, 1987.

Catalog of the Edward Ayer Collection of American Indians in the Newberry Library. Chicago: The Newberry Library, 1961.

Cerny, Johni and Arlene Eakle. *Guide to Research, Case Studies in American Genealogy.* Salt Lake City: Ancestry, 1985.

Chepesiuk, Ron and Arnold Shankman. *American Indian Archival Material: Guide to the Holdings in the Southeast.* Westport, CT: Greenwood Press, 1982. 325p. Includes bibliographic references and index.

DeWitt, Donald L. *American Indian Resource Materials in the Western History Collections, University of Oklahoma.* Norman, OK: University of Oklahoma Press, 1990. 272p. Includes bibliographic references and index.

Ebbott, Elizabeth. *Indians In Minnesota.* Fourth edition. Minneapolis: University of Minnesota Press, 1985. 326p. Includes bibliography and index.

Epstein, Ellen Robinson and Rona Mendelsohn. *Record and Remember: Tracing Your Roots Through Oral History.* New York: Sovereign Books, 1978. 119p. Includes bibliography.

Folwell, William Watts. *A History of Minnesota.* Four volumes. St. Paul, MN: Minnesota Historical Society, 1921–1930. Revised edition, 1956–1969. Contains a complete description of the commission's work and the related lawsuits. Includes bibliographic references and an index.

Henry, Jeannette. *The American Indian Reader: History.* Book four. San Francisco: The Indian Historian Press, 1974. Includes bibliography.

Hill, Edward E. *Guide to Records in the National Archives of the United States Relating to American Indians.* Washington, D.C.: National Archives and Records Services Administration, 1981. 467p. A guide to the history and development of agencies and subagencies of the Office of Indian Affairs and their records. Includes a listing of records of other branches of the federal government pertaining to the American Indian as well as an index.

Hodge, William H. *A Bibliography of Contemporary North American Indians.* Selected and partially annotated with study guide. New York: Interland Publishing, 1976. 310p. Includes index.

Hoxie, Frederick E. and Harvey Markowitz. *Native Americans: An Annotated Bibliography.* D'Arcey McNickle Center for the History of the American Indian. Pasadena, CA: Salem Press, 1991. 325p. Includes index.

Huntington, Henry E., Library and Art Gallery. *Guide to American Historical Manuscripts in the Huntington Library.* San Marino, CA: Kingsport Press for the Huntington Library, 1979. 442p. Includes index.

Johnson, Steven L. *Guide to American Indian Documents in the Congressional Serial Set, 1817–1899.* A project of the Institute for the Development of Indian Law. New York: Clearwater Publishing Company, 1977. 503p. Includes index.

Karriker, Robert C. and Eleanor R. Karriker. *Guide to the Microfilm Edition of The Pacific Northwest Tribes Missions Collection of the Oregon Province Archives of the Society of Jesus.* Wilmington, DE: Scholarly Resources, 1987.

Lists Showing the Degree of Indian Blood of Certain Persons Holding Land Upon the White Earth Indian Reservation in Minnesota and a List Showing the Date of Death of Certain Persons Who Held Land Upon Such Reservation. Hinton Roll. Washington, D.C.: United States Government Printing Office, 1911.

Meyer, Melissa L. "'We Can Not Get a Living as We Used To:' Dispossession and the White Earth Anishinaabeg, 1889–1920." In *The American Historical Review*, vol. 96:2 (April 1991), pp. 368–394.

Morgan, Dale L. and George P. Hammond. *A Guide to the Manuscript Collections.* Vol. 1: Pacific and Western Manuscripts; vol. 2: Manuscripts Relating Chiefly to Mexico and Central America. Bancroft Library Publications. Bibliographical series. Berkeley, CA: Published for the Bancroft Library by the University of California Press, 1963.

Morris, John W., Charles R. Goins, and Edwin C. McReynolds. *Historical Atlas of Oklahoma.* Third edition. Norman, OK: University of Oklahoma Press, 1986. Includes bibliography and index as well as several maps delineating the various portions of Indian Territory.

National Anthropological Archives. *Catalog to Manuscripts at the National Anthropological Archives, Department of Anthropology, National Museum of Natural History, Smithsonian Institution, Washington, D.C.* Boston: G.K. Hall, 1975.

Smithsonian Institution. Bureau of American Ethnology. *List of Publications of the Bureau of American Ethnology with Index to Authors and Titles.* Washington, D.C.: Government Printing Office, 1962.

United States Department of the Interior Library. *Bibliographical and Historical Index of American Indians and Persons Involved in Indian Affairs.* Eight volumes. Boston: G.K. Hall, 1966. Subject index developed in the library of the Bureau of Indian Affairs which was consolidated in 1949 with other bureau libraries to form the library of the Department of the Interior. From 1951–1965, the work of the index was continued. This work includes extensive listings of Indian agents, other personnel of the Bureau of Indian Affairs, Indian chiefs, and historically prominent Native Americans, as well as obscure information related to tribal matters. The scope is broader than that of the department collections since it includes material found in journals, books, and documents contained in other libraries and personal collections. Arranged alphabetically by subject, i.e. Native American tribes, individual names, events, and other items of a historical nature, the entries do not always follow standard bibliographical form, and frequently the alphabetizing is informal within a single letter. There is no listing by author or title of works cited, except as these happen to occur as subjects.

Weil, Richard H. "Destroying a Homeland: White Earth, Minnesota." In *American Indian Culture and Research Journal*, vol. 13:2 (1989), pp. 69–95.

Withington, Mary C. *A Catalogue of Manuscripts in the Collection of Western Americana Founded by William Robertson Coe, Yale University Library.* New Haven: Yale University Press, 1952. 398p. Title on spine: *Western Americana Manuscripts in Yale University Library.*

Youngbear-Tibbetts, Holly. "Without Due Process: The Alienation of Individual Trust Allotments of the White Earth Anishinaabeg." In *American Indian Culture and Research Journal*, vol. 15:2 (1991), pp. 93–138.

Records Specific to Native Americans

Jimmy B. Parker

Lecturer, accredited genealogist, and author of numerous books, pamphlets, and articles on Native American records and research, U.S. genealogy, and family history, Jimmy B. Parker is the Manager of the Family History Library in Salt Lake City. He is a fellow of the Utah Genealogical Association, a board member or past president of various organizations, including the Association of Professional Genealogists, and in 1978 won the Award of Merit from the National Genealogical Society. Mr. Parker received his bachelor's degree from Brigham Young University in 1961 and is a graduate of the Institute of Genealogical Research in Washington, D.C.

Historical Background

When the Europeans made contact with the North American continent in the fifteenth, sixteenth, and seventeenth centuries, they found a people already living there. These natives were mostly friendly to the newcomers, curious about the strangers who came aboard strange-looking boats and dressed so differently from them. Usually both groups made efforts to trade goods and information. The natives were willing to teach the new arrivals about survival in their new surroundings in return for being taught about the weapons, trinkets, and ways of the colonists.

During the colonial period, most of the records involving the Native Americans were kept by local governments or the churches which dealt with them. However, since there was no central governmental agency which dealt with Native American affairs, very few records were kept during the colonial period. Fewer of those that were kept have survived.

After the federal government was established, and it became more and more important for Native American rights to be extinguished so settlers could move west, the War Department was assigned the responsibility of "Indian affairs." The administration of Indian affairs from 1789 until 1824 was under the direct supervision of the Secretary of War. The system of "factories," or trading posts, run by the government for the purpose of trading with the Native Americans, was administered by a Superintendent of Indian Trade who reported directly to the Secretary of War. The records generated during this time period were records of the War Department.

The governor of newly created territories often served as *ex officio* Superintendent of Indian Affairs for his territory. Some of the records thus generated may have become part of the records of the territory or the personal collection of the person who served as governor.

By order of the Secretary of War, John C. Calhoun, on March 11, 1824, the Bureau of Indian Affairs (BIA) was established. It was commonly called the Office of Indian Affairs until 1947. This new office operated under the Secretary of War informally until 1832 when Congress authorized the appointment of a Commissioner of Indian Affairs. This commissioner reported to the Secretary of War until 1849, when the Office of Indian Affairs was transferred to the new Department of the Interior.

It is important to understand the history of these offices, for the offices named were responsible for the generation and maintenance of the records of the relationship between the federal government and Native Americans.

Almost all of the record keeping for individual Native Americans occurred originally at the local agency level. Agents at factories or on reservations dealt with the Native Americans in their charge on a daily basis. The agents were responsible for seeing that the directives of the Commissioner of Indian Affairs were carried out—the payment to Native Americans as stipulated by provisions of their treaties, taking of the census, allotting and subsequent transfers of titles of land, determining heirs, educating Native American children, removing Native Americans from one area to another, hiring Native American employees, providing health care and sanitation to the Native Americans, etc.

Because the agents were the most closely involved government officials, and almost all of the records of individuals were generated at the agency level, it is absolutely essential that the name of the agency where the individual was enrolled be known. In order to know that, it is also necessary that a family historian or genealogist know the tribal affiliation of the one for whom information is being sought, the history of the organization, the areas of jurisdiction of the agencies involved with that tribe, and the locality where the individual lived during given time periods.

It is especially advantageous to a researcher to study the history of the Bureau of Indian Affairs, the major creator of records involving Native Americans in the United States. It is also very important to study the holdings of the National Archives in Washington, D.C., the largest single repository of the records of the Native Americans of the United States.

Researchers should also familiarize themselves with the branches of the National Archives and Records Administration, for each of them (at least in areas where there were large concentrations of Native Americans), holds many of the records of the local agencies.

Records

Church Records

When the new colonies in America were established, most of the colonists desired to teach the Native Americans, whom they considered to be ''savages,'' their way of life, their religious views, their ideas of land ownership, etc. To achieve these goals, they organized evangelistic activities among the natives and sent missionaries among them. Several denominations were prominent in their missionary endeavors to Native Americans and have continued their efforts, even to the present time. The records generated by the churches in their missionary efforts are covered in the preceding chapter.

Land Records

The policy of the colonists to assimilate the natives also generated land records. Attempts were made early to purchase land from the natives. Most Native Americans, however, did not understand land ownership in the sense that Europeans did. The result was that deeds from the Native Americans to the Europeans were made, but much miscommunication occurred.

It appears that the misconception of ''ownership'' of land continued to plague the Native Americans as they dealt with individual Anglo settlers and with their governments. Treaties were signed and agreements made which meant to the non-Indian settler that they had exclusive rights and/or ownership to parcels of land, but which meant to the Native Americans that the purchaser had only the right to share the use of lands which always belonged to the ''Great Spirit.''

When the settlers drove the Native Americans off the lands transferred by a treaty or other agreement, the Native Americans resisted, for they understood the agreement differently. With such resistance, the non-Indians felt justified in further removing or restricting them.

The later policy of removal of the Native Americans to west of the Mississippi River (the Jacksonian policy), tended to reinforce the Native American concept of land ownership. They were being told that they were being allowed to use the lands west of the Mississippi as they saw fit and that the Anglos would stay east of the Mississippi.

When the non-Indians continued to migrate westward onto Native American lands, the Native Americans again were told that they had to confine themselves to a particular area of land called a ''reservation.'' This was not only a reversal of the Anglo government's policy, but it was based on the concept of land ''ownership'' which was difficult for Native Americans to understand.

When the more restrictive policy of land allotments (the granting of an allotment of a particular parcel of land to an individual Native American) was put into place by the federal government on many reservations, it was even more difficult for the Native American to accept.

Early Indian deeds and transfers of land ''ownership'' to encroaching settlers were recorded by the local governments and were either kept in the records of land transactions along with all other deeds, etc., or in separate books of ''Indian Deeds.'' In either case, they are records of non-Indian governments and are therefore researched the same way that any ancestor regardless of ethnic background could be researched.

Later deeds and accompanying papers for sales of reserves of individual Native Americans required the approval of the Secretary of the Interior. These records were all part of the records of the Commissioner of Indian Affairs Office in Washington, D.C. and have been transferred to the National Archives. Though they are in several sets of copies and abstracts of records, there is a consolidated index to most of them. These records cover 1824 to 1967. One set includes deeds from 1824 to 1956. Another set, 1880–1932, consists of deeds for railroad rights-of-way to the U.S. government for official purposes, logging contracts, leases, and other types of documents. Still another set, 1903–1967, covers sales of inherited allotments and allotments of noncompetents.

There are also sets of land transactions for a number of tribes, kept as separate sets for each tribe.

There are other less general records in the National Archives which are important to specific tribes. For example, there are records of homestead entries by the Winnebago Indians of Wisconsin, 1873–1895. There is a volume of proceedings of the Wyandot Executive Council, 1855–1862, which apparently was used to determine eligibility for allotments in that tribe.

Scrip certificates which could be exchanged for allotments were issued according to the provisions of some treaties. These records typically give the certificate number, name of allottee, location and amount of land, date of issue, and information concerning delivery of the certificate.

Land allotment records are one of the most complete and accurate records concerning the Native Americans. The idea of allotments was set forth in the early 1800s. By the 1850s, when efforts were being made to persuade tribes in Kansas, Nebraska, and elsewhere to move to new reservations in Indian Territory (presently Oklahoma), many tribal members were given the option of accepting a land allotment in Indian Territory, or giving up tribal status, and living as citizens of the United States.

The General Allotment Act was passed by the U.S. Congress on February 8, 1887. This act detailed a new policy in which the individual Native Americans of the United States would supposedly be given an opportunity to become independent of government supervision. The concept was that an individual would be granted an allotment of land, to be held in trust by the government for him. A Native American head of family residing on a reservation was entitled to 160 acres; each unmarried person over the age of eighteen was entitled to eighty acres; and every other person under eighteen years of age was entitled to forty acres. After twenty-five years, the individual would then be issued a patent by the federal government to that parcel of land. Not all reservations allotted their lands, so not every tribal group has this record.

The provisions of the General Allotment Act also included a means of passing the rights to that allotment to heirs. It also allowed some sales of the allotments, under specific conditions, most notably with the permission of the Commissioner of Indian Affairs. Generally all parties holding any fractional rights to an allotment had to agree to the sale of those rights. And, usually, the tribal group had the right of first option to purchase the allotment rights to any land on its reservation.

When an allottee died, his or her right to an allotment passed to the heirs according to the degree of relationship of the heirs. However, instead of the acreage in an allotment being divided among the heirs with each receiving a full title to a portion of the acreage, each heir received a portion of the rights of the allotment to the entire parcel of land. So, an heir entitled to one quarter of an allotment of 160 acres did not receive rights to the allotment of forty acres. Rather, he received one quarter right to the entire 160 acres.

Each degree of relationship was entitled to a specific portion of the rights to the allotment, depending upon how many heirs of that degree of relationship survived the death of the allottee. Obviously, the rights to an allotment could get very fragmented. However, because the precise degree of relationship was so important to the amount of rights allowed to an heir, the records of blood relationships in the allotment records are quite precise.

There are a number of types of documents kept as part of the allotment records. The allotment register is the record of all of the allotments made on a specific reservation. It names the allottee, age, sex, and relationship in the family, the legal description of the parcel of land allotted, the number of acres allotted, and the names and degrees of relationship of potential heirs. Sometimes plats, census rolls, or appraisements are bound with the allotment schedules, as well as affidavits and correspondence.

In order to keep the degrees of relationship straight, many agents of the Bureau of Indian Affairs kept a record called the ''register of families.'' This was a volume in which family relationships were recorded and kept updated. It was referred to in determining cases of allotment relationships, heirship documentation, etc. Registers of families included much more than the immediate family—it included extended family relationships, such as aunts, uncles, and cousins. Registers of families are also discussed under the heading of ''Vital Records'' in this chapter.

Once the individual Native American proved his competency to manage his allotment, a patent was issued to him by the U.S. government. Note that the criteria for proving competency were never clearly defined, and much discretion was given to the local agents for these decisions. The percentage of Native Americans who actually received a patent for an allotted piece of land was fairly low. However, once a person obtained a patent, he had the right to sell his property to anyone.

Allotment records were kept by the agency office of the Bureau of Indian Affairs. Most of them remain there. Some of the allotment records have been microfilmed and/or have been transferred to the National Archives or one of its branches.

In order to find the information being sought in these records, the name of the allottee and the tribal affiliation must be known. Usually there is an index of some kind to the allotment register and/or the register of families.

Land records, especially the later allotment records where they apply, often are the most accurate and dependable records available to prove Native American relationships. They are public records and generally are not restricted, especially to tribal members.

Factory (Trading Post) Records

An experiment was launched in 1795 by the federal government via an appropriation by the Congress for $50,000 for goods to be sold to or traded with the Native Americans. The purpose of this experiment was to establish more harmonious relations with the Native Americans and to increase their dependency upon government goods (making them more subject to its control). If the experiment worked, it would supposedly reduce the costs of defending the frontier. Two trading posts, called "factories," were established in 1795, one at Colerain, Georgia, on the St. Mary's River, to serve the Creek Indians and the other at Tellico, Tennessee, for the Cherokee and Choctaw.

Over the next twenty-seven years, about twenty such factories were established and operated at various times among different tribes. Those who were in charge of the factories were called factors or agents. They exchanged tobacco, blankets, cloth, clothing, weapons, ammunition, and utensils for Indian-supplied goods, mostly furs and skins.

The factories and their years of operation are listed in *Guide to Records in the National Archives of the United States Relating to American Indians* (Hill 1984, 20).

The factors or agents were supposed to keep a daybook, journal, ledger, letter book, cashbook, and invoice book. At the end of each quarter they were to abstract their account books and inventories of their goods to the Office of Indian Trade, which operated under the Secretary of War. The Superintendent of Indian Trade was also supposed to maintain records similar to those in the individual factories. Some of these records still exist, but many of them either were not kept as directed or have not survived.

Of the records which still exist, there are not many references to individual Native Americans. Although they are sometimes named in the accounts, often the entries state only "bartered with Indians" or simply "bartered." Occasionally individually named Native Americans are included in the correspondence between the factors and the superintendent. The best that can be hoped for from these records is to identify an individual as being in a particular location (near one of the factories) and, therefore, associated with a particular tribe on a given date.

Nearly all of the existing records for the factories are now located at the National Archives. They are arranged by factory name, type of record, and date. There are records for individual factories and records for the Superintendent's Office. Some private papers for individual agents and superintendents are in various historical society or university archives.

To access the records, it is necessary to know the tribal group or name of factory and the approximate time period to be searched. Few of the records are indexed, so it would be necessary to search most of them page by page.

Most of the information in factory records will have only general applicability to Native Americans. A great deal of general history of the respective tribes involved in this government trading system can be gathered from the records, but, again, little information on individual Native Americans will be found. However, for the time period, these records are among the few in existence. The information in these records is not restricted in any way.

Treaties

Whenever two groups with different goals and ways of accomplishing those goals meet, there is always a need for arriving at a mutual understanding and agreement. In the early days of the American colonies, each colony was a separate political entity and each dealt with the natives of its respective area. As agreements were negotiated and reached between each colony and the indigenous people, a treaty was often created.

After the colonial period, treaties were made between the federal government and the Native American tribes. These treaties were ratified by the U.S. Senate just as a treaty with a foreign government would have been ratified, and, as a result, were published in various forms in government documents such as *Statutes at Large*, the *Congressional Record,* the *Federal Register,* reports of the Commissioner of Indian Affairs, etc. The practice of recognizing Native American tribes as nations and the negotiating of treaties with them was discontinued by an act of March 3, 1871 (16 Stat. 544, 566). After 1871 agreements were made which were similar to treaties, requiring approval by both houses of Congress.

Treaties were generated primarily to negate Native American titles to lands, but there were other provisions as well. Examples of special provisions were the guarantee of special rights such as hunting and fishing rights in ceded lands, the allotment of lands to individual, the dissolution of tribes, the cessation of hostilities and maintenance of peace, the status of tribes as dependent nations, codification of criminal and civil jurisdiction, control of tribal affairs, regulation of trade, claims of and against Native Americans, and rights-of-way across Native American lands. Almost always, the treaties specified what the Native Americans were giving up (usually the right to a certain area or parcel of land) and what consideration (amount of money in cash payment or annuity) was being given by the government entity.

Some of the treaties resulted from the voluntary relinquishment of rights by the natives for some monetary or other reason, but more often they were created because lands were taken at the defeat of the Native Americans by local militia or more formal armies.

For the colonial period, treaties between the Native American groups and the colonies were kept within the individual colonies and are most likely found in each state's archive. Some states, too, negotiated agreements with the tribal groups within their boundaries. Those agreements would also be found in the respective state archives.

The originals of most formal treaties for the federal period are kept in the Department of State because when these treaties were negotiated the Indian nations were considered "foreign." They were filed in chronological order, each treaty having been assigned a number. The earliest treaty in this file was one signed at Ft. George, New York, in 1722 between the Five Nations and the governors of New York, Pennsylvania, and Virginia. The last numbered treaty was signed in 1868 between the federal government and the Nez Perce tribe. This set of records also includes several treaties which were never ratified and therefore did not go into effect.

The Bureau of Indian Affairs also maintained a file on each treaty which often consists of an original signed copy of the treaty, the presidential proclamation of it, the Senate resolution approving ratification, and a printed copy of it. Sometimes other documents are also included, such as messages from the president to the Senate, instructions to the treaty commissioners, or other correspondence.

To locate treaties, the researcher must know the time period and location of the treaty, tribal name, and the name of the government with whom the treaty was negotiated. The treaties in the National Archives have many finding aids, including a chronological list and indexes by place and by tribe. They have been microfilmed as Microcopy 668, *Ratified Indian Treaties, 1722–1869.* The texts of treaties from 1778 to 1868 and some agreements which never were recognized as treaties, 1792–1883, have been printed in *Indian Treaties, 1778–1783* (Kappler 1972). There are no restrictions on the use of these federal records in the National Archives.

Usually treaties contain limited genealogical information—normally only the name of Native Americans recognized as the head-men or chiefs of the group with whom the government was negotiating, tribal affiliation, names of the government representatives, and the date and location of the treaty. Of course, the provisions of the treaty are also included but contain no information about individual Native Americans. Occasionally, there were specific provisions in a treaty which required additional information to be gathered and attached to the treaty. For example, Article 2 of the 1848 treaty with the Stockbridge tribe of Wisconsin specified that "a roll or census shall be taken and appended to this agreement." Article 4 of the same treaty specified that the members of the tribe "who have become citizens of the United States (a schedule of which is hereunto annexed)" should have patents to their land issued to them. Accordingly, a "Schedule of lands to be patented to individuals under the 4th Article of the above agreement" was compiled and attached to the treaty. Article 6 of the same treaty specified that "the United States shall also pay to said tribe, within six months after the ratification of this agreement, the sum of fourteen thousand five hundred and four dollars and eighty-five cents, being the appraised value of their improvements upon the lands herein ceded and relinquished to the United States, and to be paid to the individuals claiming said improvements according to the schedule and assessment herewith transmitted." Attached to the treaty in compliance with Article 6 is a schedule of the "Valuation of Improvements" which lists the individuals making the claim, number of acres owned, and the value of the improvements on that land.

One item of caution when using treaties for research: do not rely on the names of those listed as the "chiefs" or "head-men" of the tribes. To many of the tribes, each family head was a "chief." The concept of a tribal chief was, to many tribes, unknown until the non-Indians taught it. Many times those who signed the treaties were those whom the governments wanted to recognize as the tribal leaders because they were willing to give up the rights to the land, when, in fact, they were not those recognized by tribal members as their leaders. As a result, there may have been members of a tribe which was party to a treaty, who did not feel they were represented and therefore did not honor a treaty.

Annuity Rolls

Annuity rolls (also called annuity payrolls) are records of payments made by the government to Native Americans in fulfillment of provisions of treaties and agreements between the two parties. Most of the treaties between Native American tribes and the United States government included provisions that the government was to pay the tribal members a specified amount of money and/or goods for a specified period of time.

The origin of payment of annuities as a stipulation of treaties dates as early as 1790 when a treaty with the Creek Nation specified that it would surrender its claim to certain lands for an annual payment of $1,500. During the early years, payments were made to the chiefs or headmen of the tribes, who distributed the payment as they saw fit. President Thomas Jefferson advocated making payments directly to heads of families, but this was not used as an optional method of payment until after 1834 (Rev.Stat. June 30, 1834, 4 Stat. at L. 737). Finally, in 1875, the distribution of annuity payments to heads of families became mandatory under the law (March 3, 1875, 18 Stat. at L. 449).

The content and format of these records vary, depending upon the time period and tribal group involved. Generally, at least names of heads of families are given in the annuity rolls as is an indication of the number of children, date of payment, and amount paid.

During the years when payments were made to the chiefs of the tribes or bands, usually the only record created were receipts. These, of course, contained only the name of the chief or head-man receiving the money. These receipts were not kept as a separate record, but were simply interfiled with the correspondence of the Commissioner of Indian Affairs and his forerunners.

Later, as payments were made to individual family heads, censuses were taken as a basis for identifying families entitled to the annuity payments. The most valuable of these "annuity rolls" to the genealogist or historian are those dating prior to 1884, the beginning date for the largest collection of census rolls. For the pre-1884 time period, they are almost the only record with "census type" data. Often the information in annuity rolls is more complete than the information in the contemporary census rolls.

Many of the annuity rolls for 1841 through 1938 are among the records of the Bureau of Indian Affairs housed at the National Archives, although many of them also are still in the regional branches of the National Archives and Records Administration. Some are still in the local agencies of the Bureau of Indian Affairs. An inventory of those in the National Archives in Washington, D.C., was compiled in 1954 and included a tribal and band index.

In order to access the records it is necessary to know the tribal group, the agency, and the dates of the annuity payments. With that information, annuity payrolls help to identify the location of a particular family at a specific agency at a certain time.

The information in annuity payrolls is not restricted. However, questions have arisen regarding their accuracy. It has been alleged that there is some duplication in the records due to some Native American heads of families receiving annuities under two different names or from two or more different agencies. Furthermore, the spelling of the names in the records may vary considerably, depending on the proficiency of the agent with the tribe's language.

Census Records

Early census rolls: At various times and for numerous reasons, it was necessary for government representatives to know how many Native Americans resided in a given area. Census records provide name, age, sex, and other personal information about Native Americans, as well as identify their place of residence at the time of enumeration of the census.

When the Jacksonian policy of Indian removal became the national policy, it was obvious that it would become necessary to round up the Native Americans living in the eastern part of the United States and forcibly remove them to the West. In order for the army to know how many they were dealing with, a census (count or listing) was made in 1835 for the Cherokees called the Henderson Roll, and in 1832 for the Creeks, called the Parsons and Abbott Roll. These census schedules included the name of heads of families, the number of members of each family, and some information about the family and its property. These rolls are arranged by the village of residence.

These schedules are part of Record Group 75, Records of the Bureau of Indian Affairs, in the National Archives. They have been microfilmed as Microcopies 496 and 275, respectively, and are also available at all of the regional archives of the National Archives and Records Administration and on microfilm at many of the major research libraries.

For some of the removed tribes there were census rolls taken after their arrival in the West. These rolls were taken to establish eligibility for payments due under the treaties. For example, the Cherokees were counted in a number of rolls recorded at various times: Mullay Roll, 1848; Siler Roll, 1851; Chapman Roll (actually a receipt roll for payments made), 1852; Powell Roll, 1867; Swetland Rolls, 1869; and Hester Roll, 1884.

Under the Act of July 4, 1884 (23 Stat. at L. 98), the taking of an annual census of Indians on reservations was required. The instructions sent to each agent were copied from Section 9 of the act and read as follows:

> That hereafter each Indian agent be required, in his annual report, to submit a census of the Indians at his agency or upon the reservation under his charge, the number of males above eighteen years of age, the number of females above fourteen years of age, the number of school children between the ages of six and sixteen years, the number of school houses at his agency, the number of schools in operation and the attendance of each, and the name of teachers employed and salaries paid such teachers.

The information required by the first part of these instructions ("to submit a census of the Indians . . .") was gathered first in columnar form by the agents. Later, about 1890, the Bureau of Indian Affairs began furnishing printed forms on which to record the necessary information. (See the ''Basic Genealogical Research Methods and Their Application to Native Americans'' chapter for an explanation and illustrations of these forms.)

Beginning in 1925, two supplements to the census rolls were compiled. One recorded births occurring between July 1st of the year previous to the census and June thirtieth of the census year.

Many of the census returns from the various reservations were sent to the Bureau of Indian Affairs in Washington, D.C., and have since been deposited with the National Archives. The National Archives has condensed as many of the census returns as it could readily locate in its collection into a microfilm publication of 692 rolls under the title ''Indian Census Rolls'' (microcopy M-595). Complete sets of these census rolls are available for search at the National Archives, the regional branches of the National Archives, the Family History Library in Salt Lake City, and at many other research institutions.

Original copies of the census rolls included in the above mentioned microfilmed set are often found in the agency offices and in the regional branches of the National Archives as are others which will fill in gaps in the National Archives' collection. Most of these have not yet been microfilmed, although many in the regional branches have been.

It must be kept in mind that several tribes were exempted from annual census taking. Such groups as the Five Civilized Tribes of Oklahoma have **no** censuses taken under this act included in the records of the National Archives, nor do those who were on state reservations (run by state Indian affairs offices, not the federal government's), such as some of those in New York State. Then, too, some tribes which were included in the Census Act did not, for one reason or another, take an annual census. For instance, the Navajo tribe had a census taken in 1885. Due to the difficulties of taking a census on a very large reservation with scattered pockets of population, the next one was not taken until 1915.

To access Indian census records, the name of the family head and the tribal affiliation must be known, as well as the agency under whose jurisdiction the family was residing. Census information is generally not restricted, but there are many difficulties in using the records. The same individual can be listed in census records under different names—his or her Indian name, English name, Christian name, or one of perhaps a number of aliases or alternate spellings. The former roll number column in some of the census rolls is a great help, but does not solve all of the problems. Furthermore, many of the relationships given in the census rolls are simply incorrect. Often Native Americans raised their brother's or sister's children as their own, and other cultural problems and kinship systems simply did not adequately account for relationships asked for in the census rolls.

Even with their problems, census records provide a family structure from which to work. Using them as the foundation of research and in conjunction with the other records of Native Americans one begins to establish knowledge of family groups.

Removal Records

From the time of the Louisiana Purchase in 1803, there were those in government who encouraged the removal of Native Americans from the East to the area west of the Mississippi River. In 1830, President Andrew Jackson, a self-proclaimed Indian hater, supported the official government policy of removing the Native Americans to the West. The act of May 28, 1830 (4 Stat. 411), authorized the president to exchange land in the unorganized territory west of the Mississippi River for any Native American land in a state or territory, providing the Native Americans moved. President Jackson pursued this policy vigorously for the next several years, particularly with regard to four of the Five Civilized Tribes (Cherokee, Chickasaw, Choctaw, and Creek). (The Seminoles were excluded for two reasons: their land was in present-day Florida, which was still heavily influenced by Spain; and the Seminoles' lands were in the Everglades, from which they were very adept at conducting surprise military attacks, as they did on Jackson's troops in 1818.)

From 1830 to 1836 treaties were negotiated with the four tribes, most of which included provisions for paying the Native Americans for their lands (and improvements on these lands) in the East, assisting them in their removal to the West, and providing financial assistance to them for one year thereafter. The actual removals were supposedly conducted by the Office of the Commissary General of Subsistence, but it had plenty of help from the U.S. Army.

Even before the 1830 act, removal was being pursued by certain elements of the federal government. The Cherokee Nation was the first tribe which ceded lands east of the Mississippi River in exchange for lands in the West. That treaty was signed on July 8, 1817. One of the provisions of the treaty was to allow 640 acre reservations for Native American heads of families who wished to stay in the East.

Several types of records were generated because of the removal policy. Censuses were taken of the tribal members in the East (which are discussed in this chapter under ''Census Records''). These rolls usually listed only heads of families and information regarding the family and its property.

As the Native Americans were gathered for the march west, muster lists of Indians (also called emigration rolls or records) were prepared to account for those making the move. The emigration rolls usually list individual Native Americans who wished to emigrate, rolls of actual emigrants, muster rolls of conducted parties, and lists of Native Americans able to emigrate unescorted. Some rolls are actually signed by the Native Americans to verify relinquishment of lands in the East. Sometimes the value of property being left, amount of debt, and other such information is included.

Following their removal, there were many claims filed by individual Native Americans involving their lands, other property, and the proper payment for them, such as the Eastern Cherokee Claims. See the section under "Indian Claims Records."

Even when no provision was made in a treaty, sometimes an individual Native American who wished to stay in the East could accept a reserve of land and remain, usually as a citizen of the United States. There were many who chose to stay in the East, some simply moving among the non-Indian settlers of the frontier and abandoning their tribal connections. Most of these were probably part-bloods who could blend in with non-Indian settlers. There were some Native Americans who also eluded the Army and stayed in the East, maintaining their tribal affiliations and eventually reestablishing themselves as tribal entities. Examples include members of the Eastern Cherokee and Mississippi Choctaw tribes.

Once established in the West, census rolls (or rolls listing those entitled to payments under the various treaties) were taken. Many of these rolls have been maintained among the removal records, although they are technically census rolls and often extend well beyond the removal period. They have been discussed in this chapter under the heading of "Census Records."

Most of the removal records, especially for the Five Civilized Tribes, are now part of the collections of the Bureau of Indian Affairs in the National Archives in Washington, D.C. There are many guides to the records of the National Archives, the most important of which is the *Guide to Records in the National Archives of the United States Relating to American Indians* (Hill 1984). The records of removal are a bit scattered throughout the records of the Bureau of Indian Affairs. Some are in the collections of removal records for the respective tribal groups while others are found in the general correspondence of the bureau. Occasionally, reports on the removal of tribes ended up as a congressional report, such as the U.S. House of Representatives Report No. 519, *Removal of the Chippewa, Ottawa, and Pottawatomie Indians,* published in 1844.

To access removal records, the name of the tribe, locality of residence, and name of the individual being sought must be known. Removal records are unique in that they prove the movement of Native Americans from one area to another. Most of the time, when they moved on their own, no record of their migrations was generated.

Removal records are not restricted and are generally available through the National Archives and its branches. Some of the congressional reports and reports of the Bureau of Indian Affairs are available through the many government documents libraries at various universities throughout the United States. (See Addendum at the end of this chapter for more information on the Five Civilized Tribes.)

Correspondence Files

Since most of the business of the Bureau of Indian Affairs was conducted by field offices and since the central office was in Washington, D.C., a large amount of correspondence passed back and forth between the Commissioner's office and the agencies.

This correspondence was kept in basically two series from 1824 to 1907: incoming and outgoing. Most of the correspondence was with the field officials of the Bureau, not with individual Native Americans. Only after the passage of the General Allotment Act in 1887 did correspondence from Native Americans become very significant, thereafter including letters from individuals concerning their enrollment in a particular tribe, allotments, or rights to an annuity or claims payment.

The incoming correspondence has been divided into time periods and subject headings. There is a set of letters received by the Office of the Secretary of War relating to Indian Affairs, 1800–1823. This collection has been microfilmed by the National Archives on its Microcopy 271 and consists of four microfilm rolls. Another set of incoming correspondence received by the Superintendent of Indian Trade, 1806–1824, has also been microfilmed by the National Archives as its Microcopy T58.

The letters received for 1824–1881, along with the registers, 1824–1880, form another collection of correspondence. That collection has been microfilmed by the National Archives as its Microcopy 234, consisting of 1088 reels of 35 mm microfilm.

For the years 1824–1880, incoming correspondence was entered in a register upon receipt. Letters which were answered within the bureau became part of the collection of incoming correspondence filed in several sub-collections. Letters which needed to be referred to other government departments or agencies were entered in the register, but the original letter was then referred to the other office and became part of its correspondence file.

The Register of Incoming Correspondence for the early years lists the name of the writer, the date the letter was written, and the date it was received. The format changed slightly in 1834 when the place it was written, a summary of its contents, and the jurisdiction or other heading under which the letter was filed were added. In 1836 the file number assigned to each letter upon its receipt was also added.

The letters for 1824–1881 are arranged alphabetically by name of field jurisdiction (superintendency or agency) or other subject heading, thereunder by year, and thereunder in registry order (alphabetically by initial letter of surname or other designation of writer and thereunder chronologically by date of receipt). Letters relating to an agency for all or part of its existence may be filed under the agency's name or under the name of its supervising organization. Two of the major subject headings included in this incoming correspondence collection are "Emigration" and "Reserves."

A new system of registering and filing incoming correspondence was adopted in 1881 and used until 1907. It involved registering each letter in chronological order as it was received and assigning each letter a file number without regard to source or content. The division of the bureau to which the letter was sent is also noted.

Often enclosed with the correspondence sent to the Commissioner's Office from the various agencies and superintendencies were reports, petitions, muster rolls, census rolls, land records, heirship information, school census lists, journals, and many other records. (The major types of records important for family history and genealogical research are discussed under their respective headings.)

Outgoing correspondence was also carefully kept by the Secretary of War's Office and later by the Commissioner of Indian Affairs Office. There are several sets of outgoing correspondence, mostly divided by time periods of the various filing systems used.

A roughly chronological arrangement of a War Office Letter Book for the years 1791–1797 was maintained. This letter book was microfilmed by the National Archives on one roll of microfilm.

Six volumes of handwritten copies of letters to territorial governors, Indian superintendents, Indian agents and subagents, factors at trading posts, and to a host of other individuals, including a few Native Americans, have been microfilmed by the National Archives as their Microcopy 15. This collection is filed chronologically and is indexed primarily by the name of the addressee. The six volumes cover November 1800 to April 1824.

A separate collection of outgoing correspondence relating to the factory system was maintained by the Superintendent of Indian Trade and was microfilmed by the National Archives as its Microcopy 16. It includes correspondence from October 1807 to April 1823.

Handwritten copies of outgoing correspondence, 1824–1881, were recorded by the Office of Indian Affairs and included instructions of field officials and replies to incoming correspondence. From 1824 to 1869, the letters were copied in chronological order. After that date, letters relating to certain broad subjects such as land, finance, etc., were kept in separate books, but still in chronological order. Most of the volumes are indexed. This collection of outgoing correspondence has been microfilmed on 166 rolls by the National Archives as its Microcopy 21.

In 1870 the Bureau of Indian Affairs began making press copies (duplicate records, like carbon copies, made using onion skin) of outgoing letters. By the 1880s the press copies were the official copies of outgoing correspondence and handwritten copies were no longer made. These press copies were bound into volumes for each division of the Bureau of Indian Affairs—2068 volumes for eight divisions of the bureau, covering 1870 to 1908.

After August 20, 1907, the bureau began filing all incoming and outgoing correspondence in a single decimal-subject classification system. Copies of correspondence are filed first by jurisdiction, then by the decimal classification number, and then chronologically. In these "flat files," as they are called, were placed any reports, petitions, affidavits, wills, photographs, applications, other legal documents, etc.

The Bureau of Indian Affairs used a system of orders, circulars, and circular letters to issue instructions to agents and other field personnel and to provide and/or request information. When instructions needed to be sent to all agents, for instance, a circular letter would be issued and sent to all agents on all reservations. Instructions on the taking of the census, issues of health and sanitation, keeping records of allotments are examples of items which were included in these documents. This is the single most important set of records for the understanding of what the agents were being instructed to do on the Indian reservations. Files of these orders or instructions are usually found in the agencies. Some have made their way also into regional archives of the National Archives and Records Administration.

The Office of Indian Affairs kept some administrative files in addition to the correspondence files discussed above. These files contain only a few references to individual Native Americans, but they provide excellent background about the agencies under which the Native Americans lived.

The special files of the Office of Indian Affairs, 1807–1904, consist of correspondence, reports, accounts, affidavits, and other records that were brought together for easier reference. They relate principally to claims or investigations. The collection is indexed by name and subject. The special files have been microfilmed by the National Archives as its Microcopy 574 on eighty-five rolls of microfilm.

Whenever the Commissioner of Indian Affairs communicated to the Secretary of War or later to the Secretary of the Interior, the communications were considered reports. They range from rather extensive narratives to brief letters. These reports have been preserved as *Report Books of the Office of Indian Affairs, 1838–1885.* The fifty-three volumes of reports have been microfilmed by the National Archives as its Microcopy 348. The subjects of these reports vary as widely as the activities of the Indian Affairs Office—the negotiation and enforcement of treaties, claims, establishment of reservations, allotments, appraisements of land, appointments and employees, location of agencies, etc. Some of the volumes are indexed by subject.

Reports of inspection of the field jurisdictions of the Office of Indian Affairs, 1873–1900, have been taken from the Office of Indian Affairs for 1873–1880 and from the Indian Division of the Office of the Secretary of the Interior, 1880–1900. Inspectors investigated a number of subjects pertaining to the Native Americans, their conditions, how they were being treated, how they were adopting non-Indian civilization, reservation boundaries, etc. Some of the later inspection reports included names of employees and their titles at the agency being inspected, and the residence, age, sex, and rate of compensation of those employees. Comments on the character, education, personal habits, qualifications, and fitness for their employment with the agency may also be included. Other topics covered in the written reports may also include the health of the Native Americans, the removal and treatment of the Native Americans by the agents and other officials, etc. The inspection reports are arranged by the name of the field jurisdiction and thereunder chronologically. They have been microfilmed by the National Archives as its Microcopy 1070 on sixty rolls of microfilm.

The annual narrative and statistical reports, 1907–1938, are reports of each of the field jurisdictions and are an excellent source for the history of an agency or tribe. The narrative reports relate to activities in each agency, school, hospital, or other field jurisdiction. They are often illustrated with photographs and cover a variety of subjects such as education, health, population, land ownership, tribal organization, and many other subjects. The statistical reports relate to school enrollment, population, health, land ownership, and other subjects. Both these reports have been reproduced on 174 rolls of microfilm by the National Archives as its Microcopy 1011.

Vital Records

As the work of the Bureau of Indian Affairs proceeded, both the agents and the Commissioner of Indian Affairs found that there were a number of reasons to record vital events: births, marriages, deaths, and divorces. The forms used and the years covered varied considerably from one agency to another. Generally, births and deaths were not recorded until about 1880. Marriage records began even later, for many of the Native Americans married according to Native American custom, rather than by ''white-man's'' law. For example, the law regulating marriages and divorces among allotted Native Americans in Oklahoma was not passed until 1897. This law specified that a record of marriages after July 1st of that year was to be made by the probate judges of the territory.

In some states and territories, vital records were recorded by the regular office of vital records for that state. Some agencies kept birth and death registers as part of the records of the agency, particularly until the supplemental vital records rolls were added to the annual census in 1928. For example, the Coeur d'Alene Agency in northern Idaho recorded births and deaths from 1918 to 1928 in a register. Births, deaths, marriages, and divorces were also reported for the purpose of keeping enrollment lists current by simply noting the event in a letter from the outlying agency employees (such as reservation farmer, school official, health official, etc.) to the agent. In a similar manner, divorces are often noted in letters among agency officials.

By 1886 the Bureau of Indian Affairs agents had been requested to record information about all the Native Americans who came into the health service for any kind of treatment: physical or mental. The agents were to enter the date the sickness began, the date the sickness ended, the cause of the sickness, how long the patient was treated, and in the case of deaths, the date of death. For births, the date of birth and the names of parents were recorded. This record is known as the ''Sanitary Record of Sick, Wounded, Births, Deaths,'' etc. and is usually found among the records of the local agency. (See also the section ''Indian Health Service Records.'')

A number of other records of the Bureau of Indian Affairs recorded vital statistics, even though they were not kept nor thought of as ''vital records'' in the same sense as non-Indians would think of that term. For example, the supplemental rolls kept in connection with the Indian census rolls recorded births and deaths, and even prior to the supplemental rolls, some of the birth and death dates of the Native Americans were recorded on the census rolls. Agents also kept a record called the ''register of families,'' especially on allotted reservations. On this register, births and deaths were recorded as they occurred, in order that the register be kept current.

After the Indian Reorganization Act of 1934, some of the tribal governments established their own offices of vital statistics and recorded the births and deaths of their own tribal members. When they did, they usually patterned their vital statistics forms after those being used by the states in which they resided.

There are some restrictions on the later vital statistics, in the same way there are restrictions on state records of vital events. But vital records in the collections of the Bureau of Indian Affairs collections are not normally restricted.

Some tribes print their own newspapers, such as *The Chickasaw Times*, which chronicle the news and events of the tribe, and print obituaries of tribal members.

Indian Wills and Heirship Matters

The concept of passing rights to property on to relatives or others after death was also new to Native Americans. When the non-Indian government officials imposed this concept upon them, the Indians only gradually learned it. The laws governing Native American rights (passed by non-Indians), especially allotments, specified that rights could be passed on to heirs following the death of a Native American. They even specified how each fractional interest should be allowed for each degree of heirship. Therefore, it became extremely important that proper degrees of relationship be identified and recorded for each person on a reservation, particularly for those receiving allotments.The agents did the best they could by keeping a variety of records which were intended to help them with determining heirs.

A Native American who desired to make a will after 1910 could do so with the approval of the Commissioner of Indian Affairs. Those wills, referred to the bureau and to the Office of the Secretary of the Interior for approval, have been collected into eight volumes for the years 1911 to 1921. There are also many original wills and related records in the central classified files (decimal system or flat files).

The estate files collected by the various levels of the Bureau of Indian Affairs consist of more than just wills, for they include reports on heirship and related papers and usually include such information as name, tribe, agency, allotment number, description of allotment, place of residence, date of death, age at death, names of heirs, and their share of the estate. Other genealogical information which may be included in the report on heirship includes the name of the spouse, date of marriage, names and date of marriage of parents, and names of brothers, sisters, and children. Most of the early heirship records are now in the collections of the various offices of the Bureau of Indian Affairs and in the probate courts handling Native American estates for the bureau.

Heirship records are particularly important to the family historian in that they are a legal document stating correct relationships. They are somewhat difficult to find since many of them are still in the offices of the local agencies.

To access these records it is necessary to know the name of the decedent, his or her date and place of death, and the agency and/or tribal group involved.

See the chapter ''Basic Genealogical Research Methods—Probate and Heirship Records'' for more information.

Records of Indian Employees

Throughout the history of the Bureau of Indian Affairs, efforts were made to employ as many Native Americans as possible to assist with the work of the agency. The dedication with which that policy was carried out was largely dependent upon the attitude of the individual agents and/or the specific Commissioner of Indian Affairs.

Each agency kept a record of its employees, as did the central office in Washington, D.C. In the Commissioner's Office there are registers of applications and recommendations for appointments, 1833–1849 and 1866–1868. There are also bonds of field employees, 1867–1935; rosters of field employees, 1848–1850; superintendents and agents, 1853–1863; field officials, 1849–1911; agency employees, 1853–1909; school employees, 1884–1909; school employees in Indian Territory, 1899–1909; Indian police, 1878–1906; employees of the Commission to the Five Civilized Tribes, 1899–1909; and others. Obviously, not all of these employees were Native Americans but for those who were, the tribal affiliation of the Native American employee was usually noted in the remarks column.

The information given concerning the individual employee varies, but may include name, position, salary, name of tribe to which appointed, former occupation, dates of service, age, sex, race, marital status, birthplace, and legal residence or state from which appointed. For Indian police, additional information including tribal affiliation, degree of Native American blood, and physical measurements is usually given.

In the respective agencies there often are separate records of employees containing the same type of information mentioned above. As an example, for employees being paid more than $300.00 annually, the bureau required a ''Personal Record'' be kept which included the name of the employee, year and state of birth, position, agency, salary, race, whether married, number of children, legal residence, height, weight, and several items about positions held, musical ability, schools or colleges attended, military service, knowledge and experience of mechanical trade, business, etc. Records of Indian police are especially likely to have been kept on the larger reservations.

Many of the reports sent in from the agents to the Commissioner's Office have lists of employees attached and are included in the general correspondence files and some names of employees were included in the annual reports of the Commissioner of Indian Affairs. Many of those who worked for the Bureau of Indian Affairs as agents or in other capacities have been included in the *Biographical and Historical Index of American Indians and Persons Involved in Indian Affairs* (United States Department of the Interior Library).

Indian Boarding Schools and Other School Records

The Bureau of Indian Affairs established an Education Division in September 1885 and with its creation came a renewed effort on the part of the bureau to see that Native American children were educated. There had been forerunners to the Education Division and they tried to establish the teaching of Native Americans about such things as agricultural and mechanical training, health, sanitation, the effects of liquor, and a number of other subjects. They also were concerned about educating the Native Americans (especially the children) in reading, writing, and arithmetic. These efforts were intensified with the establishment of the Education Division.

School census records (which resulted from this desire to educate Native American children) list their names, ages, place of birth, and, in some cases, the names of their parents. Agents at the local Bureau of Indian Affairs Office were required to send reports to the Commissioner's Office regarding enrollment of children who were of the proper age to be in school. The National Archives has a very large set of annual school census reports sent in from the agencies, 1912–1939. These reports are actually census rolls of children of school age, whether or not they were enrolled in school. Entries give the name of the child, sex, age, tribe, and degree of Indian blood, name of reservation or agency, distance of home from a public school, and name of parent or guardian. If the child was attending school, additional information about the school attended, grade, length of term, and number of grades was included. For those not enrolled, the reason was given. Local agencies have additional school census records, some dating from the 1870s and 1880s.

Many of the local agencies had boarding schools on or near the reservations they served. These schools maintained individual pupil files which contained all of the information the school census rolls did, plus additional information about attendance, subjects taken, names of the teachers of those subjects, grades by term, dental health, vocational training, name and location of the school, health history, etc.

The agents also often kept a record called the ''Descriptive Statement of Pupils Transferred'' for the particular school which included the pupil's Indian and/or English name, degree of Indian blood, tribe, band, father's (or guardian's) name and rank, whether father and mother were living, sex, age, height, weight, ''forced inspiration'' (chest size when he or she inhaled), ''forced expiration'' (chest size when he or she exhaled), time of service, and remarks.

There were a few special advanced schools for Native American students, such as the Haskell Institute in Kansas or Sherman Institute in California. These schools kept very complete records on their students, including all of the personal data cited above as well as information about his or her residence at the school, tribal affiliation, and agency from which he or she was sent. Most records can still be found at the schools.

School records are usually unrestricted, especially the older ones. Again, there are some errors regarding parentage of the pupils, for the same reasons there are errors in relationships in the census rolls. Many children were raised by aunts and uncles as if they were their children, especially if their parents were dead or had been divorced.

Individual History Cards

Some agencies kept a set of records known as ''Individual History Cards'' to assist in determining relationships for allotments and heirship for estates. Information included the Indian and/or English name of the individual, tribe, sex, birth date, names of father and paternal grandparents, names of mother and maternal grandparents, death date, and census and allotment numbers. On the bottom half of the card (really a full-size page) were recorded the names of siblings and half-siblings with their census and allotment numbers, and aunts and uncles on both sides, all with census and allotment numbers. Some Individual History Cards even have pictures of homes attached.

These records apparently were not kept on all reservations. Where they were, they remain with the records of the agency or have been transferred to the appropriate regional archives of the National Archives and Records Administration.

There are no restrictions on the records. The name, tribal group, and agency are needed to access them.

Indian Health Service Records

The Bureau of Indian Affairs was concerned with the health and sanitation of the Native Americans under its charge. Several attempts were made to organize the best possible health care for the least amount of cost. The Indian Health Service was for a number of years part of the Education Division of the Bureau of Indian Affairs. It was primarily concerned with the education of Native Americans in the prevention of diseases such as tuberculosis, and those that were transmitted sexually.

There were a number of health-related records kept: physician's reports, clinic and hospital records, the ''Sanitary Record of Sick, Wounded, Births, Deaths'' (see also the section ''Vital Records'' above), etc., and individual records. As physicians, nurses, and other health professionals tended the sick and injured on the reservations or at boarding schools, they reported their problems to the agent in charge. As requested, they sent letters to the Commissioner's Office, reporting on the challenges of health and sanitation in the field. These reports and letters often dealt with individual Native American cases, often by name. Normally, these records contain the name of the patient, the approximate location of their residence, the agency and tribal affiliation, and something about his or her health problem(s).

The most complete records of health kept prior to 1934 are the ''Sanitary Records of Sick, Wounded, Births, Deaths,'' etc. They are sometimes called by other names in descriptive inventories—''sick ledgers,'' ''physician's reports,'' etc. These books list the name of the patient, sex, disease, when taken sick, when recovered, when deceased, age (over or under five), sex of the child for birth records, whether the child was Indian, half-breed, or white, and, if vaccinated, whether vaccination was successful.

The later Individual Health Record recorded the name of the Indian, sex, tribe, birth date, address, communicable disease history, immunizations, medical tests, and history of visits to the health clinics or hospitals. When a health official felt it was necessary, a visit was made to the home and a ''Household Record'' was completed which listed tribe, the name of the family and each member residing therein, sex, year of birth of each household member, relationship of others living in the household beyond the core family, occupation or school, and other data regarding health problems, type of housing, and notes of the visiting official.

All of the records of personal health are part of the agency records, except for the reports or correspondence sent to the Commissioner's Office, which became part of the correspondence files there. Most of the health records are not indexed and cover only a small percentage of tribal members.

Indian Claims Records

Several claims have been filed against the U.S. government by Native Americans, some of the earliest of which are Cherokee claims authorized by an act of July 1, 1902 (32 Stat. 726). These cases were filed individually as Congress allowed a particular Indian tribe to bring suit against the U.S. government.

The Cherokee Claims Commission, headed by Guion Miller, began its work in 1906. Its members gathered over 45,000 applications from people who felt they were entitled to be a part of the claim against the U.S. government. These applications and packets of supporting information are a part of the National Archives collection in Washington, and have been microfilmed on 348 rolls as Microcopy 1104. There is a two-volume index which was microfilmed as part of the collection. In order to prove that they had a right to receive a portion of the claim they were seeking, each tribal member had to prove his descendance from one of his or her ancestors who appeared on an earlier roll of that tribe. These claim files have often contained the names of the claimant, his date and place of birth, residence, and names and genealogical information about his brothers, sisters, parents, grandparents, and children.

Transcripts of the applications gathered by Guion Miller, without the supporting packets of information, but including miscellaneous testimony taken before special commissioners, have been microfilmed as National Archives Microcopy 685. This microcopy also includes copies of many of the earlier rolls including the Chapman, Drennen, Old Settler, and Hester Rolls, all taken in the 1850s. At the end of the Guion Miller Commission, a ''Roll of Eastern Cherokees Entitled to Participate in the Fund Arising from the Court of Claims of May 28, 1906'' was printed by the federal government.

Another claims case which involved a Native American tribe was the case of the Chippewa Indians in the early 1900s. At the Regional Archives in Kansas City, the records of the U.S. attorneys and marshall for the District of Minnesota are housed. In those records are the documents pertaining to the case for the Chippewas. The claim required the Indians living at the time the case was pursued to prove their ancestry several generations previous. In the records of the attorneys are hundreds of genealogical charts. For example, pedigrees show the ancestry of the White Earth Chippewas back, in many cases, to the late 1700s and early 1800s. The case files also have allotment registers, reports of the special agent assigned to the case, and the rolls of tribal membership upon which the case was built.

By 1946 there were so many cases filed in the U.S. Court of Claims that it could not process all of them. To expedite the processing of the claims, an Indian Claims

Commission was created by an act of Congress. Its purpose was to hear, investigate, and determine the validity of claims against the United States filed prior to August 13, 1846, by a tribe or any other group of Native Americans living in the United States. Essentially, it was charged with jurisdiction over those claims filed up to the time of its creation. The U.S. Court of Claims kept its jurisdiction to hear cases filed after the creation of the Indian Claims Commission.

The Indian Claims Commission originally had three members and a statutory life of ten years. Its term of life was extended several times, ultimately until 1978, at which time it stopped taking cases, and had five members. All cases remaining unheard by then were transferred back to the U.S. Court of Claims.

The cases heard by the Indian Claims Commission were based on 370 original petitions which were divided into 611 different claims. These claims were based upon real and supposed violations of the treaties or agreements reached between the government and the individual Native American tribes. Most involved claims that lands of the Native Americans had been taken without the compensation due according to the provisions of treaties or agreements.

There were basically three parts of a case heard before the Indian Claims Commission. The first was to determine whether a wrong had occurred. Since most of the claims were based on events of many years earlier, there usually were no eyewitnesses, so proof of the alleged wrong was based on historical and ethnological writings and upon contemporary accounts of the event. This phase of the case involved determining the area occupied by the tribe at the time, and the Native Americans' rights to that land area, the events surrounding the alleged malfeasance, and evidence thereof.

Once the validity of the claim was established, the next step was to present evidence of the value of the property at the time of the treaty or agreement and the amount paid by the government to the Native Americans for that property.

The final step was to determine any payments or other compensation made by the government since the signing of the treaty or agreement which would offset the amount of wrong done the tribe.

There were other types of cases heard by the Indian Claims Commission. The most common type was one in which a Native American tribe would ask the government to account for the management of the tribe's assets.

The records of the Indian Claims Commission are grouped into several collections. One set presents the cases heard by the Indian Claims Commission dating from a treaty signed in 1785 to the closing of the commission's office in 1978. It includes the treaties upon which the cases are based. This set of records has been produced in microform by University Publications of America on 420 microfiche.

A second set of records covers the decisions reached by the Indian Claims Commission from 1948 to 1981. (Although the office stopped accepting new claims in 1978, it took until 1981 to process the claims that had been filed before the deadline.) There is a three-part index to this collection. There is a tribal index which is an alphabetical listing of the tribes involved in cases heard before the commission and a reference to the docket numbers for cases in which that tribe was involved. There is also an index which lists the dockets in numerical order and gives the name of the plaintiff in the case. The table of cases lists the cases in the order heard by the Indian Claims Commission, with docket numbers for the case, the volume and page number for the decision in the case, and the nature and date of each decision. This set has also been produced on microform by University Publications of America on 346 microfiche.

Another set of records covers the expert testimony before the Indian Claims Commission. This collection of written reports submitted to the commission as evidence in the cases has four separate indexes. The tribal index lists the tribes involved in the cases in alphabetical order with all the docket numbers for all cases involving that tribe. The author index lists the authors of all the reports included in the collection. The state index is a partial index to the states covered by the written reports, but only covers those states mentioned in the title page or table of contents of the reports. The docket index lists all the dockets in numerical order and the name of the plaintiff in each case. This collection has been produced in microform on 1,674 microfiche by the National Archives.

Several of the cases heard by the Indian Claims Commission were appealed to the U.S. Court of Claims. The decisions of that court are contained in another set of records also produced on twenty-eight microfiche by University Publications of America. These cases are indexed by tribal name and volume and page number of the decisions reached. If the U.S. Court of Claims decision was appealed, the citation to the Supreme Court's decision is also indicated.

There have been many other cases before the U.S. Court of Claims, especially since 1946. Many of the records of the U.S. Court of Claims for tribes from throughout the United States are in the Washington National Records Center in Suitland, Maryland.

In all of the claims cases the tribes had the right to choose their attorney so long as he or she was approved by the Bureau of Indian Affairs. Some of these records are still in the possession of the attorneys who represented the Native American tribes in each court case.

Once the claims cases were decided, especially those heard by the Indian Claims Commission and the U.S. Court of Claims, the tribes had to determine which of their tribal members were entitled to the settlement funds. Under the Indian Reorganization Act of 1934 the tribe had the power to determine that for itself, so in each case, the tribal councils decided on the minimum degree of Indian blood required to be a member of the tribe. In some cases, the setting of eligibility requirements to receive these funds has caused some discord between the full-bloods and the part-bloods.

The claims cases contain a great deal of history about a specific tribe, its land holdings, and its relationship with the federal government. But it is the enrollment record following the case that contain the valuable personal information about individual Native Americans.

Enrollment Records

Enrolling individuals as members of a tribe was done for several reasons. Native Americans were enrolled for the purposes of allotment, to provide a base for tribal membership (for those tribes which were granted self-governing privileges before the 1934 Indian Reorganization Act to establish tribal populations), to determine eligibility for payments from claims cases, and to establish the descendants of recognized adult tribal members.

As treaties were signed, claims were granted, or land or money was made available to a particular tribe, guidelines were set to determine who was to be considered a member of the tribe in question and, therefore, eligible for the benefits. The eligibility requirements were randomly set by the Bureau of Indian Affairs, the U.S. Court of Claims, or the tribe itself.

Once a determination of the eligibility requirements was made, efforts were made to ''enroll'' everyone who met the requirements. These enrollment standards may have included such things as degree of Indian blood, descendance from a member of the tribe living at the time of some event upon which a claim was based, residency on the tribal reservation, or any of myriad possibilities.

Enrollment records usually include personal information about the individual being enrolled such as name, age, sex, degree of Indian blood, agency where enrolled, and other data. Names of relatives and their relationship may also be indicated on the enrollment records.

Historically, there have been special acts passed by Congress or special commissions to enroll a particular tribe. For example, in 1893 Congress passed an act which authorized negotiations with the Cherokee, Chickasaw, Choctaw, Creek, and Seminole Tribes (commonly called the ''Five Civilized Tribes'') to dissolve their tribal governments and allot land to each member of those tribes. Senator Henry Dawes of Massachusetts was appointed chairman of the Enrollment Commission which thereafter was called the Dawes Commission.

The Dawes Commission was authorized to prepare tribal membership (or citizenship) rolls for each of the five tribes. The rolls finally agreed upon would then be used for the basis of allotment. More than 250,000 people applied for enrollment. Just over 100,000 were approved. This enrollment was closed on March 4, 1907; however, there were 312 additional individuals added to the rolls under an act approved in 1914.

There were a number of categories of citizenship used by the Dawes Commission: citizens by blood, citizens by marriage, newborn citizens by blood, minor citizens by blood, freedmen (former black slaves of Native Americans who were freed and admitted to tribal membership), newborn freedmen, and minor freedmen. Part of the Delaware Indians who had lived among the Cherokee tribe were also enrolled as a special category of Cherokee tribal membership.

For each of the above categories of citizenship, the Dawes Commission maintained three types of cards: ''Straight'' cards for those whose applications for citizenship were approved; ''R'' cards for those whose applications were rejected; and ''D'' cards for those whose applications were doubtful and needed additional review. All of the ''D'' cards eventually ended up in either the ''Straight'' or ''R'' category.

The applications for enrollment made to the Dawes Commission for the Five Civilized Tribes have been published on 468 reels of microfilm as Microcopy 1301 of the National Archives. The enrollment cards prepared by the commission staff of the Commission for the Five Civilized Tribes have also been published as Microcopy 1186 on 93 rolls of microfilm. *The Final Rolls of Citizens and Freedmen of the Five Civilized Tribes in Indian Territory* were printed by the Government Printing Office in Washington, D.C., immediately following the conclusion of the work of the Dawes Commission. They serve as an index to the enrollment cards discussed above.

The Eastern Cherokees went through an enrollment under the Guion Miller Commission as a result of a claim against the U.S. government in 1906. That claims case is discussed above under the heading of ''Indian Claims Records.'' There was also an additional enrollment for the Eastern Cherokees which took place in the 1920s. To provide a base from which to work, a roll of the Eastern Cherokees called the Baker Roll was taken in 1924. There then followed a period of enrollment from 1926 to 1928, during which decisions were made concerning the enrollment of those who wished to be included on the rolls of the Eastern Cherokees. A revised roll was compiled from the cases heard. The records of the Baker Roll and the revised roll, as well as the decisions in the enrollment cases are all at the North Carolina Department of Cultural Resources, Department of Archives and History, in Raleigh.

Other tribes had similar enrolling commissions responsible for determining who was entitled to be a member, although none of the other tribes had as big an enrollment problem as the Five Civilized Tribes.

If the necessity for a determination of citizenship was the result of a case heard in the U.S. Court of Claims, the enrollment records are part of the claims records (see that heading above for further discussion of enrollment documents).

To access these records, it is essential to know the tribal name and the name of the individual Indian being researched. They are available at the National Archives, its branches, and at many of the larger research institutions with an American Indian collection. (See the Addendum which follows this chapter for more information on the Five Civilized Tribes.)

Reservation/Tribal Government Records

The Wheeler-Howard Act of June 18, 1934, also known as the Indian Reorganization Act (48 Stat. 984) reaffirmed Native Americans' right to manage their own affairs through tribal councils and essentially ended allotments on reservations. Many tribes had already been operating with a tribal council, but this act confirmed their right to enact ordinances to regulate various things on reservations and to determine penalties for non-compliance with those ordinances. It reinforced the power of Indian tribal courts, and the right of each tribe to determine who was eligible to be a tribal member. This regulatory power includes the right to regulate the recording of births and deaths.

Many tribes now set their own standards for enrollment as a member of the tribe, keep their own enrollment records, and also record their own vital records (those of births, marriages, deaths, and divorces). These are usually very similar to the vital statistics kept by the states. Some tribal governments have their own police and court systems, and therefore keep their own court records. The dates these records commence, the types of records kept, and their content varies by tribe.

The records of the tribal governments of the Five Civilized Tribes of Oklahoma may constitute a unique set of documents with respect to Native American research. For example, the Cherokee Nation in Indian Territory operated its affairs as a separate nation with its capital at Tahlequah. It had its own council and senate, court system, etc. When the Curtis Act of 1898 provided that the governments of each of the Five Civilized Tribes be abolished, no particular provision was made for the disposition of the records of the nations. They were stored in the federal building at Muskogee, Oklahoma, where they later came to the attention of Dr. Grant Foreman. He was so convinced of their historical value that he got permission from the Commissioner's Office in Washington, D.C., to calendar (inventory) the documents in 1929. He and others got the collection placed in the Oklahoma Historical Building in Oklahoma City. In an unprecedented move, an act of Congress in 1934 transferred the records to the care of the Oklahoma Historical Society, even though the ownership of the records was left to the federal government. The records of the governments of the Five Civilized Tribes remain in the trust and care of the Oklahoma Historical Society, although there have been efforts to remove them and place them in the National Archives and Records Administration's branch archives.

There are 730 bound volumes of the Cherokee national records, the records of the nine Cherokee districts (Canadian, Cooweescoowee, Delaware, Flint, Going Snake, Illinois, Saline, Sequoyah, and Tahlequah), and many unbound documents dating from as early as 1840 and as late as 1907. Examples of the types of records included in this collection are the acts of the National Council, journals, registers, minutes of the board of education, school records, registers of claims, estray property (livestock which had wandered off its owner's property), records of wills, civil and criminal court records, marriage records, etc. Besides the records of the Cherokee national government and the records of each of its district governments (the two sets of records for that nation placed in trust by the federal government), the historical society also has a third set of Cherokee records not under that trust agreement consisting of documents or collections which have been purchased or received as gifts since the trust agreement of 1934.

Similar records exist for the Chickasaw Nation circa 1860–1907, the Creek Nation 1834–1906, the Choctaw Nation circa 1860–1906, and the Seminole Nation, 1866–1907.

Records Custodians

There are a number of possible records custodians which should be considered in Native American family history research. Each one of them is uniquely important. Although they have been mentioned in connection with the various types of records, an understanding of their structure and the types of holdings of each is important enough to warrant separate mention. Some of them will contain records that are not official Native American records, but these can serve as secondary sources, and they all have the potential of having at least some official BIA records in their possession.

The Family

One of the first places to start when tracing an ancestral line is with the family. Find out as much information as possible from family members. This is not different from research on any other ethnic group. This is usually the place to start with any genealogical or family history research task. However, a couple of problems may be encountered as relatives are asked about the ancestral line.

First of all, many Native Americans are hesitant to talk about the dead. There are many reasons and customs contributing to this reluctancy. Second, they may have a reluctance to talk about what they consider to be moral issues such as multiple marriages, a woman having had children by several different men during her lifetime, etc.

Bureau of Indian Affairs Offices

The Bureau of Indian Affairs offices are one of the most important custodians of American Indian records. There are three levels of BIA offices.

The local BIA office is the agency or subagency. Generally, if the researcher can visit the agency, this would be the best source of genealogical or historical information. Usually, the agencies and subagencies have a number of records dating back to the establishment of that agency and the records are often most complete in the agency office itself. There are some problems in using the agency offices. One is the long distance that one sometimes has to travel to get to the agency. In many cases, the records may be better arranged, indexed, and inventoried, and therefore easier to use, elsewhere. Quite often the attitude of the agent may be less than helpful unless the request is coming from a Native American enrolled at that agency.

The second level of the Bureau of Indian Affairs is the area office. The area office of the Bureau of Indian Affairs has only a limited number of records of value to genealogists. These are primarily land records or lease records or other records relating to land allotments and health reports. Although they are often only duplicate copies of records available at the agency, sometimes the area office combines reports from a number of agencies into a single report. For example, the Portland Oregon Area Office houses such records as memorandum of trust land and deceased heir cards 1925–1939, cancelled allotments 1887–1920, farming and grazing leases 1941–1952, crippled Indian children 1934, hospital roll 1939, in-patient cards 1946, student eye-exam lists 1934–1938, trachomatous (having chronic conjunctivitis) children list 1938, dependent children applications 1940, a list of Blackfeet Indians employed in Yakima Valley hop fields 1944, a list of school personnel 1940–1942, a list of Indians residing in southwest Oregon 1940–, and a small set of family index cards. Almost all of the documents cited above appear to be reports from the various agencies or schools to the area office.

The third level is, of course, the Commissioner's Office in Washington, D.C. The Commissioner's Office has had, over the years, a number of good genealogical records. However, most of them have been transferred to the National Archives and are available for search there. Most of the records categories important to family historians and genealogists have already been discussed above.

Tribal Offices

Another important records custodian is the tribal office. Since the Wheeler-Howard Act (or Indian Reorganization Act) in 1934, some tribes have begun keeping their own records. In many cases, they have good records which should be searched for genealogy and family history purposes. Tribal offices are often housed in the same building as the Bureau of Indian Affairs' agent's office or sometimes in an adjacent building on the reservation.

National Archives and Records Administration

The largest collection of Native American records in the United States is in the custody of the National Archives and Records Administration. The National Archives in Washington, D.C., is the largest single holder of Indian records. It has a large collection of agency records which have been transferred from agencies all over the country. It also has most of the Bureau of Indian Affairs Commissioner's Office records which would be of any value to a genealogist or a historian. These include such things as the correspondence of the commissioner, the correspondence of agents to the Commissioner's Office, reports coming from the various agencies with such attachments as the annual census and annuity rolls, wills which were mentioned earlier, and many other records.

The National Archives collection has a fairly complete inventory of its holdings and it is fairly easy to use the collection. It has also microfilmed many of its records and has them available for sale. The guides to the National Archives' holdings and the catalog of microfilm publications are listed in the bibliography.

The National Archives Regional Archives are the largest collective holder of Native American records. Their collections consist primarily of the agency records for their respective regions. One thing that should be mentioned is that their regional boundaries have changed over the years, so one needs to determine what their present regional boundaries are and then determine also what other states they might have included at an earlier time period. Often, the records for a geographical area formerly covered are transferred to the newly assigned regional archives. Generally, the branch directors are very helpful to researchers using the archives. The ten regional branches throughout the country and the states they serve are: New England, serving Connecticut, Maine, Massachusetts, New Hampshire, Rhode Island, and Vermont; Northeast, serving New Jersey, New York, Puerto Rico, and the Virgin Islands; Mid-Atlantic, serving Delaware, Maryland, Virginia, West Virginia, Pennsylvania, and the District of Columbia; Southeast, serving Alabama, Florida, Georgia, Kentucky, Mississippi, North Carolina, South Carolina, and Tennessee; Great Lakes, serving Illinois, Indiana, Michigan, Minnesota, Ohio, and Wisconsin; Central Plains, serving Iowa, Kansas, Missouri, Nebraska, [Minnesota, North Dakota, and South Dakota]; Southwest, serving Arkansas, Louisiana, New Mexico, Oklahoma, and Texas; Rocky Mountain, serving Colorado, Montana, North Dakota, South Dakota, Utah, Wyoming, [New Mexico, and Arizona]; Pacific Sierra, serving California (Northern), Hawaii, Nevada (except Clark Co.), American Samoa, and Pacific Ocean area; Pacific Southwest, serving Arizona, California (Southern), and Nevada (Clark County only); Pacific Northwest, serving Idaho, Oregon, Washington, [Alaska, and Montana]; and Alaska, serving Alaska. Those states listed in brackets were served by the preceding regional archive, and although all records for that state were to have been transferred to the regional archive which is now responsible for it, some records have not been. Address all inquiries to the archive director. The address and additional information can be found in the section entitled "Libraries and Archives" in Part II.

State Archives

Many state archives have collections of Indian documents, especially of the relationship between the state and the Native Americans residing within it. New York has maintained a peculiar relationship with the Native Americans within the state as most of its relations are governed by the state, not the federal government, and therefore has many records of Indian affairs in its holdings.

The Tennessee State Library and Archives, Manuscript Division, has a separate Cherokee Collection. Many other states have similar collections among their holdings.

Churches

As stated earlier, there were many denominations which were active in converting Native Americans to Christianity. Some of the denominations which were particularly active were the Quakers, Moravians, Presbyterians, Baptists, Catholics, Mormons. The content of their records vary considerably according to the denomination. A study into the historical background of the particular tribe being researched would be necessary to determine which of those denominations should be consulted.

Private Collections

There are a number of private collections of Native American materials throughout North America, such as those found in historical societies, universities, and genealogical libraries. The collections housed in these repositories are considered private in the sense that they are not the records of a government entity, maintained through the National Archives and Records Administration or some other government agency. Some of the documents in these private collections may have been public documents which found their way into the hands of a private collector of such materials.

University collections often contain documents pertaining to Native American affairs. One of the best Native American collections is at, of course, the University of Oklahoma in Norman. Others, especially those holding regional histories and records, should be consulted for their respective areas. An example of a university with this kind of regionally important material is the Society of Jesus, Oregon Province Archives at Gonzaga University in Spokane, Washington which houses histories and records of Catholic missions among Native Americans of the Pacific Northwest.

In late 1966, Miss Doris Duke of New York awarded grants to six American universities to collect oral histories from the American Indians. The main objective was to record American history from the Native American point of view. Some of the original universities were Arizona (U. of A.), California (U.C.L.A.), New Mexico, Oklahoma, and South Dakota. Since the original grant, several other universities such as Utah, Florida at Gainesville, and others have joined in the project. These oral history interviews help with the historical background of the tribe involved and sometimes includes family information, as well. The oral history interviews conducted under the auspices of Duke University have been published in microform (310 microfiche) by Kraus Microforms.

One of the best collections anywhere in the country, as far as size, ease of use, and good indexing are concerned, is in the Oklahoma Historical Society. While the Oklahoma Historical Society is considered to be a private collector, many of the documents in its collections are official records of the Bureau of Indian Affairs which it preserved before the federal government had established its archives network. In fact, in 1934 the federal government recognized the work of the Oklahoma Historical Society in preserving Native American records by making it a repository for federal records, to be held in trust by them. Because of that special arrangement, the Oklahoma Historical Society has over three million documents of Native American records, some of which are indexed. In some cases they have fairly complete sets of agency records, such as the Cheyenne and Arapaho records, 1869–1933. These agency records include census, allotment, annuity, church, school, and other records kept by the agent of the Bureau of Indian Affairs. Records of other agencies are also found in this repository.

Other historical societies in the localities where tribal groups are located should be checked to see if they have such collections for their respective tribal interests, although none will be of the magnitude of the Oklahoma Historical Society.

The Genealogical Society of Utah has in its collection microfilm copies of many of the records from these other custodians already mentioned. The Family History Library in Salt Lake City houses many of the records microfilmed by the National Archives in Washington, D.C. Many of the Indian records, agency and otherwise, housed in the various regional archives have been microfilmed and are available in the Family History Library. They are also available through the family history centers of the Family History Library. In addition, the Family History Library has a large collection of books on Native Americans. They also have microfilmed copies of the records of the missions of a number of religious denominations which worked among Native Americans, as well as copies of part of the holdings of the Oklahoma Historical Society, other research libraries, and personal collections such as those listed below.

Some individuals who have been involved in Indian affairs or who have just had an interest in Native Americans have compiled information into personal collections. While these personal collections might be considered non-official, copies and originals of official records often found their way into them. Examples of such collections are the Major James McLaughlin Collection, the John G. Pratt Collection, the papers of Ransom Judd Powell at the Minnesota Historical Society, or the Lyman Draper Manuscript Collection.

The Major James McLaughlin Collection is a collection of the major's personal correspondence as well as copies of documents such as applications for patents in fee (land titles), letter books, censuses, and other documents. James McLaughlin was an agent for the Bureau of Indian Affairs at Devils Lake Agency in Dakota Territory and at Standing Rock. He became the Inspector General for the Bureau of Indian Affairs, a position which he held for nearly thirty years, until his death in 1923. The collection is housed at Assumption Abbey in Richardton, North Dakota.

The John G. Pratt Collection is a collection of the papers of Pratt who served as an agent to the Delaware Indians in Kansas. It contains personal papers including correspondence, business papers, account books, and sermons, but it also includes the correspondence and papers of the Delaware Agency, including an allotment book recording the allotment of land to the Delaware Indians in 1865. It was published as a microfilm publication by the Kansas State Historical Society on thirteen rolls of microfilm.

The papers of Ransom Judd Powell Collection relates to his involvement as a member of the government commission established by Congress in 1913 to compile a roll of land allotments within the White Earth Reservation of Chippewa Indians, including the establishment of the blood status of each allottee. He was also legal counsel to lumber companies seeking title to Ojibwa (Chippewa) lands. His collection of files includes Ojibwa genealogies and censuses, transcripts of legal testimonies, letters, deeds, etc. The collection is divided into five series: correspondence and related papers, legal case files, subject files, volumes, and plat maps. It is housed at the Minnesota Historical Society's Division of Library and Archives.

The Lyman Draper Manuscript Collection is a collection of interviews, writings, and original documents gathered by Lyman Copeland Draper. The bulk of the collection is at the State Historical Society of Wisconsin in Madison. Some of the Draper Collection has been published in book form and parts of the collection have been published as a microform publication by Microfilming Corporation of America, which is now part of University Microfilms International (UMI) in Ann Arbor, Michigan.

These are only examples of the types of collections that are in existence and that might be of benefit to those doing Native American research. Access to these collections is primarily through local historical societies and research institutions in close proximity to the reservations for the tribe of interest. Again, this reaffirms the need to know the tribal affiliation of the subject of research.

Secondary Sources

Access to published materials about Native Americans is facilitated, as with all other published materials, by the finding aids and catalogs available in libraries.

Published Genealogies and Histories

There has not been much interest in publishing collections of family histories, genealogies, and biographies for the Native American until fairly recently. It has only been in the 1980s and early 1990s that significant numbers of such volumes have begun to be published. The most common type of these publications is collections of biographical materials.

The value of published biographical material is that it provides in an easy-to-use format a synopsis of the life of an individual Native American. As is the case with all published or compiled material, it must be used with caution, since some of the information may be inaccurate. Compiled material is considered a secondary source—usually used as a basis for further documentation, and needing to be supported by facts located in original documents.

Very little has been done in the linkage of families for the Native American. It is quite common in the non-Indian world to find published genealogies and family histories. So far, publications about Native Americans have focused more on historical events and the involvement of individuals in those events, rather than on family relationships and settings. That probably can be explained by the difficulty of documenting precise family relationships and of the relative small number of family historians who understand and have experience with Native American records.

Periodicals

American Indian periodicals are also now being published. Most of these periodicals are historical in nature, but at least one, the *Journal of American Indian Family Research,* published by Larry S. Watson, is publishing transcripts of sources, historical narratives, tips on research methodology and sources, etc. Occasionally, *Prologue: Quarterly of the National Archives,* publishes copies of documents relating to Native Americans, guides on how to use the records in the National Archives and its branches, and lists of acquisitions and holdings. Local historical and genealogical societies in the proximity of Indian reservations also publish transcriptions of records and other material of interest to the Native American family historian. For example, the Ottawa County Genealogical Society in Miami, Oklahoma, publishes *Smoke Signals*. In their Spring 1994 issue they included the final roll of the Quapaw Tribe as approved February 8, 1890.

Bibliography

Additional information on these sources may be found in Part II.

Anderson, William L. and James A. Lewis. *A Guide to Cherokee Documents in Foreign Archives.* Native American Bibliography Series, no. 4. Metuchen, NJ: Scarecrow Press, 1983. 751p. Includes index.

Biographical Dictionary of Indians of the Americas. Two volumes. Vol. 1: A-L; vol. 2: M-Z. Newport Beach, CA: American Indian Publishers, 1983. 570p. Second edition, 1991. Biographical information about prominent Indians of North, Central, and South America from the 1400s to the present. Includes bibliographic references and an index to tribes.

Blackfeet Heritage, 1907–1908: Blackfeet Indian Reservation, Browning, Montana. Browning, MT: Blackfeet Heritage Program, n.d. Biographical sketches of prominent members of the Blackfeet tribe.

Blankenship, Bob. *Cherokee Roots.* Second edition. Two volumes. Vol. 1: Eastern Cherokee rolls; vol. 2: Western Cherokee rolls. Cherokee, NC: Bob Blankenship, P.O. Box 525, Cherokee, NC, 28719; 1992.

Bogle, Dixie. *Cherokee Nation Births and Deaths, 1884–1901.* Owensboro, KY: Cook & McDowell Publications, 1980. 129p. Abstracts from *Indian Chieftain* and *Daily Chieftain* newspapers.

Bogle, Dixie. *Cherokee Nation Marriages, 1884–1901.* Owensboro, KY: Cook & McDowell Publications, 1980. 120p. Abstracts from *Indian Chieftain* newspaper. Includes bibliography.

Chase, Marybelle W. *1842 Cherokee Claims.* Vol. 1: *Goingsnake District*, vol. 2: *Delaware District*, vol. 3: *Flint District*. Tulsa, OK: M.W. Chase, 1989.

Chase, Marybelle W. *1842 Cherokee Claims; Saline District.* Nashville, TN: Tennessee State Library, 1988.

Chase, Marybelle W. *1842 Cherokee Claims; Skin Bayou District.* Nashville, TN: Tennessee State Library, 1988.

Chase, Marybelle W. *1842 Cherokee Claims; Tahlequah District.* Nashville, TN: Tennessee State Library, 1989.

Clark, Dick. *Cherokee Ancestor Research.* Modesto, CA: Rich-Nor-Lin Publications, 1979. Although this work is specific to Cherokee research, some information is applicable to other tribes, as well.

Confederation of American Indians. *Indian Reservations: A State and Federal Handbook.* Jefferson, NC: McFarland & Co., 1986. 329p. A listing of all Indian reservations in the United States which indicates whether a specific reservation is under state or federal jurisdiction. Includes index.

Crumpton, Barbara J. *1851 Chapman Roll of the Eastern Cherokee.* Duncan, OK: Creative Copies, 1986. Covers the 1851 Chapman enrollment used by Guion Miller in certifying the eligibility of the Cherokee; original roll by Alfred Chapman. Includes name and location indexes.

Crumpton, Barbara J. *1884 Hester Roll of the Eastern Cherokee.* Duncan, OK: Creative Copies, 1986. Transcribed from federal record group 75, microcopy 685, roll 12. Covers the 1884 Hester enrollment used by Guion Miller in certifying the eligibility of the Cherokee. Includes name and locality index.

DePuy, Henry Farr. *A Bibliography of the English Colonial Treaties with the American Indians, Including a Synopsis of Each Treaty.* New York: Printed for the Lenox Club, 1917.

Drennen, John. *1851 Drennen Roll of the Cherokee Indians.* Tulsa, OK: Indian Nation Press. Roll of Eastern Cherokees, sometimes referred to as the Immigrant Roll, who went west after 1835 and were residing in what became Oklahoma by 1851.

Ellsworth, Carole and Sue Emler. *1900 U.S. Census of the Cherokee Indian Nation.* Five volumes. Vol. 1: area now in Sequoyah and Muskogee Counties, vol. 2: area now part of Sequoyah County and town of Sallisaw, vol. 3: area now part of Sequoyah County, vol. 4: area now part of Muskogee and McIntosh Counties, vol. 5: area now part of Muskogee and Wagoner Counties. Gore, OK: Oklahoma Roots Research, 1982–.

Foreman, Grant. *Indian Removal: The Emigration of the Five Civilized Tribes of Indians.* Norman, OK: University of Oklahoma Press, 1972. 423p. Includes bibliography.

Freeman, John F. *A Guide to Manuscripts Relating to the American Indian in the Library of the American Philosophical Society.* Philadelphia: American Philosophical Society, 1966. 491p. A descriptive guide to the manuscripts held by this old and revered society which began collecting Native American manuscripts as early as 1802 when Thomas Jefferson was its president.

Furtaw, Julia C. *Native Americans Information Directory.* A guide to organizations, agencies, institutions, programs, publications, services, and other resources concerned with the indigenous peoples of the United States and Canada, including American Indians, Alaska Natives, Native Hawaiians, [and] Aboriginal Canadians. First edition. Detroit: Gale Research, 1993. 371p.

Goss, Joe R. *A Complete Roll of All Choctaw Claimants and Their Heirs Existing Under the Treaties Between the United States and the Choctaw Nation As Far As Shown By the Records of the United States and of the Choctaw Nation.* Conway, AR: Oldbuck Press, 1992.

Hill, Edward E. *Guide to Records in the National Archives of the United States Relating to American Indians.* Washington, D.C.: National Archives and Records Services Administration, 1981. 467p. A guide to the history and development of agencies and subagencies of the Office of Indian Affairs and their records. Includes a listing of records of other branches of the federal government pertaining to the American Indian as well as an index.

Hill, Edward E. *The Office of Indian Affairs, 1824–1880: Historical Sketches.* New York: Clearwater Publishing Company, 1974. 246p. Historical sketches of the agencies and superintendencies of the Office of Indian Affairs, the forerunner to the Bureau of Indian Affairs. Originally prepared to enable researchers to locate correspondence contained in microcopy 234, ''Letters Received by the Office of Indian Affairs, 1824–1880,'' a microfilm publication of the National Archives and Records Service. Sketches, providing brief histories of the field units of the Office of Indian Affairs for that period, describe the geographical area covered by the office, names of tribes assigned, the interrelationship of Indian Affairs field offices, etc. Individual sketches are distributed by the Archives in pamphlet form to purchasers of selected rolls of microfilm from among the 962 rolls in the complete collection. The edition for 1967 was published under the title: *Historical Sketches for Jurisdictional and Subject Headings Used For the Letters Received By the Office of Indian Affairs, 1824–80.*

Hodge, Frederick Webb. *Handbook of American Indians North of Mexico.* Two volumes. Reprint of Bulletin 30 of the Smithsonian Institution, Bureau of American Ethnology, first published 1907–1910. New York: Pageant Books, 1959. 1225p. Alphabetically arranged list of tribal groups, clans, villages and settlements with biographies of tribal leaders. Includes a very comprehensive cross-reference to variant name spellings for all North American Indian tribes. Volume 2 includes a bibliography.

Hutchins, Alma. *Indian Territory Marriages, 1867–1898.* Tahlequah, OK: A. Hutchins, 1988.

Jackson, Curtis E. and Marcia J. Galli. *A History of the Bureau of Indian Affairs and Its Activities among Indians.* San Francisco: R & E Research Associates, 1977. 167p. It is imperative for a researcher who is trying to understand the genealogical and historical records of the American Indian to understand the history of the various offices of the federal government responsible for Indian affairs. This book provides that understanding. Includes bibliography.

Jenness, Diamond. *The Indians of Canada.* Originally published in 1932 as Bulletin no. 65, Anthropological series (Ottawa, Ontario) no. 15 of the National Museum of Canada. Seventh edition. Buffalo: University of Toronto Press, 1977. 432p. Includes bibliographic references and index.

Johnson, Steven L. *Guide to American Indian Documents in the Congressional Serial Set, 1817–1899.* A project of the Institute for the Development of Indian Law. New York: Clearwater Publishing Company, 1977. 503p. Includes index.

Jordan, Jerry Wright. *Cherokee by Blood: Records of Eastern Cherokee Ancestry in the U.S. Court of Claims, 1906–1910.* Eight volumes. Continuing series. Bowie, MD: Heritage Books, 1987–. Based on the ''Report of Guion Miller, Special Commissioner to the U.S. Court of Claims, 1906–1910.'' Includes index.

Kappler, Charles J. *Indian Treaties, 1778–1883.* New York: Interland Publishing Co., 1972. 1099p. Reprint of *Indian Affairs: Laws and Treaties*, vol. 2, published by the Government Printing Office in 1904. Treaties usually were the basis upon which the federal government dealt with the Native American tribe and often marked the beginning of the keeping of federal records about tribal members. Includes names of tribal leaders who signed the treaties.

Kelsay, Laura E. *Cartographic Records of the Bureau of Indian Affairs.* United States National Archives and Records Service Special List, no. 13. Washington, D.C.: National Archives and Records Service, General Services Administration, 1977. 187p. A guide to maps in the National Archives relating to Native Americans. The 1954 edition was issued with the title *List of Cartographic Records of the Bureau of Indian Affairs.*

Kerner, Gaiselle. *Preliminary Inventory of the Records of the United States Court of Claims.* Washington, D.C.: National Archives, 1953. Includes entries relating to Native American claims cases.

Kirkham, E. Kay. *Our Native Americans and Their Records of Genealogical Value.* Logan, UT: Everton Publishers, 1980. A listing of sources for family history on the American Indian.

Klein, Barry T. *Reference Encyclopedia of the American Indian.* Second edition. Two volumes. Rye, NY: Todd Pub., 1973. Includes information about reservations, biographies of some prominent Native Americans or those associated with Native American history and affairs, and a rather extensive bibliography.

Kutsche, Paul. *A Guide to Cherokee Documents in the Northeastern United States.* Native American Bibliography Series, no. 7. Metuchen, NJ: Scarecrow Press, 1986. 531p. A summary of the holdings of some twenty collections of Cherokee material which includes such diverse places as the Houghton Library at

Harvard University, New York Public Library, Newberry Library in Chicago, Presbyterian Historical Society in Philadelphia, and the State Historical Society of Wisconsin in Madison. It not only lists sources but carries an annotated note with each entry describing the research material. This work is the result of research conducted by Professor Kutsche from 1962 to 1983. Includes index.

Mason, Alma Burke. *1896 Tobucksy County, Choctaw Nation, Indian Territory.* McAlester, OK: Pittsburg County Genealogical and Historical Society, 1988.

Mauldin, Dorothy J. (Tincup). *Federal Population Schedule of the United States Census, 1860, Indian Lands West of Arkansas.* Tulsa, OK: Oklahoma Yesterday Pub., [198–]. Covers the Creek, Cherokee, Chickasaw, Choctaw, and Seminole Nations.

National Archives Microfilm Resources for Research: A Comprehensive Catalog. Washington, D.C.: National Archives and Records Administration, 1989. A listing of Native American records at the National Archives that have been microfilmed including most of the major classes of records.

O'Beirne, Harry F. *Leaders and Leading Men of the Indian Territory, with Interesting Biographical Sketches.* Chicago: American Publishers Association, 1891. Includes index.

Olsen, Monty. *Choctaw Emigration Records.* Calera, OK: Bryan County Heritage Association, 1990. Covers 1831–1856.

Paulson, T. Emogene and Lloyd R. Moses. *Who's Who among the Sioux.* Vermillion, SD: University of South Dakota, n.d. Biographical sketches of prominent members of the Sioux Tribe during the 19th and 20th centuries.

Prucha, Francis Paul. *A Bibliographical Guide to the History of Indian-White Relations in the United States.* A publication of the Center for the History of the American Indian of the Newberry Library. Chicago: University of Chicago Press, 1977. 454p. A monumental work. Part 1 lists guides to sources and Part 2 contains a classified and selected bibliography of published works. Includes index.

Prucha, Francis Paul. *Atlas of American Indian Affairs.* Lincoln, NE: University of Nebraska Press, 1990. 191p. A cartographic guide to information and statistics regarding the history of Native Americans which includes information on land cessions, population, reservations, agencies, schools, hospitals and skirmishes with the U.S. Army.

Rolls of Certain Indian Tribes in Oregon and Washington. Fairfield, WA: Ye Galleon Press, 1969.

Ruby, Robert H. and John A. Brown. *A Guide to the Indian Tribes of the Pacific Northwest.* Revised edition. Civilization of the American Indian Series. Norman, OK: University of Oklahoma Press, 1992. 289p. History, location, population estimates, government, claims, contemporary life and culture, special events, and suggested readings are all addressed in this regional guide. Includes bibliographic references and index.

Schmeckebier, Laurence F. *The Office of Indian Affairs: Its History, Activities, and Organization.* Baltimore: Johns Hopkins Press, 1927. Reprint. AMS Press; New York; Brookings Institution, Institute for Government Research, Service Monographs of the U.S. Government, no. 48; 1972. 591p. Although much of this book is outdated, the section dealing with the history of the Office of Indian Affairs is not. Includes bibliography.

Smith, E.B. *Indian Tribal Claims Decided in the Court of Claims of the United States . . . to June 30, 1947.* Washington, D.C.: University Publications of America, 1947. Many Indian tribes have had claims against the federal government settled in this court. Knowing when a case was settled is important since genealogical records were often generated in order to determine how the claims settlement would be divided.

Smith, Jane F. and Robert M. Kvasnicka. *Indian-White Relations; A Persistent Paradox.* Washington, D.C.: Howard University Press, 1976. 278p. Proceedings of the National Archives Conference on Research in the History of Indian-White Relations held June 15–16, 1972, at the National Archives in Washington, D.C. Includes index.

Sovereign Cherokee Nation Tejas (Texas). *History and Enrollments of the Sovereign Cherokee Nation Tejas.* Three volumes. Troup, TX: Sovereign Cherokee Nation Tejas, 1992.

Spindel, Donna. *Introductory Guide to Indian-Related Records (to 1876) in the North Carolina State Archives.* Raleigh, NC: Division of Archives and History, 1977. A description of sources containing North Carolina Indian information, many of which would be very difficult and time-consuming to find without this guide.

Starr, Emmet McDonald. *Old Cherokee Families and Their Genealogy.* Norman, OK: University of Oklahoma Foundation, 1968. 90p. Reprinted from *History of the Cherokee Indians and Their Legends and Folk Lore* with a comprehensive index compiled by J.J. Hill. Original manuscripts used for the printed volumes are in the Oklahoma Historical Society Archives and Manuscript Division and contain information not in the printed version. The manuscript version has been microfilmed.

Sturtevant, William C. *Handbook of North American Indians.* Twenty volumes are projected. Washington, D.C.: Smithsonian Institution, 1978–. Vol. 1: *Introduction*; vol. 2: *Indians in Contemporary Society*; vol. 3: *Environment, Origins, and Population*; vol. 4: *History of Indian-White Relations*; vol. 5: *Arctic*; vol. 6: *Subarctic*; vol. 7: *Northwest Coast*; vol. 8: *California* (published in 1978); vol. 9: *Southwest* (published in 1979); vol. 10: *Southwest*; vol. 11: *Great Basin*; vol. 12: *Plateau*; vol. 13: *Plains*; vol. 14: *Southeast*; vol. 15: *Northeast* (published in 1978); vol. 16: *Technology and Visual Arts*; vol. 17: *Languages*; vols. 18 and 19: *Biographical Dictionary*; vol. 20: *Index.* Other volumes besides the three indicated above may now be published. Includes bibliographies and indexes.

Swanton, John Reed. *The Indian Tribes of North America.* United States, 81st Congress, 2nd Session, 1950–1951, House Document, no. 383; Bulletin (Smithsonian Institution), Bureau of American Ethnology, no. 145. Washington, D.C.: U.S. Government Printing Office, 1952. 726p. Reprint. Classics of Smithsonian Anthropology. Smithsonian Institution Press, Washington, D.C., 1969, 1984. History, location, and population details for all major tribes. Arranged alphabetically by state and thereunder by tribal name with cross-references if a tribe resided in more than one state. Includes bibliography.

Talbot, Virgil. *The Goingsnake Marriages.* Westville, OK: Goingsnake District Heritage Association, 1984. Includes marriages, 1869–1910.

Thernstrom, Stephan. *Harvard Encyclopedia of American Ethnic Groups.* Cambridge, MA: Belknap Press of Harvard University, 1980. 1076p. Includes sixty-four pages on Native Americans. Every researcher should read this section which includes a section on federal policy toward Native Americans. Includes bibliographies.

Tyner, James W. *Those Who Cried; the 16,000: A Record of the Individual Cherokees Listed in the United States Official Census of the Cherokee Nation Conducted in 1835.* Chi-ga-u,

1974. Covers Alabama, Georgia, North Carolina, and Tennessee. This is a census taken before the removal of the Cherokee to western lands.

Tyner, James W. and Alice Tyner Timmons. *Our People and Where They Rest.* Volumes 1–9, 12. Oklahoma: J.W. Tyner, 1969–1985. M.H. Tyner contributed to vols. 9 and 12. Vols. 2–8 have the imprint "Norman, OK: American Indian Institute, University of Oklahoma;" vols. 9 and 12 list Chi-ga-u as publisher. Consists of records of burials in seventeen counties of northeastern Oklahoma within the Oklahoma Cherokee Nation boundary. Includes indexes.

United States Department of the Interior Library. *Bibliographical and Historical Index of American Indians and Persons Involved in Indian Affairs.* Eight volumes. Boston: G.K. Hall, 1966. Subject index developed in the library of the Bureau of Indian Affairs which was consolidated in 1949 with other bureau libraries to form the library of the Department of the Interior. From 1951–1965, the work of the index was continued. This work includes extensive listings of Indian agents, other personnel of the Bureau of Indian Affairs, Indian chiefs, and historically prominent Indians, as well as obscure information related to tribal matters. The scope is broader than that of the department collections since it includes material found in journals, books, and documents contained in other libraries and personal collections. Arranged alphabetically by subject, i.e. Indian tribes, individual names, events, and other items of a historical nature, the entries do not always follow standard bibliographical form, and frequently the alphabetizing is informal within a single letter. There is no listing by author or title of works cited, except as these happen to occur as subjects.

United States Superintendent of Documents. *Checklist of United States Public Documents, 1789–1909, Congressional: to Close of Sixtieth Congress; Departmental: to End of Calendar Year 1909.* Washington, D.C.: Government Printing Office, 1911. 1707p. Reprint. J.W. Edwards, Ann Arbor, MI, 1953; Kraus Reprint Corporation, New York, 1962. Includes lists of the annual and special reports of the Indian Affairs Office and the Indian Affairs Committee of the U.S. Congress as well as an index.

Waldman, Carl. *Who Was Who in Native American History: Indians and Non-Indians from Early Contacts Through 1900.* New York: Facts on File, 1990. 410p. Biographical sketches of those who were prominent in Indian affairs prior to 1900.

Watson, Larry S. *Cherokee Emigration Records, 1829–1835: Reprint of Senate Document No. 403, 24th Congress, 1st Session.* Laguna Hills, CA: Histree, 1990.

Records Specific to Native Americans—Addendum

George J. Nixon

See the chapter "Basic Genealogical Research Methods and their Application to Native Americans" for a brief biography of the author.

The Five Civilized Tribes

These tribes consisted of the Cherokee, Choctaw, Chickasaw, Creek, and Seminole Nations.

The Dawes Commission

The Commission to the Five Civilized Tribes or the Dawes Commission records are very important to anyone who has Cherokee, Choctaw, Chickasaw, Creek, or Seminole ancestors. The commission generated some of the most important genealogical records available for members of these tribes.

The General Allotment Act, also known as the Dawes Act, paved the way to statehood for Oklahoma and was also one of the most detrimental blows dealt to Native Americans by the United States.

The act, approved by Congress on March 3, 1893 (27 Stat. L. 645), provided for the appointment of three commissioners to negotiate with the Five Civilized Tribes for the extinguishment of the tribal title (land held in common) and the allotment of lands in single family plots. The commission, generally known as the Dawes Commission, after former Senator Henry L. Dawes of Massachusetts who was appointed chairman, reported directly to the Secretary of the Interior. In 1895 the number of members was increased to five. At that time, the work of the commission was limited to two fields: changing the method of land ownership and the abolition of the tribal governments. The commission experienced little success in these two endeavors and on June 10, 1898 (29 Stat. L. 339), the scope of the work of the commission was enlarged by an authorization and direction to "hear and determine the application of all persons who may apply to them for citizenship in any of said nations" (29 Stat. L. 339), requiring the commission to file the list of tribal members with the Commissioner of Indian Affairs "for use as the final judgment of the duly constituted authorities."

On June 28, 1898 (30 Stat. L. 495), a law known as the "Curtis Act" was approved. The Curtis Act is the basis of all later legislation relating to the affairs of these Indians. Its main features are: (1) the allotment of land in severalty; (2) leasing of tribal lands by the Secretary of the Interior; (3) incorporation of cities and towns, survey of town sites, and sale of town lots to the lessees at half their appraised value; (4) prohibition of any payment to tribal governments, and provision for making per capita payments directly to individuals; (5) provision for the payments of all rents and royalties into the Treasury of the United States to the credit of the tribe; (6) enlargement of the power of the U.S. courts and the abolition of tribal courts.

Agreements had been made with the Choctaws and Chickasaws on April 23, 1897, with the Creeks on September 27, 1897, and with the Seminoles on December 16, 1897. The Choctaw-Chickasaw and the Creek agreements were embodied in the Curtis Act. The agreement was confirmed on August 24, 1898, but the Creeks rejected it. The agreement with the Seminole tribe was ratified by Congress in the act of July 1, 1898 (30 Stat. L. 567).

A new agreement with the Creeks was made on March 8, 1900, and ratified March 1, 1901. The Cherokees were the last to accept the new conditions, but an act was ratified by them on August 7, 1902, and proclaimed by President Teddy Roosevelt on August 12, 1902.

The agreements provided for each member of the Choctaw and Chickasaw Nations to receive "land equal in value to 320 acres of the average allottable land," in Indian Territory out of which 160 acres were to be designated as a homestead, which was to be inalienable during the life of the allottee, but not beyond twenty-one years from the date of the certificate of allotment. Lands not included in the homestead were to be alienable for one-fourth the acreage in one year, one-fourth in three years, and, the balance in five years from the date of patent (deed to the land). Each freedman was to be allotted "land equal in value to forty acres of the average allottable land" according to the Curtis Act.

The Seminole agreement provided for the division of the land into three classes to be appraised at $1.25, $2.50, and $5.00 per acre, and for allotments such that each member should have an average of 120 acres in dollar value. Each allottee was required to designate a tract of forty acres, which was, according to the Curtis Act, "made inalienable and nontaxable as a homestead in perpetuity."

In the Cherokee Nation the allotments were to be 110 acres of the average allottable land on the basis of the appraisal to be made by the Dawes Commission. Provision was made for a homestead of forty acres, which was to be inalienable and nontaxable during the lifetime of the allottee, but not longer than twenty-one years.

In the Seminole, Creek, and Cherokee Nations the freedmen (former slaves of the tribe) received the same allotments as the Indians by blood.

The closing of the tribal affairs of the Five Civilized Tribes involved among other tasks, the preparation of a correct tribal roll and division of the land among the members according to the varying provisions of the separate agreements. Applications for enrollment were received from about 250,000 persons in all parts of the United States, but the final rolls contained the names of approximately 101,000, of whom about one-fourth were full-blood.

The enrollment records consist of the application made for enrollment, together with all of the records, evidence, and papers filed in connection with the decision of the commissioner.

During the early stages of enrollment, appointments were made by the commission at various places in the different nations where the Indians and freedmen appeared to make application for enrollment. At that time the applicants were sworn before a notary public. Their testimony was taken orally and placed upon a card which constitutes the enrollment card. The Cherokees, where written testimony was taken in all cases, were the exception.

In a great majority of the early enrollments, except Cherokee cases, the only records shown are the oral statements that were taken from the applicants, together with any other evidence that may have been obtained. In many instances, when there was doubt as to the rights of the applicants to enrollment, and they could not be identified from the tribal rolls, written testimony of the applicants was taken and made part of the record. Additional testimony was taken later. Written testimony was also taken in all applications made for the identification of Mississippi Choctaws and in practically all other cases as the work neared completion.

The tribal rolls of the various nations came into the possession of the Commissioner to the Five Civilized Tribes, and were used for identification and as a basis for enrollment.

When the enrollments were completed, the names of all persons whom the commission had decided were entitled to enrollment were placed on rolls. These rolls show the name, age, sex, degree of blood, and the number of the census card (which is generally known as the "enrollment card") on which each citizen was enrolled. A number was placed opposite each name appearing on this roll, beginning at one and running consecutively to the final name listed. This roll was made out in quintuplicate and forwarded to the Secretary of the Interior for his approval. The secretary returned three copies for the files of the Commissioner to the Five Civilized Tribes. The roll thus approved was known as the "approval roll," and was used as the basis for allotments (except in the cases of a large number of Creeks, to whom allotments were made before the approval of their enrollment). These allotments were subsequently confirmed by Congress.

The enrollment records consist of:

(1) the census card, or the card on which the applicant was listed for enrollment. Sometimes early in the enrollment process, persons were listed on what is known as a "doubtful card." Later, the names appearing on the doubtful cards were transferred to a regular census card;
(2) all testimony taken in the matter of the application at various times prior to the decision on the application;
(3) birth affidavits, affidavits of death, and other evidence and papers filed in connection with the application made for enrollment; and
(4) the enrollment as shown on the approved roll.

Many of the records of the Dawes Commission are still in the custody of the Muskogee Area Office of the Bureau of Indian Affairs in Muskogee, Oklahoma.

General Records of the Commission to the Five Civilized Tribes

Most of the correspondence received by the commission prior to 1901 and copies of letters sent prior to 1906 are in the custody of the Oklahoma Historical Society. This correspondence can also be found in the records of the Indian Division of the Office of the Secretary of the Interior (Record Group 48) and the Bureau of Indian Affairs (Record Group 75).

The following are found at the National Archives, and those on microfilm are available at other federal records centers:

Index to Letters Received from the Department of the Interior. 1907–1914. This index is divided into chronological segments: 1907–1908, 1909–1910, 1911–1912, and 1913–1914. Entries are arranged alphabetically by subject and thereunder chronologically by the date the letter was written. Information given for each letter includes the date it was written, the file number assigned, and a short summary of the subject.

Register of Letters Received from the Department of the Interior (''Special Index''). 1903–1914. Arranged chronologically by date of receipt. Information given for each letter includes the date it was written, the date received, the name of the sender, the file number assigned, and a short summary of the subject.

Letters Received from the Department of the Interior (''Departmental Letters''). 1901–1914. Arranged numerically by file number assigned chronologically by date of receipt within each fiscal year. The letters relate to all phases of the commission's activities including administration, enrollment, allotment, the leasing and sale of allotted and unallotted land, and the establishment of town sites.

Instructions received from the Department of the Interior. 1900. Arranged chronologically by date of receipt, indexed by subject. Carbon copies of letters received from the Department of the Interior relating to enrollment and enrollment procedures, the leasing of allotted land, and the removal of non-Indians from allotted land. Many letters transmit opinions of the Assistant Attorney General on legal issues relating to enrollment and allotment.

Index to Letters Received. 1897–1913. The index is divided into yearly segments. Within each segment, entries are arranged alphabetically by the first two letters of the sender's surname. Information given includes the name of the sender, the date the letter was written, the file number assigned, and a brief summary of the subject.

Registers of Letters Received. 1908–1914. Arranged chronologically by date of receipt. The information given for each letter includes the name and address of the sender, the date the letter was written, the date received, the file number assigned, a brief summary of the subject, and occasionally remarks about actions taken.

Registers of Letters Received from the Union Agency. 1906–1909. (The Union Agency was the principal agency in Indian Territory; the Dawes Commission was headquartered here). Arranged chronologically by date of receipt. The information given for each letter includes the date it was written, the date received, the file number assigned, and a brief summary of the subject.

Letters Received (''General Office Letters''). 1900–1914. Arranged numerically by file number assigned chronologically by date of receipt within each fiscal year. Original letters and telegrams received from the U. S. Indian Inspector for Indian Territory, the Union Agency, other Indian agencies, field offices of the Dawes Commission including the land offices maintained for each tribe, officials of tribal governments, and the general public. The letters relate to all phases of the commission's activities.

Letters Received by Commissioner Tams Bixby. 1897–1906. Arranged alphabetically by name of sender until 1901 and thereafter numerically by file number assigned chronologically by date of receipt. The letters relate to the status of applications for enrollment or allotment, the sale and leasing of land, applications for employment. Many of the books are marked ''personal and confidential.''

Letters Sent to the Secretary of the Interior. 1906–1914. Arranged chronologically by date sent. Indexed by subject. Press copies (precursor of carbon copies) of letters sent to the Secretary of the Interior through the Commissioner of Indian Affairs.

Letters Sent to the Commissioner of Indian Affairs. 1907–1911. Arranged in rough chronological order and indexed by subject.

Letters Sent (''Miscellaneous Letters''). 1895–1914. Arranged chronologically by date sent. Press copies of letters sent to the U.S. Indian Inspector for Indian Territory, the Union Agency, other Indian Agencies, field offices of the Dawes Commission, officials of tribal governments, and the general public.

Letters Sent by Commissioner Tams Bixby. 1902–1907. Arranged chronologically by date sent. Press copies of letters sent by Commissioner Bixby from Washington, D.C., to Commissioner in Charge T. B. Needles in Muskogee and letters sent by Bixby from Muskogee to the Secretary of the Interior, the Commissioner of Indian Affairs, and members of Congress.

Annual Narrative Reports. 1894–1914. Arranged chronologically by date of report. No reports for 1897 or 1899 to 1903. Printed copies of the annual reports of the commission's activities submitted to the Secretary of the Interior. The reports provide detailed information about the activities of the commission.

Index to Reference Documents. Arranged alphabetically by subject. The index provides the category and file number of each document. The categories used are A: Cherokee and Delaware; B: Choctaw and Chickasaw; C: Creek; D: Enrollment; E: Leases; F: Reports; and G: Miscellaneous.

Reference Documents (''Miscellaneous Documents''). 1896–1904. Arranged in three groups. Within each group, documents are arranged numerically by a file number assigned by the commission. Correspondence, printed congressional documents, copies of agreements with tribal governments, rules and instructions issued by the Secretary of the Interior or the commission, receipts for rolls and other papers supplied by tribal governments, copies of documents filed in cases heard by the U.S. Supreme Court and other federal courts, lists of persons admitted to tribal citizenship by U.S. courts. There are also transcripts of hearings in citizenship cases.

Index to Enrollment Cards. 1899–1907. Arranged by tribe and thereunder by enrollment category. Entries within each volume are arranged alphabetically by the first two letters of the applicant's surname. Generally, the index provides only the number of the card on which the applicant's name appears but some volumes also provide the individual's enrollment number. Many of the volumes include the names of persons listed on "Doubtful" and "Rejected" cards.

[The card shown in Figure 3.1 is the enrollment card of Daniel Beaver and his wife, Susan. Daniel Beaver, twenty-five, was a full-blood Cherokee Indian. His father was Chualuke Beaver (deceased), and his mother was Ne-cu-hah Beaver (deceased). Susan was also twenty-five and a full-blood Cherokee Indian. Her father was John Waker (deceased). Her mother was To-you-na-ah Beaver (deceased). Daniel and Susan received certificates of citizenship (Cherokee Nation) on June 30, 1905. Daniel appears on the 1880 Cherokee Roll as "Ahtola," and on the 1896 Cherokee Roll as Daniel Chuwaluke (see the Eastern Cherokee Application of Daniel Chu-wa-loo-kie, Figure 3.2). Susan appears in the 1896 Cherokee Roll as Susie Chuwaluke.]

Enrollment Cards ("Census Cards"). 1899–1907. Arranged by tribe and thereunder by enrollment category. Within each category there are generally three groups: "Straight" (persons who were enrolled without question), "Doubtful," and "Rejected." Within each group, the cards are arranged numerically by numbers assigned chronologically by area by the commission. Original 7 × 14 inch printed cards are annotated with information about persons applying for enrollment. Cards were prepared for each family group and used by enrollment parties traveling throughout Indian Territory to record information about the applicants and actions taken by the commission. The information given for each applicant generally includes name, enrollment number, age, sex, degree of Indian blood, relationship to the head of the family group, references to enrollment on earlier tribal rolls used by the Commission to verify eligibility, and the parents' names. The card often includes notations about an applicant's birth or death, changes in marital status,

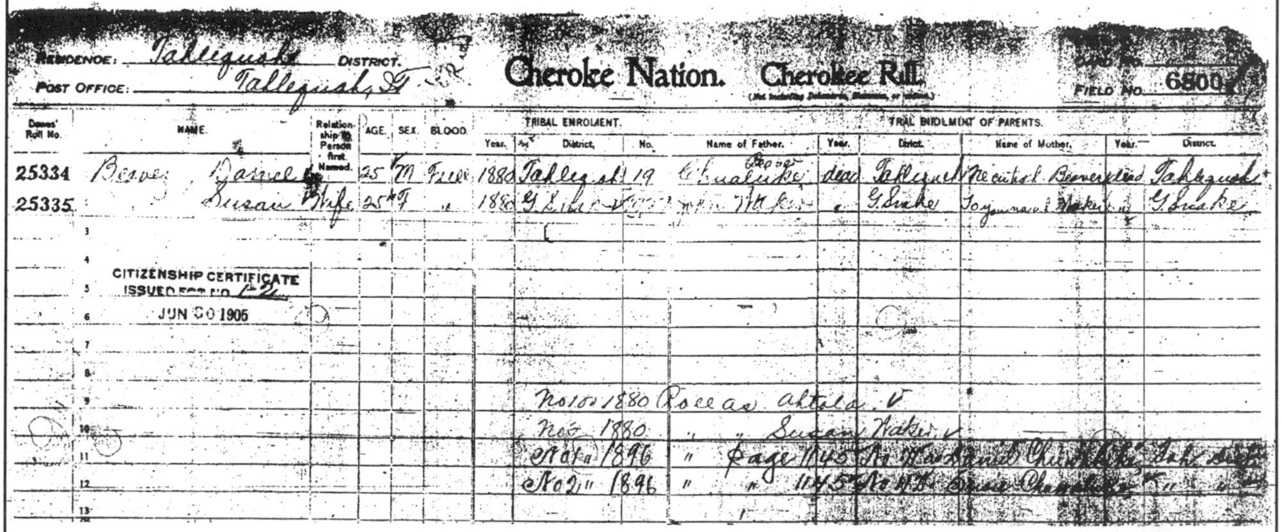

Figure 3.1. Commission to the Five Civilized Tribes. Enrollment Card of Daniel Beaver.

DEPARTMENT OF THE INTERIOR.
COMMISSION TO THE FIVE CIVILIZED TRIBES.
TAHLEQUAH, I.T., DECEMBER 15th, 1900.

IN THE MATTER OF THE APPLICATION OF Daniel Beaver for the enrollment of himself and wife as citizens of the Cherokee Nation, and he being sworn and examined by Commissioner, T.B. Needles, testified through interpreter, Joe Sequichie, as follows:

Q What is your name? A Daniel Beaver.
Q How old are you? A Twenty five.
Q What is your Post office? A Tahlequah.
Q What district do you live in? A Tahlequah.
Q Are you a full blood Cherokee? A Yes sir.
Q Whom do you want to enroll? A Myself and wife.
Q What is your wife's name? A Susan.
Q What was her name before you married her? A I do not know; I think Waker.
Q How old is she? A About twenty five.

(1896 Roll, Page 1145, #411, Daniel Chuwaluke, Tahlequah D'st)
(1896 Roll, Page 1145, #412, Susie Chuwaluke, Tahlequah D'st)

Figure 3.2. Daniel Beaver. Application for Enrollment as Citizen of the Cherokee Nation.

references to related enrollment cards, and actions taken by the commission or the Secretary of the Interior. The cards relating to applicants who were "freedmen" also contain the name of the person who owned the applicant as a slave and the owner of the applicant's parents. These cards have been microfilmed.

Duplicate Enrollment Cards. 1918–1919. Arranged by tribe, thereunder by enrollment category, and thereunder by type of card ("Straight," "Doubtful," or "Rejected"). Within each type, the cards are arranged numerically (number assigned by the Dawes Commission). Duplicate paper copies of the cards were prepared to reduce the use of the original cards and contain all of the information recorded on the original. There are no copies of Creek, Seminole, or Cherokee by blood cards.

Letters Sent Transmitting Enrollment Schedules. 1901–1907. Arranged by tribe and thereunder by enrollment category. Within each volume, the letters are arranged chronologically by date sent. Press copies of letters sent to the Secretary of the Interior through the Commissioner of Indian Affairs transmitting schedules of the names of persons recommended for enrollment and press copies of the schedules. The information given in the schedules includes the person's name, enrollment number, tribal district of residence, and the tribal roll used to verify eligibility. There are occasionally remarks about relationships to other person listed in the schedule.

Enrollment Schedules. 1900–1907. Arranged by tribal enrollment category, names within the schedule are arranged numerically by enrollment number. These records include carbon copies of typed schedules of the names of persons recommended for enrollment. The schedules were submitted to the Secretary of the Interior in triplicate for approval and one copy was returned to the commission for reference. The information given for each person includes name, age, sex, degree of blood, and enrollment number. The schedules for the Seminoles also include the band name and a reference to an 1897 Seminole census roll.

Report on Enrollment. 1909. Press copy of a report prepared by Joseph W. Howell on the enrollment of the Five Civilized Tribes which was submitted to the Secretary of the Interior. The report provides a detailed description of the enrollment procedures, controversial decisions, and the difficulties of obtaining records from the tribal governments. There are several appendices which provide lists of tribal rolls used by the commission.

List of Claimants. 1907. Names within the list are arranged alphabetically by surname. A typed "Departmental List of Persons Who Claim to be Entitled to Enrollment as Citizens and Freedmen of the Five Civilized Tribes Prepared with a View to Remedial Legislation,'' contains the names of 741 persons and includes the tribal affiliation claimed by each and a summary of the facts in each case.

Index to Citizenship Docket. Arranged alphabetically by the first letter of the claimant's surname. Index to an unidentified citizenship docket which provides only a case number for each claimant under the heading ''Nation Number.''

Records of the Dawes Commission Relating to Cherokee Citizenship

List of Rejected Claimants. 1878–1880. Arranged chronologically by court term and thereunder by the reason for rejection and thereunder by case number. A handwritten copy of a list of persons whose claim to citizenship was rejected by the Cherokee Commission on Citizenship. The only information given for each claimant is the case number and the reason for rejection (by decree, default, or withdrawal).

List of Persons Admitted to Citizenship. Arranged roughly in alphabetical order by surname. A printed ''List of persons admitted and re-admitted to Cherokee citizenship by the National Council and Commissions on Citizenship in the year 1880, and since that year.'' The list covers the period from 1880 to 1899 and appears to have been printed for use by the commission. The only information given is the person's name and the date admitted.

Cherokee Citizenship Commission Dockets. 1880–1984; 1887–1889. Arranged numerically by case number assigned chronologically by the date the case was opened. Indexed by name of applicant. A record of actions taken by the tribal commission on applications for citizenship. Each docket entry generally includes the applicant's name, age, sex, name(s) of attorney(s), the text of the application, a summary of the proceedings held, and the text of the commission's decision.

Record of Births. 1897. Arranged by districts of the Cherokee Nation. A record of children born from 1895 to 1897. The list appears to have been completed in 1897, and contains the child's name, date of birth, and parent's names. Most of the children listed were born in 1897.

Dawes Commission Dockets. 1902. Arranged numerically by case number assigned chronologically by the date the case was opened. A record of actions taken by the Dawes Commission on applications for citizenship. The information given for each application includes the date it was filed, the names of the persons covered by the application, the date the attorneys for the Cherokee filed an answer, the commission's decision, the date of appeal to the U.S. Court and the court's decision.

Docket of Cases Appealed. 1896–1899. Arranged numerically by case number assigned chronologically by the date the case was opened. Indexed by name of applicant. A record of actions taken by the U.S. Court for the Northern District of Indian Territory on appeals from decisions of the Dawes Commission on applications under the act of June 10, 1896. The information given for each case includes the names of the parties and their attorneys, a summary of proceedings and motions filed, and the decision of the court.

Lists of Applicants. 1902. There are separate lists for admitted and rejected applicants. Within each list, names are arranged alphabetically by surname. Typed lists of persons admitted or rejected for citizenship by the U.S. Courts for the Northern and Southern Districts of Indian Territory. There are lists for the following actions: applicants admitted by the Dawes Commission and affirmed by the courts, applicants admitted by the Court for the Southern District who had been rejected by the commission, applicants denied by the Court for the Northern District who had been admitted by the commission, and applicants admitted by the Court for the Northern District who had been denied by the commission. The information given for each applicant generally includes the Dawes Commission case number, U.S. court docket number, and the Dawes Commission enrollment card number.

Decisions of the U.S. Court. 1897–1899. Arranged in roughly chronological order by the date of the decision. Each volume is indexed by name of applicant involved in the decision. Press copies of decisions of Judge William M. Springer of the U.S. Court for the Northern District of Indian Territory on appeals of decisions of the Dawes Commission on applications for enrollment under the act of 1896. The decision of the judge often includes a report on the case prepared by a special master appointed by the court.

Records Relating to Appeals. 1897–1898. Arranged by case number assigned by the date the case was opened. Bonds for appeals to the U.S. Supreme Court from decisions of the U.S. Court for the Northern District of Indian Territory, petitions for appeals, and assignments of errors. These records appear to be copies which were filed with the court and subsequently given to the Dawes Commission for reference.

Lists of Applicants as Freedmen. 1897. Names within each list are arranged in roughly alphabetical order by applicant's surname. Lists of applicants for participation in an award by the U.S. Court of Claims to Cherokee Freedmen who had not been included in the roll prepared for payment of the award. The lists include each applicant's name, roll number from the 1880 Cherokee census, roll number from the Wallace Roll of Cherokee

Freedmen, an exhibit number which corresponds to the exhibit number in the Applications for Enrollment as Freedmen, district of residence within the Cherokee Nation, and occasionally remarks about other enrollments. These lists were submitted as evidence to the Dawes Commission by the Cherokee National Council in enrollment proceedings.

Applications for Enrollment as Freedmen. 1897. Arranged numerically by exhibit number assigned in roughly chronological order by date of application. Notarized applications prepared on printed forms submitted by persons claiming a share of a payment made to Cherokee freedmen in accordance with an award of the U.S. Court of Claims in the case of *Moses Whitmire, Trustee* vs. *the Cherokee Nation.* The applications and supporting material were submitted by James M. Keys to the Commissioner of Indian Affairs between May 10 and June 30, 1897, and may have been a part of the general correspondence of the bureau. It appears that the records were returned to the Dawes Commission for use in enrollment proceedings. The application provides the applicant's name, age, and district of residence in the Cherokee Nation and the names and ages of other family members. There are some letters from claimants and officials of the Cherokee tribal government included with the application form.

Index to Applications for Enrollment through Intermarriage. Arranged alphabetically by the first letter of the applicant's surname. A handwritten index to the Applications for Enrollment through Intermarriage. The only information given is the application number.

Applications for Enrollment through Intermarriage. Arranged numerically by application number assigned in roughly alphabetical order by the first letter of the applicant's surname. Original applications submitted to the Dawes Commission for enrollment which required any person married to a Cherokee citizen to apply for himself or herself and his or her children. The applications or petitions are notarized and provide the name, age, sex, and address of each child and information supporting the claim to citizenship, such as date of marriage and enrollment on other tribal rolls. In addition to the application, there are occasionally copies of marriage licenses, statements of witnesses to the marriage, notice of service of a copy of the application on the chief of the Cherokee tribe, and the answer of the tribal government (generally rejecting the claim). The Dawes Commission held hearings on the applications at Fort Gibson but no record of the hearings has been located.

Dockets to Rejected and Doubtful Applications. 1904–1905. There is one docket for Cherokees by blood and one for freedmen. Within each docket there are separate sections for ''Doubtful'' and ''Rejected'' applications. Within each section, entries are arranged numerically by case number assigned chronologically by the date the case was opened. Each docket contains an index to the name of the applicant. A record of actions taken on applications classified by the commission as ''Doubtful'' and ''Rejected;'' the information for each application includes the name of the applicant and his or her attorney(s), the decision of the commission, date prepared, date forwarded to the Commissioner of Indian Affairs, and date approved by the Secretary of the Interior. Many of the ''Doubtful'' and some of the ''Rejected'' applicants were eventually enrolled, and in these cases there are references to enrollment card numbers. The case numbers in these dockets match the application numbers in the Applications for Enrollment as well as enrollment card numbers.

Applications for Enrollment. 1898–1907. Arranged by enrollment category and thereunder numerically by application number assigned chronologically by date of application. There are numerous gaps in the applications and some applications are missing. Original applications for enrollment and supporting evidence submitted to the Dawes Commission. The records include carbon copies of the testimony taken at hearings held by the commission, notices and letters sent to the applicants and the attorneys for both the applicants and the Cherokee tribe, correspondence with the Secretary of the Interior about the applications, and copies of the commission's decisions. There are only applications for the following categories: ''Doubtful Citizens by Blood,'' ''Rejected Citizens by Blood,'' ''Doubtful Freedmen,'' ''Rejected Freedmen,'' and ''Newborn Freedmen. There are also some ''memorandum cases'' which contain applications rejected under an act of Congress which restricted the commission's jurisdiction. Applications for the majority of the Cherokee categories are still in the custody of the Bureau of Indian Affairs and have been microfilmed.

[In the application of Daniel Beaver for enrollment as a citizen of the Cherokee Nation dated December 15, 1900, Daniel testified that he was twenty-five years of age and a resident of Tahlequah District, Cherokee Nation. His wife, Susan, was ''about twenty-five'' years of age. Daniel testified that, as far as he knew, Susan's maiden name was Waker. They had no children. He also states that his Indian name was ''Ahtola.'' Figure 3.3 is a portion of a letter from Special Commissioner Guion Miller to the Commissioner to the Five Civilized Tribes, dated March 15, 1909, requesting information about the enrollment of Daniel (or Ay-to-lay-hi) Chu-wa-loo-kie, age about thirty-six. Information about Daniel's brothers was also requested. (See Eastern Cherokee Application of Daniel Chu-wa-loo-kie, Figure 3.5). In response to the letter, the Commissioner to the Five Civilized Tribes responded on March 22, 1909, that Daniel (or Ay-to-la-

Sir:

Kindly inform this Office if you have any record of the enrolled by the Commission or Commissioner to the Five Civilized Tribes of Daniel (or Ay-to-lay-hi) Chu-wa-loo-kie, of Wauhillau, Oklahoma. His age is about 36 years and he has the following brothers:

Tee-hoo-yah Willey (or Weeley),
Kah-ter-yu-ie Willey (or Weeley), and
William Weeley.

The wife of the applicant is named as Susie Chu-wa-lo-kie.

Kindly refer in reply to FST 21749-17573.

Figure 3.3. Letter from Special Commissioner Guion Miller to the Commissioner of the Five Civilized Tribes.

hi) was enrolled in the Cherokee Nation as Daniel Beaver, opposite No. 25334. The third document (Figure 3.4) found in the file is the ''Statement of Applicant Taken under Oath,'' which reflects the same information provided in Daniel's testimony.]

Transcripts of Testimony of Applicants. 1910. Arranged numerically by application number assigned chronologically by date of application. Carbon copies of transcripts of testimony taken at hearings held by the commission. The majority of the applications relate to children of persons previously enrolled by the commission and persons listed on a roll of ''Eastern Cherokees'' who were not enrolled.

Record of Decisions. 1901–1902. Arranged chronologically by date of decision. Indexed by applicant. A record of actions taken by the commission on applications for enrollment. The information given for each action includes the names of the applicants, names of attorneys for the applicants and the Cherokee tribe, the nature of the decision, and a reference to the enrollment cards.

Index to the Cherokee Final Rolls. Arranged alphabetically by the first two letters of the enrollee's surname. Two indexes to names appearing on the ''Final Roll of the Cherokees.'' One index is contained in a single volume and the second index is divided into two volumes (A-K and L-Z). The only information given in the index is the enrollee's Dawes enrollment number.

Records Relating to Choctaw and Chickasaw Citizenship

Acts of the Choctaw National Council. 1893–1895. Arranged chronologically by date of passage. Handwritten copies of ''Acts of the General Council Admitting Parties to Citizenship.'' The text of the acts includes the names of persons and the authority for admission.

Lists of Applicants for Choctaw Citizenship. 1902. Arranged alphabetically by applicant's surname. A typed list of persons who applied for Choctaw citizenship. The information given for each applicant includes the Dawes Commission case number and a reference to the enrollment cards. The list is annotated with an ''A'' for persons who were admitted and a ''D'' for persons who were denied admission.

Lists of Persons Involved in Appeals to U.S. Courts. 1900. Arranged by type of action taken by the court. The names within each list are arranged in roughly alphabetical order by surname. Lists of applicants for citizenship whose cases were appealed to the U.S. Court for the Central District of Indian Territory at South McAlester or the Southern District at Ardmore. There are lists for

CHEROKEES BY BLOOD AND ADOPTION.

Date DEC 15 1900 1900.

Name Daniel Beaver Tahlequah Ind Ter

District TAHLEQUAH Year 1880 Page 732 No. 19

Citizen by blood yes Mother's citizenship

Intermarried citizen

Married under what law Date of marriage

License 25 Certificate

Wife's name Susan Beaver

District GOING SNAKE Year 1880 Page 488 No. 1927

Citizen by blood yes Mother's citizenship

Intermarried citizen no

Married under what law Date of marriage

Figure 3.4. Statement of Applicant taken under oath.

persons admitted by the court, persons admitted by the court who were previously denied by the Dawes Commission, and persons denied by the court who were previously admitted by the commission. The information given for each person generally includes the Dawes Commission case number, the U.S. Court docket number, and references to the Choctaw-Chickasaw Citizenship Court case number. There are also two lists of cases heard by the U.S. Court for the Central District. One is arranged numerically by case number and the other is alphabetical by the name of the first person listed in the appeal.

Indexes to Applicants. 1900–1906. Arranged by type of application. Entries within each index are alphabetical by surname. Indexes to applications for enrollment under various acts of Congress including: Choctaws applying under the act of May 31, 1900; Choctaw and Chickasaw freedmen testifying at Atoka and Colbert between June 4 and June 16, 1900; Choctaw and Chickasaw applicants under the act of July 1, 1902; Choctaw children applying after September 25, 1902; Choctaws also enrolled as Cherokees; Choctaw and Chickasaw applicants listed on "Rejected" and "Doubtful" enrollment cards; and Choctaws and Chickasaws found on earlier rolls who had not applied for enrollment. Each index generally provides only references to the enrollment cards.

Lists of Chickasaw Applicants. 1899–1902. Arranged in rough chronological order by the date compiled. Lists of applicants for enrollment by the Dawes Commission as Chickasaws, persons listed on tribal rolls who had not applied for enrollment, persons admitted by U.S. courts, and persons denied by the Dawes Commission. There are a few copies of marriage certificates and other documents submitted as evidence in enrollment proceedings. Some of the lists are annotated with enrollment numbers.

Lists of Choctaw Applicants. 1899–1902. Arranged in rough chronological order by the date compiled. Lists of applicants or potential applicants for enrollment by the Dawes Commission as Choctaws. There are lists of "Choctaws on the 1896 roll—unenrolled by the Dawes Commission," "Choctaws not having appeared before the Dawes Commission by 28 October 1899," "Applicants admitted by the Dawes Commission," and "Parties on Choctaw Cards who may be on Cherokee Cards." The information given in the lists generally includes the person's name, Dawes Commission enrollment number, and a reference to one of the earlier Choctaw rolls used to determine eligibility for enrollment.

Lists of Pending Applications. 1902–1905. There are separate lists for Choctaws by blood, Chickasaws by blood, Choctaw freedmen, and Chickasaw freedmen.

Within each list, the names are arranged numerically by enrollment card number. Lists of names of applicants whose applications were pending at the time the lists were compiled. The information given for each applicant includes name, age, sex, and enrollment card number.

Dockets of Special Enrollment Cases. 1905–1907. There is a separate docket for each type of case. Entries within each docket are arranged numerically by case number assigned chronologically by the date the case was opened. The information given for each case includes the names of all applicants, names of attorneys, a chronological summary of papers filed and proceedings held, the decision of the commission, actions taken by the Secretary of the Interior, and references to related cases.

Record of Decisions. 1902–1904; 1906–1907. There are separate volumes for Choctaws and Chickasaws. Within each volume, entries are in rough chronological order by date of decision. A record of decisions on enrollment applications made by the commission and forwarded to the Secretary of the Interior for approval. The information given for each decision includes the names of the applicants, enrollment card number, date of decision, action taken by the Secretary of the Interior, and date of notification to the applicant.

Records of the Choctaw-Chickasaw Citizenship Court. Section 31 of an act of Congress of July 1, 1902 (32 Stat. 641) established a Choctaw-Chickasaw Citizenship Court and authorized either tribe to file a bill of equity to regain enrollment in the court to seek annulment of the negative decisions made by the U.S. Courts in Indian Territory under the act of June 10, 1896. Cases originating in the U.S. Court for the Central District of Indian Territory were heard by the Citizenship Court at South McAlester and cases from the Southern District were heard at Tishomingo (both of which were within Indian Territory). The Citizenship Court heard 256 cases involving more than 3,400 people and admitted 161 to citizenship. The case files of the court are still in the custody of the Muskogee (OK) Area Office of the Bureau of Indian Affairs. (See "Oklahoma" section in "Private and Public Organizations," Part II, for more information.)

Lists of Claimants. 1902. There are separate lists for Choctaws and Chickasaws. Within each list, the names are arranged alphabetically by surname. The information given for each person claiming citizenship includes name, sex, age, degree of Indian blood, Dawes enrollment card number, and some remarks relating to decisions of the Citizenship Court. Some of the lists described under "Lists of Persons Involved in Appeals to U.S. Courts." Some 1,900 have been annotated with case numbers from the Citizenship Court.

Index to Dockets. 1903. There is one index to the South McAlester docket, one index to the Tishomingo docket, and one consolidated index to both dockets. The information given for each person involved in a case before the Citizenship Court is the case number and the Dawes enrollment card number.

General Dockets. 1903–1904. There is one docket for cases heard at South McAlester and one docket for cases heard at Tishomingo. Entries within each docket are arranged numerically by case number assigned chronologically by the date the case was opened. Indexed by surname of principal party. Information given for each case includes the names of all parties involved, names of attorneys, nature of the case, a chronological summary of papers filed and proceedings held, and references to the minute books.

Appearance Dockets. 1902–1904. There is a separate docket for cases heard at South McAlester and Tishomingo. Entries within each docket are arranged numerically by case number assigned chronologically by the date the case was opened, indexed by surname of principal party. Information given for each case includes the names of all parties involved, the names of attorneys, and a summary of the orders, writs, and other documents filed with the court. The summaries in these dockets are more detailed than the summaries contained in the dockets described under "General Dockets. 1903–1904."

Case Files. 1902–1904. Arranged by docket number assigned in chronological order by the date the case was opened. Original papers filed in proceedings held by the Citizenship Court including briefs, memorandum of arguments submitted by attorneys for the Choctaw and Chickasaw Nations, and opinions of the court. The majority of the cases were heard at South McAlester.

Records Relating to the Identification of Mississippi Choctaws. The Dawes Commission was required by an act of Congress to investigate the right of the Mississippi Choctaws to enrollment and allotment. The commission received 24,634 applications from all over the United States before the deadline of March 25, 1903.

Lists of Claimants under the Treaty of 1830. Arranged alphabetically by surname. Manuscript copies of lists of persons who remained in Mississippi under article 14 of the treaty of 1830 and claimed land. Each list generally includes the claimant's name, date of application, and the legal description of the land claimed. Some lists have been annotated with Dawes enrollment numbers and enrollment card numbers. Essentially, by accepting allotments in the East, the Native Americans gave up any right to future land allotments in the West.

Index and Record of Testimony. 1899. Arranged alphabetically by surname of the applicant. Copies of an index to Mississippi Choctaw applicants who appeared before the commission in 1899 in the Mississippi towns of Carthage, Philadelphia, and Decatur and typed transcripts of the testimony given by the applicants.

Indexes to Field Cards. Arranged alphabetically by surname of applicant. Index to enrollment cards. The only information provided is the field number of the applicant's enrollment card.

Indexes to Applicants. 1902–1906. Arranged alphabetically by surname of applicant. Indexes to applicants for enrollment under various acts of Congress. The indexes include the following categories: identified and rejected; rejected and reviewed by the Secretary of the Interior; decisions during the year ending June 30, 1903; applications for children whose parents were rejected; newborn and minor children. The indexes generally provide only a reference to the applicant's enrollment card number and occasionally an enrollment number.

Decisions of the Commission. 1902–1904. Arranged chronologically by date of decision. The first volume contains an index to all applicants covered by the decisions. The decisions of the commission on applications for identification as Mississippi Choctaws generally review the facts contained in each application considered.

Roll of Identified Mississippi Choctaws. 1905. The names on the roll are arranged by enrollment card number. Indexed by surname. List of persons who were identified as Mississippi Choctaws. The information provided for each person includes enrollment number and enrollment card number.

Lists of Identified Full-Blood Mississippi Choctaws. Arranged alphabetically by surname. Information given for each person includes enrollment card number, age, sex, post office address, county or parish of residence, and date of removal to the Choctaw Nation. The lists have been annotated to indicate persons who were removed at government expense, refused to remove, could not be located, or died prior to removal to the Choctaw Nation.

Lists of Persons Removed. 1904. Names of persons who removed are arranged alphabetically. Names of persons who refused to remove are arranged numerically by identified roll number. Included is a list of persons identified as Mississippi Choctaws who were removed from Mississippi and Louisiana at government expense, and a list of persons who were identified but refused to remove. The information given for each person includes age, sex, post office address, county or parish of residence, and date of removal or identification.

Records Relating to Creek Citizenship

List of Applicants. 1895–1896. Arranged alphabetically by surname. List of applicants considered by the Creek Citizenship Commission in 1895 and 1896. The information given for each applicant includes type of citizenship claimed, date of application, date of judgment, decision rendered, and a reference to a ''Record Book.'' The lists have been annotated with the field numbers of Dawes enrollment cards.

Citizenship Commission Docket. 1895. Arranged numerically by case number assigned chronologically by the date the case was opened. Indexed by surname of applicant. A record of cases heard by the Citizenship Commission. The information given for each case includes the names of all persons involved and occasionally a reference to the action taken by the Citizenship Commission.

Record Books. 1885–1888, 1895–1896. Arranged in rough numerical order by case number assigned in chronological order by the date the case was opened. Record of actions taken by the tribal Citizenship Commission on applications for citizenship. The information given for each case generally includes the text of the application, transcripts of testimony, and the commission's recommendation. There are occasional references to the docket described under ''Citizenship Commission Docket. 1895.'' Part of the record was prepared on unbound printed forms (''Census of the Non-Citizens of the Muskogee Nation''). There is also a list of names, along with each person's age and a description of his or her property.

Lists of Admitted Applicants. 1902. Arranged alphabetically by surname of applicant. Lists of persons admitted to citizenship by the Dawes Commission or the U.S. Court for the Northern District of Indian Territory. The list gives only the person's name and Dawes Commission case number. Some of the lists have been annotated with field numbers of Dawes enrollment cards.

Indexes to Unenrolled Creeks. 1900. Arranged alphabetically by surname. Creeks on the authenticated roll of 1890 and Creeks on the authenticated roll of 1895 who had not been enrolled by the Dawes Commission as of August 15, 1900. Information given for each person includes town of residence and the roll number from the 1890 and 1895 rolls.

List of Unenrolled Creeks. A list of the names of Creeks who appeared on various tribal rolls but had not been enrolled by the Dawes Commission. The only information given is the person's name.

Miscellaneous Indexes. 1902–1906. Arranged alphabetically by surname of enrollee. Indexes to various enrollment categories including citizens by blood, freedmen, minors, and newborns. The indexes generally provide only the enrollee's enrollment number or enrollment card number.

Lists of Applicants. 1900–1907. Arranged alphabetically by surname. Lists of Creeks whose names appear on various tribal rolls and applicants for whom birth or death affidavits were submitted. Some of the lists have been annotated with enrollment card numbers.

Index to Freedmen Enrollment Cards. 1898. Arranged alphabetically by surname of enrollee. Index to the "Old Series" of freedmen enrollment cards.

Enrollment Cards ("Old Series Cards"). 1898. Arranged numerically by card number. Original enrollment cards prepared from the authenticated 1895 Creek Census. Each card contains the names of the members of a family group and each person's age, sex, degree of Indian blood, post office address, district or town of residence, 1895 payroll number, and relationship to the head of the family group. The card also includes remarks about names used on earlier rolls and actions taken by the Dawes Commission and references to the field numbers of the enrollment cards.

Record of Enrollment. Arranged numerically by field number (the temporary number assigned until they were arranged chronologically). A record prepared on a printed form similar to the enrollment cards which contains the names of all members of a family group and remarks of actions taken by the Dawes Commission. The field numbers on these cards do not match the number on the enrollment cards.

Records Relating to Seminole Citizenship

Index to Newborns. 1905. Arranged alphabetically by enrollee's surname. Persons enrolled under the act of Congress of March 3, 1905. The only information given is the person's enrollment number and enrollment card number.

Enrollment Schedules. 1900. Arranged numerically by enrollment card number. Schedules prepared on printed forms of the names of persons enrolled as Seminole citizens by blood and Seminole freedmen. The information given for each person includes age, sex, band name, roll number from the 1897 Seminole census, post office address, and parents' names and 1897 enrollment numbers.

Records of the Five Civilized Tribes, Not Part of the Dawes Commission

It is important to realize that the Cherokee, Choctaw, Chickasaw, Creek, and Seminole tribes had each established their own governments with constitutions and courts. The national records of these tribes predate and overlap those of the Commission to the Five Civilized Tribes. Consequently, the researcher needs to consider these records in conjunction with the records of the Dawes Commission. These records can be found at the Oklahoma Historical Society.

Cherokee Nation

Members of this nation migrated in varying amounts over the years. In response to a request from Cherokees who had fought for the British during the American Revolution, the Spanish governor at New Orleans, in 1794, granted permission allowing them to settle in the St. Francis River valley (present day southeastern Missouri). In 1811–1812 some Cherokees moved en masse to the Arkansas region. In both moves, other members of the Nation later joined the original emigrants.

An 1817 treaty with the U.S. government called for the Cherokees to cede tracts of land east of the Mississippi River for an area of equal value in the West between the Arkansas and White Rivers. The 1,100 and more Cherokees who emigrated during 1818–1819 were promised various material gifts, compensation for any improvements made to the new location, transportation, and subsistance. The lands in Arkansas were ceded for lands in modern Oklahoma in a treaty signed in 1828. The rolls for those who removed under these two treaties are located at the National Archives and include a register of Cherokees who wished to remain in the East, 1817–1819 (two volumes); emigration registers of Indians who wished to migrate, 1817–1838 (eighteen volumes); and applications for reservations, 1819.

The New Echota Treaty, dated December 29, 1835, provided for the final cession of all Cherokee lands east of the Mississippi River and the beginning of the forced western migration resulting in the infamous "Trail of Tears," during which nearly twenty-five percent of the tribe died from disease and exposure. Cherokees who had emigrated prior to this treaty were called *Old Settler Cherokees.*

Cherokee Removal Records. Cherokee removal records include a register of Cherokees who wished to remain in the East, 1817–1819; applications for reservations, 1819; Eastern Cherokee census rolls, 1835–1884; emigration rolls, 1817–1836; and miscellaneous Cherokee removal records, 1820–1854.

Board of Cherokee Commissioners. Four commissions were appointed at various times to settle claims arising from the New Echota Treaty:

Records of the First Board of Cherokee Commissioners, 1836–1839, include letters sent, property valuations and changes in their valuation, reservation claims and claim papers, records of judgments against Cherokee Indians, decisions on claims of attorneys against the Cherokee Nation, certificate stubs, and a general abstract of valuations and spoliation (or plunder) allowed and of balances due.

Records of the Second and Third Board of Cherokee Commissioners, 1842–1845, include include letters sent, proceedings and a schedule of claims (Second Board), claim papers of the Second and Third Boards, claims presented in the West, and a register of payments.

Records of the Fourth Board of Cherokee Commissioners, 1846–1847, include letters sent, minutes, claim papers, and a register of payments.

Rolls of Cherokee Nation Residing West of the Mississippi River. Cherokee territory west of the Mississippi River consisted of the political districts of Cooweescoowee, Delaware, Saline, Going Snake, Tahlequah, Flint, Illinois, Sequoyah, and Canadian .

Old Settler Roll (1851). This roll lists each individual and offspring by district (unless the mother was an emigrant Cherokee—one who went West after 1835). Some non-resident family groups are also listed.

Drennen Roll. 1852. Arranged by Cherokee District and thereunder by family group. A receipt roll for a per capita payment made to Cherokees living in the West who removed as a result of the Treaty of 1835. The roll was prepared by John Drennen and contains the payee's name, amount received by the head of each household, and the name of the witness.

Drennen Roll Index. 1852. Arranged alphabetically by first two letters of the name. This index contains the individual's surname, given name, and a page number reference to the receipt roll.

Complete list of names of Emigrant Cherokee who drew Emigrant Money in 1852. Flint, Sequoyah, and Illinois districts.

Tompkins Roll of 1867. Arranged by Cherokee District. A census roll of Cherokees residing in Cherokee Nation taken by H. Tompkins. The census roll provides the name, age, and sex of the individual. It also indicates if the individual is "white," "half-breed," or "colored."

Tompkins Roll Freedmen Indices. 1897. Arranged alphabetically by the first two letters of the name. Indices of the freedmen listed by H. Tompkins in 1867. One index is alphabetical by surname and the other is alphabetical by given name. The indices provide the name, page number of the roll, and the district of residence.

Receipt Roll for Per Capita Payment. 1874. Lists head of household, family members, total in family, amount paid, to whom paid, and name of witness.

Lists of Rejected Claimants. 1878–1880. Arranged by type of decision and thereunder by case number. List of persons who appeared before the Cherokee Commission on Citizenship and whose claims were rejected. The list provides the name of the claimant and the decision rendered by the commission. The notation "Colored" has been made in the margin preceding some of the names.

Cherokee Census of 1880. Authorized by the Cherokee National Council in 1879, the Dawes Commission listed any Indian or intermarried white on this census in the final rolls, annotating each individual's location and name on the census. The census was arranged by district into one of six schedules: Cherokee citizens (natives, adopted whites, Shawnees, Delawares, and freedmen; orphans under 16; those rejected; those with pending citizenship claims; unauthorized white squatters; and those within the Cherokee Nation by permission of the Cherokee Council. Information provided consists of an individual's name by family group, age, race, occupation, sex, and roll number.

Cherokee Census Index, 1880. Arranged by Cherokee District and thereunder (roughly) alphabetically. A printed index to the 1880 Cherokee Census, which contains the name, roll number, place of birth, age, and sex of each individual. The volume also includes lists of Shawnee and Delaware who were residing in the Cherokee Nation, North Carolina Cherokee who removed to the Cherokee Nation, and persons admitted or re-admitted to citizenship by the Cherokee National Council. There is also an "Orphan Roll."

Lipe Receipt Roll. 1880. Arranged by Cherokee District and thereunder by roll number. A per capita receipt roll by government agent D.W. Lipe. The roll provides the name of the payee, number in the family, total amount paid to the family, name of the person receiving the payment, and the name of the witness.

Receipt Roll of Per Capita Payment. 1881. Lists head of household and family members, nationality, and remarks.

Lists of North Carolina Cherokees Who Removed to the Cherokee Nation West. 1881. Lists roll number, family number, English name, Cherokee name (in Cherokee), age, sex, nationality, residence (in Cherokee), and remarks.

Roll of North Carolina Immigrants Allowed Per Capita Payment. 1881. Lists name of head of household and family members.

Payroll By Right of Cherokee Blood. 1883. Lists roll number, name of head of household and family members, age, and remarks.

Lists of North Carolina Cherokees. 1882–1883. Lists name of head of household, family members, nationality, and age.

The Cherokee Census of 1883 and 1886. Authorized by the Cherokee National Council on May 19, 1883, the 1883 census is arranged by district (like the 1880 census) and includes an orphan's roll, Cherokee nation prisoners, and a supplemental roll. Name and age are provided. In addition, a receipt roll lists each individual's name and roll number, the total number in the household, the total amount paid each household from rentals of land, and the names of the person receiving the payment and of the witness to the payment. The 1886 census is similar to that of 1883, but additionally states each individual's relationship to the head of household.

Supplemental Roll of Those Left off the Rolls of 1880 Per Capita Payment. 1884. Lists heads of household, family members, and remarks.

Citizenship Commission Docket Book, 1880–1884. Arranged by session and thereunder by case number. Docket of the Citizenship Commission of the Cherokee Nation which contains the names of claimants, nature of the claim, and the decision of the commission.

The 1890 Cherokee Census. Provides the most information (105 columns) of any census initiated by the Cherokee Nation. It is arranged by district and includes the same six schedules used in the 1880 census detailed above.

The 1893 Cherokee Census. Classifies as Cherokee citizens those who were Cherokee by blood, adopted whites, freedmen, Shawnees, Delawares, intermarried persons, and Creeks. Also arranged by district, each individual's name, age, sex, admission reference, guardian, and place of residence is given as well as the name of person providing identification.

The Wallace Roll of Cherokee Freedmen, 1890–1893. Arranged by enrollment number. A copy of a Cherokee freedmen census made in 1890 of those eligible to receive a per capita payment. The roll was prepared by BIA Special Agent John Wallace and was based on an 1883 census of Cherokee freedmen. The roll includes lists of authenticated freedmen who appear on the 1883 roll, individuals who died between 1883 and 1890, individuals admitted by Wallace, and "Free Negroes." The volume also contains a list of individuals whose rights were questioned by the Commissioner of Indian Affairs and supplemental lists of individuals who were admitted by the Secretary of the Interior. The roll contains the individual's name, age, sex, and residence. The entries have been annotated with the enrollment numbers from the Clifton Roll of Cherokee Freedmen of 1896, and in some cases, with the enrollment numbers from the Dawes Roll of 1907. This roll was set aside as "fraudulent" by a decree of May 8, 1895, of the U.S. Court of Claims and was never recognized by the Cherokee Nation.

Cherokee Freedmen Roll Index, 1893. Arranged alphabetically by first two letters of the surname. The index lists the individual's surname, given name, and district of residence. The index contains page number references to another 1893 roll.

Cherokee Freedmen Roll Index. 1890–1893. Arranged alphabetically by last name. An index to the Cherokee Freedmen Roll (Wallace Roll). The index lists the individual's roll number, district of residence, and a page number reference to the 1890 roll.

The Starr Roll (1894). In 1891 the U.S. Congress passed an act that resulted in the sale of the 12,000 square mile Cherokee Outlet (part of present day Oklahoma) to the United States. E. E. Starr, treasurer of the Cherokee Nation, prepared a receipt roll to distribute the per capita payment received from the sale. It was arranged by district, followed by enrollment number and provided the names of the head of household, the person receiving payment, and the witness to the transaction. An orphans' roll was also created.

Cherokee Payroll Index. 1894. (Authenticated Roll of 1894). Arranged alphabetically by surname. This index lists the individual's name, roll number, and district of residence. It also contains page number references to the 1894 receipt roll (Starr Roll). The roll number and names also correspond with the names and roll numbers on the 1894 Cherokee Census Roll.

Cherokee Census Roll. 1894. Arranged by Cherokee District and thereunder by enrollment number. A census of the Cherokee Nation made in 1894. The roll is based on the 1894 payroll. The roll contains the individual's enrollment number, name, age, and sex. Under "remarks," the name of deceased parents and other names used on previous enrollments are listed.

Lists of Cherokee Children, 1895–1897. Arranged by Cherokee District. These lists contain the names of children born between 1895 and 1897, their date of birth, and parents' names.

Old Settlers Roll, 1896. Arranged numerically by agency pay number. A receipt roll for a per capita payment based on the 1851 "Old Settlers' Roll" of the "Western Cherokees" (those removing prior to the New Echota Treaty). The names of persons who were still living at the time of the payment are listed first and are followed by the names of those who were deceased and the names of their heirs who were paid. This payment resulted from a decision of the U.S. Court of Claims made on June 6, 1893. The roll contains each payee's name, 1851 roll number, agency pay number, age, sex, amount received, post office address, signature, date of payment, and names of witnesses. The relations of heirs to the original payee is given. Information regarding guardianship, related correspondence files, and correction of names is provided under "remarks." There are also three versions of a supplemental list of original enrollees from the 1851 roll whose shares were not claimed. One version lists just the names of the heirs of the enrollees, the second version lists the names of the heirs of the individuals and the amount of payment they received, and the third version is a working copy.

Cherokee Census Roll. 1896. Arranged by Cherokee District and thereunder by roll number. This census roll of citizens of the Cherokee Nation contains the individual's name, roll number, age, sex, precinct, proportion of blood, and place of birth.

The 1896 Payment Roll (Lipe Roll). Based on the 1851 Old Settler Roll, it lists the names of those still living in 1896; followed by those deceased, their heirs, and the relationship which existed between each heir and the decedent. Other information provided includes each payee's 1851 roll number, name, age, sex, and post office address with the agency pay number and the amount received.

Shawnee-Cherokee Census. 1896. Arranged roughly alphabetically by name. This roll contains the names of Cherokee Shawnee who were entitled to participate in the distribution of funds to equalize a per capita payment. The roll contains the individual's name, roll number, "Cherokee Number" (assigned to Cherokee to indicate that they were not Shawnee living on Cherokee land), age, sex, address, and names used on previous rolls. A notation was made after the names of deceased individuals. The roll includes two supplemental lists of Cherokee Shawnee entitled to funds and a list of persons "Omitted from Government Pay Rolls of the Cherokee Shawnee Tribe of Indians."

Cherokee Freedmen Roll (Clifton Roll). 1896. Arranged numerically by roll number. List of Cherokee freedmen and their descendants prepared by a commission appointed by the Secretary of the Interior. The roll was based on testimony taken by the Commission in the Cherokee Nation between May 4 and August 10, 1897. The list contains the individual's name, relationship to the head of the household, sex, age, and district of residence. There is a supplemental list of individuals whose claims to citizenship were rejected by the Cherokee Nation but approved by the commission.

Delaware Payroll. 1896. Arranged alphabetically by first letter of surname. A list of persons entitled to funds to equalize a per capita payment. The information given for each person includes name; census number; payroll number; age; amounts received in payments made in 1890, 1894, and 1896; name of person receiving payment; and names of witnesses. There are some remarks about deaths, relations to others on the list, and some names have been annotated with Dawes Commission enrollment numbers.

Cherokee Citizenship Records. This group includes:

Lists of Rejected Claimants. 1878–1880. Arranged by type of decision and thereunder by case number. List of persons who appeared before the Cherokee Commission on Citizenship and whose claims were rejected. The list provides the name of the claimant and the decision rendered by the commission. The notation "Colored" has been made in the margin preceding some of the names.

List of Applicants Admitted to Citizenship. 1896. Arranged alphabetically by name. List of names of applicants admitted to citizenship in the Cherokee Nation by the Dawes Commission. The list contains the applicant's name, references to case numbers from the U.S. Court in Indian Territory, Dawes Commission file and card numbers, other names used by the applicant, and notations concerning applicants living outside Indian Territory.

Lists of Applicants for Cherokee Citizenship. 1896. Arranged alphabetically by name. This volume contains a list of names of applicants for citizenship in the Cherokee Nation under an act of Congress of June 10, 1896. There are lists of applicants admitted to citizenship by the Dawes Commission, applicants rejected by the Dawes Commission but admitted by the U.S. Courts in Indian Territory, and applicants admitted by the Dawes Commission but rejected by the U.S. courts. The information given in each lists varies but generally includes the applicant's name, a reference to a Dawes case number, and a court case number.

Cherokee District Records. These records include:

Canadian District. Court records 1867–1898.

Cooweescoowee District. Marriages, Permits, Wills, and Estates, 1858–1898; Cherokee Marriages, 1868–1897; District Estate Records, 1875–1897; Permits to Non-citizens, 1893–1899; Land Records and Estray (livestock that has wandered off its owner's property) Property Records, 1875–1914; Cherokee Townsites, 1876–1898; District, Circuit, and Supreme Court Records, 1868–1895; Cherokee Courts, 1857–1898; Divorce, 1890.

Delaware District. Marriages, 1867–1896; Delaware District Permits, 1868–1895; Cherokee Permits, 1886; District Estates, 1867–1898; District, Circuit, and Supreme Court Records, 1868–1895; Divorce, 1902; Improvements, 1859–1898; Marks and Brands, 1876–1898; Estray Property, 1875–1895.

Flint District. Estates, 1876–1893; Estray Property, 1876–1898; Marks and Brands, 1876–1897; Improvements, 1881–1892; Supreme, Circuit, and District Court Records, 1877–1897; Marriages, 1893.

Going Snake District. Marriages, 1880–1898; Estates, 1868–1904; Improvements and Estray Property, 1880–1898; Supreme, Circuit, and District Court Records, 1876–1898.

Illinois District. Marriages, Estates, and Permits, 1859–1897; Estates, 1876–1898; Permits, 1895–1896; Improvements, Marks and Brands, Estray Property, and Supreme, Circuit, and District Court Records, 1965–1898; Supreme, Circuit, and District Court Records, 1862–1898.

Saline District. Marriages, Estates, Permits, Property Improvements, Estray Property, and Marks and Brands, 1866–1898; Permits, 1876–1897; Supreme, Circuit, and District Court Records, 1872–1898.

Sequoyah District. Marriages, Estates, Estray Property, and Property Improvements, 1874–1898; Supreme, Circuit, and District Court Records, 1876–1898.

Tahlequah District. Marriages, Estates, and Permits, 1856–1898; Property Improvements, Estray Property, and Marks and Brands, 1872–1898; Supreme, Circuit, and District Court Records, 1865–1904.

Documents Pertaining to Determination of Tribal Membership, 1870–1909.

Cherokee Citizenship, 1841–1911. Letters Sent and Letters Received and Other Documents, 1829–1914.

Records Relating the Enrollment of Eastern Cherokee. The treaties of 1835–1836 and 1845 created a fund to be awarded to Cherokees (or their heirs) who lived in the East during that time. Guion Miller was appointed by the U.S. Court of Claims to determine eligibility. While the majority of the affected group was residing in Indian Territory at the time of Miller's commission, many Eastern Cherokees remained in North Carolina. Miller submitted his report and roll in 1909, following up with two supplementary reports the next year. The rolls are known as the Guion Miller Rolls.

These records are also commonly referred to as "Eastern Cherokee Applications." This title is misleading in that the researcher is led to believe that the records pertain only to the Eastern Cherokee Tribe of North Carolina.

The records consist of: the Guion Miller Report and Exhibits, 1908–1910 (twenty-nine volumes), ten volumes of transcripts of testimony; a report concerning exceptions to findings; a printed copy of the Guion Miller roll including the supplements; copies of the Drennen and Chapman rolls with a consolidated index, and a copy of the "Old Settlers" rolls, also indexed. These records are included in classified file "33931-11-053 Cherokee Nation."

Between 1906 and 1909, more than 45,000 claimants submitted applications providing detailed information on their families. A typical application includes the applicant's English name, Indian name, residence, date and place of birth, marriage status, and name of husband or wife. The applicant also gave the name of his or her mother and father, their places of birth and residence in 1851 and dates of death; names, dates of birth, and death dates of brothers and sisters; names of his or her paternal and maternal grandparents and their children, their places of birth and residence in 1851; and the name of the ancestor from whom they claimed to be a descendant.

[Figure 3.5 shows the first page of the Eastern Cherokee application of Daniel Chu-wa-loo-kie. The application is dated March 30, 1907. Daniel was a resident of Tahlequah District, Cherokee Nation, Indian Territory. His post office address was Wau-hillaw, Cherokee Nation, Indian Territory. His Indian name was Ay-to-lay-hi. Daniel was born about 1873 in Tahlequah District, Cherokee Nation. He based his claim to share "For my fathers share—'Chu-wa-loo-kie' and an interest in my mothers share Nic-o-ti-yi also for the following shares, viz: Toy-ya-lee-si, grand father—Ay-to-lay-hi, uncle—Ah-que-sa, aunt—Walker, 1st cousin, Oo-wah-nur-ki, uncle—Stand (or Ja-ka-to-qah), 1st cousin—Ben, and Logan and all others on census roll of 1851 in the said Oo-wa-nur-ki's family." He was married. His wife was Susie Chu-wa-loo-kie, born about 1870. Daniel's father was Chu-wa-loo-ki, born "In the Cherokee Nation East." He died about 1893. His mother was Nic-o-ti-yi, born in the Tahlequah District, Cherokee Nation, and died about 1874. The application also contains information about Daniel's brothers and sisters: Tee-hee-yah Willey, who died in September 1905; Kah-ter-yer-ie, who died in 1874; and William Wee-ley, who was living in 1907. William's application number is written in the left margin of the page. Daniel's paternal grandfather was Toy-ya-lee-si (or "Beaver Toter"). The names of his paternal grandmother and his maternal grandparents were not known. Toy-ya-lee-si was born in "The Cherokee Nation East—in Georgia." Children of Toy-ya-lee-si were: Oo-wa-nur-kee, Ay-to-lay-hi, and Choo-wa-lee-kie (Daniel's father). Daniel concluded his application:

> In regard to my uncle Oo-wa-nur-key and family for whom I claim, I am unable to enumerate his entire family by name, but I am creditably informed that he had at least 5 children in family commencing with, Stand or Ta-ka-tah-ga the eldest. I give the English names of some of them: Ben and Logan, but am unable to find what their Cherokee names were.

The application is signed in Daniel's own handwriting, indicating that he could read and write English.]

Records of the Choctaw Nation

The Choctaw Nation in Indian Territory maintained its own constitutional government and records for many years in the nineteenth century, and in limited form after 1906 (and Oklahoma's statehood which began in 1907). The Choctaw National Constitution was adopted on June 3, 1834, and the government consisted of a Principal

Commissioner of Indian Affairs,
Washington, D. C.

Sir:

I hereby make application for such share as may be due me of the fund appropriated by the Act of Congress approved June 30, 1906, in accordance with the decrees of the Court of Claims of May 18, 1905, and May 28, 1906, in favor of the Eastern Cherokees. The evidence of identity is herewith subjoined.

---

1. State full name—
   English name: Daniel Chu wa loo-kie
   Indian name: Ay-to-lay hi
2. Residence: Tahlequah District Cherokee Nation
3. Town and post office: Wau-hillau P.O.
4. County: Cherokee
5. State: Indian Territory
6. Date and place of birth: Tahlequah District – age 34 years
7. By what right do you claim to share? If you claim through more than one relative living in 1851, set forth each claim separately: For my fathers share – "Chu-wa-loo-kie" and an interest in my mothers share Nic-o-ti-yi also for the following shares, viz – Toy-ya lee si Grandfather – Ay to lay hi' uncle". Ah quo sa' Aunt. Walker 1st cousin Oowah nuy ki, uncle Stand (or Ta-ka-to-gah) 1st cousin Ben, and Logan and all others on census roll of 1851. in the said Oowa nuv ki's Family, –
8. Are you married? yes
9. Name and age of wife or husband: Susie Chu wa loo kie, age 37
10. Give names of your father and mother, and your mother's name before marriage.
    Father—English name:
    Indian name: Chu-wa-loo-ki
    Mother—English name:
    Indian name: Nic-o-ti-yi
    Maiden name:
11. Where were they born?
    ~~Father: In the Cherokee Nation "East."~~
    Mother: " " " " "
12. Where did they reside in 1851, if living at that time?
    Father: Tahlequah District Cherokee Nation
    Mother: " "
13. Date of death of your father and mother—
    Father: about 1893 Mother: about 1871

Figure 3.5. Eastern Cherokee Application (page 1). Daniel Chu-wa-loo-kie.

Chief, a General Council composed of a Senate and House of Representatives, and a court system consisting of a Supreme Court and District Courts. The nation was divided into three geographical and political districts. District One, Masholatubbe, consisted of Tobucksy, Gaines, Sans Bois, Skullyville, and Sugar Loaf counties. District Two, Apuckshunnubbee, consisted of Cedar, Nashoba, Towson, Boktuklo, Eagle, Wade, and Red River counties. District Three, Pushmataha, consisted of Atoka, Jacks Fork, Blue, Jackson and Kiamichi counties. The district capitals were at Gaines, Alichi and Mayhew. The national capital has been at Tushkahomma for most of the years of the nation's existence.

Records consist of:

Choctaws paid by Chickasaw, Treaty of June 22, 1855. Contains names of individuals; their marks; identification of the individual as man, woman, or child; total number in the family; the amount of the individual share; and the total dollar amount per family. There are tallies in the middle and the bottom of the pages and at the end of the county list and district list. The orphans list contains the names of individuals, names of the representatives for orphans, marks, the amount received per representative, the total amount received per orphan, and remarks. Remarks are primarily confined to "death after 4th installment." There are tallies on each page and at the end of the list.

Index to 1885 Choctaw Census. Contains individual's name, county of residence, age, and number in census book for county.

Choctaw Census. 1885. Arranged by county. A census of Choctaw citizens living in Atoka, Blue, Boktoklo, Cedar, Eagle, Gains, Jacks Fork, Kiomitia, Nashoba, Red River, Sans Bois, Sckullyville, Sugar Loaf, Towson, Tobuksko, and Wade counties of the Choctaw Nation. The information given for each person includes name, age, sex, race ("White," "Indian," "Colored"), occupation, and agricultural schedule.

Choctaw-Chickasaw Freedmen Rolls, 1885. Arranged by first, second, and third Choctaw Districts, thereafter consecutively by family group. Contains names of persons admitted to citizenship, heads of families and children, sex and age group, nationality of parents, previous owner of freed slaves, number of livestock, and acres of land in cultivation.

Choctaw Payroll. 1893. Arranged alphabetically by county, thereafter alphabetically by individual's name. Manuscript list of individuals (Choctaw by blood) receiving annuity payments. Contains names of citizens by blood, name and sex of children, individual receiving payment, amount of payment, and remarks. Remarks primarily confined to identification of orphans.

Census of Choctaw Nation. 1896. Arranged numerically by district, thereafter alphabetically by the initial of surname of individuals living within a particular county or Chickasaw district. Contains names of adults, names and sex of children, age, relationship, and remarks. Remarks include such things as wife of intermarried citizen, orphan, widow, stricken from roll, child of a Choctaw, deceased, and transfers to other rolls.

Census Roll of Freedmen. 1896. Arranged alphabetically. Contains consecutive numbers, notation if Chickasaw, name, age, county of residence, and other notations. Other notations consist primarily of "dead," parents' names, and Dawes numbers.

Census and Citizenship Records. Mississippi Choctaw Census and Citizenship, 1830–1899; Census records and lists, 1830–1896; Census of Choctaws by blood and intermarried citizens, 1868–1896; residents of the Chickasaw Nation, 1896; restricted Choctaws, 1929; Choctaw Citizenship, 1897–1930; Choctaw Citizenship, 1897–1930; Undated, 1884–1904; Choctaw Citizenship Cases, 1896–1904; Rejected Cases, First District, 1896–1897; Census and Citizenship, Choctaw Freedmen, 1885–1897.

County Court Records. Atoka County Courts, 1886–1906; Blue County Courts, 1868–1906; Boktuklo County Courts, 1858–1905; Cedar County Courts, 1875–1905; Eagle County Courts, 1889–1906; Gaines County Courts, 1859–1906; Jacks County Courts, 1860–1906; Jackson County Courts, 1887–1906; Kiamichi County Courts, 1888–1905; Nashoba County Courts, 1856–1905; Red River County Courts, 1866–1905; Sans Bois County Courts, 1888–1906; Skullyville County Courts, 1868–1906; Sugar Loaf County Courts, 1874–1906; Tobucksy County Courts, 1867–1906; Towson County Courts, 1881–1906; Wade County Courts, 1858–1906.

District, Circuit, and Chancery Records. First District (Mosholatubbe), 1848–1905; Second District (Apuckshunnabbee), 1871–1905; Third District (Pushmataha), 1859–1906.

Records of the Chickasaw Nation

An agreement between the Chickasaws and Choctaws signed at Doaksville, Indian Territory, on January 17, 1837 (11 Stat. 573), permitted the Chickasaws to settle in the Choctaw Nation with all the rights of Choctaw citizens. A further provision created an area to be set aside as the Chickasaw District, with the land to be held in common by the two tribes. Residents of the district were to have equal representation in the Choctaw General Council and were to be governed by the laws of the Choctaw Nation.

This arrangement proved to be unsatisfactory for the Chickasaws. In 1855 another treaty was signed (11 Stat. 611) which gave the Chickasaws the unrestricted right of self-government and defined the boundaries of the Chickasaw Nation. In 1856 and 1857 constitutions were adopted, with the government organized into three departments. The executive authority was vested in the office of Governor and the legislative in a Senate and House of Representatives. A Supreme Court was established as well as District and County Courts. This form of government was retained until the advent of statehood for Oklahoma in 1907.

The original counties of the Chickasaw District were Panola, Wichita, Caddo, and Perry. When the Chickasaw Nation proper was organized under the treaty of 1855, the country was again divided into four counties called from that time onward Panola, Pickens, Tishomingo, and Pontotoc.

On April 23, 1897, the Chickasaws, under the Atoka Agreement, consented to the provisions of allotment of their lands in severalty.

Records consist of:

Chickasaw Annuity Roll. 1878. Arranged by consecutive numbers. List of Chickasaws registered in Panola, Pickens, Pontotoc, and Tishomingo Counties in the Chickasaw Nation and Masholatubby and Pushmatahal Districts in the Choctaw Nation for the annuity payment of 1878. Contains names of head of family, indication of wife, number of children, total number in family, and name of person receiving payment.

Chickasaw Annuity Roll. 1878. Arranged alphabetically by county, thereafter alphabetically by surname. List of persons registered in Masholatubby District for Chickasaw Annuity of 1878 resulting from thc Leased District claim. Contains unidentified number; name; number of men, women, and children; and total number in family.

Chickasaw Census Roll. 1890. Arranged by county, thereafter unarranged. Census rolls of Pickens and Pontotoc counties, Chickasaw Nation. Contains names of heads of families; indication of wives; post office address; age of head of family; number of male and female children; Chickasaw or Choctaw by blood or marriage; whether a U.S. Citizen, State Negro (former Indian-owned slave, no Indian blood), Indian Negro (former slave, with mixed blood), or ''Intruder;'' and total number in family.

Chickasaw Payroll. 1893. One list is arranged consecutively by family groups. Another list is arranged alphabetically by surname. Payroll of individuals in Chickasaw Nation. Includes Maytubby's Roll of 1893 and Iishatubby's Roll of 1893. Information given includes family number, names, ages, number in family, and checkmark for payment. Notations include Dawes card number, dead, full payment, and dates.

Chickasaw Census. 1896. List of Chickasaws in the Chickasaw Nation and those residing in Choctaw Nation. Contains names of heads of family (both parents) and children, ages, sex, whether Chickasaw by blood or intermarriage, date of intermarriage, and remarks. Remarks consist primarily of ''married to. . . .''

Chickasaw Census Index. 1897. Arranged alphabetically by individual's surname, thereafter by county. Contains name and page number in census roll.

Chickasaw Census. 1897. Arranged alphabetically by county, numerically by district in Choctaw Nation. List of Chickasaws registered within Chickasaw and Choctaw Nations. Separate lists for intermarried whites and doubtful citizens within each county. List of names from 1893 Chickasaw roll but not on the 1896 Chickasaw roll. Contains name and census card number.

Census and Citizenship Records. Documents Concerning Census, 1896; Letters and Documents Concerning Citizenship, 1861–1907; 1818 Census; 1890 Census of Pickens County and Tishomingo County; Choctaws in the Chickasaw Nation, 1896; Journals of the Citizenship Committee and Court of Claims, 1889–1895; Proceedings of Investigation Committee, 1893; Records of the Chickasaw Commission, 1896; Dawes Commission Citizenship Cases, 1896–1904; Incompetent Record and List of Original Claimants, 1839–1890; Journal of the Commission on Incompetent Funds, 1889–1890; Incompetent Fund Records, 1889–1890; Evidence Book, 1889–1890; Competent and Incompetent Roll; Chickasaw Per Capita, 1889–1890.

Records of the Executive Department, Senate, and House of Representatives. Constitutions, Acts, and Laws, 1848–1901; Senate Journals, 1860–1902; House of Representatives, 1866–1894; Journals of the House of Representatives, 1894–1909; Lists of National, District, and County Officers, 1856–1905; Official and Unofficial Papers of the Executive Department; Chickasaw Tribal Officers, Cyrus Harris and D. H. Johnston, 1856–1936.

Court Records. Panola County, 1878–1894; Pickens and Wichita Counties, 1849–1881; Pickins County, 1864–1906; Pontotoc County, 1884–1904; District Court, unidentified county, 1891–1892; Tishimingo County, 1866–1906; Supreme Court records, District Court records, Reports and Other Records of the Attorneys General of the Indian Nations, 1856–1907.

School Records. Reports and Minutes of the School Committee, 1872–1905; Attendance and Financial Records, 1890–1902; Letters and Documents Concerning Academies, 1867–1928.

Permit Records. Permits to Non-Citizens, 1868–1897; Taxes, Permits to Non-Citizens, 1874–1906;

Chickasaw Permits, 1878–1904; Traders, 1889–1902; Doctors, 1894–1902.

Financial Records. National Treasurer and Auditor, 1858–1902; Financial Records of the National Treasurer and Auditor, 1884–1898.

Land Use and Revenue. Taxes, Special National Agent, Land, Agricultural Leases, Cattle, Hay, Timber, Minerals, Roads, Railroads, Ferries, Telephones, and Townsites, 1878–1909.

Letters Sent from and Received by Tribe and Other Documents. 1873–1919.

Records of the Creek Nation

The Creek Nation in the Indian Territory was composed of the Upper and Lower Creek divisions which were not fully united until 1867 when the Muskogee Nation was established with a written constitution and code of laws which remained in force until 1906. Under the constitution a principal chief and a second chief were elected by popular vote every four years. The legislature, called the National Council, consisted of the House of Kings and the House of Warriors. These bodies met each year in regular session at the national capital. The judicial system included a Supreme Court and courts for each of the nation's six districts. The districts were Coweta, Muskogee (originally called Arkansas District), Eufaula, Wewoka, Deep Fork, and Okmulgee.

There was considerable opposition to allotment in severalty among the Creeks, and an agreement concluded with the Dawes Commission on September 27, 1897, was opposed by the chief and rejected by the National Council. This agreement was amended and in 1897 became Section 30 of the Curtis Act. A further agreement was reached providing for the allotment of 160 acres to every tribal member, including freedmen, and for the dissolution of the tribal government on or before March 4, 1906.

Records consist of:

Creek Old Settlers Roll, 1857. Arranged by town and thereunder by family group. Contains the name of the head of each household and the names of the other members, the amount each received, the total amount paid to the family, and the payee's mark.

Creek Payrolls, 1858–1859. Arranged by town and thereunder by family. Contains the name of the head of the family and the names of the other family members, the amount each received, and some remarks.

Creek Payroll. 1867. Arranged by town and thereunder by family group. Contains payee's name, amount received, and mark.

Index to Creek Freedmen. 1869. Arranged alphabetically by surname. The index provides a page reference to an unidentified volume. The page numbers do not match the copy of the Dunn Roll of 1869.

Payroll of Creek Freedmen and Index. (Dunn Roll) 1869. Arranged by district. Index is arranged alphabetically by given name. The payroll contains the payee's name, amount received, and mark. The index contains the payee's roll number.

Creek Census. 1890. Arranged by town and thereunder by family group. Census rolls of the following towns compiled during 1890: Arbeka (Deep Fork), Arkansas (doubtful), Kialachee, Arbeka (doubtful), Northfork (colored, or "freedmen"), Tuckabache (partial census); typed lists for Arbeka, Alabama, Cussetah, Coweta, North Fork (colored), Concharty, Hutcherchuppa, Tucabache, Cussetah, Thlopthlocco, Tuckabatchee, Weogufke. The rolls contain only an individual's name and, in a few cases, an amount of money to be received (presumably in 1891).

Annuity Roll. 1891. Arranged alphabetically by town and thereunder by family group. Receipt roll for a per capita payment in 1891. Contains payee's name, amount received, mark, signature of witnesses, and date of payment. The roll has been annotated with Dawes enrollment card numbers.

Supplemental Annuity Roll. Arranged alphabetically by town and thereunder by family group. Contains payee's name, amount received, mark, names of witnesses, and date of payment. The roll has been annotated with Dawes enrollment card numbers.

Creek Census Roll (Omitted Roll). 1891. Arranged roughly alphabetically by town and thereunder by family group. The roll contains an individual's name, roll number, and the notation "O" for omitted and "NB" for newborn.

Creek Census Roll. 1891. Arranged by town. A manuscript list of "Citizens Not Enrolled and Their Respective Towns" which was apparently prepared by the clerk of the Special Committee of the National Council which was established to identify individuals who did not participate in the 1891 per capita payment and children born after April 3, 1891. The roll contains an individual's name, the notation "Omitted" or "Newborn," and occasionally remarks about actions of the Special Committee.

Creek Census. 1893. Arranged by family group. A manuscript of individuals who apparently were not citizens of the Creek Nation but were living there. The list, which was made on a printed form titled "Census of the Non-Citizens of the Muskogee Nation Under Act of Council, 6 Nov. 1893," is incomplete.

Creek Census. 1895. Arranged by town. Manuscript census rolls submitted by the Special Committee on Census Rolls to the National Council for approval between May 31 and June 6, 1895. There are rolls for the following towns: Alabama, Arbeka (Deep Fork), Arkansas (colored), Artussee, Big Spring, Canadian (colored), Coweta, Cussehta, Conchart, Euchee, Eufaula (Canadian), Eufaula (Deep Fork), Fish Pond, Greenleaf, Hickory Ground, Hillabee (Canadian), Hitchitte, Hutchechuppa, Kechapataka, Kialigee, Little River Tulsa, Lochapoka, North Fork (colored), Okchiye, Okfuskee (Deep Fork), Okfusky (Canadian), Osoche, Pukken Tallehassee, Quassarte #1 and #2, Thlewaithle, Thlopthlocco, Tokpofke, Tuckabache, Tullahassochee, Tulmochussee, Tulsa (Canadian), Tulwathlocco, Tuskegee, Weogufkee, Wewoka (Doubtful).

Creek Census. 1895. Arranged by town. A manuscript census roll of Creek citizens. The roll contains an individual's name and roll number. The roll has been annotated with card numbers of Dawes enrollment cards.

Creek Census. (Supplemental Roll). 1895. Arranged by town. A list of persons who were omitted from the 1895 payroll and "newborns." The list was apparently prepared by the Special Committee of the National Council. The roll contains an individual's name, the name of the individual's mother and her 1895 roll number, and the designation "Newborn" or "Omitted."

Creek Census. (Omitted Roll). 1895. Arranged by town. List of individuals who were omitted from the 1895 payroll and "newborns" which was submitted to the National Council by the Special Committee on Census Rolls on December 4, 1895. The roll contains an individual's name, the name of the individual's mother and father, 1895 census roll number, and the designation "Newborn" or "Omitted." The roll numbers in these rolls match the roll numbers in the Supplemental Roll.

Creek Payrolls. 1895. Arranged by town. Payrolls for a per capita payment. The payment was based on the 1895 census. There are payrolls for the following towns: Alabama, Arbeka (Deep Fork), Arbekochee, Arkansas, Artussee, Big Springs, Broken Arrow, Canadian (colored), Cheyaha, Coweta, Cussehta, Conchart, Euchee, Eufaula (Deep Fork), Hitchitte, Hutchechuppa, Kechapataka, Kialigee, Lochapoka, North Fork (colored), Nutaka, Okchiye, Okfuskee (Canadian), Okfuskee (Deep Fork), Osoche, Pukken, Tallehassee, Quassarte #1 and #2, Thlewaithle, Thlopthlocco, Tokpafka, Tuckabatchee, Tuladegee, Tallahassoche, Tulmochussee, Tulwathlocco, Tuskegee, Weogufkee, Wewoka. The roll contains each payee's name, amount received, signature of payee and witnesses, and date of payment. The roll has been annotated with field numbers of Dawes enrollment cards and card numbers of the "old series" of Dawes enrollment cards.

Colbert Census Roll of Creek Nation, 1896. Arranged by town. Census rolls submitted by the Special Committee on Census Rolls to the National Council. There are rolls for the following towns: Arbeka (North Fork), Arbekochee, Arkansas (colored), Artussee, Big Spring, Canadian (colored), Concharty, Cussehta, Euchee, Eufaula (Canadian), Eufaula (Deep Fork), Fish Pond, Greenleaf, Hickory Ground, Kialigee, Little River Tulsa, Nuyaka, Okchiye, Okfuskee (Deep Forks), Osoche, Pakkon Tallahasse, Quassarte #1 and #2, Tallahassoche, Thlewaithle, Thlopthlocco, Tokpafka, Tuckabache, Tulladegee, Tuskegee, Weogufke, Wewoka.

Citizenship Commission Docket Book, 1895. Arranged by case number and includes an alphabetical index.

Census and Citizenship Records. Letters and documents concerning census, 1832–1900; Okmulgee District, enrollment of Shawnee Indians, undated; Census of Non-Citizens, undated; Creek Reservations under the treaty of March 24, 1832, entries 1–2000; Pension list, Muskogee Nation, 1872–1873; 1892 Census Roll, Arkansas District; Census of the town of Wagoner, 1894; List of non-citizen cattlemen and roll of Shawnee Indians, Deep Fork District, 1897; Letters and documents concerning citizenship, 1874–1910; Permit lists and citizenship records, 1880–1906; Permit lists; Citizenship applications; Creek freedmen; Creek per capita payments, 1869–1904; Letters and documents pertaining to per capita payments, 1870–1888; List of Civil War officers and record of issues to indigent refugee Creeks in the Chickasaw Nation, 1862–1865; Annuity Payroll of Creeks who were orphans in 1832 or their heirs, 1883–1889.

Records of the Creek National Council, House of Kings and House of Warriors. Journal of the House of Warriors, 1868–1903; Journal of the House of Kings, 1882–1895; Records of the General Council, Creek Agency, 1861–1862; Acts and resolutions of the National Council, 1873–1892; Appropriation acts of the National Council, 1895–1899; Constitution and laws; Undated and Creek miscellaneous documents, 1883–1909.

Supreme Court Records. 1870–1897; Court record book, 1884–1898; Records and documents, 1868–1899; U.S. Courts, 1871–1909; North Fork, Deep Fork, and Arkansas District Courts, 1874.

District Court Records. Arkansas District Courts, 1870–1895; Muskogee District Courts, 1876–1898; Coweta District Courts, 1877–1895; Deep Fork District Courts, 1872–1896; Eufaula District Courts, 1882–1898; North Fork District Courts, 1868–1873; Okmulgee District Courts, 1884–1898; Wewoka District Courts, 1871–1897.

Executive Office Records. Correspondence and records of the Principal Chiefs, 1878–1914.

Records of the Seminole Nation

Seminole Payment and Census rolls, 1868, 1895–1897. Arranged by band and thereunder by family. Gives payee's name and annotated with Dawes enrollment card number.

Seminole Payment Rolls. 1895–1896. Arranged by band and thereunder by family group. The roll contains each payee's name and amounts of money listed under columns labeled ''Wewoka,'' ''Sasakwa,'' and Balance. Wewoka was the capital of the Seminole Nation and Sasakwa was the place of business of the principal chief.

Seminole Payment Rolls. 1895–1897. Arranged by band and thereunder by family group. Copies of an 1895 and 1897 ''Head Right'' (referring to the family group, and the right to the payment that the family has for residing there) payment roll. The 1897 payment roll is not an exact copy but contains most of the same names and amounts as the 1895 roll.

National Council, Federal Relations and Per Capita. Laws and Acts of the National Council, 1886–1905; Federal Relations, 1900; Per Capita Payments, 1898–1907; Seminole Miscellaneous Papers.

Financial and School Records. Financial Records, 1893–1907; Miscellaneous Documents, 1866–1923; School Financial Records, 1906.

Mekusukey Academy 1910–1929. Student Applications, Rosters, Progress Cards, Letters Sent and Received by the Superintendent, Medical, and other records.

Part II
Directory of Genealogical Information

Libraries & Archives

Private & Public Organizations

Print Resources

Other Media

Libraries and Archives

This chapter lists libraries, archives, and repositories both within and outside the United States which hold materials relevant to genealogists whether their focus is on genealogy in general or on a specific ethnic group. A description of special collections and services available to users may be provided for each institution. Federal institutions and those private and public institutions whose name implies a national focus appear first, followed by state institutions with a regional focus which may also have a national focus. Institutions which either have an international focus or are located outside of the United States, if present, appear at the end of the chapter. All institutions are listed alphabetically within each category.

National and Regional

American Baptist Historical Society Archives

Box 851
Valley Forge, PA 19482-0851
Phone: (215)768-2378
Beverly Carson, Administrator/Archivist

Special collections: Historical records of Board of National Ministries, Board of International Ministries, Board of Educational Ministries, Ministers and Missionary Benefit Board, Office of General Secretary.

American Congregational Association Congregational Library

14 Beacon St.
Boston, MA 02108
Phone: (617)523-0470
Fax: (617)523-0491
Rev. Dr. Harold F. Worthley, Librarian

Staff: Prof 2; Other 3. **Description:** Contains town histories, local church histories, and church records. **Founded:** 1853. **Holdings:** 125,000 books; 100,000 pamphlets and periodicals. **Subscriptions:** 80 journals and other serials. **Services:** Interlibrary loan; copying; direct mail service available to individuals in the U.S.; library open to the public.

American Family Records Association Library

PO Box 15505
Kansas City, MO 64106
Phone: (816)252-0950
Fax: (816)252-0950

Founded: 1985. **Subjects:** Genealogy, history, adoptive relationships. **Special collections:** Genealogy circulating collection. **Holdings:** 3000 volumes. **Services:** Interlibrary loan; library open to the public. **Remarks:** Association promotes preservation of and access to public and private genealogical records. Collection is located in the North Independence Branch of Mid-Continent Public Library, Independence, MO. **Publications:** *Genealogy from the Heartland*, 1992.

Bethel College Mennonite Library and Archives

300 E. 27th
North Newton, KS 67117-9989
Phone: (316)283-2500
Fax: (316)284-5286

TF Professional 2; Other 2. **Founded:** 1935. **Subjects:** Anabaptists; Mennonites in Europe, America, Latin America, and Asia; peace; Kansas. **Special collections:** Manuscript collection (1500 shelf feet); General Conference Church Archives (2000 shelf feet); oral history of World War I and II conscientious objectors; rare Anabaptist books; H.R. Voth Manuscript and Photograph Collection on Hopi Indians; Rodolphe Petter manuscript collection on Cheyenne Indians. **Holdings:** 25,300 books; 3200 bound periodical volumes; 1000 reels of microfilm; 1000 audiotapes; 150 maps. **Subscriptions:** 300 journals and other serials; 80 newspapers. **Services:** Interlibrary loan; copying; library open to the public. **Computerized services:** OCLC; internal database. **Publications:** *Mennonite Life,* quarterly; *Guide to Mennonite Library and Archives*, 1981.

Church of Jesus Christ of Latter-day Saints Family History Library

35 N. West Temple
Salt Lake City, UT 84150
Phone: (801)240-2331
Fax: (801)240-5551
Stephen Kendall, Director

Staff: Professional 120; Other 98. **Founded:** 1894. **Subjects:** Genealogy, family history, church and civil records, local history. **Special collections:** Family Group Records Collection (8 million family reconstitution forms from the U.S. and other countries); oral genealogy tapes; international collection of manuscripts identifying individuals in historic populations (microfilm); military rosters; baptismal records; wills; civil registration records; notarial collections; International Genealogical Index (over 200 million names; microfiche, CD-ROM); U.S. census from 1790-1920. **Holdings:** 240,000 volumes; 3000 bound periodical volumes; 1.8 million reels of microfilm; 350,000 microfiche. **Subscriptions:** 135 journals and other serials. **Services:** Copying; orientation film; research classes; center open to the public. **Computerized services:** Produces Family Search CD-ROM. **Special catalogs:** Family History Catalog (COM & CD-ROM); Catálogo de Pasajeros a Indias (microfilm). **Remarks:** Branch family history centers (over 2000 in 60 countries) having access to most films are added to the system on a continuing basis. Largest collection of Hispanic genealogical materials in the world. **Publications:** *Genealogical Research Papers*, irregular; *News of the Family History Library*—to genealogical societies; Personal Ancestral File (genealogical software); see also Ancestral File, International Genealogical Index, Social Security Death Index and Military Index, Family History Library Catalog, and Family Search in "Other Media."

Daughters of the American Revolution National Society Library

1776 D St. NW
Washington, DC 20006-5392
Phone: (202)879-3229
Fax: (202)879-3252
Eric G. Grundset, Library Director

Staff: Professional 6; Other 12. **Founded:** 1896. **Subjects:** Genealogy, U.S. local history, U.S. history, American Indian history, American women's history. **Special collections:** Genealogies; United States, state, county, local histories; published rosters of Revolutionary War soldiers; published vital records; cemetery inscriptions; Bible records; transcripts of various county records (such as wills), compiled by the Genealogical Records Committees of DAR; published archives of some of the thirteen original states; abstracts of some Revolutionary War pension files; American Indian history, genealogy, culture; U.S. City Directory Collection, 20th century. **Holdings:** 120,000 books; 12,000 bound periodical volumes; 250,000 files of manuscript material, genealogical records, pamphlets. **Subscriptions:** 650 journals and other serials. **Services:** Copying; library open to the public on a fee basis. **Special catalogs:** DAR Library Catalog, volume 1: Family Histories and Genealogies, 1982; supplement to volume 1, 1984; volume 2: State and Local Histories and Records, 1986; volume 3: Acquisitions 1985-1991, 1991. **Publications:** *Continental Columns* (newsletter).

Department of the Army U.S. Army Military History Institute

Carlisle Barracks
Carlisle, PA 17013-5008

Remarks: Accepts and provides information on nearly all military units involved in the history of the United States.

Thomas Gilcrease Institute of American History and Art Library

1400 Gilcrease Museum Rd.
Tulsa, OK 74127
Phone: (918)596-2700
Fax: (918)596-2770
Sarah Erwin, Curator, Archival Collections

Staff: Professional 1. **Founded:** 1955. **Subjects:** History—Colonial, Western, Spanish Southwest, Indian. **Special collections:** Hispanic documents, 1500-1800; John Ross papers (Chief of Cherokees); Peter P. Pitchlynn papers (Chief of Choctaws); Grant Foreman Collection. **Holdings:** 50,000 books; 50 VF drawers of historic photographs and manuscripts; broadsides; maps; photostats. **Subscriptions:** 10 journals and other serials. **Services:** Copying (limited); library open to the public by appointment. **Special catalogs:** Gilcrease-Hargrett Catalog; Hispanic Documents Catalog (out of print); Guidebook to Manuscripts (out of print).

Huntington Free Library National Museum of the American Indian Library

9 Westchester Sq.
Bronx, NY 10461
Phone: (212)829-7770
Mary B. Davis, Librarian

Staff: Professional 1; Other 3. **Founded:** 1930. **Subjects:** Archeology and ethnology of Indians of the Western Hemisphere; linguistics; anthropology; history; current affairs. **Special collections:** American Indian newspapers; Cherokee nation rolls; U.S. Department of Interior records; extensive biographical file. **Holdings:** 40,000 volumes; 140 VF drawers; 50 manuscripts. **Subscriptions:** 250 journals and other serials; 50 Indian newspapers. **Services:** Copying; library open to the public by appointment. **Remarks:** Museum also maintains archives.

Indian Action Council Library

PO Box 1287
Eureka, CA 95502-1287

Library of Congress American Folklife Center

Thomas Jefferson Bldg.
Washington, DC 20540-8100
Phone: (202)707-6590
Alan Jabbour, Director

Staff: Prof. 13; Other 5. **Founded:** 1976. **Subjects:** American folklife with emphasis on research, public programs, and technical assistance; folksong; folk music; folklife; ethnomusicology; oral history. **Special collections:** Archive of Folk Culture. **Holdings:** 4000 books; 1300 serial titles; 40,000 hours of unpublished field recordings; manuscript collection (600,000 pages); results of current research projects including fieldnotes, sound recordings, photographs, and videotapes; 200,000 ephemera; 170,000 photographs. **Services:** Copying (limited); reading room open to the public; listening by appointment; correspondence and telephone inquiries. **Computerized services:** Computerized public access catalog, internal databases. **Special catalogs:** Catalog of issued LPs/cassettes (pamphlet); catalog of recorded collections (card); catalog of individual titles on some recordings (card); catalog of manuscript and microform collections (card). **Remarks:** Publishes *Folklife Center News,* quarterly; mailing list composed of folklife organizations, institutions, and individuals—additions made upon request; *Folklife Sourcebook: A Directory of Folklife and Fieldwork* (English and Spanish editions); *American Folk*

Music and Folklore Recordings: A Selected List; LC recordings of folk music and lore; 200 reference and finding aids—available upon request; Federal Cyclinder Project Catalogs; list of publications—available upon request.

Library of Congress Humanities and Social Sciences Division Local History and Genealogy Section

Thomas Jefferson Bldg., Rm. G20
Washington, DC 20540-5554
Phone: (202)707-5537
Judith P. Austin, Head

Staff: 9. **Remarks:** The Library of Congress has more than 400,000 volumes of U.S. and European genealogy, heraldry, and U.S. local history, including compiled genealogies, city directories, and published vital statistics, military records, and church registers. The Local History and Genealogy Room has a 10,000 volume reference collection, 40 current periodicals, and several card catalogs, including a 200,000 entry index to biographical histories from 50 states. The section offers its services to persons over high school age. Researchers may be referred to other divisions.

Library of Congress Humanities and Social Sciences Division Microform Reading Room Section

Thomas Jefferson Bldg.
LJ-107
Washington, DC 20540-5550
Phone: (202)707-5522
Fax: (202)707-1957
Robert Costenbader, Head

Staff: 7. **Subjects:** Areas include early state records; early English and American periodicals; American and British black journals; underground newspapers; oral histories; U.S. nondepository documents; copyright records of the U.S. District Courts, 1790-1870; Barbour Collection of Connecticut vital records; State labor reports, 1865-1900; American labor union constitutions and proceedings; English books to 1700; Western Americana; pre-1900 Canadiana; manuscripts of American interest filmed by the American Council of Learned Societies; archives of the Japanese Ministry of the Foreign Affairs and other ministries, 1868-1945; translations from Mainland China, Japan, Indonesia; Schomburg clipping file on black history; Spanish Civil War pamphlets. **Holdings:** 5.5 million reels and strips of microfilm, microfiche, and micro-opaques. **Services:** Reading room is open to persons above high school age. **Remarks:** A guide to selected microform sets is available on request; see the *Guide to the American Indian Doctoral Dissertations* and *Inventory to the National Indian Collection of Indian Manuscripts.*

Library of Congress Manuscript Division

James Madison Memorial Bldg., LM 101-102
101 Independence Ave., SE
Washington, DC 20540
Phone: (202)707-5383
James H. Hutson, Chief

Subjects: Collections of the papers of most of the presidents, from George Washington through Calvin Coolidge, other political, military, scientific, and literary leaders, and records of numerous enterprises and institutions, totaling more than 45 million pieces. Among them: National Association for the Advancement of Colored People, American Colonization Society, National American Woman Suffrage Association, National Urban League, Kraus Collection (Latin America), Harkness Collection (Mexico and Peru), WPA collection (Federal Writer's Project and Historical Records Survey, which includes transcripts of laws relating to slaves, notices and records of slave sales, newspaper advertisements of slave auctions and runaways, tax enumerations on slaves, and records of slave transfer and manumission). **Services:** Reading room is open to adults and high school students with a letter of introduction from faculty advisors.

Library of Congress Prints & Photographs Division

James Madison Memorial Bldg., LM 339
Washington, DC 20540
Phone: (202)707-5836
Fax: (202)707-5844
Stephen Edward Ostrow, Chief

Staff: Prof. 22; Other 8. **Founded:** 1897. **Subjects:** Architecture, design, engineering, popular and applied graphic art, documentary photographs, fine prints, master photographs, postures. **Special collections:** Civil War drawings by Edwin Forbes, A.R. Waud, and others (originals); Mathew B. Brady and the Brady-Handy Collection (Civil War, portraits, the American scene); the Carnegie Survey of the Architecture of the South, Archive of Hispanic Culture (photographs of Latin American art and architecture); Detroit Publishing Company archives, 1898-1914; collection of slave photographs. **Holdings:** 190,000 prints and drawings; 80,000 posters, 12 million photographic prints and negatives, daguerreotypes, slides; 1.8 million architectural drawings and related materials; 50,000 images on video disc. **Services:** Photoduplication; open to the public. **Computerized services:** Multiple Use MARC System (MUMS), SCORPIO. **Remarks:** The division houses 15 million images other than painting and sculpture.

National Archives National Archives and Records Administration

8th & Constitution Ave. NW
Washington, DC 20408
Phone: (202)501-5400
Fax: (202)501-5005
Dr. Trudy Huskamp Peterson, Acting Archv.

Staff: 625. **Founded:** 1934. **Subjects:** United States history, archives and manuscripts, genealogical research, government publications, U.S. politics and government. **Special collections:** Printed Archives of the Federal Government (GPO Collection); Gift Collection; Polar Archives. **Holdings:** 1.64 million cubic feet of textual cartographic, audiovisual, and machine readable records, 1774 to present; 4 billion documents; 235,000 reels of microfilm; 170,000 reels of motion picture film; 180,000 sound recordings; 7 million still pictures; 2 million maps and charts; 9 million aerial photographs; 6000 magnetic computer electronic data sets. **Subscriptions:** 700 journals and other serials. **Services:** Copying; archives open to public. **Special indexes:** List of special indexes available on request. **Publications:** List of publications available on request.

National Archives—Alaska Region National Archives and Records Administration

654 W 3rd Ave.
Rm. 012
Anchorage, AK 99501
Phone: (907)271-2441
(907)271-2443
Fax: (907)271-2443
Thomas E. Wiltsey, Director

Staff: Prof 4. **Founded:** 1991. **Subjects:** U.S. District Courts, Bureau of Indian Affairs, Alaska Road Commission, Bureau of

Land Management, U.S. Customs Service, Military. **Special collections:** Records of federal agencies in Alaska. **Holdings:** 9000 cubic feet of archival items; 5000 sheets of microfiche; 65,000 reels of microfilm. **Subscriptions:** 6 journals and other serials. **Services:** Copying; library open to public. **Publications:** Finding aids, inventories, guides to records and film holdings.

National Archives and Records Administration General Reference Branch

7th and Pennsylvania Ave NW
Washington, DC 20408
Phone: (202)501-5170

Description: Maintains pension application files, based on Federal service before World War I; bounty-land warrant application files based on Federal service before 1856; and military service records based on service in the United States Army (officers who served before June 30, 1917, enlisted men who served before October 31, 1912), Navy (officers serving before 1903, enlisted men serving before 1886), Marine Corps (officers serving before 1896 and enlisted men serving before 1905), and Confederate Armed Forces (1861-1865) as well as persons who served in regular forces raised by the federal government, volunteers fighting in various wars from the Revolutionary War through the Philippine Insurrection (1775-1902). **Services:** Upon receipt of a National Archives Trust Fund Form (NATF) 80, Order for Copies of Veterans Records, will copy complete compiled military service or bounty-land application files or any documents in the pension files containing genealogical information. Pension application files contain the most complete information regarding a military career and should be requested first. **Remarks:** Once file is located, notice of fee charged for copying is sent.

National Archives and Records Administration Washington National Records Center

4205 Suitland Rd., Rm. 121
Suitland, MD 20746
Phone: (301)763-7000
Ferris E. Stovel, Director

Staff: Professional 125. **Founded:** 1968. **Subjects:** Records of U.S. Government agencies in the District of Columbia, Maryland, Virginia, West Virginia; records of the United States Army, Air Force, and Navy worldwide. **Holdings:** 3.2 million cubic feet of records. **Subscriptions:** 15 journals and other serials. **Services:** Access to information is obtained by contacting the Federal agency that created the records. **Computerized services:** Internal databases. Performs searches free of charge. Contact Person: Andrew Jones.

National Archives—Central Plains Region National Archives and Records Administration

2312 E Bannister Rd.
Kansas City, MO 64131
Phone: (816)926-6272
Fax: (816)926-6982
Diana L. Duff, Director
Mark A. Corriston, Assistant Director

Staff: Prof 5; Other 7. **Founded:** 1968. **Subjects:** Noncurrent administrative and program records of historical and informational value accessioned from Federal Agencies in the states of Iowa, Nebraska, Kansas, Missouri, and North and South Dakota. **Special collections:** Pre-1900 records from the Bureau of Customs, Geological Survey, Internal Revenue Service, Forest Service, U.S. Coast Guard, U.S. Attorneys and Marshals, Weather Bureau, U.S. Army Engineers, Bureau of Indian Affairs Reservations (located in the present states of North and South Dakota, Minnesota, Nebraska, and Kansas, 1850-1965), U.S. District and Territorial Courts, 1824-1965. **Holdings:** 30,000 cubic feet of records. **Services:** Copying, reference service; reading and research rooms open to the public. **Computerized services:** Archival Information Service (internal database). **Special catalogs:** Inhouse archives inventories and shelf lists. **Publications:** *Guide to Research in the Central Plains Region,* book.

National Archives—Great Lakes Region National Archives and Records Administration

7358 S Pulaski Rd.
Chicago, IL 60629
Phone: (312)581-7816
Peter W. Bunce, Director

Staff: Prof 4; Other 6. **Founded:** 1969. **Subjects:** Federal Government records for Illinois, Wisconsin, Michigan, Indiana, Ohio, and Minnesota. **Special collections:** Judicial Branch records—U.S. Circuit and District Courts, 1870-1974; U.S. Circuit Court of Appeals, 6th and 7th Circuits, 1891-1965; Executive Branch records of various civilian and military agencies, 1800-1987. **Holdings:** 60,140 cubic feet of records, 50,000 reels of microfilm. **Services:** Copying; genealogy workshops; professional workshops; exhibit program; archives open to public with restrictions. **Computerized services:** NARS A-1 (internal database). **Publications:** *Guide to Records in the National Archives—Great Lakes Region, Microfilm Publications in the National Archives—Great Lakes Region.*

National Archives—Mid-Atlantic Region National Archives and Records Administration

9th & Market Sts., Rm. 1350
Philadelphia, PA 19107
Phone: (215)597-3000
Fax: (215)597-2303
Robert J. Plowman, Director
Joseph J. Sheehan, Assistant Director

Staff: Prof 7. **Founded:** 1969. **Subjects:** Archives and records of federal agencies located in Pennsylvania, Delaware, Maryland, Virginia, and West Virginia. **Special collections:** Records of U.S. District Court, U.S. Court of Appeals for 3rd and 4th Circuit, U.S. Corps of Engineers, Bureau of Census, National Park Service, Bureau of Mines, U.S. Attorneys and Marshals, Bureau of Customs. **Holdings:** 42,000 cubic feet of federal government archives; 27,500 reels of microfilm. **Subscriptions:** 25 journals and other serials. **Services:** Copying; branch open to public with restrictions, dependent on agency regulations. **Special catalogs:** List of microfilm holdings; list of textual record holdings. **Publications:** *Branch News,* biennial.

National Archives—New England Region National Archives and Records Administration

380 Trapelo Rd.
Waltham, MA 02154
Phone: (617)647-8100
James K. Owens, Director

Staff: Prof 3; Other 3. **Founded:** 1969. **Subjects:** Noncurrent permanent federal government records for agencies located in Connecticut, Maine, Massachusetts, New Hampshire, Rhode Island, and Vermont. **Holdings:** 23,000 cubic feet of records of federal agencies in New England, 1789-1977: U.S. District and

Circuit Courts, U.S. Court of Appeals, customs and Coast Guard activities, Life Saving Service Stations Logs, Naval Shore Establishments including Boston and Portsmouth, NH naval shipyards, Bureau of Public Roads, U.S. Army Corps of Engineers, War Manpower Commission (World War II); Office of Scientific Research and Development (Harvard/MIT Labs); 65,000 reels of microfilm of National Archives publications; U.S. Census reports, 1790-1910 on microfilm. **Subscriptions:** 12 journals and other serials. **Services:** Copying; branch open to the public. **Computerized services:** National Archives—Archival Information System (internal database). **Publications:** *Guide to Records in the National Archives—New England Region, Microfilm Publications in the National Archives—New England Region,* and *Sources for Family History in the National Archives—New England Region,* (leaflet).

National Archives—Northeast Region National Archives and Records Administration

201 Varick St.
New York, NY 10014
Phone: (212)337-1300
Fax: (212)337-1306
Robert C. Morris, Director

Staff: Professional 5; Other 5. **Founded:** 1970. **Subjects:** Permanently valuable records of federal agencies in New York State, New Jersey, Puerto Rico, and the Virgin Islands, 1790-1978. **Holdings:** 62,000 cubic feet of archival materials; 42,000 reels of National Archives microfilm. **Services:** Copying; branch open to the public for research. **Computerized services:** NARS-5, NARS-A1 (internal databases).

National Archives—Pacific Northwest Region National Archives and Records Administration

6125 Sand Point Way NE
Seattle, WA 98115
Phone: (206)526-6507
(206)526-6347
Phillip E. Lothyan, Director

Staff: 7. **Founded:** 1969. **Subjects:** Historical records of federal agencies for Montana, Idaho, Oregon, and Washington; Bureau of Customs; Bureau of Land Management; Bureau of Indian Affairs; U.S. Army Corps of Engineers; U.S. District Courts; Bonneville Power Administration. **Special collections:** Census records for all states and territories, 1790-1920. **Holdings:** 30,000 cubic feet of records; 60,000 reels of microfilm. **Services:** Copying; branch open to public with restrictions. **Computerized services:** InterNet (electronic mail service). **Remarks:** Electronic Mail address: YGO@CU.NIH.GOV (InterNet). **Publications:** Guide, 1988; Preliminary Inventories; Special Lists; Research Opportunities at the National Archives—Seattle Branch, 1985.

National Archives—Pacific Sierra Region National Archives and Records Administration

1000 Commodore Dr.
San Bruno, CA 94066
Phone: (415)876-9009
Fax: (415)876-9233
Waverly B. Lowell, Director

Staff: Professional 5; Other 6. **Founded:** 1969. **Subjects:** Archival records of the Federal Government in Nevada (except Clark County), Northern California, Hawaii, the Pacific Ocean areas. **Special collections:** Records of the Government of American Samoa; records of the Bureau of Indian Affairs, California and Nevada; Chinese immigration records; records of Federal district courts in Northern California, Hawaii, and Nevada, and of the U.S. Courts of Appeals for the Ninth Circuit; records relating to migratory labor. **Holdings:** 41,000 cubic feet of original records; 31,000 reels of microfilm. **Subscriptions:** 6 journals and other serials. **Services:** Copying; branch open to the public. **Computerized services:** Chinese Immigration to Hawaii, 1898-1947 (internal database). **Special indexes:** Admiralty case files of the U.S. District Court for the Northern District California, 1850-1990 (microfilm). **Publications:** *Guide to Records in the National Archives, Pacific Sierra Region*; *Microfilm Publications Concerning Spanish Private Land Grant Claims*; reference information papers on Federal records relating to ethnic groups; reference information paper on records of Federal district and appellate courts.

National Archives—Pacific Southwest Region National Archives and Records Administration

24000 Avila Rd.
Box 6719
Laguna Niguel, CA 92607-6719
Phone: (714)643-4241
(714)643-4242
Fax: (714)643-4832
Diane S. Nixon, Regional Director

Staff: Prof 4; Other 6. **Founded:** 1969. **Subjects:** Inactive and noncurrent Federal Government records for Arizona, southern California, and Clark County, Nevada. **Special collections:** National Archives microfilm publications of national significance; records of Bureau of Indian Affairs, Bureau of Customs, U.S. Navy, U.S. District Court. **Holdings:** 22,000 cubic feet of original records. **Services:** Copying; branch open to public with restrictions. **Publications:** *Guide to the National Archives—Pacific Southwest Region.*

National Archives—Rocky Mountain Region National Archives and Records Administration

Denver Federal Center
Bldg. 48
Denver, CO 80225
Phone: (303)236-0817
Fax: (303)236-9354
Joel Barker, Director

Staff: Prof 3; Other 4. **Founded:** 1969. **Subjects:** Archival records of the federal government for Colorado, Montana, Arizona, New Mexico, North and South Dakota, Utah, and Wyoming. **Special collections:** Records of 60 federal agencies, including the U.S. District Courts, Bureau of Indian Affairs. **Holdings:** 23,000 cubic feet of archives; 60,000 reels of microfilm; census on microfilm. **Services:** Copying; reference service to researchers; branch open to public.

National Archives—Southeast Region National Archives and Records Administration

1557 St. Joseph Ave.
East Point, GA 30344
Phone: (404)763-7477
Fax: (404)763-7815
Gayle P. Peters, Director

Staff: Prof 4; Other 9. **Founded:** 1969. **Subjects:** Historically valuable records, 1716-1978, of the Federal Government from field offices and courts in Alabama, Georgia, Florida, Kentucky, Tennessee, Mississippi, and North and South Carolina. **Special collections:** Selective Service System for the entire United States.

Holdings: 45,000 cubic feet of records; 46,000 reels of microfilm. **Services:** Copying; branch open to the public. **Computerized services:** National Archives A-1 (internal database). **Special catalogs:** Catalog of Federal Court records; shelf list finding aids on material in regional archives and in Records Center. **Publications:** Research Opportunities and list of microfilm available, biennial.

National Archives—Southwest Region National Archives and Records Administration

Ft. Worth Federal Ctr., Bldg. 1
Box 6216
Fort Worth, TX 76115
Phone: (817)334-5525
Kent Carter, Director, Archives Branch

Staff: Professional 3; Other 5. **Founded:** 1969. **Subjects:** Inactive records of U.S. government agencies in Texas, Oklahoma, Arkansas, New Mexico, Louisiana. **Special collections:** U.S. census reports, 1790-1920; index to some Civil War service records; passenger records from various ports; Bureau of Indian Affairs records from the state of Oklahoma. **Holdings:** 65,000 cubic feet of records; 70,000 reels of microfilm. **Services:** Copying; archives open to the public except for restricted records.

National Genealogical Society Library

4527 17th St. N.
Arlington, VA 22207-2399
Phone: (703)525-0050
Fax: (703)525-0052
Dereka Smith, Librarian

Staff: Professional 1; Other 8. **Description:** Individuals are members; libraries and societies are subscribers. Promotes genealogical research; stimulates and fosters preservation and publication of records of genealogical interest including national, state, county, township, city, town, church, cemetery, Bible, and family records. Members list with the society the families in which they are working and on which they can exchange data with one another. **Founded:** 1903. **Subjects:** Genealogy, local history, bibliography, biography. **Special collections:** Manuscript collections of former members. **Holdings:** 23,000 books; 5000 bound periodical volumes; 300 boxes of manuscript materials; 40 VF drawers of documents, clippings, pamphlets; microfilm; microfiche. **Subscriptions:** 20 journals and other serials. **Services:** Copying; library open to the public. Operates speakers bureau and National Genealogy Hall of Fame; bestows awards. **Computerized services:** OCLC. **Publications:** *National Genealogical Society Quarterly*; *National Genealogical Society Newsletter*, bimonthly; 109 special publications, book list revised 1988 with supplements, 1989.

National Museum of the American Indian

Suitland, MD

Description: State-of-the-art collections research center. **Remarks:** Scheduled to open in 1997.

National Personnel Records Center (Military Records) National Archives and Records Administration

9700 Page Ave.
St. Louis, MO 63132-5100
Phone: (314)538-4201
David L. Petree, Director

Staff: 500. **Founded:** 1952. **Subjects:** Service and medical records of persons who have served in the Armed Forces, noncurrent records of organizations which have been a part of the military establishment, personnel and medical records of former federal civilian employees. **Holdings:** 1.8 milion cubic feet of military and personnel records (MPR) and organizational records; 1.9 million cubic feet of civilian personnel records (CPR) and agency organizational records. **Services:** Library not open to the public. Answers written requests for information (Standard Form 180: Request Pertaining to Military Records); for a fee, provides copies. **Remarks:** Maintains and services the records of separated military personnel of the Army (1912 to present), Navy (1885 to present), Air Force (1947 to present), Marine Corps (1905 to present), Coast Guard (1906 to present). The National Personnel Records Center (CPR) maintains and services the personnel and medical records of former civilian employees and is located at 111 Winnebago St., St. Louis, 63118-4199.

Navajo Nation Library System

Drawer K
Window Rock, AZ 86515
Phone: (602)871-6376
Fax: (602)871-7304
Irving Nelson, Manager

Staff: Professional 1; Other 10. **Founded:** 1941. **Subjects:** Navajos, Indians of the Southwest, Indians of North America, archeology, Arizona history. **Special collections:** Navajo History; Native American Research Library; J.L. Correll Collection (30 filing cabinets); *Navajo Times* (80 acid-free boxes). **Holdings:** 22,000 books; 1000 manuscripts; 60 films; 250 tape recordings; microfilm. **Subscriptions:** 80 journals and other serials. **Services:** Interlibrary loan; copying; facsimile services; library open to the public. **Computerized services:** CD-ROM. **Special indexes:** Navajo Times index (tribal newspaper); ONEO Oral History Index. **Remarks:** Maintains two branch libraries in Window Rock, AZ, and one branch library in Navajo, NM.

Presbyterian Church Department of History Library

425 Lombard St.
Philadelphia, PA 19147
Phone: (215)627-1852
Fax: (215)627-0509
Frederick J. Heyser Jr., Director

Staff: Prof 10; Other 10. **Description:** Contains church records and histories. **Founded:** 1852. **Subjects:** American Presbyterian history. **Special collections:** American Indian Missionary Correspondence and Papers (manuscripts and microfilm); American Sunday School Union (manuscripts); Archives of Presbyterian Church and Predecessor Denominations; Board of Foreign Missions (manuscripts and microfilm); Early American and European Imprints, before 1800; Sheldon Jackson Collections, Alaska; Missions; National Council of Church Archives. **Holdings:** 250,000 books; 1875 reels of microfilm; 9000 pictures of churches and ministers; 5000 communion tokens; 21 million arranged archival materials. **Subscriptions:** 407 journals and other serials. **Ser-**

vices: Copying; library open to the public. **Formerly:** Presbyterian Historical Society—Library.

United Methodist Church
General Commission on Archives and History
Libraries and Archives

36 Madison Ave.
Box 127
Madison, NJ 07940

Phone: (201)822-2787
Fax: (201)408-3909
Kenneth E. Rowe, Librarian

Staff: Prof 3; Other 3. **Founded:** 1866. **Subjects:** Church records of Methodist Episcopal Church, Methodist Episcopal Church (South), Methodist Protestant Church, Methodist Church, Evangelical United Brethren Church, United Brethren in Christ Church, Evangelical Church, Evangelical Association, United Evangelical Church; United Methodist Church. **Special collections:** Board of Mission correspondence from missionaries and overseas conference journals; private papers of Methodist leaders and bishops. **Holdings:** 70,000 books; 1600 bound periodical volumes; 4 million archival items; 100,000 feet of microfilm; 100 tubes of blueprints. **Subscriptions:** 600 journals and other serials. **Services:** Interlibrary loan; copying; library open to the public with restrictions. **Computerized services:** OCLC, RLIN, DIALOG Information Services. **Remarks:** Includes the holdings of the Association of Methodist Historical Societies and the former E.U.B. Historical Society.

United States Department of the Interior
Bureau of Land Management

2800 Cottage Way
Sacramento, CA 95825

Description: Holds land grant records which includes genealogical material.

U.S. Department of the Interior
Natural Resources Library

1849 18th St. NW
Washington, DC 20240

Phone: (202)208-5815
Fax: (202)208-5048
Vicki Nozero, Manager/ Librarian

Subjects: Archival materials of the Dept. of Interior; materials which did belong to the Bureau of Indian Affairs. Emphasis on federal government-Indian relations; indexes include names. **Holdings:** Over 600,000 materials. **Services:** Open to the public with restrictions. **Special catalogs:** *Bibliographical and Historical Index of American Indians,* G.K. Hall & Co.: 1966.

Washington National Records Center

4205 Suitland Rd.
Suitland, MD 20746

Phone: (301)763-7000

Remarks: Affiliated with the National Archives, the Washington National Records Center houses records of various government agencies and courts. Most of the records stored at the center are in the legal custody of the agency that created them, and to use them written authorization must be provided before the center will release the records. Usually, the authorization will contain the accession number, center location, box number, and file designation. This authorization should arrive at the Reference Service Branch of the Washington National Records Center at least one day before the researcher's visit. If the records are classified, the agency must provide written evidence of security clearance. If the records are in the custody of the National Archives, access to these is administered by the Suitland Reference Branch of the Textual Reference Division of the Office of the National Archives.

Alabama

Alabama A & M University
J.F. Drake Memorial Learning Resources Center

Box 489
Normal, AL 35762

Phone: (205)851-5760
Fax: (205)851-5768
Dr. Birdie O. Weir, Director

Staff: Professional 10; Other 14. **Founded:** 1904. **Subjects:** Education, business and economics, agriculture, the sciences, computer science, literature. **Special collections:** Black Collection (3551 items); Archival Collection (3004 items); Schomburg Collection; Carnegie-Mydral Collection. **Holdings:** 231,304 books; 21,140 bound periodical volumes; 4008 AV programs; 16,452 periodicals on microfilm; 769 college catalogs; 661 telephone directories; 10,951 vertical files; 497,806 ERIC microfiche; 136,532 government documents; Wall Street Journal on microfiche (11,015); NewsBank on microfiche (21,566); Business NewsBank on microfiche (2735). **Subscriptions:** 1580 journals and other serials; 93 newspapers; 652 microfilm subscriptions. **Services:** Interlibrary loan; copying; videotaping; center open to the public; courtesy card must be purchased for check out of materials by persons not enrolled at the university or at one of the cooperating institutions. **Computerized services:** DIALOG Information Services; Internet (electronic mail service). Performs searches on fee basis. Contact Person: Prudence W. Bryant, Supervisor, Reference & Information Services. **Publications:** *Mixed Media* (newsletter), annual; *In the News* (newsletter)—for internal distribution only; *LRC Fast Facts*; *LRC Handbook of Programs and Services*; brochures.

Alabama (State) Department of Archives and History
Reference Room

PO Box 300
100n Ave.
Montgomery, AL 36130-0100

Phone: (205)242-4435
Debbie Pendleton, Head, Public Services Division

Staff: Professional 4; Other 2. **Founded:** 1901. **Subjects:** Alabama—history, politics and government, economic conditions, family history, social life and customs. **Special collections:** Federal records include mortality schedules 1850-1880, population schedules 1820-1880, 1860 slave schedules. **Holdings:** State and local government records; state publications; private records; maps; photographs; newspapers. **Subscriptions:** 90 journals and other serials. **Services:** Interlibrary loan (limited); copying; room open to the public with restrictions (registration required). **Computerized services:** OCLC, RLIN; RLG (electronic mail service).

Mobile Public Library
Local History and Genealogy Division

704 Government St.
Mobile, AL 36602-1499
Phone: (205)434-7093
Fax: (205)434-5866
George H. Schroeter, Head

Staff: Professional 1; Other 3. **Founded:** 1961. **Subjects:** Genealogy, Mobile history. **Special collections:** Panton-Leslie colonial trade papers, 1770-1840; Hunley Civil War papers. **Holdings:** 15,112 books; 1700 bound periodical volumes; 1814 reels of microfilm of Mobile newspapers; 6900 reels of microfilm of federal census records; 56 reels of microfilm of French and Spanish colonial records; 206 reels of microfilm on miscellaneous subjects including Indian Rolls (1832-1905). **Subscriptions:** 41 journals and other serials; 7 newspapers. **Services:** Copying; library open to the public for reference use only. **Special indexes:** Vertical file index (card); map index (card); index to Mobile Register Obituaries, 1986 to present (book).

Samford University
Harwell Goodwin Davis Library
Special Collections

800 Lakeshore Dr.
Birmingham, AL 35229
Phone: (205)870-2749
Fax: (205)870-2642
Elizabeth C. Wells, Special Collections Librarian

Staff: Professional 1; Other 3. **Founded:** 1957. **Subjects:** Alabama history, literature, and imprints; Early Southeast—Indians, travel, law; genealogical source records; Southern Reconstruction; Irish history and genealogy. **Special collections:** William H. Brantley Collection (books; 19th and 20th century manuscripts; 18th and 19th century maps); Douglas C. McMurtrie Collection; John Ruskin Collection; John Masefield Collection; Alfred Tennyson Collection; Lafcadio Hearn Collection. **Holdings:** 25,653 books; 2562 bound periodical volumes; 806 microcards; 349 phonograph records; 2725 maps; 1477 linear feet of manuscripts; 7739 reels of microfilm; 7828 prints and photographs; 3113 microfiche; 150 oral histories; 37 atlases; 1 globe; 60 relief models. **Subscriptions:** 330 journals and other serials. **Services:** Interlibrary loan; copying; collections open to the public. **Computerized services:** DIALOG Information Services. **Special catalogs:** Map Catalog; Catalog of the Casey Collection of Irish History and Genealogy. **Special indexes:** Analytical Information Index; index to *The Alabama Baptist* (newspaper).

Alaska

Alaska Collection and Archives

4101 University Dr.
Anchorage, AK 99508

Alaska (State) Department of Education
Division of Libraries, Archives and Museums
Archives & Records Management Services (ARMS)

141 Willoughby Ave.
Juneau, AK 99801-1720
Phone: (907)465-2275
Fax: (907)465-2465
Virginia A. Newton Ph.D., State Archivist

Staff: Professional 6; Other 7. **Founded:** 1971. **Subjects:** Alaska territorial and state government. **Holdings:** 6,000 cubic feet of territorial and state government records. **Services:** Copying; archives open to the public. **Computerized services:** WLN; internal database. **Special catalogs:** Finding aids to records. **Special indexes:** Microfilm index (card); index to noncurrent foreign and domestic corporation records (online); Alaska State Government Records Management Manual; Alaska Local Government General Records Retention Schedules; Alaska School District General Retention Schedules; Records Management Resources for Local Governments in Alaska. **Remarks:** The archives are the official repository for all permanently valuable records of the executive, legislative, and judicial branches of Alaska's state government. **Publications:** *Alaska State Archives: A Guide.*

Alaska State Library
Alaska Historical Collections

PO Box 110571
Juneau, AK 99811-0571
Phone: (907)465-2925
Fax: (907)465-2990
Kathryn H. Shelton, Head, Historical Collections

Staff: Professional 3; Other 4. **Founded:** 1900. **Subjects:** Alaska, Yukon, Arctic; Russian, especially Siberian, culture. **Special collections:** Alaska government publications; James Wickersham Collection; Snow Family Papers; L.H. Bayers Maritime Collection; Winter and Pond photograph collection; John Granger Alaska postcard collection. **Holdings:** 35,000 volumes, manuscripts, tapes, video cassettes, maps; 110,000 photographs; microfilm. **Services:** Mail or telephone reference and copying services; noncirculating collection open to the public for research. **Computerized services:** DIALOG Information Services, OCLC. **Formerly:** Alaska (State) Department of Education, Division of Libraries, Archives and Museums—Historical Library Section. **Publications:** *Some Books About Alaska Received*, annual; *Polar Libraries Bulletin*, biannual; historical monograph series, guides, and bibliographies.

Anchorage Museum of History and Art
Archives

121 W. 7th Ave.
Anchorage, AK 99501
Phone: (907)343-6189
Fax: (907)343-6149
M. Diane Brenner, Museum Archivist

Staff: Professional 1. **Founded:** 1968. **Subjects:** Alaskana—prehistoric, native, Russian, Gold Rush, current; fine arts. **Special collections:** Valdez photographs, 1900-1910 (12 albums); Alaska Railroad historical photographs (10,000); Ward Wells photograph collection (100,000); FAA Collection (10,000); Stephen D. McCutcheon photograph collection (50,000). **Holdings:** 6000 books; 200,000 photographs; 16 boxes of Alaskana archives; 10,000 slides of contemporary Alaskan art; 8 VF drawers; 8 drawers of biographies of Alaska artists; 200 maps. **Subscriptions:** 15 journals and other serials. **Services:** Interlibrary loan (limited); copying; archives open to the public. **Computerized services:** BITNET, Internet (electronic mail services). **Special indexes:** Index to Alaska Railroad Microfiche Project; Ward Wells Stock Series Indexing Project (Alaska Historical Commission Studies in History, No. 186). **Remarks:** Electronic mail addresses: anmdb@ alaska (BITNET); anmdb@cad2.alaska.edu (Internet).

Arizona

Arizona (State) Department of Library, Archives & Public Records

State Capitol, Rm. 200
1700 W. Washington
Phoenix, AZ 85007
Phone: (602)542-5630
Fax: (602)542-4400
Sharon G. Womack, Director

Staff: Professional 44; Other 72. **Founded:** 1864. **Subjects:** Arizona and southwestern history, law, genealogy. **Special collections:** State Archives. **Holdings:** 1.1 million volumes; federal document depository; state document center; state reference center (Arizona public libraries only). **Subscriptions:** 1700 journals and other serials; 130 newspapers. **Services:** Interlibrary loan; library open to the public for reference use only. **Computerized services:** DIALOG Information Services. Performs searches on fee basis.

Church of Jesus Christ of Latter-day Saints Genealogical Society Branch Library

1536 E. Cherokee Ln.
Safford, AZ 85546
Phone: (602)428-3194
Leven B. Ferrin

Staff: 50. **Founded:** 1939. **Subjects:** Genealogy. **Special collections:** Indian Tribes (pamphlets); World Conference, 1969 (18 volumes); World Conference, 1981 (13 volumes); Genealogical Society Series (12 volumes). **Holdings:** 5000 books; 1087 bound periodical volumes; 3000 films; microfiche for genealogical research. **Subscriptions:** 21 journals and other serials. **Services:** Interlibrary loan; copying; center open to the public. **Computerized services:** Ancestral Search, Computers, Personal Ancestral File (internal databases).

Fort Bowie Library

PO Box 158
Bowie, AZ 85605
Phone: (602)847-2500
Larry Ludwig, Park Ranger

Description: Located at the National Historic Site of Fort Bowie. **Holdings:** Over 700 books, cemetery records for the Fort, post records, and records of Chiricahua Apaches.

Hubbell Trading Post National Park Service Library

PO Box 150
Ganado, AZ 86505
Phone: (602)755-3575
Shirley A. Harding, Park Curator

Description: Located on the National Historic Site with exhibits of Native American arts and crafts and tours of the John Lorenzo Hubbell house. **Holdings:** Nearly 500 volumes describing Navajo culture and history. Includes photo albums, oral histories, and manuscripts.

Phoenix Public Library Arizona Room

12 E. McDowell Rd.
Phoenix, AZ 85004
Phone: (602)262-4636

Staff: Professional 1; Other 1. **Subjects:** Phoenix and Arizona history, Southwestern Indians, Southwestern water and land use, Mexican Americans, Southwestern art. **Special collections:** James Harvey McClintock papers, 1864-1934. **Holdings:** 20,000 books; 225 bound periodical volumes; Phoenix municipal records. **Subscriptions:** 45 journals and other serials. **Services:** Copying; room open to the public.

Arkansas

Arkansas State Library

One Capitol Mall
Little Rock, AR 72201
Phone: (501)682-1527
Fax: (501)682-1529
Jack C. Mulkey, Associate Director

Staff: Professional 12; Other 35. **Founded:** 1935. **Special collections:** Arkansas. **Holdings:** 144,278 volumes; 24 VF drawers. **Subscriptions:** 285 journals and other serials. **Services:** Library open to the public. **Computerized services:** OCLC. **Remarks:** Electronic mail address: ALA 0967 (ALANET).

Arkansas State University Museum Library/Archives

Box 490
State University, AR 72467
Phone: (501)972-2074
Fax: (501)972-5706
Madeleine Kirkland, Curator

Staff: 4. **Founded:** 1936. **Subjects:** History - Indian, American military, Arkansas, United States, European; old textbooks; religion; children's rare books; minerals and fossils. **Special collections:** Rare newspapers, 1750-1960 (1500); Sharp County, Arkansas Courthouse Ledgers. **Holdings:** 5000 books; 6500 other cataloged items. **Subscriptions:** 3 journals and other serials. **Services:** Interlibrary loan; library open to the public.

Southwest Arkansas Regional Archives

Box 134
Washington, AR 71862
Phone: (501)983-2633

Staff: Professional 1. **Founded:** 1978. **Subjects:** History of Southwest Arkansas, Caddo Indians. **Special collections:** Rare books collection on Southwest Arkansas and Texas; census and court records for twelve southwest Arkansas counties; newspapers of southwest Arkansas; index and service records for Civil War soldiers who served in Arkansas units. **Holdings:** 1500 books; 3000 reels of microfilm; original court records of Hempstead County, 1819-1910; pictures; manuscripts; family histories; theses; sheet music; newspapers; maps; pamphlets; journals; genealogical records. **Services:** Copying; archives open to the public for reference use only. **Publications:** *SARA Newsletter*, quarterly.

California

California State Archives

201 N. Sunrise Ave.
Roseville, CA 95661
Phone: (916)773-3000
Fax: (916)773-8249
John F. Burns, Chief of Archives

Staff: Professional 7; Other 11. **Founded:** 1850. **Subjects:** California government and politics. **Special collections:** Spanish land grants (19 volumes); State government Oral History Program transcripts (100 volumes). **Holdings:** 60,000 cubic feet of documents, photographs, microforms, maps, audiotapes, films, videotapes, computer materials, and artifacts. **Subscriptions:** 20 journals and other serials. **Services:** Copying; archives open to the public. **Computerized services:** RLIN. **Remarks:** Maintained by California State Secretary of State. **Publications:** *California Originals* (newsletter), quarterly available upon request.

California State Library

Library & Courts Bldg.
914 Capitol Mall
Box 942837
Sacramento, CA 94237-0001
Phone: (916)654-0183
Fax: (916)654-0064
Gary E. Strong, State Librarian

Staff: Professional 86; Other 102. **Founded:** 1850. **Subjects:** General research collection in support of state government, Californiana, law, genealogy (holdings compiled by D.A.R. containing cemetery records, the 1852 State Census, etc; pre-statehood newspapers on microfilm are some of the items concerning genealogy), population, public administration, statistics. **Holdings:** 708,542 volumes; 780,449 documents; 2.6 million microforms; 74,700 maps and charts; 11 16mm films; 165 video recordings; 310,231 audio recordings; federal and state government document depository. **Subscriptions:** 7006 journals, serials, and newspapers. **Services:** Interlibrary loan; copying; consultant service for public libraries; library open to the public. **Computerized services:** DIALOG Information Services, InfoPro Technologies, ORBIT Search Service, Mead Data Central; OnTyme Electronic Message Network Service, Internet (electronic mail services). **Special indexes:** California State Publications, monthly (hardcopy; cumulations on COM). **Remarks:** Electronic mail addresses: CSLILL (OnTyme Electronic Message Network Service); csl_ill@library.ca.gov (Internet). Includes the holdings of the State Law Library. **Publications:** List of publications—available on request.

California State Library Sutro Library

480 Winston Dr.
San Francisco, CA 94132
Phone: (415)557-0421
Fax: (415)557-9325
Clyde Janes, Supervising Librarian

Staff: Professional 2; Other 5. **Founded:** 1917. **Subjects:** American genealogy and local history, English history, history of science and technology, Americana, bibliography, voyages and travels, Mexican history, valuable collection of printed works containing Hispanic material, Hebraica, natural history. **Special collections:** Papers of Sir Joseph Banks, 1760-1820; the Mexican Pamphlet Collection. **Holdings:** 150,000 volumes; 20,000 manuscripts. **Subscriptions:** 87 journals and other serials. **Services:** Interlibrary loan; copying; library open to the public. **Remarks:** Library specializes in works published prior to 1900. **Publications:** *Anatomy of a Library* (brochure on the collection); *New Arrivals in American Local History and Genealogy*, quarterly—free upon request.

Compton Library

240 West Compton Blvd.
Compton, CA 90220

County of Los Angeles Public Library American Indian Resource Center

Huntington Park Library
6518 Miles Ave.
Huntington Park, CA 90255
Phone: (213)583-1461
Fax: (213)587-2061

Staff: Professional 1; Other 2. **Founded:** 1979. **Subjects:** Indians of North America, including Southwest, Plains, Woodlands, and California Indians history, tribal cultural histories, fine arts, religion, literature, laws and treaties. **Special collections:** Federal Census Records (1880-1940). **Holdings:** 2000 books; 60 16mm films; 65 titles in microform; 110 videotapes; 400 audiocassettes; 300 federal and state documents. **Subscriptions:** 45 periodical titles. **Services:** Interlibrary loan; copying; center open to the public.

Family History Center, Los Angeles

10741 Santa Monica Blvd.
Los Angeles, CA 90025
Phone: (310)474-2202

Description: Branch of the Family History Library of the Church of Jesus Christ of Latter-day Saints. **Subjects:** Genealogy, family history, church and civil records, local history. **Remarks:** Access to main library microfilm.

Family History Center, Oakland

4780 Lincoln Ave.
Oakland, CA 94602
Phone: (510)531-3905

Description: Branch of the Family History Library of the Church of Jesus Christ of Latter-day Saints. **Subjects:** Genealogy, family history, church and civil records, local history. **Remarks:** Access to main library microfilm.

Family History Center, Pasadena

770 N. Sierra Madre Villa
Pasadena, CA 91107
Phone: (818)351-8517

Description: Branch of the Family History Library of the Church of Jesus Christ of Latter-day Saints. **Subjects:** Genealogy, family history, church and civil records, local history. **Remarks:** Access to main library microfilm.

Family History Center, Sacramento

2745 Eastern Ave.
Sacramento, CA 95821
Phone: (916)621-2090

Description: Branch of the Family History Library of the Church of Jesus Christ of Latter-day Saints. **Subjects:** Genealogy, family history, church and civil records, local history. **Remarks:** Access to main library microfilm.

Family History Center, San Diego

15750 Bernardo Heights
San Diego, CA 92128
Phone: (619)487-2304

Description: Branch of the Family History Library of the Church of Jesus Christ of Latter-day Saints. **Subjects:** Genealogy, family history, church and civil records, local history. **Remarks:** Access to main library microfilm.

Family History Center, San Diego

3705 10th Ave.
San Diego, CA 92103
Phone: (619)295-9808

Description: Branch of the Family History Library of the Church of Jesus Christ of Latter-day Saints. **Subjects:** Genealogy, family history, church and civil records, local history. **Remarks:** Access to main library microfilm.

Family History Center, San Francisco

730 Sharp Park Rd.
Pacifica, CA 94044
Phone: (415)355-4986

Description: Branch of the Family History Library of the Church of Jesus Christ of Latter-day Saints. **Subjects:** Genealogy, family history, church and civil records, local history. **Remarks:** Access to main library microfilm.

Family History Center, San Jose

2175 Santiago St.
San Jose, CA 95122
Phone: (408)274-8592

Description: Branch of the Family History Library of the Church of Jesus Christ of Latter-day Saints. **Subjects:** Genealogy, family history, church and civil records, local history. **Remarks:** Access to main library microfilm.

Fresno County Free Library Special Collections

2420 Mariposa St.
Fresno, CA 93721
Phone: (209)488-3195
Fax: (209)488-1971
John K. Kallenberg, Librarian

Founded: 1910. **Subjects:** Fresno County—local history, architecture; American Indians—Mono, Miwok, Yokut. **Special collections:** Local History Collection (15 linear feet of oral history manuscripts, vertical files of ephemera, biographical sketches, broadsides, maps, pamphlets); Ta-Kwa-Teu-Nee-Ya-Y Collection (200 books); South East Asian Acculturation Collection (300 books). **Holdings:** 122 bound periodical volumes; 15 linear feet of archival materials; 15,000 microfiche; Fresno newspapers on microfilm (1860 to present). **Subscriptions:** 4 journals and other serials; 5 newspapers. **Services:** Copying; library open to the public. **Computerized services:** VU/TEXT Information Services; internal database. Performs searches. Contact Person: Linda Sitterding, Local History Librarian. **Special indexes:** Historical Landmarks and Records Commission Index; Fresno papers index (1851 to present); Photograph Index; Oral History Index. **Publications:** *Ta-Kwa-Teu-Nee-Ya-Y Bibliography*; *South East Asian Cultural Materials Bibliography.*

Gardena Library Los Angeles County Public Library

1731 West Gardena Boulevard
Gardena, CA 90247

Held-Poage Memorial Home & Research Library

603 W. Perkins St.
Ukiah, CA 95482-4726
Phone: (707)462-6969
Lila J. Lee, Librarian

Staff: 2. **Founded:** 1970. **Subjects:** History - Mendocino County, California, U.S., Civil War; Pomo and other Indians. **Special collections:** Writings of Edith Van Allen Murphey, Dr. John Whiz Hudson, Helen Carpenter. **Holdings:** 5000 books; 16,000 negatives; photographs; maps; bound county records; clippings; genealogies. **Subscriptions:** 13 journals and other serials. **Services:** Interlibrary loan; copying; library open to the public on a limited schedule for reference use only, by appointment. **Remarks:** Maintained by Mendocino County Historical Society.

Huntington Library

1151 Oxford Rd.
San Marino, CA 91108
Phone: (818)405-2191
Fax: (818)405-0225

Staff: Prof. 25, Other 25. **Description:** Large historical collection including genealogical documents, books, etc. **Founded:** 1919. **Special collections:** Hudson's Bay Co. papers, and papers from the Puget Sound Agricultural Co. (some of which list Indian employees) **Holdings:** 357,643 rare books; 321,362 reference books; 3 million manuscripts, etc. **Remarks:** Published guides and articles about collections they hold are available. Some of their holdings are available on microfilm at other libraries and archives. See *Reader's Guide to the Huntington Library.*

Los Angeles Public Library History and Genealogy Department

630 W. 5th St.
Los Angeles, CA 90071
Phone: (213)228-7400
Fax: (213)228-7409
Jane Nowak, Department Manager

Staff: Professional 8; Other 13.5. **Subjects:** History, travel, biography, Californiana, genealogy, local history, heraldry, newspapers. **Special collections:** Genealogy (38,000 volumes); Californiana (20,000 items); maps and atlases; American Indians; Security Pacific Bank historic photograph collection; Herald Examiner Newspaper and Photograph Morgues. **Holdings:** 290,000 volumes; 91,000 maps; 2.7 million photographs; 800 historical specimen newspapers; 25,000 reels of microfilm of newspapers; 4 CD-ROMs; U.S. city directories; census records. **Subscriptions:** 1300 journals and other serials; 65 newspapers. **Services:** Interlibrary loan; copying (limited). **Computerized services:** DIALOG Information Services, EasyNet; internal databases; Internet (electronic mail service). Performs searches on fee basis. **Special indexes:** California biography; California subject; Western outlaws and sheriffs; collected biography; American Indians; family history; local history; coats of arms; photograph collection (accessed on microcomputer). **Remarks:** Electronic mail address: laplgene@class.org (Internet).

Los Angeles Public Library Social Sciences, Philosophy and Religion Department

630 W. 5th St.
Los Angeles, CA 90071
Phone: (213)228-7300
Fax: (213)228-7319
Marilyn C. Wherley, Department Manager

Staff: Professional 6.5. **Subjects:** Philosophy, religion, psychology, social problems, government, foreign affairs, international relations, law, criminology, education, women's movements, family relations, ethnic groups, interpersonal relations. **Special collections:** California, U.S., and U.N. documents depository; African-American history and culture; Mexican-American Affairs. **Holdings:** 400,000 volumes. 10 CD-ROMs. **Subscriptions:** 2850 journals and other serials. **Services:** Interlibrary loan; copying; department open to the public. **Computerized services:** DIALOG Information Services, EasyNet. Internet (electronic mail service). Performs searches on fee basis. **Remarks:** Electronic mail address: laplsocs@class.org (Internet).

Monterey County Historical Society Boronda History Center Research Center and Archive

333 Boronda St.
PO Box 3576
Salinas, CA 93912

Phone: (408)757-8085
Mona Gudgel, Director

Description: Archive of material concerning Monterey County. Holds three-quarters of the material in the Monterey County Archives, concerning Indian, Spanish and Mexican California historical and genealogical research.

Oakland Public Library History/Literature and Oakland History Room

125 14th St.
Oakland, CA 94612

Phone: (510)238-3136
Sherrill Reeves, Senior Librarian

Staff: Professional 5; Other 3. **Subjects:** History, travel, biography, English and foreign languages and literature, genealogy, maps. **Special collections:** Schomburg Collection of Black Literature and History (in microform); Negroes of New York, 1939 (Writers Program; in microform); Sutro Library Family History and Local History Subject Catalogs (in microform); Index to Biographies in State and Local Histories in the Library of Congress (in microform). **Holdings:** 100,663 books; genealogy microfilms. **Subscriptions:** 114 journals and other serials. **Services:** Interlibrary loan; copying; division open to the public. **Special indexes:** Local History. **Publications:** *New Releases.*

Richmond Public Library Special Collections

325 Civic Center Plaza
Richmond, CA 94804

Phone: (510)620-6561
Adelia Lines, Director

Founded: 1905. **Special collections:** Local history; Afro-American history; Hispanic geographical areas. **Services:** Interlibrary loan; collections open to the public. **Computerized services:** DIALOG Information Services; CLSI (internal database); OnTyme Electronic Message Network Service (electronic mail service). Performs searches on fee basis. Contact Person: Douglas Holtzman.

Santa Barbara Historical Museums Gledhill Library

136 E. De La Guerra St.
Box 578
Santa Barbara, CA 93102-0578

Phone: (805)966-1601
Fax: (805)966-1603
Michael Redmon, Head Librarian

Staff: Professional 1; Other 8. **Founded:** 1967. **Subjects:** Local history and genealogy. Growing collection concerning Hispanic families of Santa Barbara and the surrounding area. **Holdings:** 5000 books; 30,000 photographs; 360 oral history tapes. **Subscriptions:** 20 journals and other serials. **Services:** Copying; photograph reproduction; library open to the public.

Santa Barbara Mission Archive-Library

Old Mission, Upper Laguna St.
Santa Barbara, CA 93105

Phone: (805)682-4713
Father Virgilio Biasiol O.F.M., Director

Staff: Professional 1. **Founded:** 1786. **Subjects:** Early missions and missionaries in the Santa Barbara area, Californiana and Mexicana, Spain and Hispanic America. **Special collections:** De la Guerra Collection (12,000 pages of documents on California); Wilson Collection (rare books; globes; works of art); Alexander Taylor Collection (copies of 2300 documents from the Archdiocesan Archives in San Francisco); photographs of the late mission period in California, Spain, and Mexico (4000); original mission music (1000 brochures); original mission documents (3500). **Holdings:** 15,000 books; 200 scrapbooks, newspaper clippings; 3000 pamphlets. **Services:** Library open to the public on a limited schedule. **Special catalogs:** Catalog of documents and old books. **Remarks:** Maintained by the Franciscan Fathers of California. **Publications:** Newsletter, irregular—to Friends of Archive-Library; list of other publications—available on request.

University of California, Berkeley Bancroft Library

Berkeley, CA 94704

Description: Collection of original documents and manuscripts, microforms, printed materials, etc., for California, and the entire Southwest, as well as Mexico and Spain. Includes copies of landgrant records from the California Archives, as well as from the Federal Archives, etc. Also has collection of dictation given to Bancroft employees by historic figures and their descendants (1880s). Collection has a great deal of Indian history prior to 1883. **Special catalogs:** Detailed in-house guides of specific collections and various card catalogs. See *Catalog of Printed Books in the Bancroft Library,* and *A Guide to the Manuscript Collections at the Bancroft Library.* **Remarks:** Friends of the Bancroft Library publish newsletter as well as an annual keepsake book.

University of California, Davis Michael and Margaret B. Harrison Western Research Center

Department of Special Collections
Shields Library
Davis, CA 95616

Phone: (916)752-1621
Michael Harrison, Director

Staff: Professional 1. **Founded:** 1981. **Subjects:** History and development of the trans-Mississippi West, mid-19th century to present; American Indians; ethnic studies; military, local, and economic history; sociology; census records; Forbes Collection (Native American studies organized by tribe); religious studies, especially the Catholic and Mormon churches; literature; art and architecture; history of printing. **Holdings:** 19,689 volumes. **Subscriptions:** 107 journals and other serials. **Services:** Center open to the public by appointment only.

University of California, Los Angeles American Indian Studies Center Library

3220 Campbell Hall
Los Angeles, CA 90024-1548
Phone: (310)825-7315
Fax: (310)206-7060
Velma S. Salabiye, Librarian

Staff: Professional 1; Other 1. **Founded:** 1970. **Subjects:** American Indians government relations, history, literature, art, language; Indians in California; works of Indian authorship. **Special collections:** Indian newspapers and journals. **Holdings:** 6100 volumes; 5700 pamphlets. **Subscriptions:** 60 serials. **Services:** Copying; library open to the public with restrictions. **Computerized services:** ORION (internal database).

University of the Pacific Holt-Atherton Department of Special Collections

Stockton, CA 95211
Phone: (209)946-2404
Fax: (209)946-2810
Daryl Morrison, Head, Special Collections

Staff: Professional 1; Other 2. **Founded:** 1947. **Subjects:** Californiana, Western Americana, Pacific Northwest, Northern San Joaquin Valley, gold mining, Western authors, Native Americans, economic development of the West, ethnic history in California. **Special collections:** Early California exploration. **Holdings:** 30,000 books; 2928 bound periodical volumes; 75 linear feet of VF pamphlets; 45,000 photographs; 1670 maps; 2670 linear feet of manuscripts. **Subscriptions:** 116 journals and other serials. **Services:** Interlibrary loan (limited); copying; library open to the public. **Computerized services:** OCLC. **Also known as:** Stuart Library of Western Americana and Pacific Center for Western Studies. **Publications:** Monographs; *Bibliographic Guides to Archives.*

Colorado

Colorado (State) Division of State Archives and Public Records

Dept. of Administration
1313 Sherman St., Rm. 1B20
Denver, CO 80203
Phone: (303)866-2358
Fax: (303)866-2257
Terry Ketelsen, State Archivist

Staff: 11. **Founded:** 1943. **Subjects:** Noncurrent official public records and printed publications of the Territory and State of Colorado. **Holdings:** 80,000 cubic feet of public records. **Services:** Copying; certification; open to all who wish to consult records for legitimate purposes. **Publications:** *Guide to the Resources of the Colorado State Archives* (loose-leaf), updated periodically; brochures.

Colorado State Library Colorado State Publications Library

State Office Bldg., Rm. 314
201 E. Colfax Ave.
Denver, CO 80203
Phone: (303)866-6725
Fax: (303)866-6940
Maureen Crocker, Librarian

Staff: Professional 1; Other 2. **Founded:** 1980. **Subjects:** State publications. **Holdings:** 12,000 volumes. **Services:** Interlibrary loan; copying; library open to the public. **Computerized services:** OCLC. **Publications:** Accessions checklist; microfiche checklist; Selective Bibliography Series; *Colorado State Publications Classification Schedule.*

Denver Public Library Genealogy Department

1357 Broadway
Denver, CO 80203
Phone: (303)640-8870
Fax: (303)640-8818
James Jeffrey, Collection Specialist

Staff: Professional 8. **Founded:** 1910. **Subjects:** County, state, town histories; census schedules, 1790-1910; genealogy; military rosters; heraldry. **Special collections:** Denver obituaries, 1939 to present (21 reels of microfilm; 15 volumes; 15 file drawers; 34 microfiche); genealogical manuscripts and clippings (13 VF drawers); genealogical charts (2 map cases); Draper Manuscript Collection (134 reels of microfilm); Corbin Collection (New England; 60 reels of microfilm); Barbour Collection (Connecticut; 98 reels of microfilm); Archives of the Catholic Archdiocese of Santa Fe, 1678-1976 (90 reels of microfilm); Spanish Archives of New Mexico, 1621-1821 (22 reels of microfilm); Mexican Archives of New Mexico, 1821-1846 (42 reels of microfilm); Territorial Archives of New Mexico, 1846-1914 (189 reels of microfilm); Hale Collection of Connecticut Vital Records (358 reels of microfilm); Enrollment card collection of the five civilized tribes, 1896-1914 (93 reels of microfilm); Registers of signatures of the depositors in branches of the Freedman's Savings and Trust Company, 1865-1874 (32 reels of microfilm). **Holdings:** 40,000 books; 3250 bound periodical volumes; 5200 reels of microfilm of census schedules and other material; 30,000 microcards and microfiche; vital records; census indexes; 7 VF drawers of Denver Tramway personnel records; 150 audiocassettes. **Subscriptions:** 450 journals and other serials. **Services:** Interlibrary loan; copying; genealogical research. **Special catalogs:** FHLC Family History Library Catalog. **Special indexes:** Index to obituaries published in 2 major Denver newspapers (1939-present); index to anniversary announcements published in 2 major Denver newspapers; family name file; coat of arms file; IGI (International Genealogical Index) (all on microfiche); index to the Freedman's Savings and Trust Company registers (on microfilm).

University of Denver Penrose Library Special Collections

2150 E. Evans Ave.
Denver, CO 80208-0287
Phone: (303)871-3428
Steven Fisher, Curator

Founded: 1864. **Special collections:** Miller Civil War Collection (1000 items); Davidson Folklore Collection (1000 items). **Services:** Interlibrary loan; copying; collections open to the public. **Computerized services:** Online systems.

Connecticut

Connecticut State Library

231 Capitol Ave.
Hartford, CT 06106
Phone: (203)566-4971
Fax: (203)566-8940
Richard G. Akeroyd Jr., State Librarian

Staff: Professional 43; Other 94. **Founded:** 1854. **Subjects:** Connecticut, local history and genealogy, state and federal law, politics and government, legislative reference. **Special collections:** Barbour Index of Connecticut Vital Records to 1850; indexes to original sources of genealogical data; Connecticut newspapers, town documents; State Archives (includes records of Judicial Dept., Governor's Office, General Assembly, and several executive branch agencies); local government records; land records; selectmen's records; non-government records from individuals, families, businesses, and organizations. **Holdings:** 715,000 books; 34,000 bound periodical volumes; 28,000 cubic feet of archival records; newspaper clipping files, 1927 to present; 26,000 reels of microfilm; 6000 maps; regional federal documents depository of 1.5 million documents; state documents depository of 50,000 state documents. **Subscriptions:** 9053 journals and other serials; 100 newspapers. **Services:** Interlibrary loan; copying; library open to the public. **Computerized services:** OCLC, DIALOG Information Services, InfoPro Technologies, RLIN; internal database. **Publications:** *Checklist of Publications of Connecticut State Agencies*; *Agency Newsletter.*

Indian and Colonial Research Center, Inc. Eva Butler Library

PO Box 525
Old Mystic, CT 06372
Phone: (203)536-9771
Kathleen Greenhalgh, Librarian

Staff: Professional 2; Other 15. **Founded:** 1965. **Subjects:** Indians, genealogy, colonial history. **Special collections:** Elmer Waite collection of glass plate negatives of the area; rare American school books, 1700-1850 (300). **Holdings:** 2000 books; 954 manuscripts; 90 maps and atlases; 2000 early American notebooks; 69 boxes of bulletins and pamphlets; 2000 photographs. **Subscriptions:** 2 journals and other serials. **Services:** Copying; library open to the public. **Remarks:** Also maintains a museum. **Publications:** *Our Woodland Indians* (coloring book).

Kent Historical Society Library

R.D. 1
Box 321
Kent, CT 06757
Phone: (203)927-3055
Emily Hopson, Information Director

Staff: 3. **Founded:** 1935. **Subjects:** Local history, settlement, development; Scaticook Indians; iron industry; genealogy. **Special collections:** Photographs of early Kent (1000). **Holdings:** 20 VF drawers; ledgers. **Services:** Library open to the public.

Yale University Beinecke Rare Book and Manuscript Library

Wall and High Streets
New Haven, CT 06520
Phone: (203)432-2977
Fax: (203)432-4047
Ralph W. Franklin, Director

Staff: Prof. 20, Other 20. **Description:** Native American history and languages; early newspapers; literature. **Founded:** 1963. **Holdings:** 500,000 volumes; 2.25 million manuscripts. **Special catalogs:** See *Catalog of Western Americana Manuscripts in the Yale University Library* by Mary Withington.

Delaware

Delaware (State) Division of Historical & Cultural Affairs Delaware State Archives

Hall of Records
Dover, DE 19901
Phone: (302)739-5318
Fax: (302)739-6710
Howard P. Lowell, State Archivist/Records Administrator

Staff: Professional 4; Other 2. **Founded:** 1905. **Subjects:** Delaware history and government, county and city records.

Florida

Florida State Archives

R.A. Gray Bldg.
500 S. Bronough St.
Tallahassee, FL 32399-0250
Phone: (904)487-2073
Fax: (904)488-4894
Jim Berberich, Chief

Staff: Professional 12; Other 6. **Subjects:** Florida history. **Special collections:** Florida Photographic Collection (history and culture of Florida; 750,000 photographic images); Florida Genealogical Collection (6000 volumes; 5000 reels of microfilm). **Holdings:** 25,000 cubic feet of state historical records, 1822 to present; 1250 cubic feet of manuscripts. **Services:** Copying; archives open to the public. **Computerized services:** Internal database. **Remarks:** Contains the holdings of the former Florida Photographic Collection.

St. Augustine Historical Society Library

271 Charlotte St.
St. Augustine, FL 32084
Phone: (904)824-2872
Sheherzad Navidi, Library Director

Staff: 7. **Founded:** 1883. **Subjects:** History of St. Augustine and environs, history of Florida, genealogy. **Special collections:** Cathedral Parish records, St. Augustine, 1594-1763 and 1784-1882 (marriages, baptisms, burials); archives (manuscripts; city papers; St. Johns County court records); East Florida Papers, 1784-1821 (175 reels). **Holdings:** 10,000 books; photocopies; manuscripts; documents; microfilm; 10,000 photographs; 1000 maps; pictures; card calendar of Spanish documents, 1512-1821; card index of St.

Augustine people, 1594 to present. **Subscriptions:** 12 journals and other serials. **Services:** Copying; library open to the public for reference use only. **Publications:** *El Escribano*, annual—by subscription; *East Florida Gazette* (periodical).

State Library of Florida

R.A. Gray Bldg.
500 S. Bronough St.
Tallahassee, FL 32399-0250
Phone: (904)487-2651
Fax: (904)488-2746
Barratt Wilkins, State Librarian

Staff: Professional 32; Other 37. **Founded:** 1845. **Subjects:** Florida, history, social sciences, library science. **Special collections:** Floridana (21,809 items). **Holdings:** 272,067 books; 8503 bound periodical volumes; 115,972 Florida public documents; 140,636 U.S. documents; 18,549 reels of microfilm; 278,846 microfiche; 4801 films; 3574 videotapes. **Subscriptions:** 827 journals and other serials; 13 newspapers. **Services:** Interlibrary loan; copying; SDI; library open to the public. **Computerized services:** OCLC; DIALOG Information Services, Mead Data Central; Internet (electronic mail service). **Special indexes:** KWIC Index to Florida Public Documents, semiannual. **Remarks:** Electronic mail address(es): WILKINB@FIRNVX.FIRN.EDU (Internet). **Publications:** *Florida Library Directory with Statistics*, annual—free to libraries; *Florida Public Documents*, monthly.

University of Florida
Southeastern Indian Oral History Project Library

126 Florida State Museum
Gainesville, FL 32611
Phone: (904)392-1721
Fax: (904)392-7168
Dr. Samuel Proctor

Staff: 5. **Founded:** 1967. **Subjects:** Southern history, southeastern Indians, Florida history. **Holdings:** 3000 cassette interviews. **Services:** Library open to the public for reference use only.

University of South Florida
Special Collections Department

4202 E Fowler Ave.
Tampa, FL 33620
Phone: (813)974-2731
Fax: (813)974-5153
Thomas Jay Kemp

Staff: Prof. 4; Other 12. **Founded:** 1962. **Special collections:** Florida Collection (35,000 volumes; 150,000 maps; photographs; other items); papers of Florida governor LeRoy Collins, Congressman Sam Gibbons; papers of the Centro Asturiano, Centro Espanol, La Union MARTI-MACEO; Armwood Family papers; Black publishers archives; 19th century American Almanacs (900); Nation's Bank Black American Music Collection (15,000 pieces of sheet music). **Holdings:** 100,000 manuscripts; 75,000 archives. **Services:** Copying, collections open to public. **Computerized services:** Computerized cataloging.

West Florida Regional Library

200 W Gregory St.
Pensacola, FL 32501-4778
Phone: (904)435-1763
Dolly Pollard, Librarian

Staff: Prof. 1. **Description:** Public library with some Native American coverage, minor African American coverage. **Founded:** 1947. **Special collections:** Creek and Cherokee Indian genealogy; some information on other southeastern tribes, especially Choctaw. **Holdings:** 2,500 books, 60 bound periodical vols., 3,000 microfiche, 2,000 microfilm, and 5 active periodical subscriptions. **Services:** Limited copying, list of researchers for hire, limited genealogical assistance, and educational programs. Open to public.

Georgia

Atlanta-Fulton Public Library
Special Collections Department

1 Margaret Mitchell Sq.
Atlanta, GA 30303
Phone: (404)730-1700
Fax: (404)730-1989
Janice White Sikes, Manager

Staff: Professional 5; Other 3. **Founded:** 1925. **Subjects:** African-American studies, genealogy, Georgia history and literature, oral history, Margaret Mitchell. **Special collections:** Hattie Wilson High Memorial Genealogical Collection (6800 books, 372 bound periodical volumes, 129 unbound periodicals, 214 city directories, 1200 maps, 160 reels of microfilm); Samuel Williams Collection of materials by and about Afro-Americans (40,000 books, 1600 bound periodical volumes, 2100 reels of microfilm, 1000 microfiche); Atlanta-Fulton Public Library Archives; rare books. **Holdings:** 54,300 books; 3930 bound periodical volumes; 4396 reels of microfilm; 11,000 microfiche; 300 audiocassettes; 790 other cataloged items. **Subscriptions:** 350 journals and newsletters; 15 newspapers. **Services:** Copying; department open to the public for reference use only. **Publications:** Bibliographies and guides.

Georgia (State) Department of Archives and History
Reference Services

330 Capitol Ave. SE
Atlanta, GA 30334
Phone: (404)656-2393
Fax: (404)651-9270
Brenda S. Banks, Dir., Ref./Preservation

Staff: Professional 9; Other 4. **Founded:** 1918. **Subjects:** Georgia, southeastern U.S., genealogy. **Special collections:** Federal records include population schedules 1800-1820, the Negro in the Military Service of the U.S. 1639-1886, schedule of slave owners 1850 and 1860, African slave trade and Negro colonization records 1854-1872; Georgia state records (82,000 cubic feet); county records (7500 cubic feet; 20,000 reels of microfilm); private papers (2500 cubic feet). **Holdings:** 20,000 volumes; 2000 reels of microfilm of newspapers; 10,500 maps; 2000 manuscript volumes; 20,000 prints and photographs. **Subscriptions:** 425 journals and other serials; 91 newspapers. **Services:** Copying; services open to the public. **Computerized services:** RLIN; BITNET (electronic mail service). **Special catalogs:** Civil War Pension Index (microfilm); Family Surname File; descriptive inventories for individual official record groups and of manuscript collections. **Remarks:** Electronic mail address: GSP@RLG (BITNET). Contains the holdings of the former Georgia (State) Department of Archives and History—Land Records Office. **Publications:** List of publications of the Georgia State Department of Archives and History—free upon request.

Sara Hightower Regional Library Special Collections

205 Riverside Pkwy.
Rome, GA 30161
Phone: (706)236-4607
Fax: (706)236-4605
Jacqueline D. Kinzer, Curator

Staff: 2. **Founded:** 1911. **Subjects:** Cherokee Indians, Georgia and local history, genealogy, Southern history, Civil War. **Special collections:** J.F. Brooks Cherokeeana Collection (401 books); Ellen Louise Axson Wilson Collection; John L. Harris Papers (3 VF drawers); George M. Battey, III, Papers (5 VF drawers); Civil War collection; Yancey Lipscomb Collection (4 VF Drawers); Rome News-Tribune Resource Collection. **Holdings:** 14,000 books; 30 VF drawers; 350 maps; 7800 microforms; 600 unbound periodicals. **Subscriptions:** 71 journals and other serials. **Services:** Interlibrary loan; copying; collections open to the public with restrictions.

Hawaii

Family History Center, Hilo

1373 Kilauea Ave.
Hilo, HI 96720
Phone: (808)935-0711

Description: Branch of the Family History Library of the Church of Jesus Christ of Latter-day Saints. **Subjects:** Genealogy, family history, church and civil records, local history. **Remarks:** Access to main library microfilm.

Family History Center, Honolulu

1560 S. Beretania St.
Honolulu, HI 96826
Phone: (808)955-8910

Description: Branch of the Family History Library of the Church of Jesus Christ of Latter-day Saints. **Subjects:** Genealogy, family history, church and civil records, local history. **Remarks:** Access to main library microfilm.

Family History Center, Honolulu

1723 Beckley St.
Honolulu, HI 96819
Phone: (808)841-4118

Description: Branch of the Family History Library of the Church of Jesus Christ of Latter-day Saints. **Subjects:** Genealogy, family history, church and civil records, local history. **Remarks:** Access to main library microfilm.

Family History Center, Kaneohe

46-117 Halaulani St.
Kaneohe, HI 96744
Phone: (808)247-3134

Description: Branch of the Family History Library of the Church of Jesus Christ of Latter-day Saints. **Subjects:** Genealogy, family history, church and civil records, local history. **Remarks:** Access to main library microfilm.

Genealogical Resource Center Alu Like Native Hawaiian Libraries Project

1024 Mapunapuna St.
Honolulu, HI 96819-8940

Idaho

Idaho State Library

325 W. State St.
Boise, ID 83702
Phone: (208)334-2150
Fax: (208)334-4016
Charles Bolles, State Librarian

Staff: Professional 20; Other 30. **Founded:** 1901. **Subjects:** Idaho and Pacific Northwest, library science, public administration. **Holdings:** 103,000 books; 5200 phonograph records and cassettes; 3000 films and videotapes; federal and state document depository. **Subscriptions:** 1100 journals and other serials. **Services:** Interlibrary loan; copying; library open to the public. **Computerized services:** DIALOG Information Services. **Special catalogs:** Film and video catalog, biennial—to Idaho librarians. **Publications:** *Newsletter*, monthly—to Idaho librarians and trustees; *Idaho Library Directory*; *State Documents Checklist*.

Illinois

Illinois State Archives

Archives Bldg.
Springfield, IL 62756
Phone: (217)782-4682
Fax: (217)524-3930
John Daly, Director

Staff: Professional 31; Other 16. **Founded:** 1921. **Subjects:** Illinois history and official records. **Holdings:** 52,000 cubic feet of state agency reports, land patents, manuscript records, county and state agency records. **Subscriptions:** 3 journals and other serials. **Services:** Copying; genealogical, war records, historical, and land record research; archives open to the public, mental health records closed by law. **Computerized services:** Internal databases. **Publications:** *A Descriptive Inventory of the Archives of the State of Illinois*; *Illinois Public Domain Land Sales*; *A Summary Guide to Local Records in the Illinois Regional Archives*; *A Guide to County Records in the Illinois Regional Archives*; *Windows to the Past, 1818-1880*; *Early Chicago, 1833-1871; From the Ashes 1871-1900.*

Illinois State Historical Library

Old State Capitol
Springfield, IL 62701
Phone: (217)782-4836
Janice A. Petterchak, Head

Staff: Professional 15; Other 7. **Founded:** 1889. **Subjects:** Illinois history, Lincolniana, Civil War history, Midwest Americana, Mormon history, Indian history, genealogy. **Special collections:** Picture and Print Collection (250,000). **Holdings:** 170,000 volumes; 9 million manuscripts; 70,000 reels of newspapers on microfilm; 3000 maps; 3500 broadsides. **Subscriptions:** 600 journals and other serials; 300 newspapers. **Services:** Interlibrary loan (limited); copying; library open to the public. **Computerized services:** OCLC. **Remarks:** Maintained by Illinois (State) Historic Preservation Agency.

Illinois State Library

300 S. 2nd St.
Springfield, IL 62701-1796
Phone: (217)782-2994
Fax: (217)785-4326
Bridget L. Lamont, Director

Staff: Professional 60; Other 66. **Founded:** 1839. **Subjects:** U.S. and Illinois state government, business. **Special collections:** State documents (475,000); federal documents (1.6 million); U.S. patents; maps (140,000). **Holdings:** 5 million items. **Subscriptions:** 2250 journals and other serials; 27 newspapers. **Services:** Interlibrary loan; copying; current awareness; library open to the public. **Computerized services:** InfoPro Technologies, DIALOG Information Services, OCLC, ILLINET. **Remarks:** Headquarters of the network ILLINET. **Publications:** *Illinois Libraries*, 10/year; *Insight*, 12/year.

Kendall College
Mitchell Indian Museum Library

2408 Orrington Ave.
Evanston, IL 60201
Phone: (708)866-1395
Fax: (708)866-1320
Jane T. Edwards, Director/Curator

Staff: 2. **Founded:** 1977. **Subjects:** Native Americans—history, anthropology, art, literature, ethnography. **Special collections:** Jesuit Relations; Bureau of Ethnology reports. **Holdings:** 1100 books; 14 AV programs. **Subscriptions:** 5 journals and other serials; 3 newspapers. **Services:** Interlibrary loan; copying; SDI; library open to the public.

Newberry Library

60 W. Walton St.
Chicago, IL 60610
Phone: (312)943-9090
Charles T. Cullen, President & Librarian

Staff: Professional 42; Other 60. **Description:** Private reference and research library containing one of the most extensive collections of local history and genealogy in the U.S. Has resources for research in the Midwest, New England, mid-Atlantic, Southern, and border states as well as other regions of the U.S. and Canada. **Founded:** 1887. **Subjects:** Genealogy; European, English, and American history and literature; local and family history; church history; bibliography; history of cartography. **Special collections:** Western Americana; American Indian; Midwest manuscripts; over 16,000 printed family histories; county and town histories and published local records (birth, marriage, death registers; tax lists; land records); U.S. census records and city directories; military records; Darcy McNichol Collection (Native Americans). **Holdings:** 1.4 million volumes; 5 million manuscripts; 225,000 microforms. **Subscriptions:** 1500 journals and other serials. **Services:** Copying; library open to the public with identification. **Computerized services:** OCLC, Association of Research Libraries (ARL). **Publications:** *An Uncommon Collection of Uncommon Collections*; *Newberry Library Center for the History of the American Indian Bibliographical Series*; *Catalog of the Edward E. Ayer Collection of American Indians in the Newberry Library;* newsletter; bulletins.

Indiana

Allen County Public Library
Fred J. Reynolds Historical Genealogy Collection

900 Webster St.
PO Box 2270
Fort Wayne, IN 46802
Phone: (219)424-7241
Fax: (219)422-9688
Curt B. Witcher, Manager

Staff: Professional 5; Other 11. **Founded:** 1961. **Subjects:** North American genealogy and family history, Indiana history, heraldry. **Special collections:** Collection of passenger and immigration records, including thousands of rolls of ships' passenger lists for major U.S. ports; collection of North American historical and genealogical society serial publications; U.S. Census population schedules, 1790-1910; Soundexes, 1880-1910 (microfilm); North Carolina Core Collection (county records through 1868; 4500 reels of microfilm); Canadian census schedules, 1825-1891; ships passenger lists, 1820-1945; Black American family history; Native American family history. **Holdings:** 183,000 books; 8500 bound periodical volumes; 500 vertical file materials and clippings; 210,000 microforms; 9 AV programs; 273,000 clippings and pamphlets. **Subscriptions:** 3182 journals and other serials. **Services:** Interlibrary loan; copying; collection open to the public. **Computerized services:** DIALOG Information Services, InfoPro Technologies, CompuServe Information Service, OCLC, OCLC FirstSearch Catalog; internal database. Performs searches on fee basis. Contact Person: Susan M. Riehm, Online Services Coordinator. **Special indexes:** Subject index to genealogical periodical literature. **Remarks:** Is said to house the largest group of genealogical materials in a North American public library. **Publications:** Bibliographies; pathfinders; *Periodical Source Index.*

Earlham College
Friends Collection

Lilly Library
Richmond, IN 47374
Phone: (317)983-1511
Fax: (317)983-1304
Thomas Hamm, Archivist

Staff: Professional 1; Other 1. **Founded:** 1847. **Subjects:** Society of Friends (Quakers); Earlham College. **Special collections:** Indian Affairs; correspondence involving the work of the Quakers with a number of tribes in Oklahoma, Nebraska, and Iowa; collections of Chas. F. Coffin, Allen Jay, Barnabas C. Hobbs, Thomas E. Jones, David M. Edwards, William C. Dennis, Landrum Bolling, Josiah Parker, Elbert Russell, Marcus Mote, Clifford Crump, Esther Griffin White, Harlow Lindley; Earlham College Historical Collection; Willard Heiss; Homer L. Morris; Eli & Mahalah Jay; Joseph Moore; Indiana Yearly Meeting of Friends; Pusey Grave; Walter C. Woodward; Errol T. Elliott; Levi Coffin. **Holdings:** 12,000 books; 550 bound periodical volumes; 5000 pamphlets, manuscripts, photographs; 100 volumes of printed and bound theses; 250 audiocassettes; 1200 volumes of Quaker genealogy. **Subscriptions:** 70 journals and other serials. **Services:** Interlibrary loan (limited); copying; collection open to the public. **Special catalogs:** Catalog of archival materials (card).

Indiana Historical Society William Henry Smith Memorial Library

315 W. Ohio St.
Indianapolis, IN 46202-3299
Phone: (317)232-1879
Fax: (317)233-3109
Bruce L. Johnson, Director

Staff: Professional 17; Other 5. **Founded:** 1934. **Subjects:** History of Indiana and Old Northwest. **Special collections:** Black history (including Mme. C.J. Walker, Elijah Roberts, and Herbert Heller manuscript collections, Emmett Brown photograph collection; 6000 items); Indiana in the Civil War (including Lew Wallace, D.E. Beem, and Jefferson C. Davis manuscript collections; 15,000 items); Old Northwest Territory history (600 manuscripts); William Henry Harrison and Indiana Territory history (500 manuscripts); visual collection (1.5 million of graphics works, paintings, and photographs). **Holdings:** 65,000 books; 150 bound periodical volumes; 4 million manuscripts; 1000 maps; 1600 reels of microfilm. **Subscriptions:** 360 journals and other serials. **Services:** Limited photocopying; photographic reproductions; preservation consultations; library open to the public. **Computerized services:** OCLC. Performs searches free of charge. **Publications:** Indiana Historical Society annual report (accessions); *Black History News and Notes*, quarterly.

Indiana State Library

140 N. Senate Ave.
Indianapolis, IN 46204
Phone: (317)232-3675
Fax: (317)232-3728
C. Ray Ewick, Director

Staff: Professional 44; Other 40. **Founded:** 1825. **Subjects:** Genealogy, Indiana history, federal and state documents, library science. **Special collections:** Indiana Manuscript Collection. **Holdings:** 1.6 million items; regional depository for federal documents; state documents. **Subscriptions:** 15,792 journals and other serials. **Services:** Interlibrary loan; copying; library open to the public. **Computerized services:** DIALOG Information Services, OCLC, STATIS, Library of Congress Information System. **Special indexes:** Index of Indianapolis newspapers since 1898 (card); genealogical indexes; newspaper, biographical, picture, and map holdings index (card). **Publications:** *Indiana Libraries*, quarterly; *Focus on Indiana Libraries*, monthly; *Hoosier Highlights*.

Notre Dame University Archives

c/o University of Notre Dame
Notre Dame, IN 46556

Iowa

Effigy Mounds National Monument Library

R.R. 1, Box 25A
Harpers Ferry, IA 52146
Phone: (319)873-3491
Thomas A. Munson, Superintendent

Staff: Professional 1. **Founded:** 1949. **Subjects:** Archeology, anthropology, ethnology, local history, natural sciences. **Special collections:** Ellison Orr manuscriptts and library (1000 items); materials that used to belong to the BIA. **Holdings:** 2600 books. **Subscriptions:** 17 journals and other serials. **Services:** Library open to the public for reference use only.

Iowa State Archives

Capitol Complex
East 12th St. and Grand Ave.
Des Moines, IA 50319

State Historical Society of Iowa Library/Archives

600 E. Locust
Des Moines, IA 50319
Phone: (515)281-5111
Fax: (515)282-0502
Jerome Thompson, Bureau Chief

Staff: Professional 2; Other 6. **Founded:** 1894. **Subjects:** History—Iowa, agriculture, railroad, regional Indians; historic preservation; genealogy. **Special collections:** State Archives (17,000 cubic feet); historical Iowa photographs (100,000 images); Iowa historical maps (3000); Manuscript collections—Grenville Dodge, Charles Mason, Albert Cummins, William Boyd Allison, John A. Kasson. **Holdings:** 70,500 books; 2500 linear feet of manuscripts; 30,000 reels of microfilm; 42 VF drawers of pamphlets and clippings. **Subscriptions:** 200 journals and other serials; 300 newspapers. **Services:** Interlibrary loan; copying; library open to the public. **Special indexes:** Index to Iowa GAR file (microfilm); index to selected newspapers (microfilm).

State Historical Society of Iowa Library/Archives

402 Iowa Ave.
Iowa City, IA 52240-1806
Phone: (319)335-3916
Fax: (319)335-3924
Christie Dailey, Bureau Chief

Staff: Professional 7; Other 4. **Founded:** 1857. **Subjects:** History—Iowa, the frontier, agriculture, railroad, women, education, American Indians; genealogy. **Special collections:** Robert Lucas papers; Jonathan P. Dolliver papers; Gilbert Haugen papers; Cyrus Carpenter papers; labor collection historical Iowa photographs (265,000); historical Iowa maps (3000). **Holdings:** 130,000 books; 10,000 bound periodical volumes; 15,000 pamphlets; 17,000 reels of microfilm; 10,000 bound newspapers; 25 VF drawers of newspaper clippings; 1800 oral history interviews; 4000 linear feet of manuscripts. **Subscriptions:** 575 serials. **Services:** Interlibrary loan; copying; library open to the public. **Special catalogs:** Manuscript catalog; Fire Insurance Maps of Iowa Cities and Towns. **Special indexes:** Indexes to selected history and genealogy serials. **Publications:** *Bibliography of Iowa Newspapers*, 1836-1976; *Iowa History and Culture* (bibliography of materials published between 1952 and 1986); bibliographies on immigrant groups.

State Library of Iowa

E. 12th & Grand
Des Moines, IA 50319
Phone: (515)281-4118
Fax: (515)281-3384
Sharman B. Smith, Administrator, Div. of Library Services

Staff: Professional 14; Other 22. **Founded:** 1838. **Subjects:** State government, public policy, law, medicine, library science. **Special collections:** State Documents Collection; Federal Documents Depository; State Data Center. **Holdings:** 312,232 books; 10 cabinets of vertical files about Iowa; 16,841 reels of microfilm; 630,000 microfiche. **Subscriptions:** 2224 journals and other serials. **Services:** Interlibrary loan; copying; library open to the public. **Computerized services:** DIALOG Information Services,

PFDS Online, InfoPro Technologies. **Special catalogs:** Audio-Visual Catalog; *Iowa Documents Catalog* (book). **Publications:** *Iowa Locator* (compact disc), quarterly; *Footnotes*, monthly; *Iowa Library Directory*, annual.

Kansas

Kansas Heritage Center Library

PO Box 1275
Dodge City, KS 67801
Phone: (316)227-1616
Fax: (913)227-1640
Jeanie Covalt, Research Librarian

Staff: 4. **Founded:** 1966. **Subjects:** Frontier and pioneer life, Kansas, the West, Indians of North America, cowboys, cattle trade, transportation, agricultural history, folklore. **Special collections:** Historical collections from the states of Kansas, Missouri, Colorado, and New Mexico. **Holdings:** 10,000 volumes; clippings; pamphlets; microfilm; filmstrips; slides; tapes and phonograph records; 16mm films; videotapes. **Subscriptions:** 6 journals and other serials. **Services:** Interlibrary loan; copying; assembles mini-kits on various subjects; programs and workshops; library open to the public. **Computerized services:** Dodge City Newspapers abstracted 1877-1929; Ford County census 1875, 1885 (internal databases). **Special catalogs:** Reference Materials and Resources. **Publications:** *Sentinel to the Cimarron*; *The Frontier Experience of Fort Dodge, Kansas* (1970); *Up From the Prairie* (1974); *The Process of Oral History* (1976); *Dodge City* (1982); *West by Southwest* (1984); *Indians in Kansas* (1987); *Adventures with the Santa Fe Trail* (1989); bibliographies; *399 Kansas Characters* (1992).

Kansas State Historical Society Library

Historical Research Center
120 W. 10th St.
Topeka, KS 66612-1291
Phone: (913)296-3251
Fax: (913)296-1005
David A. Haury, Acting Director

Staff: Professional 6; Other 11. **Founded:** 1875. **Subjects:** Kansas history, local history of other states, genealogy, American Indians, the West, American biography, Civil War. **Special collections:** Kansas (21,529 books; 130,139 pamphlets); genealogy and local history (18,584 books; 7476 pamphlets); American Indians and the West (5006 books; 2140 pamphlets). **Holdings:** 135,119 books; 25,892 bound periodical volumes; 74,086 bound volumes of Kansas newspapers; 12,373 bound volumes of out-of-state newspapers; 1977 volumes of clippings; 51,706 reels of microfilm; 194 titles on microcard. **Subscriptions:** 300 journals and other serials. **Services:** Interlibrary loan; copying (both limited); library open to the public. **Special catalogs:** Guide to the Microfilm Collections of Kansas State Historical Society (1991).

Kansas State Library

300 SW 10th Ave., Rm. 343
Topeka, KS 66612-1593
Phone: (913)296-3296
Fax: (913)296-6650
Duane F. Johnson, State Librarian

Staff: Professional 11; Other 13. **Founded:** 1855. **Subjects:** Public administration, census, Kansas government and legislation. **Special collections:** Federal and state documents depository. **Holdings:** 60,000 books; 10,000 bound periodical volumes; 60,000 other cataloged items. **Subscriptions:** 250 journals and other serials; 10 newspapers. **Services:** Interlibrary loan; copying; SDI; library open to the public. **Computerized services:** DIALOG Information Services, InfoPro Technologies, PFDS Online, Library Information Service (LIS). Performs searches on fee basis. **Special catalogs:** Kansas Government Documents Catalog. **Publications:** *State Data Center News*, quarterly; *Kansas Libraries*, monthly.

University of Kansas Kansas Collection

220 Spencer Research Library
Lawrence, KS 66045-2800
Phone: (913)864-4274
Sheryl K. Williams, Curator

Staff: Professional 3; Other 3. **Founded:** 1892. **Subjects:** Kansas and Great Plains social movements, business and economic history, social and cultural history, politics, travel; regional African-American history. **Special collections:** Overland diaries; Kansas State documents depository; J.J. Pennell Collection of photographs and negatives, 1891-1923 (40,000 items); Wilcox Collection of Contemporary Political Movements, 1960 to present (6500 books; 6000 serials; 84,000 pieces of ephemera); Jules Bourquin Collection of photographs, 1898-1959 (30,000); J.B. Watkins Land Mortgage Company Records, 1864-1946 (627 linear feet); regional African-American history. **Computerized services:** OCLC; BITNET (electronic mail service). **Remarks:** Electronic mail address: SWILLIAM@UKANVM (BITNET).

Wyandotte County Historical Society and Museum Harry M. Trowbridge Research Library

631 N. 126th St.
Bonner Springs, KS 66012
Phone: (913)721-1078

Staff: Professional 1; Other 5. **Founded:** 1956. **Subjects:** Wyandotte County and Kansas City history; Wyandot, Shawnee, and Delaware Indians. **Special collections:** Early, Conley, and Farrow Family Collections, 1763-1960 (30 cubic feet of papers, books, photographs). **Holdings:** 4000 books; 1000 bound periodical volumes; clippings; 150 reels of microfilm; 5000 photographs; maps. **Subscriptions:** 10 journals and other serials. **Services:** Copying; library open to the public with restrictions.

Kentucky

Kentucky (State) Department for Libraries & Archives Public Records Division

PO Box 537
Frankfort, KY 40602
Phone: (502)875-7000
Fax: (502)564-5773
Richard N. Belding, Director/State Archivist

Staff: Professional 20; Other 48. **Founded:** 1958. **Subjects:** Kentucky—history, genealogy, government, politics, health services. **Holdings:** 91,000 cubic feet of state and local government records, including those of the judicial and legislative branches; 35,000 reels of microfilm; 1000 microfiche; 100 videocassettes; 200 audiocassettes; 25,000 photographic negatives. **Subscriptions:** 15 journals and other serials; 5 newspapers. **Services:** Copying; archives open to the public. **Computerized services:** Internal database. **Publications:** List of publications available on request.

Louisiana

Archdiocese of New Orleans Archives

1100 Chartres St.
New Orleans, LA 70116
Phone: (504)529-2651
Fax: (504)529-2001
Charles E. Nolan, Archivist

Staff: Prof. 5, other 1. **Description:** Nonprofit regional collection includes major coverage of African and Hispanic Americans, minor coverage of Native Americans. **Founded:** 1971. **Subjects:** Sacramental (baptism, marriage, funeral), cemetery and orphanage records from eight civil parishes (counties) comprising the present Archdiocese of New Orleans, 1718-1900, and selected local genealogical and historical publications. **Holdings:** Bound periodical volumes, periodicals, 300 books, and 810 archival volumes. **Services:** Copying, genealogical assistance, educational programs. Archives open to scholars; genealogical requests handled by mail only. **Computerized services:** SacraInd (Data Perfect): all surname entries for sacramental records, 1773-1809; continuous additions. **Special indexes:** Published indices to early sacramental records.

Archives of the Parish of East Baton Rouge Genealogy Section

Public Service Department
B1 Governmental Bldg.
222 St. Louis St.
Baton Rouge, LA 70802
Edward O. Cailleteau, Archives Department Head
Doug Welborn, Clerk of Court

Staff: Professional assistance available. **Description:** Contains one of the most extensive county records collections in the southern U.S. Holds land records from 1799; court records from 1808 (original and microfilm); possesses the 19 volume *Spanish West Florida Records* of the Baton Rouge Post, dating from 1782-1810 (originals and translations on microfilm); *American State Papers,* containing legislative and executive documents relating to public lands (1789-1834); marriage license records, 1840-; criminal records, 1814-.

Le Comite des Archives de la Louisiane

116 Main St.
PO Box 44370
Capitol Station
Baton Rouge, LA 70804

Special collections: Ship passenger lists of the French and Spanish arriving in Louisiana.

Louisiana (State) Office of the Secretary of State Division of Archives, Records Management, and History

PO Box 94125
Baton Rouge, LA 70804
Phone: (504)922-1206
Fax: (504)925-4726
Dr. Donald J. Lemieux, State Archivist/Director

Staff: Professional 10; Other 25. **Founded:** 1956. **Subjects:** State and local government records, Louisiana history, genealogy. **Special collections:** Louisiana Confederate government records (80 volumes and 8 cubic feet); Records of Board of Confederate Pension Commissioners (147 cubic feet); Louisiana Legal Archives (85 cubic feet); original acts of the Louisiana Legislature, 1804-1964 (121 bound volumes); oral history tape library (930); graphics collection (2379 images); New Orleans birth records, 1790-1893; New Orleans death records, 1804-1943; New Orleans marriage records, 1831-1943; Statewide Death Records, 1900-1943. **Holdings:** 11,100 books; 19,200 cubic feet of archival government records; 53,400 reels of microfilm. **Subscriptions:** 7 journals and other serials. **Services:** Copying; microfilming; conservation laboratory; division open to the public. **Special indexes:** *1898 and 1913 Louisiana Voter Registration Index* (book); *Records of the Opelousas Post,* 1766-1803 (book); Confederate pension applicants index (book); collections indexes (card).

State Library of Louisiana

PO Box 131
Baton Rouge, LA 70821
Phone: (504)342-4913
Fax: (504)342-3547
Thomas F. Jaques, State Librarian

Staff: Professional 28; Other 41. **Founded:** 1925. **Special collections:** Louisiana (70,113 cataloged items; 119,493 state documents; 225 VF drawers); genealogy (5238 items); U.S. Government documents (209,478). **Holdings:** 392,949 volumes; 3088 maps; 10,000 photographs; 18,730 reels of microfilm. **Subscriptions:** 1575 journals and other serials; 25 newspapers. **Services:** Interlibrary loan; copying; library open to the public. **Computerized services:** OCLC, DIALOG Information Services, DataTimes, InfoPro Technologies, EPIC, LEAP; Internet (electronic mail service). Contact Person: Margaret Schroth, Head, Reference/Bibliographies, (504)342-4913. **Special catalogs:** Louisiana Union Catalog (card, microfiche). **Remarks:** Electronic mail address: michael-mckann@solinet.net (Internet). **Publications:** *Searching for Your Ancestors on Microfilm* (brochure)—free upon request; *Recent Acquisitions*; *LaGIN Directory of State Agency Information Resources*; *LaGIN Information Resources Exchange.*

Tulane University Howard-Tilton Memorial Library Louisiana Collection

New Orleans, LA 70118

Phone: (504)865-5643
Fax: (504)865-6773
Joan G. Caldwell, Library Head

Staff: 2. **Founded:** 1952. **Subjects:** Louisiana history and culture from colonial times to present. **Special collections:** Louisiana State, Louisiana Territory, and La Louisiane region maps and charts. Books; pamphlets; maps; photographs; newspapers; vertical file of clippings and ephemeral material arranged by subjects; bibliography file, citation file. **Holdings:** 35,000 titles. **Services:** Copying; collection open to the public.

Tulane University Howard-Tilton Memorial Library Rare Books

New Orleans, LA 70118-5682

Phone: (504)865-5685
Fax: (504)865-6773
Sylvia Verdun Metzinger, Rare Books Librarian

Staff: Professional 1; Other 1. **Founded:** 1952. **Subjects:** Southern history, Civil War, literature, water transporation, natural history, English county history, Romanov Russian history and travel, American Revolution, science fiction, 19th-20th century English language first editions. **Holdings:** 50,000 rare books titles. **Subscriptions:** 20 journals and other serials. **Services:** Copying; open to the public with identification. **Computerized services:** OCLC. **Special catalogs:** Favrot Library catalog; rare book catalog. **Formerly:** Tulane University—Manuscripts, Rare Books and University Archives.

University of New Orleans Earl K. Long Library Archives & Manuscripts/Special Collections Department

Lake Front
New Orleans, LA 70148

Phone: (504)286-6543
Fax: (504)286-7277
D. Clive Hardy, Archivist, Head of Department

Staff: Professional 3; Other 16. **Founded:** 1968. **Subjects:** New Orleans—ethnic groups, labor unions, legal records, businesses, history, culture. **Holdings:** 4800 volumes; 11,000 linear feet of manuscripts and archival records. **Subscriptions:** 12 journals and other serials. **Services:** Interlibrary loan (limited); copying; department open to the public. **Computerized services:** DIALOG Information Services, InfoPro Technologies, STN International, ORBIT Search Service, OCLC. **Special catalogs:** Special Collections at the University of New Orleans.

Maine

Maine State Archives

State House Sta. 84
Augusta, ME 04333-0084

Phone: (207)287-5790
Fax: (207)287-5739
James S. Henderson, State Archivist

Staff: 14. **Founded:** 1971. **Subjects:** Maine. **Holdings:** 20,000 cubic feet of judicial, legislative, and executive branch records, land office records, military (Civil War) records, censuses, and vital statistics records. **Services:** copying; archives open to registered researchers. **Computerized services:** Computer databases for patron use only. **Remarks:** Electronic mail address: ubrown@saturn.caps.maine.edu (Internet). Maintains a Bulletin Board System: (207)287-5797. **Publications:** List of publications available upon request.

Maine State Library

Cultural Bldg.
State House Sta. 64
Augusta, ME 04333-0064

Phone: (207)287-5600
Fax: (207)287-5615
J. Gary Nichols, State Librarian

Staff: Professional 18; Other 42. **Founded:** 1839. **Subjects:** Maine—history, genealogy, state, county, and local histories. **Special collections:** Maps; manuscripts; town reports, 1892 to present (includes city directories and Maine Registers, 1820 to present); Maine newspapers (*Bangor Daily Whig and Courier*, 1836-1900; *Eastern Argus*, 1803-1921; *Le Messager*, 1880-1946); Maine Vertical File. **Holdings:** 400,000 volumes; federal and state government documents. **Subscriptions:** 200 journals and other serials; 31 newspapers. **Services:** Interlibrary loan; copying; library open to the public. **Computerized services:** OCLC, DIALOG Information Services. Performs searches free of charge. Contact Person: Emily Herrick, Reference Librarian. **Publications:** *The Maine Entry*, quarterly; *Libraries in Maine*, annual.

Maryland

Maryland State Archives Library

350 Rowe Blvd.
Annapolis, MD 21401

Phone: (410)974-3915
Fax: (301)974-3895
Shashi P. Thapar, Library Director

Staff: Professional 1. **Founded:** 1935. **Subjects:** History—Maryland, American, Black, other states; genealogy; biography. **Special collections:** Works Project Administration Historical Records Survey Publications; Maryland State Publications and Reports. **Holdings:** 15,000 books; 450 bound periodical volumes; reports; manuscripts; archives. **Subscriptions:** 100 journals and other serials. **Services:** Copying; library open to the public for reference use only. **Computerized services:** Internal databases. Performs searches on fee basis. **Publications:** Irregular publications; serials and periodicals list.

Massachusetts

Connecticut Valley Historical Museum Library and Archives

194 State St.
Springfield, MA 01103
Phone: (413)732-3080
Fax: (413)734-6158
Guy A. McLain, Head, Library & Archival Collections

Staff: Professional 4; Other 2. **Founded:** 1988. **Subjects:** Connecticut Valley history, Springfield history 1636 to present, New England genealogy, Springfield business history. **Special collections:** Roger Putnam papers (1920-1972; 96 linear feet); 17th-20th century Springfield and Connecticut Valley manuscripts. **Holdings:** 23,000 books; 2000 bound periodical volumes; 35,000 photographs; 2800 linear feet of archival records; 300 feet of vertical files, atlases, and maps; 5000 microform records. **Subscriptions:** 40 journals and other serials; 15 newspapers. **Services:** Copying; department open to the public. **Special indexes:** Springfield History Index (card). **Publications:** Pathfinders for African American genealogy; archives guides for all archives collections.

Jones Library, Inc. Special Collections

43 Amity St.
Amherst, MA 01002
Phone: (413)256-4090
Fax: (413)256-4096
Daniel J. Lombardo, Curator

Staff: Professional 1; Other 3. **Founded:** 1921. **Subjects:** Local and regional history, Amherst authors, genealogy. **Holdings:** 15,000 books; 50,000 historical photographs; 20,000 other cataloged items; 240 reels of microfilm. **Subscriptions:** 11 journals and other serials. **Services:** Copying; collections open to the public. **Special indexes:** Index of local newspapers (online). **Publications:** Finding aids.

Massachusetts (State) Archives at Columbia Point

220 Morrissey Blvd.
Boston, MA 02125
Phone: (617)727-2816
Fax: (617)727-8730
Dr. Albert H. Whitaker Jr., State Archivist

Staff: Professional 17; Other 3. **Subjects:** Massachusetts state and local government and history. **Special collections:** Judicial Archives: Superior Court of Judicature Records, 1692-1780 (dockets, record books, and file papers), Supreme Judicial Court Records, 1780-1859 (dockets, record books, and file papers), trial courts and their predecessor courts, 1634-1859, selected county probate records, selected Superior Court naturalization records; Massachusetts Archives (328 volumes of colonial and Revolutionary-era manuscripts); enacted and unenacted legislative documents, 1630 to present; gubernatorial records; maps and plans, 1630 to present; case files for Department of Correction, Mental Health and Public Health, 19th and 20th centuries. **Holdings:** 30,000 cubic feet of archival records; 9000 microforms; 24,000 photographs. **Subscriptions:** 10 journals and other serials. **Services:** Copying; archives open to the public with restrictions. **Computerized services:** RLIN. **Publications:** Collections bulletins and information sheets.

New England Historic Genealogical Society Library

99-101 Newbury St.
Boston, MA 02116
Phone: (617)536-5740
Fax: (617)536-7307

Staff: Professional 4; Other 31. **Founded:** 1845. **Subjects:** Genealogy and family history, local history, vital records, heraldry. **Special collections:** New England family and local histories; Eastern Canadian family and local histories; genealogical research materials; American Antiquarian Society newspaper index. **Holdings:** 135,000 volumes; 7000 reels of microfilm; 3500 linear feet of manuscripts; city directories; vital records; diaries; regimental histories; church histories. **Subscriptions:** 420 periodicals. **Services:** Copying; research; lectures and seminars; library open to the public on a fee basis. **Computerized services:** OCLC, Sydney Library Systems, MARCIVE. **Remarks:** Major center in the eastern United States for Canadian and Canadian American genealogy. **Publications:** *New England Historical and Genealogical Register*, quarterly; *Nexus* (newsletter), 5/year; monographs.

State Library of Massachusetts

341 State House
Boston, MA 02133
Phone: (617)727-2590
Gasper Caso, State Librarian

Staff: Professional 12; Other 20. **Founded:** 1826. **Subjects:** Public law, public affairs, Massachusetts legislation, government, politics, U.S. and Massachusetts history. **Special collections:** Massachusetts history (books; prints; photographs; broadsides; manuscripts); city directories; 18th and 19th century newspapers; maps and atlases. **Holdings:** 825,000 volumes; 12,170 reels of microfilm; 294,855 microfiche; official depository for Massachusetts publications; selective depository for federal publications. **Subscriptions:** 2465 journals and other serials; 97 newspapers. **Services:** Interlibrary loan; copying; library open to the public for reference use only. **Computerized services:** OCLC, CARL; CD-ROMs. Performs searches. **Special indexes:** Boston Newspapers, 1879-1937, 1962-1981, 1983 to present; Index and Guide to Massachusetts Legislative Documents, 1802-1882; Legislative Biographical File, colonial times to present; Guide to Massachusetts Legislative and Government Research. **Publications:** *Commonwealth of Massachusetts Publications Received*, quarterly and annual.

University of Massachusetts Library Special Collections and Archives

Amherst, MA 01003
Phone: (413)545-2780
Fax: (413)545-6873
Linda Seidman, Acting Library Head

Staff: Professional 1; Other 2. **Founded:** 1867. **Subjects:** History of botany and entomology to 1900; historical geography and cartography of Northeastern United States to 1900; history of Massachusetts and New England; antislavery movement in New England; travel and tourism in New England, New York, and eastern Canada; Massachusetts; African-American studies; labor and business history. **Holdings:** 19,000 books; 8000 linear feet of records, manuscripts, clippings, photographs, maps, building plans, microfilm, audiotapes. **Services:** Copying; collections open to the public. **Computerized services:** OCLC. **Remarks:** Electronic mail address: linda.seidman@library.umass.edu (Internet).

Michigan

Central Michigan University Clarke Historical Library

Mt. Pleasant, MI 48859
Phone: (517)774-3352
Fax: (517)774-4499
Frank Boles, Director

Staff: Professional 3; Other 4. **Founded:** 1955. **Subjects:** Michigan, Old Northwest Territory, early travel in the Midwest, Afro-Americana, history of slavery, Native Americans, children's literature, angling. **Special collections:** Wilbert Wright Collection Afro-Americana (5000 volumes). **Holdings:** 60,000 books; 1440 maps; 3274 manuscripts; 1100 broadsides; 26,400 photographs; 8072 microforms; 3564 pieces of sheet music; 900 newspapers; 12,000 pieces of ephemera; 50 tape recordings; 100 phonograph records. **Subscriptions:** 103 journals and other serials. **Services:** Library open to the public. **Special indexes:** Indexes to: newspapers on microfilm; Mt. Pleasant death records; manuscripts on microfilm. **Publications:** Annual report—to mailing list; *Resource Guides*; occasional books and bibliographies; *Michigan Historical Review*, semiannual—by subscription.

Detroit Public Library Burton Historical Collection

5201 Woodward Ave.
Detroit, MI 48202
Phone: (313)833-1480
Noel S. VanGorden, Chief

Staff: Professional 8; Other 2. **Founded:** 1914. **Subjects:** History—Detroit, Michigan, Old Northwest, local, Great Lakes, New England, New France; genealogy. **Special collections:** Edgar DeWitt Jones—Lincoln Collection. Canadian material and early French records. **Holdings:** 260,000 volumes; 12,000 pamphlets; 4800 bound volumes of newspapers; 5060 feet of manuscripts and personal papers; 10,500 feet of archival materials; 20,000 reels of microfilm; 10,000 microfiche; 1100 microcards; 50,000 pictures; 4000 maps; 5000 glass negatives; 6800 scrapbooks; 1000 color transparencies; 1000 lantern slides; 4050 maps; 325 broadsides. **Subscriptions:** 500 journals and other serials. **Services:** Copying (limited); collection open to the public. **Special indexes:** Manuscripts reported in National Union List of Manuscripts. **Publications:** *Guide to the Manuscripts in the Burton Historical Collection, Detroit Public Library*; *Genealogical Guide to the Burton Historical Collection.*

Lake Superior State University Kenneth J. Shouldice Library Michigan & Marine Collections

1000 College St.
Sault Sainte Marie, MI 49783
Phone: (906)635-2402
Fax: (906)635-2193
Dr. Frederick A. Michels, Director

Staff: Professional 5; Other 6. **Founded:** 1946. **Subjects:** History of Michigan's Upper Peninsula; Indians of Michigan's Upper Peninsula; local history of Sault Ste. Marie, Michigan. **Holdings:** 1400 books; *Sault Evening News* on microfilm; 16 VF drawers of pamphlets concerned with local and area history; Indian cemeteries card file covering the local area. **Subscriptions:** 1200 journals and other serials. **Services:** Interlibrary loan; copying; collections open to the public for reference use only. **Computerized services:** DIALOG Information Services; CD-ROMs. Performs searches on fee basis. Contact Person: Ruth Neveu, Public Services Librarian.

Library of Michigan

717 W. Allegan
PO Box 30007
Lansing, MI 48909
Phone: (517)373-1580
Fax: (517)373-3381
James W. Fry, State Librarian

Staff: Professional 38; Other 70. **Description:** One of the top ten genealogical libraries in the United States. Genealogy/Local History Collection focuses on Michigan and areas from which most of the state's earlier settlers came, including Great Lakes, New England, Mid-Atlantic, and Southern states as well as Ontario and Quebec. **Founded:** 1828. **Subjects:** Public policy and management, politics and government, automation. **Special collections:** Special Michigan collection; regional depository for federal documents; official depository for State of Michigan documents; genealogy; Michigan vital records indexes; Michigan newspapers on microfilm (75,000 reels); 250 genealogical and historical periodicals; Martich black history collection. **Holdings:** 850,000 books; 50,000 bound periodical volumes; 5 million microforms; 300 AV items; 2 million pieces of ephemera. **Subscriptions:** 2500 journals and other serials; 57 newspapers. **Services:** Interlibrary loan; copying; library open to the public. **Computerized services:** DIALOG Information Services, InfoPro Technologies, OCLC; internal databases. **Special indexes:** Michigan Documents, quarterly. **Publications:** *Access*, bimonthly; *Michigan Library Directory*, annual; *Michigan Cemetery Atlas,* 1991; *Genealogy Update,* periodic bulletin listing new acquisitions and highlighting various subjects in the genealogy area.

State Archives of Michigan

717 W. Allegan
Lansing, MI 48918-1837
Phone: (517)373-1408
Fax: (517)373-0851
David J. Johnson, State Archivist

Staff: Professional 8; Other 4. **Founded:** 1913. **Subjects:** Michigan history and government. **Special collections:** Historical photograph collection (300,000 images of Michigan); historical map collection (500,000 cartographic expressions). **Holdings:** 1000 books; 100 bound periodical volumes; 6000 reels of microfilm; 80 million documents (24,000 cubic feet of state and local government records; private papers). **Services:** Copying; archives open to the public (appointments recommended). **Publications:** *A Guide to the State Archives of Michigan: State Records*; published finding aids (1-20); circulars (1-45); genealogical information; *Michigan's Memory* (pamphlets).

University Microfilms International Library

300 N. Zeeb Rd.
Ann Arbor, MI 48106
Phone: (313)761-4700
Fax: (313)761-1204

Staff: Prof 5. **Founded:** 1938. **Subjects:** Early English printed books, incunabula, early American printed books, early English and American periodicals, out-of-print books. **Holdings:** 1 million dissertations; 175 major research collections; 19,000 periodicals on microfilm; 7000 newspapers. **Computerized services:** ABI/INFORM, Newspaper Abstracts, Business Dateline, Pharmaceutical News Index (PNI); CD-ROM (Periodical Abstracts Ondisc); DATRIX (doctoral research information; internal database). **Special catalogs:** Serials in Microform Catalog; Books on Demand Catalog. **Special indexes:** Comprehensive Dissertation Index; Japanese Technical Abstracts and Japanese Current Research. **Publications:** UMI Newsletter; Collections Guides and Indexes; Special Bibliographies; Dissertation Abstracts International; Masters Abstracts; Monograph Abstracts; American Doctoral Dissertations. **Remarks:** Library not open to the public.

Minnesota

Minnesota Historical Society Fort Snelling Branch Library

Fort Snelling History Center
St. Paul, MN 55111
Phone: (612)726-1171
Fax: (612)725-2429
Stephen E. Osman

Staff: 1. **Founded:** 1970. **Subjects:** History - Minnesota, regional, military; American Indians; American and regional archeology; 19th century America. **Holdings:** 6000 volumes; 1500 other cataloged items. **Subscriptions:** 5 journals and other serials. **Services:** Library open to the public for reference use only.

Minnesota Historical Society Library & Archives

345 Kellogg Blvd. W.
St. Paul, MN 55102-1906
Phone: (612)296-2143
Fax: (612)297-7436
Denise Carlson, Head, Reference

Staff: Professional 10; Other 11. **Founded:** 1849. **Subjects:** Minnesota, Upper Midwest, genealogy, Scandinavians in North America, ethnic groups in U.S. and Canada, transportation, agriculture, arts, commerice, family life, industry, Indians (Ojibway, Chippewa, and other Minnesota tribes). **Special collections:** Minnesota newspapers, 1849 to present; Minnesota State Archives (40,000 cubic feet); St. Paul and Minneapolis newspaper negatives (1 million); MHS manuscript collections. **Holdings:** 500,000 monographs, government documents, and microform volumes; 100 VF drawers; 250,000 photographs; 35,000 maps; 1300 atlases; 4.5 million issues of 3000 titles of newspaper volumes; 37,000 cubic feet of manuscripts. **Subscriptions:** 3000 journals and other serials; 436 newspapers. **Services:** Interlibrary loan; copying; library open to the public for reference use only. **Computerized services:** DIALOG Information Services, OCLC. **Remarks:** Absorbed holdings of Minnesota Historical Society—Archives and Manuscripts Collections. **Publications:** Pathfinders and guides, irregular.

Mississippi

Mississippi (State) Department of Archives and History Archives and Library Division

PO Box 571
Jackson, MS 39205
Phone: (601)359-6850
Fax: (601)359-6905
H.T. Holmes, Division Director

Staff: Professional 15; Other 7. **Founded:** 1902. **Subjects:** Mississippiana, genealogy, Confederate history, colonial history of Southeast United States. **Special collections:** Federal records include mortality and population schedules; territorial census for 1805, 1810, and 1816; special census 1890. **Holdings:** 58,000 volumes; 17,000 cubic feet of documents; 2000 manuscript collections; 24,000 nonbook items; 6000 cubic feet of manuscripts; 11,000 cubic feet of official state archives; 7095 maps; 12,500 reels of microfilm; 50,000 photographs; 3 million feet of newsfilm; 2203 architectural drawings; 158 VF drawers. **Subscriptions:** 370 journals and other serials; 137 newspapers. **Services:** Copying; library open to the public for reference use only. **Computerized services:** Informix, Bibliofile (internal databases). **Publications:** List of publications—available on request.

University of Southern Mississippi McCain Library and Archives

Souther Sta.
Box 5148
Hattiesburg, MS 39406-5148
Phone: (601)266-4345
Kay L. Wall, Director

Staff: Prof 6; Other 3. **Founded:** 1976. **Subjects:** Mississippiana, genealogy, Civil War, Confederate State of America, children's literature, British and American literary criticism, political cartoon. **Special collections:** Papers of Theodore G. Bilbo, William M Colmer, Governor Paul B. Johnson; Cleanth Brooks Literature Collection; papers and illustrations of Ezra Jack Keats; Ernest A. Walen Collection of Confederate Literature; Collection of Rare Cooks; genealogy collection; University Archives. **Holdings:** 73,000 volumes; 7500 linear feet of manuscripts and illustrations. **Subscriptions:** 220 journals and other serials; 64 newspapers. **Services:** Interlibrary loan; copying (both limited); library open to the public for reference use only. Computerized cataloging and serials. **Computerized services:** OCLC. Member of SOLINET.

Missouri

Mid-Continent Public Library Genealogy and Local History Department

Spring and 24 Highway
Independence, MO 64050
Phone: (816)252-0950
Fax: (816)252-0950
Martha L. Henderson, Department Head

Staff: Prof. 2, other 16. **Description:** Genealogy collection with national and regional focus. Some coverage of African and Native Americans, minor coverage of Hispanic and Asian Americans. **Founded:** 1965. **Special collections:** Federal Census Population Schedules, 1790-1920, for all states with accompanying Soundex; AFRA/MoSGA Genealogy Circulating Collection, over 4,000 titles available on interlibrary loan, free of charge, nationwide. **Holdings:** 30,000 books, 1,000 bound periodical vol., 60,000 microfiche, 50,000 microfilm, 300 periodicals, and 1,000 maps. **Services:** Interlibrary loan, list of researchers for hire, genealogical assistance (inhouse limited mail assistance), and educational programs. Open to public. Developing a pedigree database with access via a bulletin board system. **Publications:** *Genealogy from the Heartland,* (a catalog of titles in the genealogy circulating collection) 1992; *Genealogy Records on Microfilm,* 1994; *Genealogy Records on Microfiche and Electronic Media,* 1994.

Missouri Historical Society Library

PO Box 11940
St. Louis, MO 63112-0040
Phone: (314)746-4500
Peter Michel, Director of Library and Archives

Staff: Professional 3; Other 5. **Founded:** 1866. **Subjects:** History—St. Louis, Missouri, Western United States, Missouri and Mississippi Rivers; fur trade; biography; genealogy; selected city and county of St. Louis censuses; theater; music; Thomas Jefferson; early Mississippi travel; steamboats; Lewis and Clark expedition; American Indians. **Special collections:** Western Americana; maps; scrapbook collection; Missouri Gazette newspaper (complete file). **Holdings:** 70,000 book, pamphlet, and periodical titles; 2000 bound newspaper volumes; 2500 maps. **Subscriptions:** 241 journals and other serials. **Services:** Copying; library open to the public. **Publications:** *Gateway Heritage*, quarterly.

Missouri State Archives

600 W. Main
Box 778
Jefferson City, MO 65102
Phone: (314)751-3280
Fax: (314)526-3857
Kenneth H. Winn, State Archivist

Staff: 12. **Founded:** 1965. **Subjects:** Missouri history, genealogy. **Special collections:** Federal census schedules (microfilm); some partial state censuses; municipal records; French and Spanish land grants, 1790-1803; United States Land Sales, 1818-1903 (26 volumes); Township School Land, Seminary and Saline Land, Swamp Land, and 500,000 Acre Grant indexes; Missouri State Penitentiary indexes, 1837-1933 (microfilm); pardon records, 1837-1901 (microfilm); Reference & Manuscript Collection (city directories, maps, reference books, church records, George Washington Carver papers, A.P. Morehouse collection); Military Records Collection (War of 1812, Black Hawk War of 1832, Heatherly War of 1836, Seminole War of 1837, Osage War of 1837, Mormon War of 1838, Iowa or Honey War of 1839, Mexican War of 1846, Civil War 1861-1865, Spanish American War of 1898, Missouri Militia 1865-1866); county records (microfilm); Supreme Court Records of Missouri, 1804-1940. **Holdings:** 1250 linear feet of books; 20,000 cubic feet of archival material; 55,000 microfiche; 30,000 reels of microfilm. **Services:** Copying; library open to the public. **Publications:** *Researching Family & Community History at the Missouri State Archives*; *Guide to County Records on Microfilm*; *Historical Listing of Missouri Legislatures, 1812-1986*; *The Record*.

Missouri State Library

PO Box 387
Jefferson City, MO 65102
Phone: (314)751-2751
Fax: (314)751-3612
Monteria Hightower, State Librarian

Staff: Professional 19; Other 28. **Founded:** 1907. **Subjects:** State government, social services, human services, personnel administration, taxation, statistics. **Holdings:** 80,000 books; 365,000 microforms; federal and Missouri state documents. **Subscriptions:** 402 journals and other serials; 22 newspapers. **Services:** Interlibrary loan; copying; library open to the public. **Computerized services:** DIALOG Information Services, InfoPro Technologies; MCAT (Missouri statewide database) (internal database). **Publications:** *Show-Me Libraries*, quarterly; *Population & Census Newsletter*, quarterly; *Directory of Missouri Libraries*, annual; *Missouri Libraries Newsletter*, bimonthly; *Info To GO*; *Update* (current awareness bibliography); *Wolfner Library Newsletter*.

St. Joseph Museum Library

11th at Charles
St. Joseph, MO 64501
Phone: (816)232-8471
Fax: (816)232-8482
Richard A. Nolf, Director

Staff: 1. **Founded:** 1927. **Subjects:** Local and area history, Western movement, ethnology, natural history. **Special collections:** American Indian Collection; Civil War period local history collection; Nusom's Biography of Iowa Indians of Kansas and Nebraska. **Holdings:** 6500 volumes. **Subscriptions:** 40 journals and other serials. **Services:** Copying; library open to the public by appointment. **Publications:** *Happenings of the St. Joseph and Pony Express Museums*.

St. Louis Genealogical Society Library

9011 Manchester Rd., Ste. 3
St. Louis, MO 63144
Phone: (314)968-2763
Lorraine C. Cates, Librarian

Staff: 2. **Founded:** 1969. **Subjects:** Genealogy, family histories. **Special collections:** Daughters of the American Revolution Collection (lineage books and indexes; bound volumes of DAR Magazine, 1896 to present). **Holdings:** 30,000 volumes; 500 reels of microfilm; 250 microfiche; 100 cassette tapes. **Subscriptions:** 275 journals and other serials. **Services:** Copying; limited genealogical research (fee based); library open to the public. **Special indexes:** Index to 1860 St. Louis City & County Census (book). **Remarks:** Library is located at University City Public Library, 6701 Delmar Blvd., University City, MO 63130. **Publications:** List of publications—available on request.

St. Louis Public Library History and Genealogy Department

Central Library
1301 Olive St.
St. Louis, MO 63103-2389
Phone: (314)539-0385
Fax: (314)539-0393
Joseph M. Winkler, Coordinator of Research Collections

Staff: Professional 2. **Founded:** 1973. **Subjects:** U.S. history; genealogy of Missouri, Illinois, and most states east of the Mississippi River; heraldry; maps. **Special collections:** Complete set of St. Louis city directories; early printed records of Eastern States; American Colonial and State Papers: passenger lists and indexes of the 19th century (microfilm); St. Louis newspapers; Boston Evening Transcript: Genealogical Queries (microfiche); U.S. state and county histories and genealogical materials; Missouri Union and Confederate service records and indexes (microfilm); federal population censuses (microfilm) and indexes; territorial papers of U.S.; family histories (4000). **Holdings:** 143,000 volumes; 1150 genealogy files; 8482 reels of microfilm; U.S. Geological Survey depository for topographic maps; U.S. Army maps of foreign countries; U.S. and foreign gazetteers. **Subscriptions:** 395 current journals and other serials. **Services:** Interlibrary loan; copying; department open to the public. **Computerized services:** CD-ROMs (Biography Index, Place Name Index, U.S. History on CD-ROM). **Special indexes:** Heraldry Index of the St. Louis Public Library, 1980 (4 volumes); Genealogy index (card); heraldry index supplement (card); map index; surname and locations file. **Publications:** *Genealogical Materials and Local Histories in the*

St. Louis Public Library (bibliography of holdings), 1965, 1st supplement, 1971.

Western Historical Manuscript Collection University of Missouri, Columbia

23 Ellis Library
Columbia, MO 65201
Phone: (314)882-6028
Nancy Lankford, Associate Director

Staff: Professional 13; Other 3. **Founded:** 1943. **Subjects:** History—Missouri, political, economic, agricultural, urban, labor, black, women's, frontier, religious, literary, social, science, steamboating, social reform and welfare, business. **Holdings:** 13,100 linear feet of manuscripts; 7300 reels of microfilm; 3725 audiotapes and audiocassettes; 700 phonograph records; 190 video materials. **Services:** Interlibrary loan; copying; collection open to the public. **Computerized services:** Internet (electronic mail service). **Remarks:** Electronic mail address: whmscoll@ ext.missouri.edu (Internet). Collection contains the manuscript holdings of both the University of Missouri and the State Historical Society of Missouri. Offices are located at the four branches of the University of Missouri. Materials may be loaned among the four branches. **Publications:** *Guide to the Western Historical Manuscripts Collection*, 1952; supplement, 1956; finding aids (index, shelf list, and chronological file).

Western Historical Manuscript Collection University of Missouri, St. Louis

Thomas Jefferson Library
8001 Natural Bridge Rd.
St. Louis, MO 63121
Phone: (314)553-5143
Ann Morris, Associate Director

Staff: Professional 3; Other 2. **Founded:** 1968. **Subjects:** History—state and local, women's, Afro-American, ethnic, education, immigration; socialism; 19th century science; environment; peace; religion; Missouri politics; social reform and welfare; photography; journalism; business; labor. **Special collections:** Oral History Program (1000 tapes); Photograph Collection (200,000 images); African American Journalism; Afro-Americans in St. Louis; *Limelight Magazine* (black-oriented newspaper); New Age Federal Savings and Loan Association, St. Louis, 1915-1967 (first black-owned financial institution). **Holdings:** 5500 linear feet of manuscripts, photographs, oral history tapes, and university archives. **Services:** Interlibrary loan (limited); copying of manuscripts and photographs; library open to the public with restricted circulation. **Special indexes:** Unpublished inventories to collections in repository. **Remarks:** Collection contains the manuscript holdings of both the University of Missouri and the State Historical Society of Missouri. Offices are located at the four branches of the University of Missouri. Materials may be loaned among the four branches. **Publications:** *Western Historical Manuscript Collection—St. Louis* (1993 Guide).

Montana

Bitter Root Valley Historical Society Ravalli County Museum Miles Romney Memorial Library

Old Court House
205 Bedford Ave.
Hamilton, MT 59840
Phone: (406)363-3338
Helen Ann Bibler, Director

Staff: Professional 1. **Founded:** 1979. **Subjects:** Pioneer and Indian history. **Special collections:** Indian Collection; Granville Stuart Collection; Western News Files, 1890-1977; Ravalli Republican Files, 1899 to present; Northwest Tribune Files, 1906-1950; Stevensville Register Files, 1906-1914; western history (two private libraries). **Holdings:** 500 books. **Subscriptions:** 219 newspapers. **Services:** Copying; library open to the public for reference use only.

Montana Historical Society Library/Archives

225 N. Roberts
PO Box 201201
Helena, MT 59620
Phone: (406)444-2681
Fax: (406)444-2696
Robert M. Clark, Head, Library and Archives Division

Staff: Professional 9; Other 5. **Founded:** 1865. **Subjects:** Lewis and Clark Expedition; George Armstrong Custer; Charles M. Russell; military history of the Montana Indians; Montana biography/genealogy; mining; cattle and range; homesteading. **Special collections:** T.C. Power papers; F.J. and Jack Ellis Haynes Northern Pacific Railroad and Yellowstone National Park Photograph Collection; state government archives (5500 cubic feet). **Holdings:** 50,000 books; 5000 bound periodical volumes; 50,000 state publications; 6500 cubic feet of private papers; 200,000 photographs; 14,000 reels of microfilm of Montana and other newspapers; 16,000 maps; 4000 broadsides and ephemera; 1500 oral history interviews. **Subscriptions:** 300 journals and other serials; newspapers. **Services:** Interlibrary loan; copying (both limited); library open to the public for research and reference use only. **Computerized services:** Internal database; CD-ROM (Lasercat). **Special catalogs:** Union List of Montana Newspapers in Montana Repositories; Catalog of the Map Collection (microfiche). **Special indexes:** Index to archival collections (online); History of Montana, 1739-1885; Contributions to the Montana Historical Society; Montana obituary index, 1864-1930 (card); Montana biographies index (card); F. Jay Haynes Photo Collection Index (microfiche)—for sale. **Remarks:** Alternate telephone number(s): (406)444-4775 (Archives); (406)444-4739 (Photo Archives). **Publications:** *Montana: The Magazine of Western History*, quarterly; *Montana Post* (newsletter), quarterly.

Montana State Library

1515 E. 6th Ave.
Helena, MT 59620
Phone: (406)444-3004
Fax: (406)444-0581
Richard T. Miller Jr., State Librarian

Staff: Professional 7; Other 29. **Founded:** 1946. **Subjects:** General collection. **Special collections:** Federal government publications (partial depository); state government publications (complete depository). **Holdings:** 69,592 books; 502 periodical titles;

20,635 state publications; 259,137 federal publications. **Subscriptions:** 502 journals and other serials; 15 newspapers. **Services:** Interlibrary loan; copying; library open to the public. **Computerized services:** DIALOG Information Services, InfoPro Technologies, OCLC; Natural Resource Information System (internal database); Internet (electronic mail service). Performs searches free of charge. Contact Person: Darlene Staffeldt, Program Manager, Information Resources. **Remarks:** Electronic mail address: staffeld@class.org (Internet). **Publications:** *Montana State Library News*, irregular; *Montana Library Directory*, annual.

Montana State University—Libraries Merrill G. Burlingame Special Collections/ Archives

Bozeman, MT 59717-0332
Phone: (406)994-4242
Fax: (406)994-2851
Nathan E. Bender, Special Collections Librarian

Staff: Professional 1; Other 2. **Founded:** 1953. **Subjects:** Montana history, Yellowstone National Park, Senator Burton K. Wheeler, Montana Native Americans, Montana agriculture, James Williard Schultz, Montana State University, Montana architecture. **Special collections:** Haynes Collection; Montana WPA files; Burton K. Wheeler Collection; tribal newsletters from Montana. **Holdings:** 31,903 volumes; 953 reels of microfilm; 311 microfiche; 1615 aperture cards; 1654 manuscripts; 11,005 cubic feet of University records; 10,000 photographs on Montana agriculture and Montana State University. **Subscriptions:** 14 journals and other serials. **Services:** Copying; open to the public. **Computerized services:** BITNET, Internet (electronic mail services). **Remarks:** Electronic mail address: bender/lib@renne.lib.montana.edu (Internet).

Nebraska

Custer County Historical Society Library

445 S. 9th
PO Box 334
Broken Bow, NE 68822-0334
Phone: (308)872-2689
Mary Landkamer, Researcher

Staff: Professional 3; Other 3. **Founded:** 1960. **Subjects:** History—state, local; genealogy. **Special collections:** Census of the 81 cemeteries in Custer County, Nebraska. **Holdings:** 200 books; 110 volumes of bound newspapers; 700 photographs; 50 maps; 221 reels of microfilm; 24 VF drawers of obituaries and biographical materials. **Subscriptions:** 2 journals and other serials. **Services:** Copying; library open to the public. **Special indexes:** Index to Butcher Photograph Collection, city and county histories, obituaries, and cemeteries, 1874 to present. **Publications:** *Custer County Times Newsletter*, 2/year—to members.

Nebraska State Genealogical Library

PO Box 5608
Lincoln, NE 68505
Phone: (402)371-3468
Bob Plisek, President

Staff: 1. **Description:** Some coverage of all ethnic groups, with national and regional scope. Collection is held at the Beatrice Public Library, Beatrice, NE. Members may rent books by mail. **Holdings:** 300 microfilms and 110 periodicals. **Services:** Genealogical assistance. **Special catalogs:** Large special publications catalog available.

Nebraska State Historical Society Library/Archives Division

1500 R St.
Box 82554
Lincoln, NE 68501
Phone: (402)471-4771
Fax: (402)471-3100
Andrea I. Paul, Associate Director, Library and Archives

Staff: 18. **Founded:** 1878. **Subjects:** Nebraska—history, politics, agriculture; Indians of the Great Plains, archeology, Great Plains history, genealogy. **Holdings:** 80,000 volumes; 563 sets of Sanborn Fire Insurance maps of Nebraska; 2000 maps and 400 atlases relating to Nebraska, 1854 to present; 2500 photographs in Solomon D. Butcher Photograph Collection of Sod Houses; 465 photographs in John A. Anderson Photograph Collection of Brule Sioux; 247,000 other photographs; Nebraska state government publications repository, 1905 to present; 15,000 volumes of genealogical materials; 15,000 cubic feet of state and local archival materials; 8000 cubic feet of manuscripts; 28,000 reels of microfilm of newspapers, 1854-1991. **Subscriptions:** 930 journals and other serials; 200 newspapers. **Services:** Interlibrary loan (copies only); copying; library/archives open to the public. **Publications:** *Guides to the State Archives*, issued periodically.

Nevada

Nevada Historical Society Library

1650 N. Virginia St.
Reno, NV 89503-1799
Phone: (702)688-1190
Fax: (702)688-2917
Peter L. Bandurraga, Director

Staff: 7. **Founded:** 1904. **Subjects:** Nevada history, mining, Indians, agriculture, water, gambling, transportation and communication, censuses (Nevada), newspaper index. **Holdings:** 30,000 books; 5000 bound periodical volumes; 3000 manuscript collections; 5000 reels of microfilm; 250,000 photographs; 50,000 maps; manuscripts; photographs; government documents. **Subscriptions:** 260 journals and other serials. **Services:** Copying; limited written research by mail; library open to the public. **Special indexes:** An Index to the Publications of the Nevada Historical Society, 1907-1971. **Publications:** *Nevada Historical Society Quarterly*.

Nevada State Library and Archives

Capitol Complex
Carson City, NV 89710
Phone: (702)687-5160
Fax: (702)887-8330
Joan G. Kerschner, State Librarian

Staff: Professional 13; Other 15. **Founded:** 1859. **Subjects:** Public administration, history of Nevada, business. **Special collections:** Nevada Collection; state, county, and municipal documents (55,000). **Holdings:** 47,627 books; 12,596 bound periodical volumes; 250,000 U.S. Government publications; 15,233 reels of microfilm of Nevada newspapers. **Subscriptions:** 504 journals and other serials; 60 newspapers. **Services:** Interlibrary loan; copying; archives open to the public. **Computerized services:**

DIALOG Information Services, RLIN, VU/TEXT Information Services, OCLC, WILSONLINE, DataTimes. Performs searches. Contact Person: Joyce C. Lee, Assistant State Librarian. **Special catalogs:** Nevada Statewide Union catalog. **Publications:** *Info Connection*.

New Hampshire

New Hampshire (State) Department of State Division of Records Management & Archives

71 S. Fruit St.
Concord, NH 03301
Phone: (603)271-2236
Fax: (603)271-2272
Frank C. Mevers, State Archivist

Staff: Professional 2. **Subjects:** State and county archives. **Services:** Copying; archives open to the public for reference use.

New Hampshire State Library

20 Park St.
Concord, NH 03301-6303
Phone: (603)271-2397
Fax: (603)271-2205
Kendall F. Wiggin, State Librarian

Staff: Professional 18; Other 41. **Founded:** 1716. **Subjects:** New Hampshire—history, government, political science, law. **Holdings:** 450,100 books; 16,011 manuscripts; 5271 scores; 12,500 reels of microfilm; 71,770 microcards; 114,000 microfiche; 653 motion pictures; 500 sound recordings. **Subscriptions:** 850 journals and other serials; 44 newspapers. **Services:** Interlibrary loan; copying; library open to the public. **Computerized services:** DIALOG Information Services, OCLC; internal database; Internet (electronic mail service). **Remarks:** Electronic mail address: k_wiggin@uhh.unh.edu (Internet). **Publications:** *Granite State Libraries*, bimonthly to library community; *Reference Roundtable*, quarterly.

New Jersey

Bridgeton Free Public Library Special Collections

150 E. Commerce St.
Bridgeton, NJ 08302-2684
Phone: (609)451-2620
Fax: (609)455-1049
Grace M. Stirneman, Library Director

Staff: Professional 2; Other 8. **Subjects:** Cumberland County history, local genealogy, Woodland Indians. **Special collections:** New Jersey reference; Woodruff Museum books. **Holdings:** 2000 volumes, including newspapers, 1881 to present, bound and on microfilm; 20,000 Indian artifacts, 10,000 B.C. to circa 1700 A.D., collected within a 30-mile radius of the library. **Services:** Interlibrary loan; copying; collections open to the public.

Danforth Memorial Library

250 Broadway
Paterson, NJ 07501
Phone: (201)357-3000
Fax: (201)881-8338
Kwaku Amoabeng, Director

Staff: Professional 10; Other 50. **Founded:** 1985. **Subjects:** Applied science, business, career information, computers, adult literacy, literature. **Special collections:** African-American studies collection; Spanish-language collection; local history/genealogy collection; New Jersey Government Documents Depository. **Holdings:** 357,000 books; 20,500 reels of microfilm; 1394 AV materials. **Subscriptions:** 300 journals and other serials; 44 newspapers. **Services:** Interlibrary loan; copying; library open to the public. Fee for non-resident loans. **Computerized services:** OCLC, DIALOG Information Services, InfoTrac; Internet (electronic mail service). Contact Person: Usha Regy, Head of Reference Servicess. **Special indexes:** Obituary Index. **Remarks:** Electronic mail address: patersonpl@hslc (Internet). **Publications:** *Resources of Paterson History: An Annotated Bibliography* (Centennial Publications).

New Jersey State Library

185 W. State St.
CN 520
Trenton, NJ 08625-0520
Phone: (609)292-6220
Fax: (609)984-7900
Louise Minervino

Staff: Professional 38; Other 65. **Founded:** 1796. **Subjects:** Law, New Jersey history and newspapers, political science, public administration, genealogy. **Special collections:** New Jerseyana; New Jersey State Government Publications; U.S. Government documents selective depository. **Holdings:** 750,000 volumes. **Subscriptions:** 2800 journals and other serials. **Services:** Interlibrary loan; copying; library open to the public by appointment. **Computerized services:** OCLC, RLIN, LEXIS, NEXIS, InfoPro Technologies, DIALOG Information Services; CompuServe Information Service; Internet (electronic mail services). Performs searches on fee basis. **Special catalogs:** Genealogy: New Jersey Family Names. **Remarks:** Electronic mail address: hadunn@pilot.NJINNet (Internet). Library coordinates a statewide, cooperative multitype library network. **Publications:** *Checklist of Official New Jersey Publications*, bimonthly—limited distribution; *Impressions* (newsletter), monthly.

Newark Public Library Humanities Division

5 Washington St.
Box 630
Newark, NJ 07101-0630
Phone: (201)733-7820
Fax: (201)733-5648
Sallie Hannigan, Supervising Librarian

Staff: Professional 6; Other 1. **Founded:** 1889. **Subjects:** Literature, language, literary criticism, biography, bibliography, religion, philosophy, history, geography, psychology, librariana, travel, film, theater, television, sports and recreation, encyclopedias, dictionaries. **Special collections:** Black literature, history, and biography. **Holdings:** 130,000 books; 1000 bound periodical volumes; 1000 maps; dictionaries and encyclopedias in Spanish, Italian, French, German, Russian; information file. **Subscriptions:** 630 journals and other serials. **Services:** Interlibrary loan; copying; telephone and in-person reference available in Spanish; division open to the public. **Computerized services:** InfoPro Technologies, DIALOG Information Services, ORBIT Search Service, OCLC EPIC; CD-ROMs. Performs searches on fee basis.

Rowen College of New Jersey Savitz Library Stewart Room

201 Mullica Hill Rd.
Glassboro, NJ 08028
Phone: (609)863-6303
Fax: (609)863-6313
Clara M. Kirner, Special Collections Librarian

Staff: Professional 1; Other 1. **Founded:** 1948. **Subjects:** New Jersey history, early religious history, genealogy, Indians of North America, Revolutionary War, War of 1812, Grinnell Arctic expedition. **Special collections:** Family papers: Howell, Inskeep, Haines, Lippincott; Frank H. Stewart Collection (8000 volumes); Charles A. Wolverton Papers (10 boxes); Satterthwaite Genealogical Collection (24 VF drawers). **Holdings:** 16,300 books; 422 bound periodical volumes; 5000 manuscripts; 13 VF drawers of college archives; 4200 volumes of masters' theses; rare books; deeds; surveys; marriage licenses; acts of assembly. **Subscriptions:** 28 journals and other serials. **Services:** Copying (limited); room open to the public for reference use only. **Formerly:** Glassboro State College. **Publications:** *Guide to the Special Collections*—available on request.

New Mexico

Institute of American Indian and Alaska Native Culture and Arts Development Library

College of Santa Fe Campus
St. Michael's Dr.
Box 20007
Santa Fe, NM 87504
Phone: (505)988-6670
Fax: (505)988-6446
Mary Young, Dir. of Libs.

Subjects: American Indian culture, history, and technique of American Indian fine arts. **Special collections:** Exhibition catalogs. **Holdings:** 18,000 books; 8 file drawers of archival materials; 9,000 art slides; 4,000 Indian slides; 24 file drawers of art catalogs; 27,826 Smithsonian Indian photographs; 8 file drawers of Indian newspapers; 60 tapes, 88 cassettes and 585 phonograph records of Indian music recordings; Indian newspapers. **Remarks:** Institute is not affiliated with the College of Santa Fe.

New Mexico State Library

325 Don Gaspar
Santa Fe, NM 87503
Phone: (505)827-3800
Fax: (505)827-3888
Karen J. Watkins, State Librarian

Staff: Professional 17; Other 42. **Founded:** 1929. **Subjects:** Public administration, management, education, social sciences, environment. **Special collections:** Southwest/New Mexico collection. **Holdings:** 70,000 books; 900,000 federal and state documents (Federal Regional Depository). **Subscriptions:** 463 journals and other serials; 57 newspapers. **Services:** Interlibrary loan; copying; library open to the public. **Computerized services:** DIALOG Information Services, OCLC. Performs searches on fee basis for New Mexico libraries. **Publications:** *Hitchhiker*, weekly.

New Mexico State Records Center and Archives

404 Montezuma St.
Santa Fe, NM 87503
Phone: (505)827-7332
Fax: (505)827-7331
J. Richard Salazar, Chief, Archive Services

Staff: Professional 4; Other 2. **Founded:** 1960. **Subjects:** New Mexico state history, Southwestern history. **Special collections:** Spanish and Mexican Archives of New Mexico; New Mexico Territorial Archives; New Mexico Statehood Archives. **Holdings:** 4000 books; 300 bound periodical volumes. **Subscriptions:** 4 journals and other serials. **Services:** Copying; archives open to the public. **Special indexes:** Photograph index. **Publications:** *Spanish, Mexican, Territorial Archives of New Mexico.*

University of New Mexico Special Collections Department Center for Southwest Research

General Library
Albuquerque, NM 87131
Phone: (505)277-6898
Fax: (505)277-6019
David A. Baldwin, Head

Staff: Professional 3; Other 12. **Founded:** 1950. **Subjects:** History of the American West, New Mexico history and culture, history and culture of Mexico and Latin America, Indians of the Southwest, southwestern architectural history, Hispanic and Native American studies. **Special collections:** Doris Duke Collection (982 oral history tapes); Pioneer Foundation (527 tapes); Microfilm edition of the American Indian Oral History Collection (Navajo, Pueblo Transcripts). **Holdings:** 36,700 volumes; 2100 tape recordings; 3150 linear feet of manuscript material; 17,000 photographs; 250 videocassettes. **Subscriptions:** 121 journals and other serials. **Services:** Copying Mexico history and culture, Western Americana, historical and contemporary Latin American issues, and Hispanic and Native American studies. **Computerized services:** Internet (electronic mail service). **Remarks:** Electronic mail address: dbaldwin@unmb.unm.edu(Internet).

New York

Cayuga County Historian Library

Historic Old Post Office Bldg.
157 Genesee St.
Auburn, NY 13021
Phone: (315)253-1300
Thomas G. Eldred, County Historian

Staff: 4. **Founded:** 1969. **Subjects:** Local history, genealogy. **Special collections:** Cayuga County Records. **Holdings:** 300 books; 500 bound periodical volumes; 50 boxes and 27 VF drawers of reports, manuscripts, letters, broadsides, clippings; 700 reels of microfilm of newspapers; 1500 reels of microfilm of records; photographs. **Subscriptions:** 16 journals and other serials. **Services:** Copying; library open to the public for reference use only. **Publications:** *Cayuga Gazette*.

Hartwick College
Stevens-German Library
Special Collections

Oneonta, NY 13820
Phone: (607)431-4440
Fax: (607)431-4457
Robert E. Danford, Director

Staff: Professional 8; Other 11. **Founded:** 1928. **Subjects:** Indians of North America, especially Eastern Woodland Indians. **Special collections:** Yager Collection of Rare Books; Congressman James Hanley papers concerned with Native Americans (2 cubic feet); Hatrwick Seminary records (40 cubic feet); Judge William Cooper papers (15 cubic feet); Willard E. Yager Manuscript Collection (15 cubic feet); John Christopher Hartwick Library (290 titles). **Holdings:** 6200 books; 200 bound periodical volumes; 200 folders of clippings; 1000 reels of microfilm; 3000 microfiche. **Subscriptions:** 1202 journals and other serials; 17 newspapers. **Services:** Interlibrary loan; copying; collection open to the public. **Computerized services:** OCLC, FIRSTSEARCH, DIALOG Information Services; Internet, ALANET (electronic mail services). **Remarks:** Electronic mail address: DANFORDR@HARTWICK.EDU (Internet). **Publications:** *Indians of North and South America*, a bibliography based on the collection of the Willard E. Yager Library Museum, 1977; supplement, 1987.

New York Genealogical and Biographical Society
Library

122 E. 58th St., 4th Fl.
New York, NY 10022
Phone: (212)755-8532
Fax: (212)754-4218
Peter Gordon B. Stillman,
Trustee Librarian, Policy

Staff: Professional 3; Other 4. **Founded:** 1869. **Subjects:** Genealogy, biography, local history. **Special collections:** New York State church, town, and other records; family and Bible records. **Holdings:** 70,182 volumes; 23,011 manuscripts; 3174 reels of microfilm; 7859 microfiche; 30 CDs. **Subscriptions:** 1190 journals and other serials. **Services:** Copying; library open to the public with restrictions. **Publications:** *New York Genealogical and Biographical Record*; *The NYG & B Newsletter*; *Collections of the New York Genealogical and Biographical Society.*

New York Public Library
The Research Libraries
United States History, Local History and Genealogy Division

5th Ave. & 42nd St., Rm. 315S
New York, NY 10018
Phone: (212)930-0828
Ruth A. Carr, Chief

Staff: Professional 5; Other 1.5. **Subjects:** U.S. history; county, city, town histories of the United States; European and American genealogy and heraldry; works on names and flags of the world. **Special collections:** Photographic views of New York City (54,000); postcards and scrapbooks of U.S. local views; Lewis W. Hine Collection (443 prints and negatives); local history ephemera; American Antequarian Society newspaper index; U.S. election campaign materials. **Holdings:** 154,000 volumes. **Subscriptions:** 1254 journals and other serials. **Services:** Copying; division open to the public. **Computerized services:** DIALOG Information Services; CD-ROM (Family Search).

New York State Archives

Cultural Education Center, Room 11D40
Albany, NY 12230
Phone: (518)474-8955

Description: Acquires, preserves, and makes accessible state government records that have continuing historical or legal value; acquires microfilm copies of some archival records of local governments. **Holdings:** 63,000 cubic feet of records, dating from the seventeenth century to the present and taking a variety of formats, including parchment, paper, and photographic and magnetic media; microfilms. **Services:** Inter-library loan, photocopies, limited genealogical assistance regarding records. Open to the public. **Computerized services:** Information on holdings available through the State Library/State Archives local computerized catalog, and through RLIN (Research Libraries Information Network), available in major research libraries and are accessible through the Internet (jfolts%sedofis@vm.nysed.gov). **Special catalogs:** *Guide to Records in the New York State Archives* (Albany, 1993), $12.95, plus $3.00 P & H; *Genealogical Sources in the New York State Archives,* Information Leaflet 1 (1994), single copy free on request; *Guide to Records Relating to Native Americans* (in the New York State Archives), (Albany, 1988), $2.00.

New York State Library

Cultural Education Center
Empire State Plaza
Albany, NY 12230
Phone: (518)474-7646
Fax: (518)474-5786
Jerome Yavarkovsky, Director

Staff: Professional 79; Other 107. **Founded:** 1818. **Subjects:** Education, science, technology, art, architecture, economics, sociology, current affairs, bibliography, New York State documents (also original documents for California), New York State newspapers, law, medicine, state and local history, genealogy, heraldry. **Special collections:** Almanacs; New York State documents. **Holdings:** 8.2 million books, bound periodical volumes, manuscripts, pamphlets; patents; microfilm; microcards; pictures; maps. **Subscriptions:** 18,582 journals and other serials; 111 newspapers. **Services:** Interlibrary loan; copying; library open to the public. **Computerized services:** InfoPro Technologies, DIALOG Information Services; ALANET (electronic mail service). **Remarks:** Electronic mail address: ALA0198 (ALANET). **Publications:** *Bookmark*, quarterly; *Checklist of Official Publications of the State of New York*, monthly.

Rochester Public Library
Local History and Genealogy Division

115 South Ave.
Rochester, NY 14604
Phone: (716)428-7338
Fax: (716)428-7313
Wayne Arnold, Head

Staff: Professional 3; Other 1. **Subjects:** History of Rochester and Genesee area, genealogy (primarily New York and New England). **Special collections:** Local newspapers. **Holdings:** 25,000 books; 15 cases and 400 volumes of manuscripts; 1800 maps; 500 scrapbooks; 145 VF drawers of newspaper clippings; 80 VF drawers of pamphlets and ephemera; 20 VF drawers of pictures; 12 drawers of postcards; 638 reels of microfilm; 120 films. **Subscriptions:** 200 journals and other serials; 78 newspapers. **Services:** Copying (limited). **Remarks:** The majority of the holdings of the Rochester Historical Society are on permanent loan to the Local History Division.

Staten Island Institute of Arts and Sciences Archives and Library

75 Stuyvesant Pl.
Staten Island, NY 10301
Phone: (718)727-1135
Fax: (718)273-5683
Vince Sweeney, Curator of History

Staff: Professional 2; Other 1. **Founded:** 1881. **Subjects:** Natural history, Staten Island history, archeology, black history, women's history, urban planning. **Special collections:** Photographs and prints of old Staten Island; local black history; complete list of special collections available on request. **Holdings:** 12,000 books; 22,000 bound periodical volumes; 3000 maps; 1200 prints; 50,000 photographs; 1500 cubic feet of manuscripts, letters, and documents; 80 reels of microfilm of Staten Island newspapers. **Subscriptions:** 200 journals and other serials. **Services:** Copying; library open to the public by appointment. **Special indexes:** Guide to Institute Archives, 2 volumes; indexes to newspapers, iconography of Staten Island, special collections (all on cards). **Publications:** *Guide to Special Collections*, 16 volumes.

University of Rochester Government Documents and Microtext Center

Rush Rhees Library
Rochester, NY 14627
Phone: (716)275-4484
Fax: (716)473-1906
Kathleen E. Wilkinson, Government Documents Librarian

Staff: Professional 2; Other 3. **Founded:** 1880. **Subjects:** Documents—U.S. Congress, U.S. Bureau of the Census, New York State, women's studies, black studies, North American Indians, American and British literature. **Holdings:** 385 books; 445,000 uncataloged government documents in paper; 945,000 uncataloged government documents in microform; 2.4 million other microforms. **Subscriptions:** 10 journals and other serials. **Services:** Interlibrary loan; copying; center open to the public. **Computerized services:** Internet (electronic mail). **Remarks:** Electronic mail addresses: docs@dbl.cc.rochester.edu; kwlk@dbl.cc.rochester.edu (Internet).

North Carolina

North Carolina (State) Department of Cultural Resources Division of Archives and History Archives & Records Section

109 E. Jones St.
Raleigh, NC 27601-2807
Phone: (919)733-3952
Fax: (919)733-1354
David J. Olson, State Archivist

Staff: Professional 38; Other 39. **Founded:** 1903. **Subjects:** Official records, especially county records, of the state of North Carolina and its subdivisions. **Special collections:** Federal records include mortality schedules 1850-1880, population schedules 1800-1880; manuscript collections, colonial times to present; maps; photographs; audiovisual materials; microfilm. **Holdings:** 39,800 cubic feet of archive material; 135,000 reels of microfilm. **Services:** Copying; search room and archives open to the public Tuesday-Saturday. **Computerized services:** MARS (Manuscript and Archives Reference System; internal database); Internet (electronic mail service). **Publications:** List of publications—available on request.

North Carolina (State) Department of Cultural Resources Division of the State Library

109 E. Jones St.
Raleigh, NC 27601-2807
Phone: (919)733-2570
Fax: (919)733-8748
Sandra M. Cooper, Director/State Librarian

Staff: Professional 33; Other 81. **Founded:** 1812. **Subjects:** Public policy, Southern history, library science. **Special collections:** Genealogy; North Carolina state documents (123,441). **Holdings:** 200,000 volumes; 600,000 state and federal documents; 33,126 reels of microfilm; 35 titles on microfiche; 166,000 containers of talking books; 7177 16mm films; 2644 videocassettes. **Subscriptions:** 646 journals and other serials; 119 newspapers. **Services:** Interlibrary loan; copying; library open to the public with circulation of materials limited to state employees. **Computerized services:** DIALOG Information Services, InfoPro Technologies, OCLC, LC Direct, U.S. Bureau of the Census; LINC (Log Into North Carolina); BITNET, Internet (electronic mail services). Performs searches for state employees and libraries. Contact Person: David Bevan, Chief, Information Services Section, (919)733-3683. **Special catalogs:** North Carolina Union Catalog (microfilm); North Carolina Online Union Catalog; North Carolina Online Union List of Serials. **Also known as:** State Library of North Carolina. **Publications:** *Tar Heel Libraries*, bimonthly; *News Flash*, monthly—to public libraries; *Selected Acquisitions*; *Checklist of Official North Carolina State Publications*, bimonthly.

Western Carolina University Hunter Library Special Collections

Cullowhee, NC 28723
Phone: (704)227-7474
George Frizzell, Unit Head

Staff: 2. **Founded:** 1953. **Subjects:** Western North Carolina, Cherokee Indians. **Special collections:** Appalachia (1200 volumes; 220 manuscript collections); spider behavior (100 volumes); Cherokee Documents in Foreign Archives Collection, 1632-1909 (manuscript sources from foreign archives relating specifically to the Cherokee and to southern Indians in general; 821 reels of microfilm). **Holdings:** 1500 books. **Services:** Interlibrary loan (Cherokee document microfilm only); copying; collections open to the public. **Computerized services:** Online Manuscript Search Service (internal database). Performs searches free of charge. Member of SOLINET.

North Dakota

Assumption Abbey, Inc. Library

Box A
Richardton, ND 58652
Phone: (701)974-3315
Bro. Aaron Jensen, Librarian

Staff: 1. **Founded:** 1893. **Subjects:** Theology, religion, history (especially North Dakota). **Special collections:** The Major James McLaughlin Collection, a collection of the major's personal correspondence as well as copies of documents such as applications for patents in fee (land titles), letter books, censuses, and other documents. All those wishing to research the McLaughlin collection should call first. **Holdings:** 85,000 books, 2500 bound periodical volumes. **Subscriptions:** 80 journals and other serials; 8 newspapers. **Services:** Interlibray loan, copying, library open to the public with restrictions.

North Dakota State Library

Liberty Memorial Bldg.
Capitol Grounds
604 E. Boulevard Ave.
Bismarck, ND 58505-0800
Phone: (701)224-2492
Fax: (701)224-2040
William R. Strader, State Librarian

Staff: Professional 7; Other 18. **Founded:** 1907. **Subjects:** North Dakota, state government, library science, music, education. **Special collections:** Last Copy Repository. **Holdings:** 126,928 books; 14,233 tape cassettes; 72,059 state documents, 1889 to present; 15,904 federal documents; CD-ROMs. **Subscriptions:** 241 journals and other serials; 15 newspapers. **Services:** Interlibrary loan; copying; library open to the public. **Computerized services:** DIALOG Information Services, OCLC; EasyLink, Internet (electronic mail services). **Remarks:** Electronic mail addresses: 62755117 (EasyLink); strader@sendit.nodak.edu (Internet). **Publications:** *Flickertale Newsletter*, bimonthly.

State Historical Society of North Dakota State Archives and Historical Research Library

Heritage Center
612 E. Boulevard
Bismarck, ND 58505
Phone: (701)224-2668
Fax: (701)224-3710
Gerald Newborg, State Archivist/Division Director

Staff: Professional 8; Other 2. **Founded:** 1895. **Subjects:** North Dakota and Dakota Territory; social, cultural, economic, and political history; early exploration and travel; fur trade; plains military history; Northern Plains region—archeology, prehistory, ethnology, ethnohistory; historic preservation; genealogy. **Holdings:** 100,400 volumes; 2198 cubic feet of manuscripts; 11,740 cubic feet of state and county archives; 100,000 photographs; 12,500 reels of microfilm of microfilm of manuscripts, records and newspapers; 1421 titles of North Dakota newspapers; 2100 titles of periodicals; 1843 oral history interviews; sound recordings; maps; videotapes; motion pictures; newsfilm archives. **Subscriptions:** 300 journals and other serials; 103 newspapers. **Services:** Interlibrary loan (limited); copying; library open to the public for reference use only. **Computerized services:** OCLC. **Special catalogs:** The North Dakota Newspaper Inventory, 1992. **Publications:** *North Dakota History: Journal of the Northern Plains*, quarterly; *Plains Talk* (newsletter), quarterly; *Guide to the North Dakota State Archives*, 1985; *Guide to Manuscripts*, 1985.

University of North Dakota Elwyn B. Robinson Department of Special Collections

Chester Fritz Library
Box 9000
Grand Forks, ND 58202
Phone: (701)777-4625
Fax: (701)777-3319
Sandra Beidler, Head, Archives & Special Collections

Staff: Professional 2; Other 1. **Founded:** 1963. **Subjects:** History—North and South Dakota, Northern Great Plains, Plains Indian, environmental; agrarian radicalism; Nonpartisan League (North Dakota); genealogy; oral history; ethnic heritage and family history (North Dakota); Norwegian local history. **Special collections:** North Dakota Book Collection (17,661 volumes); Fred G. Aandahl Book Collection (1477 volumes); Family History/Genealogy Collection (3429 volumes); North Dakota State Documents (4000); Orin G. Libby Manuscript Collection (12,289 linear feet). **Holdings:** 21,400 books; 11,000 linear feet of manuscript material; 4150 reels of microfilm; 44,500 photographs; 3500 AV items; 6514 theses and dissertations. **Subscriptions:** 71 journals and other serials; 4 newspapers. **Services:** Copying; department open to the public for reference use only. **Computerized services:** OCLC, DIALOG Information Services, IAC; Internet (electronic mail service). **Special catalogs:** Subject Guide to the Orin G. Libby Manuscript Collection, 1979; Guide to Genealogical/Family History Sources, 1986. **Publications:** Reference Guide to North Dakota History and Literature, 1979; Reference Guide to the Orin G. Libby Manuscript Collection (Volume 1, 1975; Volume 2, 1983; Volume 3, 1985; Volume 4, 1990).

Ohio

Allen County Historical Society Elizabeth M. MacDonell Memorial Library

620 W. Market St.
Lima, OH 45801-4604
Phone: (419)222-9426
Anna B. Selfridge, Curator, Archives and Manuscripts

Staff: Professional 1. **Founded:** 1908. **Subjects:** Local history and genealogy, Ohio history, railroading, American Indian. **Holdings:** 8271 books; 585 bound periodical volumes; Lima, Ohio newspapers, 1840s to present; Lima directories, 1876 to present; 1938 reels of microfilm of newspapers and census records. **Subscriptions:** 40 journals and other serials. **Services:** Copying; library open to the public. **Remarks:** Library is part of Allen County Museum. **Publications:** *Allen County Reporter*, 3/year; newsletter, bimonthly—both to members.

Cleveland Public Library History and Geography Department

325 Superior Ave.
Cleveland, OH 44114-1271
Phone: (216)623-2864
JoAnn Petrello, Department Head

Staff: Professional 4; Other 6. **Founded:** 1869. **Subjects:** History—ancient, medieval, modern; archaeology; local history; genealogy; heraldry; geography; black history; exploration and travel; numismatics. **Special collections:** Photograph Collection (904,206). **Holdings:** 171,338 volumes; 11,738 bound periodical volumes; 18,800 Cleveland pictures on microfiche; 6000 maps and brochures with current travel data; local history clipping file; 919,526 photographs; 35 vertical files; 4750 microfiche. **Subscriptions:** 411 journals and other serials. **Services:** Interlibrary loan; copying; department open to the public. **Computerized services:** OCLC, DIALOG Information Services, InfoPro Technologies, OhioPI (Ohio Public Information Utility), Hannah Information Systems, PFDS Online; CD-ROMs. **Special indexes:** Photograph Collection index (movie stills and posters captured on an optical disk).

Rutherford B. Hayes Presidential Center

1337 Hayes Avenue
Speigel Grove
Fremont, OH 43420-2796
Phone: (419)332-2081
Fax: (419)332-4952

Special collections: Microfilm holdings: censuses for some states (especially Ohio, Georgia, Alabama), area newspapers, county histories (California, Illinois, Indiana, Michigan, New York, Pennsylvania, Wisconsin), city directories for some Ohio cities; manuscripts and archives: local area records of funeral homes, businesses, churches, townships and villages, probate records, deeds, etc.; newspapers from throughout the U.S.; social security death benefit index; international genealogical index; phonedisc. **Services:** Photocopying, microfilm prints, limited research via mail request. **Remarks:** Genealogical collection is located on the second floor. Library is open Monday through Saturday, 9:00 to 5:00.

Ohio Genealogical Society Library

34 Sturges Ave.
PO Box 2625
Mansfield, OH 44906-0625
Phone: (419)522-9077
Fax: (419)522-0224
Thomas S. Neel, Office Manager

Staff: Prof. 1, other 1. **Description:** Nonprofit library collection on Ohio pioneer materials including census, court records, county histories, Bible records, and family accounts. Both national and regional focus with some African and Native American coverage, minor Hispanic and Asian American coverage. **Founded:** 1959. **Special collections:** First Families of Ohio, lineage society to pre-1820 Ohio settlers; Ohio ancestor card file, nearly 300,000 cards tying surnames to researchers; Ohio Bible records, everyname index. **Holdings:** Two rooms of archival material, 15,000 books, 200 periodical titles, 16 file cabinets of reports, microfiche (IGI), 1500 rolls of microfilm, with active subscriptions; old newspapers. **Services:** Copying, list of researchers for hire, genealogical assistance. Open to public with fee of $3 per day for nonmembers. **Computerized services:** Phone Disk, Social Security Index, Census Indexes. **Publications:** *The Report,* quarterly, $25.00, circulation: 6350; *Ohio Records and Pioneer Families: Cross Road of our Nation,* quarterly, $18.00, circulation: 1400; *The Ohio Genealogical Society Newsletter,* monthly (with *The Report*), circulation: 6,350.

State Library of Ohio

65 S. Front St.
Columbus, OH 43266-0334
Phone: (614)644-7061
Fax: (614)466-3584
Richard M. Cheski, State Librarian

Staff: Professional 39; Other 92. **Founded:** 1817. **Subjects:** Management, social sciences, education, public administration, Ohio history. **Special collections:** Genealogy (14,000 items); Ohio and federal documents (1.5 million). **Holdings:** 622,101 books; 495,914 microforms; CD-ROMs. **Subscriptions:** 449 journals and other serials; 26 newspapers. **Services:** Interlibrary loan; copying; faxing; library open to the public. **Computerized services:** DIALOG Information Services, OCLC, LIBRIS, Library Control System (LCS), OHIONET. Performs searches for state agencies. Contact Person: Catherine Mead, Head, Reference, (614)644-6952. **Publications:** *Directory of Ohio Libraries*, annual; *Ohio Documents*, quarterly; *Recent Acquisitions*, irregular.

Western Reserve Historical Society Library

10825 East Blvd.
Cleveland, OH 44106
Phone: (216)721-5722
Fax: (216)721-0645
Kermit J. Pike, Director

Staff: Professional 7; Other 7. **Founded:** 1867. **Subjects:** Ohio history, American genealogy, Civil War, slavery and abolitionism, ethnic history, African and Native Americans. **Holdings:** 235,950 books; 25,500 volumes of newspapers; 50,300 pamphlets; 6 million manuscripts; 32,500 reels of microfilm. **Subscriptions:** 325 journals and other serials; 50 newspapers. **Services:** Interlibrary loan; copying; library open to the public. **Special catalogs:** Catalogs to manuscript, genealogy, and Shaker collections (all on cards).

Oklahoma

Cherokee National Historical Society, Inc. Cherokee National Archives

Box 515
TSA-LA-GI
Tahlequah, OK 74465
Phone: (918)456-6007
Tom Mooney, Archivist

Staff: 1. **Founded:** 1963. **Subjects:** Cherokee history. **Special collections:** W.W. Keeler (Principal Chief of Cherokees) papers; Cherokee National Executive Committee minutes, 1948 (origin) to 1970 (disbandment); Cherokee Nation papers, 1969-1975; Earl Boyd Pierce (Counsel General of the Cherokee Nation) papers, 1928-1983; manuscript collections. **Holdings:** 3000 books; 500 bound periodical volumes; 147 reels of microfilm; 5 VF drawers of pamphlets; 7 VF drawers of papers and committee minutes. **Subscriptions:** 20 journals and other serials. **Services:** Copying; archives open to the public on request. **Remarks:** $5.00 fee.

Cheyenne and Arapaho Tribal Museum and Archives

Watonga, OK 73772

Chickasaw Nation Chickasaw Council House Library

Court House Square
Box 717
Tishomingo, OK 73460
Phone: (405)371-3351
Faye Orr, Historic Property Manager

Staff: 3. **Founded:** 1970. **Subjects:** Chickasaw Indian history, biographies, and statistics; Choctaws; census; roll numbers. **Special collections:** Oklahoma Chronicles—Chickasaw Constitution and law books. **Holdings:** 50 maps; county and Chickasaw Nation records; 70 reels of microfilm; pamphlets. **Services:** Library open to the public.

Five Civilized Tribes Museum Library

Agency Hill on Honor Heights Dr.
Muskogee, OK 74401
Phone: (918)683-1701

Founded: 1966. **Subjects:** Cherokee, Chocktaw, Creek, Chickasaw, and Seminole Indians—history, current history, fiction, nonfiction. **Services:** Library open to the public by appointment.

Museum of the Great Plains Great Plains Research Library and Archives

601 Ferris
Box 68
Lawton, OK 73502
Phone: (405)581-3460
Steve Wilson, Director

Staff: Professional 2; Other 1. **Founded:** 1960. **Subjects:** Great Plains—history, natural history, archeology, anthropology, agriculture. **Special collections:** Original documents and photographs dealing with the settlement of southwestern Oklahoma and Southern Plains. **Holdings:** 25,000 books; 725 bound periodical volumes; 700 cases of manuscripts, 1880-1940, Comanche County newspapers, 1901 to present, and City of Lawton Journals; 30,000 photographs; hardware; agricultural catalogs and periodicals. **Subscriptions:** 260 journals and other serials. **Services:** Copying; library and archives open to the public. **Special indexes:** Index to photograph collections (card); index to articles in regional journals; index to agricultural catalogs and periodicals; index to collections described in *Great Plains Journal*, volume 17, 1978.

Northeastern Oklahoma State University John Vaughan Library/LRC Special Collections and Archives

Tahlequah, OK 74464
Phone: (918)456-5511
Fax: (918)458-2197
Bela Foltin, Dean

Staff: 2. **Founded:** 1909. **Special collections:** Cherokee Indian Collection (589 volumes); E. Edmondson Papers (240 boxes); Government Document Depository (332,000). **Holdings:** 10,088 books; 595 bound periodical volumes; 5172 microfiche; 1852 reels of microfilm. **Subscriptions:** 26 journals and other serials; 31 newspapers. **Services:** Copying; archives open to the public. **Computerized services:** OCLC, DIALOG Information Services, InfoPro Technologies; CD-ROM (ERIC). **Remarks:** Genealogy section has limited hours. Call extension 3221 to find out times section is open.

Oklahoma Historical Society Archives and Manuscript Division

Historical Bldg.
Oklahoma City, OK 73105
Phone: (405)521-2491
Fax: (405)525-3272
William D. Welge, Director

Staff: Professional 5; Other 8. **Founded:** 1893. **Subjects:** Oklahoma and Indian territories, Indian tribes of Oklahoma, pioneer life, missionaries, territorial court records, explorers. **Special collections:** Records from all state Indian agencies, except Osage Agency (3.5 million document pages; 6000 volumes); Dawes Commission Records (48 cubic feet; 242 bound volumes); Indian-Pioneer History (interviews; 112 volumes); Whipple Collection (8 cubic feet); Joseph Thoburn Collection (20 cubic feet). **Holdings:** 2900 reels of microfilm of Indian and Oklahoma affairs; 265,000 historical photographs; 28,000 reels of microfilm of newspapers; 4500 oral history tapes. **Subscriptions:** 10 journals and other serials. **Services:** Copying; archives open to the public. **Special catalogs:** Catalog listing films for sale. **Special indexes:** Inventories of Five Civilized Tribes documents; card index of Indian-Pioneer History. **Publications:** Microfilm of original materials for sale.

Oklahoma Historical Society Division of Library Resources

2100 N. Lincoln Blvd.
Oklahoma City, OK 73105
Phone: (405)521-2491
Fax: (405)525-3272
Edward Connie Shoemaker, Library Director

Staff: Professional 1; Other 8. **Founded:** 1893. **Subjects:** Oklahoma and American Indian history, American west, Oklahoma genealogy. **Holdings:** 62,593 books; 10,600 reels of microfilm of U.S. Census, 1790-1920; 25,000 reels of microfilm of Oklahoma newspapers, 1893 to present. **Subscriptions:** 300 journals and other serials; 280 newspapers. **Services:** Copying; library open to the public for research use only. **Computerized services:** OCLC. **Publications:** *Oklahoma History: A Bibliography*; *Five Civilized Tribes: A Bibliography*; *Family Histories: A Bibliography*; *Oklahoma Cemeteries: A Bibliography* (1993).

Oklahoma Historical Society Research Library and Archives

2100 N Lincoln Blvd.
Oklahoma City, OK 73105
Phone: (405)521-2491
Fax: (405)525-3272

Description: Archives located in basement, reference library located on first floor of Oklahoma Historical Society. **Subjects:** Archives: 3.5 million documents representing 66 of the 67 native tribes that resided in Indian Territory; 112-volume *Indian-Pioneer History,* a collection of oral histories done by the Federal Writers Project in 1937; tribal government records; Indian agency records; 1890 Special Schedule of Union Veterans and their Widows that covers both Indian and Oklahoma territories; 1900 Indian Territory and Oklahoma Territory schedule. **Holdings:** Library contains over 62,000 volumes with emphasis on Oklahoma, Native American, and western history.

Oklahoma (State) Department of Libraries

200 NE 18th St.
Oklahoma City, OK 73105
Phone: (405)521-2502
Fax: (405)525-7804
Robert L. Clark Jr., Director

Staff: Professional 40; Other 45. **Founded:** 1890. **Subjects:** Law; legislative reference materials; Oklahoma government, history, authors; librarianship; juvenile evaluation collection. **Special collections:** Oklahoma Collection (11,500 titles). **Holdings:** 320,000 books; 27,000 cubic feet of state archives and manuscript collections; 25,000 cubic feet of state records; 40,000 linear feet of U.S. Government documents (regional depository); 45,000 Oklahoma document titles; 66,000 reels of microfilm; 488 videotapes; U.S. Government documents on microfiche (270,432 linear feet); 290,840 maps; 37,000 microfiche titles; 250 file drawers of pamphlets and clippings. **Subscriptions:** 2400 journals and other serials; 18 newspapers. **Services:** Interlibrary loan; legislative and law reference; archival and state research assistance; department open to the public for reference use only; loans made to state agency personnel only. **Computerized services:** OCLC, DIALOG Information Services, Mead Data Central, InfoPro Technologies. **Publications:** *Annual Directory of Oklahoma Libraries*; *ODL Archives*, quarterly; *Oklahoma Almanac*, biennial; *GPO:*

Government Publications for Oklahoma, bimonthly; *ODL Source* (newsletter), monthly; *Oklahoma Government Publications* (checklist), quarterly; *Informacion.*

Ponca City Cultural Center & Museums Library

1000 E. Grand Ave.
Ponca City, OK 74601
Phone: (405)767-0427
LaWanda French, Supervisor

Staff: 1. **Founded:** 1938. **Subjects:** American Indian (Osages, Mission Books c. 1825-, Caws, Five Civilized Tribes, Navajo, Hopi), anthropology, archeology, American cowboy, museology. **Holdings:** 200 books; 15 bound periodical volumes; VF drawers of unbound reports, clippings, pamphlets, dissertations, documents. **Subscriptions:** 15 journals and other serials. **Services:** Copying (limited); library open to the public. **Special catalogs:** Classification, Source, Tribe, Location, and Documents Catalogs (card file). **Publications:** Museum brochure.

Will Rogers Library

121 N. Weenonah
Claremore, OK 74017
Phone: (918)341-1564
Margaret L. Guffey, Librarian

Staff: 5. **Founded:** 1936. **Subjects:** Will Rogers, American Indians, Oklahoma and regional history. **Holdings:** 50,000 books; 265 bound periodical volumes; 3 VF drawer of clippings and pamphlets. **Subscriptions:** 92 journals and other serials; 8 newspapers. **Services:** Interlibrary loan; copying; library open to the public. **Remarks:** Maintained by the City of Claremore.

Sac and Fox National Public Library

Rte. 2, Box 246
Stroud, OK 74079
Phone: (918)968-3526
Fax: (918)968-3887
Jan Vassar, Library Director

Staff: Professional 1; Other 1. **Founded:** 1987. **Subjects:** American Indians, Sac and Fox history and culture, biography. **Special collections:** Sac and Fox Photography Collection (1000); Sac and Fox Document Collection (250); Sac and Fox Oral History Collection (36 interviews). **Holdings:** 4000 books; 100 reports; 2000 archives; 46 reels of microfilm. **Subscriptions:** 2 journals and other serials; 32 newspapers. **Services:** Interlibrary loan; copying; library open to Sac and Fox jurisdiction residents. **Publications:** Brochures, pamphlets, post cards displaying Sac and Fox history; Sac and Fox News, monthly.

University of Oklahoma Western History Collections

630 Parrington Oval, Rm. 452
Norman, OK 73019
Phone: (405)325-3641
Donald L. DeWitt, Curator

Staff: Professional 4; Other 4. **Founded:** 1927. **Subjects:** American Indian, Oklahoma, American Southwest, American Trans-Mississippi West, recent U.S. history. **Special collections:** Cherokee Nation Papers. **Holdings:** 55,000 books; 9000 linear feet of manuscripts; 250,000 items in photographic archives; 20,000 microforms; 3600 maps; 1400 transcripts, tapes, and discs of oral history; 5000 pamphlets and documents; newspapers, posters, broadsides. **Subscriptions:** 52 journals and other serials; 17 newspapers. **Services:** Copying (limited); collections open to the public. **Computerized services:** RLIN, OCLC. **Special catalogs:** Catalogs of individual collections; catalog of microform holdings. **Publications:** *Guide to Regional Manuscripts in Division of Manuscripts of University of Oklahoma Library*, 1960, *American Indian Resource Materials in the Western History Collection*, 1990; *Guide to Photographs, Motion Pictures, and Sound Recording*, 1993.

University of Tulsa McFarlin Library Special Collections

2933 E. 6th St.
Tulsa, OK 74104-3123
Phone: (918)631-2496
Fax: (918)631-3791
Sidney F. Huttner, Curator

Staff: Professional 2; Other 4. **Founded:** 1894. **Subjects:** 20th century Anglo-Irish and American literature; Indian history (covers the five civilized tribes as well as other Oklahoma tribes), law, and policy; World War I; Proletarian literature; American fiction regarding Vietnam; performing arts. **Special collections:** J.W. Shleppey Indian Collection; J.B. Milam Library (Cherokee materials); Indian Claims Commission Archives; Osage allotment cards. **Holdings:** 100,000 books; 1000 bound periodical volumes; 150,000 19th and 20th century historical manuscripts (primarily regional); 150 territorial maps. **Subscriptions:** 20 journals and other serials. **Services:** Interlibrary loan; copying; collections open to the public on written application. **Computerized services:** DIALOG Information Services, OCLC; RLG, BITNET, Internet (electronic mail services). **Remarks:** Electronic mail address: SFH@VAX2.UTULSA.EDU (Internet); SHUTTNER@TULSA (BITNET); CURTIS@TULSA (BITNET); LNC@VAX2.UTULSA.EDU (Internet). **Publications:** Guides to manuscript collections—available on request; finding aids.

Oregon

Douglas County Museum Lavola Bakken Memorial Library

Box 1550
Roseburg, OR 97470
Phone: (503)440-4507
Fax: (503)440-6023
Frederick R. Reenstjerna, Research Librarian

Staff: Professional 1. **Founded:** 1969. **Subjects:** Douglas County history, Umpqua Indians, logging, sawmills and grist mills, marine history, mining, development of area towns, railroads, agriculture. **Special collections:** Photography collection (15,000 photographic prints copied from glass-plate negatives); Catholic church records. **Holdings:** 2500 books; 350 vertical files of letters, diaries, manuscripts, census, cemetery records; 400 oral histories; 175 genealogies. **Subscriptions:** 30 journals and other serials. **Services:** Copying; library open to the public for reference use only. **Computerized services:** Argus Museum Automation System.

Family History Center, Eugene

3550 NW 18th Ave.
Eugene, OR 97402
Phone: (503)343-3741

Description: Branch of the Family History Library of the Church of Jesus Christ of Latter-day Saints. **Subjects:** Genealogy, family history, church and civil records, local history. **Remarks:** Access to main library microfilm.

Family History Center, Portland

1975 SE 30th Ave.
Portland, OR 97214
Phone: (503)235-9090

Description: Branch of the Family History Library of the Church of Jesus Christ of Latter-day Saints. **Subjects:** Genealogy, family history, church and civil records, local history. **Remarks:** Access to main library microfilm.

Family History Center, Portland

2215 NE 106th St.
Portland, OR 97220
Phone: (503)252-1081

Description: Branch of the Family History Library of the Church of Jesus Christ of Latter-day Saints. **Subjects:** Genealogy, family history, church and civil records, local history. **Remarks:** Access to main library microfilm.

Klamath County Museum Research Library

1451 Main St.
Klamath Falls, OR 97601
Phone: (503)883-4208
Fax: (503)883-5163
Patsy H. McMillan, Museum Director

Staff: 2.5 **Founded:** 1954. **Subjects:** Oregon and local history, Modoc and Klamath Indians, Modoc Indian War. **Special collections:** Modoc Indian War collection; oral history collection. **Holdings:** 1650 books; photo/document archives; microfilm. **Subscriptions:** 5 journals and other serials. **Services:** Copying; library open to the public by appointment for reference use only; user fee. **Publications:** Research books on local history; *Guardhouse, Gallows, Graves* (Modoc Indian War information); *Old Fort Klamath.*

Oregon State Archives Division

800 Summer St. NE
Salem, OR 97310
Phone: (503)373-0701
Fax: (503)373-0963
Timothy Backer, Supervisor, Reference Archives

Staff: Professional 3. **Founded:** 1946. **Subjects:** Oregon government—provisional, territorial, state, county, municipal, special districts. **Special collections:** Records of Oregon state and county government departments and agencies dating from the territorial period. **Holdings:** 25,000 cubic feet of records. **Services:** Copying; archives open to the public for reference use only. **Computerized services:** RLIN; internal database. **Publications:** *Guide to Provisional & Territorial Government Records.*

Oregon State Library

State Library Bldg.
Summer & Court Sts.
Salem, OR 97310
Phone: (503)378-4277
Fax: (503)588-7119
Jim Scheppke, State Librarian

Staff: Professional 14; Other 30. **Founded:** 1905. **Subjects:** Oregon history and government, business, librarianship, social sciences, humanities, science and technology. **Special collections:** Oregoniana. **Holdings:** 1.5 million books and government documents; 1585 video cassettes; 23,893 maps; clippings; pamphlets. **Subscriptions:** 633 journals and other serials. **Services:** Interlibrary loan; copying; SDI; library open to the public. **Computerized services:** DIALOG Information Services, InfoPro Technologies, OCLC EPIC, OCLC; Internet, ALANET, OnTyme Electronic Message Network Service. **Special indexes:** ORULS; Oregon index; subject and biography index to Salem daily newspaper and other publications. **Remarks:** Electronic mail addresses: CLASS.OSL (OnTyme Electronic Message Network Service); INFO@OPAC.OSL.OR.GOV (Internet). **Publications:** *Letter to Libraries* (online); *Directory and Statistics of Oregon Libraries*, annual—to all Oregon libraries.

Pennsylvania

Fulton County Historical Society Library

PO Box 115
McConnellsburg, PA 17233
Phone: (717)485-3207
Hazel Harr, Librarian

Staff: 1. **Founded:** 1976. **Subjects:** Local history and genealogy. **Special collections:** Fulton Republican newspaper, 1865-1900; Fulton Democrat newspaper, 1866-1983; old school photographs; local family histories; county histories; church records. **Holdings:** 300 books; microfilm collection; 100 volumes of Pennsylvania Archives. **Services:** Copying; library open to the public on a limited schedule. **Special indexes:** Cemetery file (card); Index to 1850 and 1860 Fulton County census (book). **Publications:** *Annual Research Booklet.*

Genealogical Research Library Erie Branch

1244 W 22nd St.
Erie, PA 16502

Description: Genealogical materials available for research.

Historical Society of Pennsylvania Library

1300 Locust St.
Philadelphia, PA 19107
Phone: (215)732-6201
Fax: (215)732-2680
Lee Arnold, Library Director

Staff: Professional 16. **Founded:** 1824. **Subjects:** History—U.S., 1783-1865, Colonial, Revolutionary, Pennsylvania; genealogy; Afro-Americana. **Special collections:** Slavery records. **Holdings:** 564,000 volumes; 16 million manuscripts; 2800 microcards; 17,200 microfiche; 14,700 reels of microfilm; maps; prints; drawings; paintings; newspapers; ephemera. **Subscriptions:** 4000 journals and other serials. **Services:** Copying; library open to the public on fee basis. **Computerized services:** OCLC, RLIN. **Publications:** *The Pennsylvania Magazine of History and Biography*, quarterly; *Guide to the Manuscript Collections of the Historical Society of Pennsylvania*; *The Pennsylvania Correspondent* (newsletter), 5/year—to members.

Lehigh County Historical Society Scott Andrew Trexler II Memorial Library

Old Court House
5th & Hamilton Sts.
Box 1548
Allentown, PA 18105
Phone: (610)435-1072
Fax: (610)435-9812
June B. Griffiths, Librarian/Archivist

Staff: Professional 2. **Founded:** 1904. **Subjects:** Pennsylvania and Lehigh County history, genealogy. **Special collections:** Allentown Newspapers, 1810-1916; family genealogies; photographs; Civil War; Allentown imprints; native Indians. **Holdings:**

8000 books; 200 newspaper volumes; 2000 pamphlets; 200 manuscripts, archives, records of local families and businesses; deeds; maps; church records. **Subscriptions:** 12 journals and other serials. **Services:** Copying; library open to the public on fee basis. **Publications:** *Proceedings*, biennial; quarterly newsletter; *Allentown 1762-1987: A 225-Year History* (2 volumes); occasional papers.

Library Company of Philadelphia

1314 Locust St.
Philadelphia, PA 19107
Phone: (215)546-3181
Fax: (215)546-5167
John C. Van Horne, Librarian

Staff: Professional 13; Other 8. **Founded:** 1731. **Subjects:** Pre-1860 Americana, Philadelphia and Pennsylvania, pre-1820 medical material, black history before 1906, women's history. **Special collections:** Early printed books from Girard College and Christ Church (on deposit). **Holdings:** 450,000 books; 50,000 prints and photographs; 160,000 manuscripts. **Subscriptions:** 130 journals and other serials. **Services:** Interlibrary loan; copying; library open to the public for research. **Computerized services:** RLIN. **Special catalogs:** Afro-Americana, 1553-1906 in collections of the Library Company and the Historical Society of Pennsylvania; The Library of James Logan; Quarter of a Millennium: The Library Company of Philadelphia, 1731-1981; occasional catalogs of special exhibitions. **Publications:** Annual reports; newsletters—both free to libraries and individuals on request.

Pennsylvania (State) Department of Education
Commonwealth Libraries

PO Box 1601
Harrisburg, PA 17105
Phone: (717)787-2646
Fax: (717)783-5420
Sara Parker, Commissioner of Libraries

Staff: Professional 40; Other 53. **Founded:** 1745. **Subjects:** Government, law, education, public welfare and administration, Pennsylvania history and biography, Central Pennsylvania genealogy, social and behavioral science, economics, library science. **Special collections:** Early Pennsylvania Imprints; Colonial Assembly Collection. **Holdings:** 983,949 books; 900,000 federal and Pennsylvania government publications; 2.752 million microforms, including Congressional Information Service and American Statistics Index microfiche series; Newsbank, 1977 to present; ERIC microfiche. **Subscriptions:** 3881 journals and other serials; 162 newspapers. **Services:** Interlibrary loan; copying; library open to the public. **Computerized services:** DIALOG Information Services, InfoPro Technologies; Internet (electronic mail services). Contact Person: Susan Payne, Head, Main Reading Room, (717)783-5950. **Special catalogs:** Pennsylvania Imprints, 1689-1789. **Remarks:** Electronic mail addresses: parker@hslc.org; wolfe@hslc.org; hoffmand@hslc.org; emerick@hslc.org (Internet). **Publications:** *Directory-Pennsylvania Libraries*, annual; *Pennsylvania Public Library Statistics*, annual.

Pennsylvania (State) Historical & Museum Commission
Division of Archives and Manuscripts

William Penn Memorial
Museum & Archives Bldg.
Box 1026
Harrisburg, PA 17108-1026
Phone: (717)783-3281
Harry E. Whipkey, State Archivist

Staff: Professional 8; Other 6. **Founded:** 1903. **Subjects:** Archives of Pennsylvania and historical manuscripts. **Special collections:** Record groups of the holdings of state agencies and political subdivisions (57); manuscript collections (425); census material beginning in 1782, lists free blacks and slaves. **Holdings:** 17,500 books; 27,000 cubic feet of archival materials; 21,000 cubic feet of personal papers; 15,000 reels of microfilm; 4500 maps. **Subscriptions:** 180 journals and other serials. **Services:** Interlibrary loan (limited); division open to the public. **Computerized services:** OCLC, RLIN; internal databases. **Publications:** List of publications—available on request; Finding Aids.

Rhode Island

Rhode Island State Archives

337 Westminster St.
Providence, RI 02903
Phone: (401)277-2353
Fax: (401)277-3199
Timothy A. Slavin, State Archivist

Staff: 1. **Subjects:** Rhode Island history. **Holdings:** Acts and resolves of the General Assembly; colony records; Revolutionary War records; petitions and reports to the General Assembly; military and maritime charters. **Services:** Copying; archives open to the public with restrictions.

South Carolina

South Carolina (State) Department of Archives & History
Archives Search Room

Box 11669, Capitol Sta.
Columbia, SC 29211
Phone: (803)734-8577
George L. Vogt, Director

Staff: 110. **Founded:** 1905. **Subjects:** History of South Carolina—political, constitutional, legal, economic, social, religious. **Special collections:** Noncurrent public records of South Carolina, including: land records of the colony and state; Revolutionary War accounts; confederate service records; executive, legislative, and judicial records of the colony and state; special census 1890; probate records of the colony; county records (23,000 cubic feet of records; 15,000 reels of microfilm). **Holdings:** 2000 books; 250 bound periodical volumes. **Subscriptions:** 200 journals and other serials. **Services:** Copying; search room open to the public for reference use only. **Special catalogs:** Catalog of reference library (card). **Special indexes:** Published Summary Guide to Archives; consolidated computer output microfilm index to documents; bound volume indexes to land plats and grants, marriage settlements and other records; map catalog (card); Revolutionary and Confederate War service records (card). **Remarks:** Library is located at 1430 Senate St., Columbia, SC 29201. **Publications:** *Colonial Records of South Carolina*, 16 volumes; *State Records of South Carolina*, 10 volumes; *South Carolina Archives Microcopies*, 16 series; *New South Carolina State Gazette* (newsletter), 2/year; *Guide to Local Records in the South Carolina Archives*; historical booklets; curriculum resource materials; historical and technical pamphlets and brochures; *On the Record* (newsletter), quarterly; *News & Notes* (newsletter), quarterly.

South Carolina State Library

1500 Senate St.
PO Box 11469
Columbia, SC 29211
Phone: (803)734-8666
Fax: (803)734-8676
James B. Johnson Jr., Director

Staff: Professional 21; Other 32. **Founded:** 1943. **Subjects:** Reference, government, business, political science, education, history, fine arts, South Caroliniana. **Holdings:** 247,077 books; 2276 bound periodical volumes; 50,064 South Carolina state documents; 16,892 reels of microfilm of periodicals; 457,743 ERIC microfiche; 246,555 government documents; 2584 videotapes; 2384 films; 10,696 large print books. **Subscriptions:** 2636 journals and other serials; 27 newspapers. **Services:** Interlibrary loan; copying; library open to the public. **Computerized services:** DIALOG Information Services, OCLC, InfoPro Technologies; Internet (electronic mail service). Performs searches on fee basis. Contact Person: Mary Bull, Reference Librarian. **Remarks:** Electronic mail address: SOUTHCAR@CLASS.ORG (Internet). **Publications:** *News for South Carolina Libraries*, bimonthly—to public, school, and academic libraries and trustees; *New Resources*—to state government agencies and libraries.

South Dakota

Black Hills State University
E.Y. Berry Library-Learning Center
Special Collections

1200 University
Spearfish, SD 57799-9511
Phone: (605)642-6361
Fax: (605)642-6298
Dora Ann Jones, Special Collections Librarian

Staff: Professional 1. **Founded:** 1925. **Subjects:** Local and regional history, biography, Dakota Indians, western industry, transportation, North American Indians. **Special collections:** Black Hills State University Archives; Leland D. Case Library for Western Historical Studies; Library of American Civilization (microfiche); Wagner-Camp Collection (microcard); Cox Library (microfilm). **Holdings:** 12,607 volumes; 949 manuscript boxes; 54 VF drawers; 85 drawers of maps and photographs; 12,888 titles on 14,548 microforms. **Subscriptions:** 60 journals and other serials; 7 newspapers. **Services:** Copying; collections open to the public with restrictions. **Computerized services:** OCLC.

Dacotah Prairie Museum
Archives

21 S. Main St.
Box 395
Aberdeen, SD 57402-0395
Phone: (605)622-7117
Fax: (605)225-6094
Merry Coleman, Director

Staff: 5.5. **Founded:** 1969. **Subjects:** History of Brown County and the northeastern region of South Dakota, 1797 to present. **Holdings:** Ledgers; photographs; school records; oral histories; records of organizations and businesses; letters and manuscripts of missionaries in the area, 1860-1880. **Services:** Copying; archives open to the public by appointment. **Computerized services:** Internal databases.

Siouxland Heritage Museum
Pettigrew Museum Library

131 North Duluth
Sioux Falls, SD 57104

South Dakota State Historical Society
Office of History
South Dakota State Archives

900 Governors Dr.
Pierre, SD 57501
Phone: (605)773-3804
Fax: (605)773-6041
Linda M. Sommer, State Archivist

Staff: Professional 4; Other 4. **Founded:** 1986. **Subjects:** South Dakota history, culture and government; Great Plains; government administration. **Holdings:** 26,000 volumes; 6000 cubic feet of records; 70 cubic feet of photographs; 12,000 maps. **Subscriptions:** 174 journals and other serials; 140 newspapers. **Services:** Interlibrary loan; copying; office open to the public. **Computerized services:** OCLC.

South Dakota State Library

800 Governors Dr.
Pierre, SD 57501-2294
Phone: (605)773-3131
Fax: (605)773-4950
Jane Kolbe, State Librarian

Staff: Professional 10; Other 33.5. **Founded:** 1913. **Subjects:** General collection. **Special collections:** South Dakota; large print books; South Dakota documents; Native Americans (particularly Lakota). **Holdings:** 160,190 volumes; 192,961 documents; 6147 pictures; 581 maps; 8147 films, filmstrips, videotapes, and other media; 34,000 talking book titles; 481,775 microfiche; 8294 reels of microfilm. **Subscriptions:** 1244 journals and other serials; 32 newspapers. **Services:** Interlibrary loan; copying; library open to the public. **Computerized services:** DIALOG Information Services, PFDS Online, InfoPro Technologies, ALANET, OCLC, RLIN, Western Library Network (WLN); Internet (electronic mail service). **Remarks:** Electronic mail address: SDSL@CHARLIE.USD.EDU (Internet). **Publications:** *South Dakota State Government Publications*.

University of South Dakota
Institute of American Indian Studies

414 E Clark St.
Vermillion, SD 57069
Phone: (605)677-5209

Holdings: Approximately 1,400 tapes from the Doris Duke Oral History Collection. **Remarks:** The Institutue is located at Dakota Hall 12.

Tennessee

Chattanooga-Hamilton County Bicentennial Library
Local History and Genealogical Collections

1001 Broad Street
Chattanooga, TN 37402
Phone: (615)757-5317
Clara W. Swann, Department Head

Staff: Prof. 1; Other 4. **Founded:** 1888. **Subjects:** Southeast U.S. genealogy; local and state history. **Holdings:** 25,047 books; 312 manuscript collections; 160 VF drawers of clippings and photographs; 9,448 reels of microfilm of county records and local newspapers; 8,793 microfiche. **Subscriptions:** 128 journals and other serials. **Services:** Copying; collections open to the public for reference use only. **Computerized services:** Computerized cataloging; OCLC; member of SOLINET. **Special indexes:** Family surname index for materials in the department (card); local newspaper obituary indexes, 1897 to present.

Lawson McGhee Library

500 West Church Avenue
Knoxville, TN 37902
Phone: (615)544-5744
Steve Cotham, Head

Staff: Prof. 4; Other 9. **Founded:** 1921. **Subjects:** History and genealogy of Knoxville, Knox County, Tennessee and other southern states. **Special collections:** Knoxville and Tennessee newspapers, 1791 to present; 1982 World's Fair Archives (750,000 manuscripts); local architectural plans; Thompson Photographic Collection. **Holdings:** 35,416 books; 4,173 BPV; 1 million manuscripts; 1,341 maps; 8,948 reels of microfilm; 33,854 microfiche; 135 VF drawers of photographs and clippings. **Subscriptions:** 240 journals and other serials; 10 newspapers. **Services:** Copying; collection open to the public for reference only. **Computerized services:** Member of SOLINET. **Special catalogs:** *A Guide to the Manuscript Collections of the Calvin M. McClung Historical Collection of Knox County Public Library System.* **Remarks:** Collection located in East Tennessee Historical Center, 314 W. Clinch Ave., Knoxville, TN 37902-2203. The East Tennessee Historical Society, organized in 1925, has its headquarters in the East Tennessee Historical Center as well; gifts to the Society become part of the McClung Collection's holdings.

Memphis-Shelby County Public Library and Information Center
Memphis Room Collections

1850 Peabody Avenue
Memphis, TN 38104-4025
Phone: (901)725-8821
Fax: (901)725-8883
James R. Johnson, Head

Staff: Prof. 8; Other 6. **Subjects:** Memphis/Shelby County, genealogy, Mardi Gras/Cotton Carnival, yellow fever, Blues and Beale Street, Mississippi steamboats. **Special collections:** Many, including Memphis/Shelby County Archives (18,000 volumes), Wassell Randolph Genealogical Collection, E.M. Sharp Genealogical Collection, Ida Cooper Genealogical and Historical papers. **Holdings:** 11,120 books; 1,250 bound periodical volumes; 1,200 maps; 500,000 newspaper clippings; 11,000 photographs; 3,000 pages of oral history transcripts; 250 manuscript collections; 7,500 reels of microfilm. **Subscriptions:** 135 journals and other serials. **Services:** Interlibrary loan; copying; collections open to the public. **Special catalogs:** Several. **Special indexes:** Indexed guide to the collections; index to Shelby County Probate Records, 1820-1876; to Memphis City Council minutes, 1826-1855; to oral histories; to Memphis newspapers, 1975-1989; to death records, 1848-1939; marriage records, 1820-1976. **Remarks:** Maintains the second largest genealogical collection in the state.

Nashville and Davidson County Public Library
Metro Archives

1113 Elm Hill Pike
Nashville, TN 37210-3505

Remarks: Maintains extensive genealogical collection.

Nashville and Davidson County Public Library
Nashville Room

Eighth Avenue North and Union
Nashville, TN 37203-3585

Remarks: Maintains extensive genealogical collection.

Red Clay State Historical Park Library

1140 Red Clay Park Rd. SW
Cleveland, TN 37311
Phone: (615)478-0339
Lois I. Osborne, Park Manager

Staff: 4. **Founded:** 1979. **Subjects:** Cherokee history, Native Americans, Cherokee genealogy, environment. **Holdings:** 800 books. **Subscriptions:** 2 journals and other serials; 2 newspapers. **Services:** Copying; library open to the public for reference use only.

Tennessee State Library and Archives

403 7th Ave. N
Nashville, TN 37243-0312
Phone: (615)741-7996
Fax: (615)741-6471
Edwin S. Gleaves Ph.D., Librarian & Archivist

Staff: Professional 32; Other 52. **Founded:** 1854. **Subjects:** Tennesseana, U.S. and local history, state and local government, law and public administration, genealogy. **Special collections:** Papers of Jacob McGavock Dickinson, James Robertson, Andrew Jackson, George P. Buell, Henry Shelton Sanford, Richard Ewell; land records, 1777-1903 (600 volumes); state agency records and governors' papers, 1796 to present; legislative records and recordings, 1796 to present; state Supreme Court records, 1815-1955; Owsley Charts, records of farms, slaves, and equipment for Tennessee and other states in the south from the federal censuses of 1840, 1850, and 1860; petitions to Tennessee State Legislature 1796-1869; voter registration rolls; county records on microfilm; Tennessee newspapers. **Holdings:** 526,193 books; 4 million manuscript items; 22 million archival documents; 127,647 reels of microfilm; 265,193 sheets of microfiche; 47,774 audiotapes; 103,927 photographs. **Subscriptions:** 1541 periodicals; 200 newspapers on 34,670 reels of microfilm. **Services:** Interlibrary loan; copying; library open to the public. **Computerized services:** OCLC (Online Computer Library Center). **Special indexes:** Index to City Cemetery Records of Nashville; Index to Questionnaires of Civil War Veterans. **Publications:** *List of Tennessee State Publications*, quarterly; *Writings on Tennessee Counties*; *Tennessee Newspapers on Microfilm*; producers of manuscript materials; checklist of microfilm; *Guide to the Pro-*

cessed Manuscripts of the Tennessee Historical Society; *Guide to Microfilm Holdings of the Manuscripts Section*. **Remarks:** The Manuscript Division is located in the archive's 7th Ave. building.

Texas

Amarillo Public Library
Local History Collection

413 E. 4th
Box 2171
Amarillo, TX 79189-2171
Phone: (806)378-3054
Fax: (806)378-4245
Mary Kay Snell, Director, Library Services

Staff: 1. **Subjects:** Southwestern history, Indian tribes and customs, religion. **Special collections:** Bush/FitzSimon Collection of Books on the Southwest; John L. McCarty Papers (4030). **Holdings:** 5078 books; 765 unbound periodicals; 219 maps. **Services:** Interlibrary loan; copying; collection open to the public with restrictions. **Computerized services:** OCLC. **Publications:** *Bibliography of the Bush/FitzSimon/McCarty Southwestern Collections*.

Dallas Public Library
J. Erik Jonsson Central Library
Genealogy Collection

1515 Young St.
Dallas, TX 75201
Phone: (214)670-1433
Lloyd DeWitt Bockstruck, Supervisor, Genealogy Section

Staff: Professional 1; Other 7. **Subjects:** Genealogy, heraldry, onomatology, local history. **Holdings:** 59,533 books; 26,530 reels of microfilm; 1237 microcards; 46,372 microfiche. **Subscriptions:** 700 journals and other serials. **Services:** Copying; collection open to the public.

Houston Metropolitan Research Center
Houston Public Library

500 McKinney Ave.
Houston, TX 77002
Phone: (713)247-1661
Fax: (713)247-3531
Louis J. Marchiafava, Ph.D., Archivist

Staff: Prof. 5; Other 1. **Founded:** 1975. **Subjects:** Houston-business, politics, architecture, church records, city and county government, agencies. **Special collections:** John Milsaps Collection (Salvation Army); panoramic photographs collection (500); local photographs (1.8 million); county records for two-county area; Houston African-American Collection; Mexican-American Collection; Oral History Collection; Architectural collection; Texas State Archives regional depository; Texas Jazz Archive. **Holdings:** 18,000 linear feet of archival material. **Services:** Copying; center open to the public. **Remarks:** Alternate telephone number(s): 247-3562. Publishes *The Houston Review,* 3/year—by subscription; guide books to the collection.

Houston Public Library
Clayton Library
Center for Genealogical Research

5300 Caroline St.
Houston, TX 77004-6896
Phone: (713)524-0101
Maxine Alcorn, Manager

Staff: Professional 8; Other 10. **Founded:** 1921. **Subjects:** Genealogy. **Special collections:** Federal census, 1790-1900 (complete), 1910 (complete); 1900 Soundex (complete); 1910 Soundex (partial); military records; state and colonial records; county records; family histories. **Holdings:** 40,000 books; 2000 bound periodical volumes; 35,000 reels of microfilm; 50,000 microfiche; VF material. **Subscriptions:** 285 journals and other serials. **Services:** Copying; center open to the public. **Publications:** In-house Finding Aids.

Panhandle-Plains Historical Museum
Research Center

Box 967, WT. Sta.
Canyon, TX 79016
Phone: (806)656-2260
Fax: (806)656-2250
Claire R. Kuehn, Archivist/ Librarian

Staff: Professional 2; Other 2. **Founded:** 1932. **Subjects:** Texas and Southwest history; ranching; Indians of the Great Plains; archeology of Texas Panhandle; ethnology; clothing and textiles; fine arts; antiques; museum science. **Special collections:** Interviews with early settlers and other citizens collected over a period of 63 years. **Holdings:** 16,000 books; 13,000 cubic feet of manuscripts; 20 VF drawers of pamphlets; 800 maps; 1600 reels of microfilm; 45 cubic feet of manufacturers' trade literature; 300,000 historic photographs. **Subscriptions:** 250 journals and other serials; 12 newspapers. **Services:** Copying; center open to the public. **Special indexes:** Index to the Panhandle-Plains Historical Review (card); Index to the Canyon (Texas) News. **Remarks:** Center is the Regional Historical Resource Depository for noncurrent county documents for 24 Texas Panhandle counties (a Texas State Library program).

San Augustine Public Library

413 E Columbia
San Augustine, TX 75972

Southmost College
Arnulfo L. Oliveira Memorial Library

Hunter Room
83 Fort Brown
Brownsville, TX 78520

Southwest Genealogical Society and Library

412 W College St., A
Carthage, TX 75633-1406

Texas State Library
State Archives Division
Sam Houston Regional Library and Research Center

PO Box 310
Liberty, TX 77575-0310
Phone: (409)336-8821
Robert L. Schaadt, Director/Archivist

Staff: Professional 2; Other 5. **Founded:** 1977. **Subjects:** Southeast Texas history. **Special collections:** Journal of Jean Laffite; Herbert Bolton's manuscript for Athanase de Mezieres & the Louisiana-Texas Frontier, 1768-1780; French Colony Champ D'Asile, 1819; Tidelands Papers; early Texas newspapers, 1846-1860; Jean Houston Baldwin Collection of Sam Houston (591 items); private executive record of President of the Republic of Texas Sam Houston, 1841-1844 (1 volume); early Texas maps; Trinity River papers (8 feet); H.O. Compton Surveyors Books; Captain William M. Logan Papers; O'Brien Papers; Hardin Papers (52 feet); Julia Duncan Welder Collection (150 feet); family photograph collections; original and microfilm material from the 10 counties of the old Atascosito District of Southeast Texas, 1826-1960; Encino Press Collection; Carl Hertzog books; many individual family papers and collections. **Holdings:** 9729 books; 859 reels of microfilm; 20,029 photographs; 16,000 cubic feet of manuscripts, government records, and archives; county records. **Subscriptions:** 17 journals and other serials; 9 newspapers. **Services:** Interlibrary loan (microfilm only); copying; center open to the public. **Special indexes:** Llerena B. Friend card index on Sam Houston; inventories of collections in books. **Publications:** *Sam Houston Regional Library and Research Center News*, 2/year.

University of Texas at Austin
Center for American History

General Libraries, SRH 2.101
Austin, TX 78713-7330
Phone: (512)495-4515
Fax: (512)495-4542
Dr. Don E. Carleton, Director

Staff: Prof. 8; Other 15. **Subjects:** Texas history, literature, and folklore; Texas state documents; University of Texas publications and history; Southern and Western history. **Special collections:** Sound archives (2352 audiocassettes; 29,995 phonograph records; 4964 audiotapes; 1028 videocassettes; 85 videotapes); dime novel collection; Kell Frontier Collection; Austin papers; Bexar Archives; Bryan papers; T.S. Henderson papers; James S. Hogg papers; Ashbel Smith papers; John Henry Faulk papers; Pompeo Coppini-Waldine Tauch papers; Jesse Jones papers; James Wells papers; Martin M. Crane papers; Luther M. Evans collection; James Harper Starr papers; James Farmer papers; True West Archives; Field Foundation Archives; Natchez Trace Collection; Russell Lee Photograph Collection; R.C. Hickman Photograph Collection; Robert Runyon Photograph Collection. **Holdings:** 147,917 volumes; 3000 linear feet of university records; 34,987 linear feet of manuscripts and archives; 29,736 maps; 3,800 titles of historic Texas and Southern newspapers; 767,326 photographs; 12,387 slides; 100 VF drawers of clippings; 1500 scrapbooks; 22,223 reels of microfilm; 1501 microfiche; 4293 tapes of oral recordings. **Subscriptions:** 548 periodicals; 673 other serials. **Services:** Interlibrary loan; copying; center open to the public. **Formerly:** University of Texas at Austin-Barker Texas History Center. **Remarks:** Publishers newsletter, archives guide, and library guide.

Utah

Brigham Young University
Harold B. Lee Library

Provo, UT 84602
Phone: (801)378-4995

Description: Third largest collection of genealogical materials in the U.S.A.

Golden Spike Library

PO Box 897
Brigham City, UT 84302
Phone: (801)471-2209
Randy Kane

Description: Located at the National Historic Site where the first transcontinental railroad was completed on May 10, 1869. **Subjects:** Western history; railroad history, including the transcontinental railroad, nineteenth-century steam railroads, and Western railroads.

Southern Utah University Library
Special Collections Department

351 W. Center St.
Cedar City, UT 84720
Phone: (801)586-7945
Blanche C. Clegg, Archivist/Curator

Staff: Professional 1; Other 6. **Founded:** 1962. **Subjects:** Southern Paiute Indians history, local history, college history, Shakespeare. **Special collections:** William Rees Palmer Western History Collection; Document Collection (various donors); Howard Smith Collection; Homer Jones Photo Collection. **Holdings:** 7000 volumes; 925 oral history tapes; 457 phonograph records; 1445 linear feet of manuscript collections; 51,000 photographs and negatives; 804 linear feet of archives; 7530 microforms; 1743 maps. **Services:** Interlibrary loan; copying; department open to the public for reference use only. **Computerized services:** DIALOG Information Services; internal database. **Special indexes:** Document collection index; oral history index; photo collection index; index to Palmer Western History Collection.

University of Utah
Special Collections Department
Manuscripts Division

Marriott Library
Salt Lake City, UT 84112
Phone: (801)581-8864
Stan Larson, Librarian
Nancy Young, Librarian

Staff: Prof.5, other 35. **Founded:** 1935. **Subjects:** Utah, Mountain West, Mormons, Indians. **Special collections:** Doris Duke Oral History collection; others. **Holdings:** 95,100 books; 5,525 periodical titles; 30,000 theses and dissertations; 9,820 federal documents; 15,310 files of clippings; 10,150 folders of pamphlets; 13,000 linear feet of manuscripts; 600,000 photographs; 15,000 A/V items; 2,257 linear feet of archives. **Subscriptions:** 1,680 journals and other serials; 170 newspapers. **Services:** Interlibrary loan; copying (both limited); department open to the public for reference use only. **Computerized services:** Internal database. **Special catalogs:** Registers to manuscript collection; guides for subject areas; manuscript inventories. **Special indexes:** Manuscript name and subject index.

Utah State Archives

Archives Bldg.
State Capitol
Salt Lake City, UT 84114

Phone: (801)538-3012
Fax: (801)538-3354
Jeffery O. Johnson, Director

Staff: Professional 16; Other 19. **Founded:** 1951. **Subjects:** Public records of the State of Utah and its political subdivisions. **Special collections:** Military records. **Holdings:** 85,000 cubic feet of semi-active and historically valuable records; 85,000 cubic feet of records in paper copy; 95,000 reels of microfilm; 90,000 microfiche. **Subscriptions:** 35 journals and other serials; 2 newspapers. **Services:** Copying; archives open to the public. **Computerized services:** RLIN. **Special catalogs:** Records Series Catalog. **Publications:** *Records Retention Schedule.*

Utah State Historical Society Library

300 Rio Grande
Salt Lake City, UT 84101-1182

Phone: (801)533-3536
Fax: (801)533-3503

Staff: Professional 5. **Founded:** 1952. **Subjects:** History—Utah, Mormon, Western, Indian. **Holdings:** 25,000 books; 50,000 bound periodical volumes; 500,000 photographs; 22,000 pamphlets; 33,000 maps; 1500 oral history tapes; 3500 linear feet of manuscripts; 6000 reels of microfilm; 160 feet of clippings files; 5500 museum objects. **Subscriptions:** 220 journals and other serials. **Services:** Copying; library open to the public. **Computerized services:** RLIN. **Special indexes:** Utah History Index (card). **Publications:** *Guide to Unpublished Materials.*

Utah State Library

2150 South 300 West, Ste. 16
Salt Lake City, UT 84115

Phone: (801)466-5888
Fax: (801)533-4657
Amy Owen, Director

Staff: Professional 15; Other 12. **Founded:** 1957. **Subjects:** State and federal government. **Holdings:** 39,811 volumes; 49,987 federal documents; 25,892 state documents. **Subscriptions:** 105 journals and other serials. **Services:** Interlibrary loan; library open to the public with restrictions. **Computerized services:** DIALOG Information Services, OCLC, FirstSearch, Mead Data Central, Deseret News; Internet (electronic mail service). **Remarks:** Electronic mail address: lgr@usl.gov (Internet). **Publications:** *Utah Undercover*, annual; *Directory of Public Libraries in Utah*, annual.

Vermont

Vermont State Agency of Administration Department of General Services Public Records Division

Drawer 33
Montpelier, VT 05633-7601

Phone: (802)828-3700
Fax: (802)828-3710
A. John Yacavoni, Director

Staff: Professional 1; Other 17. **Subjects:** Vermont town and city land records prior to 1900s, Vermont town vital records prior to 1875, Vermont probate record volumes prior to 1850. **Special collections:** Field forms and draft material of Historical Records Survey inventories of Vermont town records and church records; Vermont Vital Record File, 1760-1982. **Holdings:** 1642 boxes of archival holdings; 31,990 reels of microfilm; 246,921 microfiche; 46,152 boxes of semiactive records center material. **Services:** Copying; division open to the public.

Vermont State Archives

26 Terrace St.
Montpelier, VT 05602

Phone: (802)828-2308
Fax: (802)828-2496
D. Gregory Sanford, State Archivist

Staff: Professional 2; Other 1. **Founded:** 1777. **Subjects:** Governors' official papers, legislative records, election records, surveyors' general papers, original acts and resolves, Vermont state papers, (1744 to present), municipal charters. **Special collections:** Stevens Collection of Vermontiana (60 feet); Houston Studio/ Country Camera Photograph Collection. **Holdings:** 500 books; 250 volumes of bound manuscripts; 60 volumes of maps, surveys, and charters; 1700 cubic feet of government records. **Services:** Copying; archives open to the public. **Computerized services:** Minaret (internal database). **Special catalogs:** Inventories for manuscript collections. **Publications:** *State Papers of Vermont.*

Virginia

Virginia State Library and Archives

11th St. at Capitol Square
Richmond, VA 23219

Phone: (804)786-8929
Fax: (804)225-4035
Dr. John C. Tyson, State Librarian

Staff: Professional 71; Other 65. **Founded:** 1823. **Subjects:** Virginiana, Southern and Confederate history, genealogy, social sciences, U.S. colonial history. **Special collections:** Population schedules; special census 1890; Virginia newspapers; Virginia public records; Virginia maps; Confederate imprints. **Holdings:** 640,549 volumes; 86,576 maps; 50,591 cubic feet of manuscripts; 15,522 microforms. **Subscriptions:** 896 journals and other serials; 104 newspapers. **Services:** Interlibrary loan; copying; library open to the public. **Computerized services:** OCLC, RLIN; Virginia Tech Library System (internal database); ALANET (electronic mail service). **Special catalogs:** CAVALIR, statewide union list (microfiche and CD-ROM). **Remarks:** Electronic mail address: ALA1166 (ALANET). **Publications:** *Virginia Cavalcade*, quarterly, available by subscription; *Virginia State Library Publications*, available by subscription and exchange; *Directory of Virginia Libraries*—free.

Washington

Chancery Office of the Catholic Archdiocese of Seattle

910 Marion St.
Seattle, WA 98104

Phone: (206)382-4560

Description: Maintains historical church records for the Indian churches within its jurisdiction. Names from these records have been entered into an ''Indian Register'' which provides the volume and page number where the original information may be found.

Family History Center, Bellevue

10675 NE 20th St.
Bellevue, WA 98004
Phone: (206)454-2690

Description: Branch of the Family History Library of the Church of Jesus Christ of Latter-day Saints. **Subjects:** Genealogy, family history, church and civil records, local history. **Remarks:** Access to main library microfilm.

Family History Center, Seattle

14022 SW Ambaum Blvd.
Seattle, WA 98166
Phone: (206)243-4028

Description: Branch of the Family History Library of the Church of Jesus Christ of Latter-day Saints. **Subjects:** Genealogy, family history, church and civil records, local history. **Remarks:** Access to main library microfilm.

Family History Center, Seattle

5701 8th Ave. NE
Seattle, WA 98105
Phone: (206)522-1233

Description: Branch of the Family History Library of the Church of Jesus Christ of Latter-day Saints. **Subjects:** Genealogy, family history, church and civil records, local history. **Remarks:** Access to main library microfilm.

Lewis County Historical Museum Library

599 NW Front Way
Chehalis, WA 98532
Phone: (206)748-0831
Brenda A. O'Connor, Director

Staff: Professional 3; Other 4. **Founded:** 1978. **Subjects:** History of Lewis County, Chehalis Indians, genealogy. **Special collections:** *Chehalis Bee-Nuggett*, 1883-1930; Lewis County cemetery history; Chehalis Indian Archival Files; genealogy research books and records; Ernst Bechley History Collection; Lewis County voting records, 1870-1930; *Daily Chronicle* newspapers, 1930-1964. **Holdings:** 12,000 photographs; 400 oral history cassette tapes; 36 feet of archival papers and newspaper clippings; 3 feet of family histories; 200 maps. **Subscriptions:** 400 journals and other serials. **Services:** Family research upon request; copies and transcripts of oral history tapes; library open to the public—must have staff present. **Special indexes:** Photograph index by subject; index of oral histories by subject (both card); index to obituary files. **Publications:** Periodical Genealogy & History books; *Lewis County Log*, quarterly—to members.

Seattle Public Library Humanities Department

1000 4th Ave.
Seattle, WA 98104
Phone: (206)386-4625
Fax: (206)386-4632
Norma Arnold, Managing Librarian

Staff: Professional 13; Other 14. **Founded:** 1891. **Subjects:** History, politics, biography, travel, law, literature, languages, philosophy, religion, poetry, fiction, government, general bibliography. **Special collections:** Northwest history; Genealogy Collection; maps. **Holdings:** 452,000 books, and bound periodical volumes; microrecords; newspapers. **Subscriptions:** 1657 journals and other serials; 129 newspapers. **Services:** Interlibrary loan; copying; CD-ROM stations for public use; department open to the public. **Computerized services:** DIALOG Information Services. Performs searches free of charge. **Special indexes:** Northwest Index (300 drawers, subject index of local newspapers).

Skagit County Historical Museum Historical Reference Library

501 S. 4th St.
PO Box 818
La Conner, WA 98257
Phone: (206)466-3365
Mari Anderson-Densmore, Librarian

Staff: Professional 7. **Founded:** 1959. **Subjects:** Skagit County—history, statistics, demographics, industry, social, economic, community life, transportation; pioneer family genealogies; local Indian histories. **Special collections:** Diaries of Grant Sisson, W.J. Cornelius, Arthur Champenois, and others, 1844-1964; Darius Kinsey Photographs. **Holdings:** 1500 books; 308 bound periodical volumes; 8000 photographs; 700 newspapers; 700 business documents; 200 letters; 200 district school accounts/records; 100 maps; 700 clippings and clipping scrapbooks; 300 programs/announcements; 80 pioneer diaries; 220 oral history tapes with transcripts; American popular music, 1866-1954; local newspapers, 1900 to present. **Subscriptions:** 4 journals and other serials; 7 newspapers. **Services:** Copying; library open to the public by appointment. **Publications:** Newsletter.

Society of Jesus, Oregon Province Archives

Foley Center, Gonzaga University
E. 502 Boone Ave.
Spokane, WA 99258
Phone: (509)328-4220
Fax: (509)484-2804
Stephanie Edwards

Staff: 1. **Founded:** 1931. **Subjects:** History - Northwest Church, Alaska Church and missions, Doukhobor, local; Alaskan and Indian languages. **Special collections:** Joset Papers; Cataldo Papers; Crimont Papers; Neil Byrne Papers; Monaghan Papers; Cowley Papers; Prando Papers; Jesuit Mission Papers. **Holdings:** 3600 books; 800 bound periodical volumes; 123,000 manuscripts; 25,000 photographs. **Subscriptions:** 35 journals and other serials; 18 newspapers. **Services:** Copying; library open to those with scholarly credentials. **Publications:** *Guides to Microfilm Editions of the Oregon Province Archives of the Society of Jesus Indian Language Collection: (1) The Alaska Native Languages; (2) The Pacific Northwest Tribes*; *The Alaska Mission Papers*; *Guide to Microfilm Editions of Papers on Pacific Northwest Jesuit Missions & Missionaries.*

Washington State Library

PO Box 42460
Olympia, WA 98504-2460
Phone: (206)753-5590
Fax: (206)586-7575
Nancy Zussy, State Librarian

Staff: Professional 58; Other 70. **Founded:** 1853. **Subjects:** Public administration, applied sciences, medicine and health, behavioral sciences, transportation, ecology, energy. **Special collections:** Pacific Northwest History (13,906 items). **Holdings:** 409,988 books; 75,750 bound periodical volumes; 1.56 million U.S. documents; 117,297 Washington state documents; 20,534 other state documents; 42,734 reels of microfilm; 483,069 microfiche; 26 VF drawers; 8744 AV titles, including 16mm films. **Subscriptions:** 7550 journals and other serials; 160 newspapers. **Services:** Interlibrary loan; copying; library open to the public. **Computerized services:** DIALOG Information Services, OCLC;

ALANET (electronic mail service). **Special catalogs:** Periodicals Holdings (microfiche). **Remarks:** Electronic mail address: WSLADMIN ALA0719 (ALANET). **Publications:** List of publications—available on request.

Washington State Office of Secretary of State
Division of Archives and Record Management

Archives & Records Center
12th & Washington
Olympia, WA 98504
Phone: (206)753-5485
Fax: (206)664-8814
Sidney McAlpin, State Archivist

Staff: Professional 12; Other 12. **Founded:** 1909. **Subjects:** State and local government records. **Special collections:** Land records, 1858 to present. **Holdings:** 8000 bound public records; 50,000 cubic feet of state and local archives; 165,000 cubic feet of records; 200,000 reels of security microfilm. **Services:** Copying; research; division open to the public. **Computerized services:** Gencat Archival Control System (internal database). **Remarks:** Territorial District Court records and other county records are held at five regional depositories operated by the division. **Publications:** *General Guide to the Washington State Archives*; list of other publications—available on request.

Yakima Nation
Environmental Restoration & Waste Management Library

Yakima National Cultural Center
PO Box 151
Toppenish, WA 98948
Wendy L. Graham, Librarian

Staff: Professional 1. **Founded:** 1991. **Subjects:** Environmental science, nuclear science, Native American history. **Holdings:** 2000 books; 50 periodical titles. **Services:** Interlibrary loan; photocopying; reference. **Computerized services:** Internal databases. **Publications:** Information packet about Yakima Indian Nation involvement in nuclear energy and cleanup issues.

West Virginia

West Virginia (State) Division of Culture and History
Archives and History Library

1900 Kanawha Blvd. E.
Charleston, WV 25305-0300
Phone: (304)558-0220
Fax: (304)558-2779
Fredrick H. Armstrong, Director

Staff: Professional 6; Other 7. **Founded:** 1905. **Subjects:** West Virginia archives, history, genealogy; history—U.S., Civil War, colonial, military. **Special collections:** Mortality and population schedules; special census 1890; manuscripts (1510 linear feet); agency records; state documents (22,200); county court records (6620 reels of microfilm); newspapers (16,900 reels of microfilm and clippings); military and land records (2500 reels of microfilm). **Holdings:** 35,800 books; 5,400 bound periodical volumes; 7050 linear feet of state archives; 180 linear feet of special collections; 28,056 reels of microfilm; 65,000 photographs; 6000 maps; 24 VF drawers of clippings. **Subscriptions:** 135 journals and other serials; 95 newspapers. **Services:** Copying; library open to the public for reference use only. **Publications:** *West Virginia History*, annual; Checklist of State Publications, semiannual.

Wisconsin

Marquette University
Department of Special Collections and University Archives
Manuscript Collections Memorial Library

Memorial Library
1415 W. Wisconsin Ave.
Milwaukee, WI 53233
Phone: (414)288-7256
Fax: (414)288-5324
Charles B. Elston, Head

Staff: Professional 4; Other 4. **Founded:** 1961. **Subjects:** Catholic social thought and action, Catholic Indian ministry, Marquette University history, Jesuits and Jesuit institutions, recent U.S. political history, Catholic religious formation and vocation ministries. **Special collections:** Bureau of Catholic Indian Missions Records, 1852 to present (300 feet); Holy Rosary Mission Records, 1852 to present (22 feet); St. Francis Mission Records, 1878 to present (23 feet). **Holdings:** 12,000 volumes; 3000 bound periodical volumes; 8600 cubic feet of archives and manuscripts; 450 reels of microfilm; 4050 feet of manuscript collections relating primarily to Catholic social action and the history of Jesuits and Jesuit institutions, 1865 to present; 4150 cubic feet of Marquette University Archives, 1881 to present; 400 cubic feet of Catholic Indian mission records, 1852 to present. **Subscriptions:** 45 journals and other serials; 20 newspapers. **Services:** Copying; department open to the public. **Computerized services:** Internet (electronic mail service). **Remarks:** Electronic mail address: ledouxs@vms.csd.mu.edu (Internet). **Publications:** In-house finding aids.

State Historical Society of Wisconsin
Archives Division

816 State St.
Madison, WI 53706
Phone: (608)264-6450
Fax: (608)264-6472
Peter Gottlieb, State Archivist

Staff: Professional 17; Other 9. **Founded:** 1846. **Subjects:** Wisconsin history; American frontier, 1750-1815; labor and industrial relations; socialism; mass communications; theater; agricultural history; civil rights; contemporary social action movements. **Special collections:** Draper Collection (frontier). **Holdings:** 53,141 cubic feet of Wisconsin state and local public records; 42,670 cubic feet of nongovernmental archives and manuscripts; 15,000 unbound maps; 2000 atlases; 500 titles on 3100 audiotapes; 110 titles on 3500 phonograph records; 1.5 million visual materials; 50 machine-readable data files of state government records. **Services:** Copying; photo and film reproduction and dubbing of recordings for television. **Computerized services:** RLIN; Internet (electronic mail service). **Remarks:** Electronic mail address: Peter.Gottlieb@MAIL.ADMIN.WISC.EDU (Internet). Administers the Wisconsin Area Research Center Network. **Publications:** Accession reports in *Wisconsin Magazine of History*, quarterly; guides and inventories.

State Historical Society of Wisconsin Library

816 State St.
Madison, WI 53706-1482

Phone: (608)264-6534
Fax: (608)264-6520
R. David Myers, Director

Staff: Professional 20; Other 13. **Founded:** 1846. **Subjects:** History—American, Canadian, Wisconsin, local, labor; radical/reform movements and groups in the U.S. and Canada; ethnic and minority groups in North America; genealogy; women's history; military history; religious history. **Special collections:** African American History Collection (newspapers; periodicals); Native American History Collection (12,000 items; government documents; Native American publications); Lyman Draper Collection of correspondence, etc. gathered by Draper, former director of the Historical Society, which contains a great deal of information about Indian leaders and frontiersmen. **Holdings:** 1.6 million books and bound periodical volumes; 100,000 cubic feet of archives; 1.4 million microfiche and reels of microfilm. **Subscriptions:** 8500 periodicals; 500 newspapers. **Services:** Interlibrary loan; copying; library open to the public. **Computerized services:** OCLC; CD-ROMs; America: History & Life (internal database); Internet (electronic mail service). **Special indexes:** Indian Culture and History (micoform); Index to Wisconsin Native American Periodicals, 1897-1981; Index to names in Wisconsin federal census, 1820-1870 and 1905 state census; Wisconsin necrology index; index of names in Wisconsin county histories. **Remarks:** Electronic mail address: maureen.hady@mail.admin.wisc.edu (Internet). The library is said to be the largest in the world devoted to North American history. This library is a U.S. Federal Government regional depository, a Wisconsin State official depository, and a Canadian Federal Government selective depository for government publications. **Publications:** *Native American Periodicals and Newspapers, 1828-1982*; *Wisconsin Public Documents* (checklist of state government documents)—free upon request; bibliographies; guides.

Outside the U.S.

Family History Center, British Columbia

5280 Kincaid
Burnaby, BC, Canada

Phone: (604)299-8656

Description: Branch of the Family History Library of the Church of Jesus Christ of Latter-day Saints. **Subjects:** Genealogy, family history, church and civil records, local history. **Remarks:** Access to main library microfilm.

Genealogical Research Library

20 Toronto St., 8th Fl.
Toronto, ON, Canada M5C 2B8

Description: Genealogical materials available for research.

Inter-American Indian Institute Library

NUBES 232
Col. Pedregal de San Angel
01900 Mexico City, DF, Mexico

Phone: 5 5680819
Fax: 5 6521274

Staff: 2. **Founded:** 1940. **Subjects:** Indians of the Americas, anthropology. **Holdings:** 30,000 books. **Subscriptions:** 11 journals and other serials. **Services:** Interlibrary loan; copying; SDI; library open to the public. **Computerized services:** Internal database. **Also known as:** Organizacion de los Estados Americanos—Instituto Indigenista Interamericano. **Formerly:** Organization of American States—Inter-American Indian Institute—Library.

Private and Public Organizations

This chapter lists those organizations of national and state significance which can provide assistance to those doing genealogical research, and a description of their various activities and services. They are arranged here categorically by scope; national/regional, followed by state listings. Organizations which either have an international scope or are located outside of the United States, if present, appear at the end of the chapter. All listings are arranged alphabetically within each category.

National and Regional

Alice's Ancestral Nostalgia

PO Box 510092
Salt Lake City, UT 84151

Description: Genealogical materials available for sale.

American Antiquarian Society (AAS)

185 Salisbury St.
Worcester, MA 01609-1634
Phone: (508)755-5221
Ellen S. Dunlap, President

Staff: 45. **Description:** Gathers, preserves, and promotes serious study of the materials of early American history and life. Maintains research library of nearly 5 million books, pamphlets, broadsides, manuscripts, prints, maps, and newspapers; the collection specializes in the period of American history through 1876. Sponsors fellowships, educational programs, and research. **Founded:** 1812. **Members:** 564.

American Genealogical Lending Library (AGLL)

PO Box 244
Dept. M
Bountiful, UT 84011
Phone: (801)298-5358

Description: State-by-state genealogical materials available for rent. Over 100,000 items available on film or fiche. **Remarks:** $2.75 per roll or fiche title for a full month. Rolls can also be purchased. Holdings include U.S. census records, military records, ship passenger lists, Indian censuses, Indian claims, Indian payment and annuity rolls, enrollment cards of the five civilized tribes (1898-1914), other Indian records, state mortality schedules, slave schedules, Freedman's Savings and Trust Company records, Negro military service records, records issued by the commissioner of the Bureau of Refugees, Freedmen, and Abandoned Lands, records for the emancipation of slaves in the District of Columbia, naturalizations of foreign protestants in American and West Indian colonies. **Publications:** Three catalogs: vol. I lists all U.S. Federal Population Census Schedules; vol. II covers military and ship passenger lists; and vol. III lists locality, surname, ethnic, and special collections, $12.50 each or $30.00 for set.

American Indian Studies Center

3220 Campbell Hall
UCLA
Los Angeles, CA 90024

Ark-La-Tex Genealogical Association (ALTGA)

PO Box 4462
Shreveport, LA 71134-0462
Phone: (318)687-3673
Victor Rose, President

Description: Genealogists whose interests lie in the South, especially in the states of Arkansas, Louisiana, and Texas. Purposes are to collect, preserve, and make available genealogical materials, documents, and records; to encourage interest in genealogy and to sponsor educational programs for its development; to promote and publicize the city of Shreveport, LA, as a major genealogical research center for genealogists and historians interested in records of the Ark-La-Tex area; to cooperate with and assist all other genealogical-historical societies and libraries in furtherance of these purposes. Supports and contributes to the Genealogy Room of the Shreve Memorial Library in Shreveport, LA. **Founded:** 1955. **Members:** 500. **Publications:** *The Genie,* quarterly.

Association of Memoirists and Family Historians (AMFH)

PO Box 44268
Tucson, AZ 85733
Ethel Jackson Price, Director

Staff: 3. **Description:** Promotes genealogical and historical research and documentation of family history. Encourages interaction of generations through memoirs. Maintains biographical archive not open to the public. **Founded:** 1991. **Members:** 835. **Remarks:** Speakers bureau, children's services, research and educational programs. **Publications:** *The Linchpin,* quarterly newsletter containing book reviews, announcements of reunions, and genealogical search requests, $10.00/year, circulation: 835; annual directory.

Borderlands Bookstore

PO Box 28497
San Antonio, TX 78228

Description: Genealogical materials available for sale.

Bureau of the Census

Federal Office Building
3 Silver Hill & Suitland Rds.
Suitland, MD 20746
Phone: (301)763-4040

Description: Maintains census records.

Bureau of the Census Personal Census Service Branch

1600 North Walnut Street
Pittsburg, KS 66762
Phone: (316)231-7100

Description: Searches the confidential records from the Federal population censuses and issues official transcripts of the results for a fee. Transcripts may contain information on a person's age, state or country of birth, relationship to householder, etc. **Remarks:** A BC-600 form, *Application for Search of Census Records,* providing the name of the household head and geographic location of the household is required for each search and is available from the Pittsburgh office, the Census History Staff in Washington, D.C. (telephone 301-763-7936), or any of the Census Bureau Regional Offices in Atlanta; Boston; Charlotte, NC; Chicago; Dallas; Denver; Detroit; Kansas City, KS; New York; Philadelphia; Seattle, WA; or Los Angeles, CA. Information services specialists are available to answer inquiries about census publications and other Bureau products. Fee is $25.00 for a search of not more than two censuses. Searches may take two months. Applicant must be a direct blood relative, surviving spouse, executor of the estate, or a beneficiary of a deceased person and must provide proof of death if birth date of ancestor is less than 100 years ago.

Cherokee Family Ties

516 N 38th St.
Mesa, AZ 85205
Phone: (602)832-1467
Donna J. Williams, President

Staff: 3 volunteers. **Description:** Gets together those who are researching Native American blood lines, especially Cherokee. Assists in the preservation of family information for future generations. Maintains a lending library open to the public consisting of books, periodicals, and A/V material; members only can check out books. **Founded:** 1989. **Members:** 54. **Remarks:** Genealogical assistance. **Publications:** *Cherokee Family Researcher,* twice yearly, included in membership ($10.00, plus $2.50 P&H).

Ciga Press

PO Box 654
Fallbrook, CA 92028
Phone: (619)728-9308
Ruth Blake, Managing Editor

Description: Publishes some genealogical materials, but mostly publishes Osage Indian materials. Reaches market through direct mail, museums, and historical societies. Subjects include Indian culture, history, genealogy, anthropology. **Publications:** *A History of the Osage People; Turn of the Wheel: A Burns-Tinker Genealogy; A System for Keeping Genealogical Research Records; Osage Indian Bands and Clans; Osage Indian Customs and Myths; Osage Mission Baptisms, Marriages and Interments 1820-1886,* all by Louis F. Burns.

Closson Press

1935 Sampson Dr.
Apollo, PA 15613

Description: Genealogical materials available for sale.

Congressional Cemetery

1801 E St. SE
Washington, DC 20003
Phone: (202)543-0539
John Hanley, Director

Description: Cemetery wherein Native Americans are interred. **Founded:** 1807. **Remarks:** Cemetery records are housed on-site; searches by office personnel only; appointment required.

Everton Publishers, Inc.

PO Box 368
Logan, UT 84321

Description: Genealogical materials available for sale.

Family History Land

6061 E Broadway, Ste. 128
Tucson, AZ 85711-4020

Description: Genealogical materials available for sale.

Family Tree Genealogical Society

450 Potter St.
Wauseon, OH 43567
Phone: (419)335-6485
Howard V. Fausey, Editor

Description: Publishes *Family Tree Digest,* which features genealogical information and responses to queries on a national basis.

Frontier Press

15 Quintana Dr., Ste. 167
Galveston, TX 77554-9350

Description: Genealogical materials available for sale.

Genealogical Books in Print

6818 Lois Dr.
Springfield, VA 22150

Description: Genealogical materials available for sale.

Genealogical Publishing Co.

1001 N. Calvert St.
Baltimore, MD 21202-3897

Description: Genealogical materials available for sale.

Genealogy Books and Consultation

1217 Oakdale
Houston, TX 77004-5813

Description: Genealogical materials available for sale.

Genealogy Booksellers, Ltd.

208 George St.
Fredericksburg, VA 22401

Description: Genealogical materials available for sale.

Gensoft, Ltd.

13215-C SE Mill Plain, No. 307
Vancouver, WA 98684

Description: Genealogical materials available for sale.

Heritage Books, Inc.

1540 E Pointer Ridge Pl.
Bowie, MD 20716

Description: Genealogical materials available for sale.

Higginson Book Co.

14 Derby Sq.
PO Box 778
Salem, MA 01970

Description: Genealogical materials available for sale.

Immigration and Naturalization Service

Chester A. Arthur Bldg.
425 Eye St. NW
Washington, DC 20001
Phone: (202)514-2783

Description: Maintains immigration records for genealogical research.

Indian University Press

Bacone College
Muskogee, OK 74401
Phone: (918)683-4581
Charles Van Tuyl, Director

Description: Publishes materials for the teaching and preservation of Indian languages, including bilingual materials. Also publishes important writing by Indians and historical materials relating to the history of Indian territory, including family histories. Accepts one unsolicited manuscript per year. Reaches market through direct mail. **Remarks:** 10 total titles in print.

International Genealogical Fellowship of Rotarians (IFRG)

5721 Antietam Dr.
Sarasota, FL 34231
Phone: (813)924-9170
Charles D. Townsend, Secretary

Description: Interested in recreational, avocational, or vocational genealogy activities. Promotes increased understanding and goodwill through the exchange of genealogical backgrounds. Furthers interchange of genealogical research ideas; develops awareness of the need for open records to aid in family research. **Founded:** 1980. **Members:** 300. **Remarks:** Provides research assistance. Sponsors programs and speakers on the subject of genealogy and genealogical research. **Publications:** *Rota-Gene,* bimonthly magazine, includes queries, news notes, book reviews, location of genealogical records, and other research information, $15.00/year, ISSN: 0730-5168; brochure.

Lineages

PO Box 417
Salt Lake City, UT 84110

Description: Genealogical materials available for sale.

Mountain Press

PO Box 400
Signal Mountain, TN 37377-0400

Description: Genealogical materials available for sale.

Mountain Press Research Center

PO Box 400
Signal Mountain, TN 37377-0400
Phone: (615)886-6369
James L. Douthat, Owner

Staff: 2. **Description:** Genealogical and historical research center. Promotes genealogical and historical research in the mid-Atlantic and Southeastern regions of the U.S. Provides research materials and information. Conducts workshops and training events. Maintains 4,500 volume library; arranges displays of genealogical and historical materials. **Founded:** 1980. **Members:** 30,000. **Publications:** *Appalachian Families,* quarterly; *Southern Genealogical Index,* quarterly; books.

National Genealogical Society (NGS)

4527 17th St. N
Arlington, VA 22207-2399
Phone: (703)525-0050
Fax: (703)525-0052

Description: Publishes *NGS Newletter* which features news of the Society and the genealogical community, articles on genealogical methods, sources, repositories, NGS's library acquisitions, and members' queries. Recurring features include a calendar of events.

R & M Publishing Co.

PO Box 1276
Holly Hill, SC 29059
Phone: (803)738-0360
Mack B. Morant, Publisher

Description: Publishes books for students and laypersons on U.S. history, politics, socio-psychology, curriculum development, art appreciation, and genealogy. Also offers a mailing list. Accepts unsolicited manuscripts. Reaches market through direct mail, trade sales: Baker & Taylor Books, Key Sea Press, and Quality Books, Inc.

Southern Historical Press, Inc.

PO Box 1267
Greenville, SC 29602-1267

Description: Genealogical materials available for sale.

Southern Society of Genealogists (SSG)

RFD 5, Box 12
Piedmont, AL 36272
Phone: (205)447-2939
Mrs. Frank Stewart, President

Staff: 1. **Description:** Genealogists; other individuals interested in southern families. Seeks to encourage genealogical research. Conducts seminars; maintains library. **Founded:** 1962. **Members:** 50. **Publications:** *SSG Bulletin,* annual. Also publishes a weekly column in the *Cherokee County Herald.*

Storbeck's Genealogy & Computers

16515 Dane Ct. E.
PO Box 891
Brookfield, WI 53008-0891

Description: Genealogical materials available for sale.

Tri-State Genealogical Society

c/o Public Library
905 5th Ave.
Belle Fourche, SD 57717
Phone: (605)892-4019
Pat Engebretson, Editor

Description: Publishes *WyMonDak Messenger* which contains genealogical material of interest to those searching for ancestors from Crook County, Wyoming; Carter County, Montana; Butte and Harding Counties in South Dakota, and parts of Perkins, Meade, and Lawrence Counties.

U.S. Department of State Passport Services Records Services

One McPherson Sq.
1425 K St., NW
Washington, DC 20005
Phone: (202)326-6124

Description: Maintains passport records for genealogical research.

U.S. Department of the Interior Bureau of Indian Affairs

1849 C St. NW
Mailstop 4140
Bureau of Indian Affairs
Washington, DC 20240
Phone: (202)208-3711
Ada E. Deer, Assistant Secretary

U.S. Department of the Interior Bureau of Indian Affairs Muskogee Area Office

Old Federal Bldg.
5th & W Okmulgee St.
Muskogee, OK 74401
Phone: (918)687-2296
Fax: (918)687-2571
Merritt E. Youngdeer, Director

Remarks: Territory includes eastern Oklahoma.

University Publications of America

4520 E West Hwy., Ste. 800
Bethesda, MD 20814-3389
Phone: (301)657-3200
Toll-Free: 800-692-6300
Fax: (301)657-3203

Description: Publishes microform research collections and books for scholars. Subjects include American studies, black studies, Indian Claims records.

Ye Olde Genealogie Shoppe

PO Box 39128
Indianapolis, IN 46239-3330

Description: Genealogical materials available for sale.

Alabama

Alabama Genealogical Society Inc. American Genealogical Society Depository and Headquarters Samford University Library

Harwell G. Davis Library
Special Collections Dept.
800 Lakeshore Dr.
Birmingham, AL 35229
Phone: (205)870-2749

Alaska

Alaska Genealogical Society

7030 Dickerson Dr.
Anchorage, AK 99504

Anchorage Genealogical Society

c/o Barbara Samuels
PO Box 212265
Anchorage, AK 99521

Arizona

Apache Genealogy Society of Cochise County

PO Box 1084
Sierra Vista, AZ 85636-1084

Arizona Society of Genealogists

6565 E Grand Rd.
Tucson, AZ 85715

Arizona State Genealogical Society

PO Box 42075
Tucson, AZ 85733-2075

Remarks: Holdings include some Mexican census records.

Family History Society of Arizona

PO Box 5566
Glendale, AZ 85312

Genealogical Society of Arizona

PO Box 27237
Tempe, AZ 85282

Arkansas

Arkansas Genealogical Society

PO Box 908
Hot Springs, AR 71902-0908
Phone: (501)262-4513

California

American Indian Historical Society

1451 Masonic Ave
San Francisco, CA 94117

California Genealogical Society

300 Brannan St.
PO Box 77105
San Francisco, CA
94107-0105
Phone: (415)777-9936
Frederick Sherman, President

Staff: 2. **Description:** Oldest genealogical society in the state of California. Helps people trace and compile their own family histories. Gathers and preserves vital records, and provides education through meetings, seminars, workshops and Computer Interest Group. Maintains reference library open to public consisting of books, periodicals, clippings, and A/V material. Some coverage of African, Hispanic, Native, and Asian Americans on both a national and regional level. **Founded:** 1898. **Members:** 700. **Remarks:** Genealogical assistance, research, and educational programs. Annual Family History Fair. **Publications:** *Index to San Francisco Marriage Returns 1850 to 1858; Member Surnames; The Nugget,* semiannnual, ISSN: 1059-9711, circulation: 700; *CGS News,* bimonthly, circulation: 700; also publishes family history books and book reviews.

California State Genealogical Alliance

PO Box 401
Wildomar, CA 92595-0401
Phone: (714)678-1231

Los Fundadores y Amigos del Condado Santa Clara

1053 South White Rd.
San Jose, CA 95127
Phone: (408)926-1165
Evelyn Romero Martinez, Managing Editor/Founder

Staff: 6 (Volunteers/Regular). **Description:** Purpose will be to preserve the history and heritage of Santa Clara County, and early California, through publication and documentation for local libraries, historical societies, and museums and to inform about local events, thereby giving recognition and raising public awareness about the history and heritage of the early families of Santa Clara County and the Californias. No library, but reference materials open to public. Holdings include books, periodicals, and genealogical charts. Major coverage of Hispanic Americans, minor coverage of Native Americans. **Founded:** 1987. **Members:** Approximately 400, 100 paid. **Local groups:** 1. **Affiliated with:** SHHAR (Society of Hispanic Historical & Ancestral Research), and CCHS (Conference of California Historical Societies). **Also known as:** The Founders & Friends of Santa Clara Co., CA. **Remarks:** Speakers bureau, genealogical assistance, research and educational programs, study groups and meetings. **Publications:** *My Family Backbone,* progenitors of (Alta) California, accepting orders, $20, circulation: Over 1,000 copies ordered.

Pocahontas Trails Genealogical Society

3628 Cherokee Lane
Modesto, CA 95356

Professional Genealogists of California

5048 J Parkway
Sacramento, CA 95823

Remarks: Register professional genealogists. No archives.

Santa Barbara Museum of Natural History

2559 Puesta del Sol Rd.
Santa Barbara, CA 93105
Phone: (805)682-4711
Dennis M. Power, Director

Description: Anthropology, including ethnobotany, genealogy, and culture of the Chumash Indians. **Publications:** Occasional Papers Series; *Museum Bulletin* (monthly), *Annual Report.*

Sonoma State University

1801 E Cotati Ave.
Rohnert Park, CA 94928

Remarks: Instrumental in the publishing of genealogical records of Sonoma County, including cemetery records.

University of California, Berkeley Native American Studies Program

3415 Dwinelle Hall
Berkeley, CA 94720

Colorado

Black Genealogy Research Group Denver Public Library Genealogy Dept.

1357 Broadway
Denver, CO 80203-2165
Harriette Brown, President

Description: Purpose is to share information about genealogy in general and Black genealogy in particular; to gather and share genealogical resource material and information about Black history; to foster interaction with individuals and groups whose purpose and goals are similar; to maintain reference materials for members. Major coverage of African-Americans, some coverage of Native-Americans and other groups. **Founded:** 1981. **Members:** About 60. **Local groups:** 1. **Also known as:** Black Genealogy Search Group of Denver, Colorado. **Remarks:** Genealogical assistance, research and educational programs, and field trips all directed toward members with research. **Publications:** *Black Tracks,* quarterly newsletter, $2.00.

Colorado Council of Genealogical Societies

PO Box 24379
Denver, CO 80224-0379

Colorado Genealogical Society (CGS)

PO Box 18221
Denver, CO 80218
Phone: (303)333-3482
Sharon Boatwright, President

Description: Promotes genealogy in Colorado. Seeks to locate, preserve, and index historical records; assists and supports state libraries. Sponsors Black Sheep Writing Contest. **Founded:** 1924. **Members:** 471. **Affiliated with:** Colorado Council of Genealogical Societies; Colorado Preservation Alliance; Colorado Society of Archivists; Federation of Genealogical Societies; National Genealogical Society. **Publications:** *CGS Membership Directory,* annual; *CGS Newsletter,* 10/year; *Colorado Genealogist,* quarterly.

Connecticut

Connecticut Society of Genealogists (CSG)

PO Box 435
Glastonbury, CT 06033
Phone: (203)569-0002
Dorothy Armistead, President

Staff: 4. **Description:** Promotes genealogical research. **Founded:** 1968. **Members:** 4500. **Publications:** *Connecticut Nutmegger,* quarterly.

Delaware

Delaware Genealogical Society

505 Market St. Mall
Wilmington, DE 19801
Donn Devine CGI, President

Description: Persons interested in genealogy. Conducts charitable programs. **Founded:** 1979. **Publications:** *Delaware Genealogical Journal,* semiannual; *Newsletter,* 7/year.

Florida

Florida Genealogical Society

PO Box 18624
Tampa, FL 33679-8624
Phone: (813)254-3045

Florida Society for Genealogical Research

8415 122nd St. N
Seminole, FL 34642
Phone: (813)867-4735
Dorothy M. Boyer, President

Description: Individuals interested in genealogical research. Maintains book collection and sponsors field trips. **Founded:** 1972. **Members:** 100. **Publications:** *Pinellas Genealogist,* periodic; newsletter.

Florida State Genealogical Society

PO Box 10249
Tallahassee, FL 32303-2249

Southern Genealogist's Exchange Society

PO Box 2801
Jacksonville, FL 32203
Phone: (904)387-9142
Faye Irvin, President

Description: Individuals interested in genealogy. Conducts seminars. **Founded:** 1967. **Members:** 225. **Publications:** *Newsletter,* bimonthly.

Georgia

Georgia Genealogical Society (GGS)

PO Box 54575
Atlanta, GA 30308-0575
Phone: (404)475-4404
Bonnie Dubberly, President

Founded: 1964. **Members:** 1,024. **Publications:** *The Cemetery Book: Cemetery Preservation, Restoration, and Recording; GGSQ,* quarterly, comes with membership; *Newsletter,* quarterly; *Subject Index to 25 Years of the GGS Quarterly, 1964-1989;* and several others.

Hawaii

Hawaii County Genealogical Society

PO Box 831
Keaau, HI 96749

Idaho

Idaho Genealogical Society, Inc.

4620 Overland Rd., No. 204
Boise, ID 83705-2867
Phone: (208)384-0542
Jane Walls Golden, President
Jolyn R. Lockhart-Lawson, Board Secretary

Staff: 10. **Description:** Furnish aid in genealogical research, preserve Idaho records, stimulate interest among members and others in the science of genealogy, acquire materials and publications which are of genealogical value. Maintain Friends of Idaho State Genealogical Library. Reference collection donated for public access which consists of 10,000 books, 200 periodicals, clippings, A/V material, 8,000 roll of microfilm, and 15,000 microfiche. Books and census records from all states, foreign reference works, and international materials. **Founded:** 1953, incorporated June 1961. **Members:** 360. **Regional groups:** 1. **State groups:** 1. **Local groups:** 5 chapters (inactive). **Computerized services:** Library: Western Library Network (WLN); and on CD-Rom the Social Security Death Record Index and the Family Search files. **Affiliated with:** Oregon Trail Project, 4620 Overland Rd., 204, Boise, ID 83705-2867, phone 208-384-0542. **Remarks:** Museum (as part of Idaho Archives have access to archival records), genealogical assistance, research and educational programs, annual conferences and workshops. **Publications:** *Idaho Genealogical Society Quarterly,* quarterly, $12.50, ISSN: 0445-2127, circulation: international, U.S. and Canada; *Footprints Through Idaho:*

Volumes of Idaho Pioneers, volumes I and II (vol. III near publication); *Oregon Trail Travelers Database,* $10.00.

Illinois

Illinois State Genealogical Society (ISGS)

PO Box 10195
Springfield, IL 62791
Phone: (217)789-1968
Joyce Standridge, Executive Secretary

Description: Individuals interested in genealogy. Seeks to further genealogical research. **Founded:** 1968. **Members:** 3000. **Publications:** *Illinois State Genealogical Quarterly; Newsletter,* monthly.

Indiana

Indiana Genealogical Society, Inc. (IGS)

PO Box 10507
Fort Wayne, IN 46852

Staff: 5. **Description:** Group's purpose is to communicate, coordinate, organize, and perpetuate genealogical organizations, projects, and materials within and concerning Indiana; and to promote preservation, education, and safeguarding of historical records, books, and other memorabilia. No library. **Founded:** 1984. **Members:** Over 500. **State groups:** 5. **Remarks:** Speakers bureau, genealogical assistance, educational programs, and annual conference. **Publications:** *Indiana Genealogical Source Directory,* $7.50; *Indiana Genealogical Society Newsletter,* 6 times/year (included in membership); *Indiana Genealogist,* 4 times/year (included with membership); *IGS Family Exchange File.*

Northwest Territory Genealogical Society (NTGS)

Lewis Historical Library, LRC22
Vincennes University
Vincennes, IN 47591
Phone: (812)885-4330
Donna Beeson, Editor

Description: Persons involved in genealogical research. Seeks to advance research in area records, preserve historical documents, and make such information more accessible to the public. Maintains library including oral histories. **Founded:** 1980. **Members:** 215. **Publications:** *Northwest Trail Tracer,* quarterly; *Index of Declarations and Naturalizations;* censuses.

Iowa

Iowa Genealogical Society

6000 Douglas
PO Box 7735
Des Moines, IA 50322

Kansas

Kansas Council of Genealogical Societies

PO Box 3858
Topeka, KS 66608-6858

Kansas Genealogical Society, Inc.

Village Square Mall, Lower Level, 2601 Central
PO Box 103
Dodge City, KS 67801
Phone: (316)225-1951
Doris D. Rooney, Executive Manager

Staff: All volunteer society. **Description:** To create interest in genealogy; preserve genealogical data; encourage an adherence to accuracy and thoroughness in research; foster careful documentation; and to require a standard of excellence and accuracy in writing of published matter sponsored by the Society. Maintain library open to public which consists of books, periodicals, clippings, and A/V material. National and regional focus. Some coverage of Hispanic and Native Americans, minor coverage of African and Asian Americans. **Founded:** 1958. **Members:** 450. **Remarks:** Biographical archives, genealogical assistance, research and educational programs, and quarterly seminars. **Publications:** *The Treesearcher,* quarterly, $15-$20, circulation: approximately 450.

Mid-America All-Indian Center Museum

650 North Seneca
Wichita, KS 67203
Phone: (316)262-5221
Fax: (316)262-4216
Jerry Martin, Museum Director

Staff: 8. **Description:** Maintains reference library open to public which consists of books, periodicals, clippings, and A/V materials. Regional focus. **Founded:** 1976. **Remarks:** Museum, research and educational programs.

Shawnee Methodist Indian Mission

3403 W 53rd
Fairway, KS 66205

Kentucky

Kentucky Genealogical Society

PO Box 153
Frankfort, KY 40602
Phone: (502)875-4452
Brian D. Harney, President

Staff: 1. **Description:** Maintains reference library open to public consisting of books, periodicals, and clippings. **Founded:** 1973. **Members:** 2200. **Computerized services:** Kentucky Genealogical Index, 2.3m records, restricted access. **Publications:** *Bluegrass Roots,* quarterly, $15/yr, on microfilm, 1973-1984.

Louisiana

Louisiana Genealogical and Historical Society (LGHS)

PO Box 3454
Baton Rouge, LA 70821-3454

Phone: (504)766-1555
Barbara C. Strickland, President
Nell T. Boersma, Editor

Staff: 19. **Description:** Seeks to preserve genealogical and historical records in Louisiana. Encourages documented genealogical research. Some coverage of all ethnic groups, with regional and national focus. **Founded:** 1953. **Members:** 600. **Remarks:** Books sent to the Society for review are donated to the Louisiana State Archives or the Louisiana State Library, where they are available to researchers. **Publications:** *Louisiana Genealogical Register,* quarterly journal, $25.00, included with membership; *Diary in Gray,* $12.50 postpaid; *Bible Records-vol. 5,* $15.00 postpaid; several others.

Maine

Maine Genealogical Society

PO Box 221
Farmington, ME 04938-0221

Maryland

Maryland Genealogical Society

201 West Monument St.
Baltimore, MD 21201

Maryland Historical Society

201 W Monument St.
Baltimore, MD 21201

Phone: (410)685-3750

Remarks: The Society houses the Peabody Genealogical Collection which consists of 5,000 books (expected to be inventoried and available for use by the end of 1994). It includes materials added to the Peabody Library (Johns Hopkins Univ.) after World War II and consists of genealogical guides; bibliographies; compendia; indexes to and abstracts of genealogical sources; family histories; patriotic society publications; and genealogical journals as well as a vertical file collection of originals and microforms.

Massachusetts

Massachusetts Genealogical Council c/o New England Historic Genealogical Soc.

101 Newbury St.
Boston, MA 02116

Massachusetts Society of Genealogists Inc.

PO Box 215
Ashland, MA 01721

Michigan

Michigan Genealogical Council (MGC)

PO Box 30007
Lansing, MI 48909

Description: Genealogical societies. Coordinates activities of members; promotes genealogical research; protects genealogical data. **Founded:** 1972. **Members:** 80. **Publications:** *Directory,* annual; *MGC Newsletter,* quarterly; *1850 Index Census; First Land Owners of Ingham County; First Land Owners of Ogemaw County; First Land Owners of St. Clair County; Michigan Surname Index;* family trees.

Fred Hart Williams Genealogical Society Detroit Public Library Burton Historical Collection

5201 Woodward Ave.
Detroit, MI 48202

Phone: (313)833-0675
Roy L. Roulhac, President

Description: Regional society with national focus. Includes major coverage of African Americans, as well as slight coverage of Native Americans. **Founded:** 1979. **Members:** 250. **Remarks:** Speakers bureau, genealogical assistance, research and educational programs. **Publications:** *Newsletter* three times a year to members.

Minnesota

Minnesota Genealogical Society

PO Box 16069
Saint Paul, MN 55116-0069

Phone: (612)645-3671
P. Warren

Description: Non-profit, educational organization whose purpose is to foster and increase an interest in genealogy by providing an association of those interested in family, state and local history; collect, preserve and publish genealogical records and information; hold meetings and workshops to educate its members on current genealogy-related topics. Maintains reference library open to public at 1650 Carroll Avenue, Saint Paul, consisting of 5500 books, periodicals, and clippings. Regional focus, some national coverage. Major coverage of Native Americans (Midwest/Eastern Canada), some coverage of Hispanic Americans, minor coverage of African and Asian Americans. **Founded:** 1969. **Members:** 1600. **Local groups:** 9 branches. **Remarks:** Speakers bureau, genealogical assistance, and research and educational programs. **Publications:** *The Minnesota Genealogist,* quarterly, included with membership, ISSN: 0581-0086, circulation: 1700; *M.G.S. Newsletter,* quarterly, included with membership, circulation: 1800. *Minnesota Place Names: Now and Then,* $12.00; *Minnesota Genealogical Periodical Index: A County Guide,* $4.00; Oakland cemetery records: Oakland, Fairview, and Brown cemeteries, prices range from $10 to $15.

Mississippi

Historical and Genealogical Association of Mississippi

618 Avalon Rd.
Jackson, MS 39206

Mississippi Genealogical Society

PO Box 5301
Jackson, MS 39206

Missouri

Missouri State Genealogical Association (MoSGA)

PO Box 883
Columbia, MO 65205-0833

Description: Purpose is to offer highest quality of education, guidance, and services to members. Maintains library available to the public at Mid-Continent Public Library, Spring and 24 Highway, Independence, MO 64050. Holdings include books, periodicals, and clippings. Regional focus. Minor coverage of African and Native Americans. **State groups:** 1. **Remarks:** Speakers bureau, educational programs, annual conference. **Publications:** *The Jourinal,* quarterly, $15.00 (included with membership); newsletter, 6 times/year, included with membership; county records publications.

Montana

Montana State Genealogical Society

PO Box 555
Chester, MT 59522

Nebraska

Nebraska State Genealogical Society

PO Box 5608
Lincoln, NE 68505
Phone: (402)266-8881

Nevada

Nevada State Genealogical Society

PO Box 20666
Reno, NV 89515

New Hampshire

New Hampshire Society of Genealogists (NHSOG)

PO Box 633
Exeter, NH 03833-0633
Phone: (603)432-8137
George F. Sanborn Jr., President

Description: Educates the public about genealogical records. **Founded:** 1978. **Members:** 800. **Remarks:** Offers assistance in conducting genealogical research. **Publications:** *New Hampshire Society of Genealogical Record,* quarterly journal; *New Hampshire Society of Genealogists Newsletter,* quarterly.

New Jersey

Genealogy Club of the Library of the New Jersey Historical Society

230 Broadway
Newark, NJ 07104

New Mexico

Indian Pueblo Cultural Center

2401 12th St NW
Albuquerque, NM 87107

New Mexico Genealogical Society

PO Box 8283
Albuquerque, NM 87198-8330

Remarks: Has published genealogical records including early censuses, family genealogies.

New York

New York Genealogical and Biographical Society

122-126 E 58th St.
New York, NY 10022-1939
Phone: (212)755-8532
William P. Johns, Exec. Dir.

Staff: 11. **Description:** To discover, procure, preserve, and perpetuate information and items relating to genealogy, biography, and family history, especially of the state of New York. Maintains research library of 68,000 books, 25,000 manuscripts, and 10,000 microforms. Maintains portrait collection; conducts educational programs. **Founded:** 1869. **Members:** 1,500. **Remarks:** Also publishes source records from New York; offers list of publications; magazine available on microform. **Publications:** *The New York Genealogical and Biographical Record,* quarterly, included in membership dues, circulation: 2,000; *NYG&B Newsletter,* quarterly.

New York State News Vital Records Index Search Service

New York State Archives
Cultural Education Center
11D40
Albany, NY 12230
Phone: (518)474-8955

Description: Searches the Department of Health microfiche indexes to marriages and deaths 1880/1-1943 and births 1880/1-1918. Covers all of the state except New York City and (prior to 1914) Albany, Buffalo, and Yonkers. Once the index entry is found, a copy may be requested from the appropriate local registrar. **Remarks:** Fee is $5 per request; there is no refund for unsuccessful searches. For a marriage or birth record, the applicant must sign a statement that the individual named is deceased. Contact the NY State Archives for the request form. Each form may be used to request a search of one index (birth, marriage, or death) for one name for up to three specific years.

Seneca Nation of Indians

1490 Route 438
Irving, NY 14081
Barbara Hemlock, Clerk

North Carolina

Blanche P. Browder

5133 Jeffries Rd.
Raleigh, NC 27606
Phone: (919)851-0679

Description: Publishes on the Cherokee Indian history of North Carolina, and on local history and genealogy. **Publications:** *DeSoto and Other Spanish Explorers and Their Historians; Cherokee Indians and Those Who Came After,* both by Nathaniel C. Browder.

North Dakota

Three Affiliated Tribes Museum, Inc.

PO Box 147
New Town, ND 58763
Phone: (701)627-4477
Herbert J. Wilson, Acting Chairman

Staff: 2. **Description:** Museum established as a non-profit organization in the summer of 1964. Provides a heritage center for the Three Affiliated Tribes in which the members could display artifacts, arts and crafts, historical data, and objects.

Ohio

Ohio Genealogical Society (OGS)

PO Box 2625
Mansfield, OH 44906
Phone: (419)522-9077
Mary Bowman, President

Staff: 2. **Description:** Genealogists, historians, libraries, and other interested individuals from throughout the U.S. Promotes genealogical research and the preservation of historical records in Ohio. Facilitates the exchange of ideas and information. Sponsors educational programs on family lineage in Ohio; conducts student essay contest. Maintains 15,000 volume library. **Founded:** 1959. **Members:** 6,350. **Regional groups:** 3; Chapters: 102. **Remarks:** Speakers bureau. **Publications:** *Chapter Directory,* periodic; *The Ohio Genealogical Society Newsletter,* monthly, includes calendar of events, chapter announcements, library acquisitions, queries, and membership information, $25.00, circulation: 6,350; *Ohio Records and Pioneer Families,* quarterly, contains cemetery and family records, court abstracts, and genealogical articles, $18.00, circulation: 1,025; *The Report,* quarterly magazine, price included in membership dues; *Ohio Cemeteries,* and *First Families of Ohio Roster.*

Oklahoma

Chickasaw Indian Nation

520 E. Arlington
Ada, OK 74820
Phone: (405)436-2603
Fax: (405)436-4287
Glenda Galvan, Library/Curator

Staff: 6. **Description:** Purpose is to educate public about Chickasaws through records, documents, etc. Have monthly programs and mail outs. Maintains reference library open to public consisting of books, periodicals, clippings and A/V material. Minor coverage of African Americans. **Founded:** 1986. **Regional groups:** 2. **Remarks:** Speakers bureau, biographical archives, museum, genealogical assistance, research and educational programs.

Federation of Oklahoma Genealogical Societies

PO Box 26151
Oklahoma City, OK 73126

Genealogical Institute of Oklahoma

3813 Cashion Pl.
Oklahoma City, OK 73112

Oklahoma Genealogical Society

PO Box 12986
Oklahoma City, OK 73157-2986
Sharron Ashton, Editor, OGSQ

Staff: Volunteer. **Description:** Created to bring together interested persons for discussion and exchange of information, to study research methodology, to issue publications, to collect and preserve data and to assist members with their genealogical research and writing. Major coverage of Native Americans; some coverage of African Americans, particularly on ''Freedmen'' — slaves and descendants of slaves who belonged to individual Indians; and minor coverage of Hispanic Americans. All genealogical material donated to Oklahoma Historical Library in Oklahoma City. Founded First Families of the Twin Territories (Indian and Oklahoma) whose members (1,800 as of April 1994) have proved lineage to individual who settled one of the territories prior to 16 November 1907. **Founded:** 1955. **Members:** 1,000. **Publications:** *Oklahoma Genealogical Society Quarterly,* quarterly, included with membership; *Record of the Choctaw Nation, 1976,* $12.00 plus $1.50 P&H; *1880 and 1890 Census, Canadian District, Cherokee Nation, Indian Territory,* 1978, $8.50 plus $1.50 P&H; *Index to Ancestors,* 1993, $10.00 plus $1.50 P&H.

Oklahoma Historical Society

2100 N Lincoln Blvd.
Oklahoma City, OK 73105
Phone: (405)521-2491

Remarks: Collection contains most of the correspondence to the Commission of the Five Civilized Tribes prior to 1906.

Oregon

Genealogical Council of Oregon

PO Box 628
Ashland, OR 97520-0021

Genealogical Forum of Oregon Inc. Headquarters and Library

2130 SW 5th Ste. 220
Portland, OR 97201
Phone: (503)227-2398
Eileen Chamberlin, President

Staff: All-volunteer. **Description:** Purpose is education, collection and publication of historical materials. Largely state and regional in focus; some national coverage. Maintains library open to public for small fee consisting of books, periodicals, clippings, and A/V material. Lends materials to members only. Minor coverage of African, Hispanic, and Native Americans. **Founded:** 1946. **Members:** 1217. **Computerized services:** CD-ROM with databases. **Remarks:** Speakers bureau, biographical archives, and genealogical assistance. **Publications:** *Oregon Donation Land Claims,* volumes 1-5, vol 6: Index and vol 1-3 (1 vol): *Oregon Provisional Land Claims,* $7.25-$20.00; *Idaho Rejected Land Claims,* volumes 1-5 from BLM record; *Multnomah County Marriage Records, 1853-1890,* vol's 1-5, $6.25-$12.00; *The Bulletin,*: quarterly $25/year (included with membership), circulation: 1217; *The Forum Insider,* 8 times a yr. (monthly between publication of *The Bulletin,* $25 yr. included with membership).

Genealogical Heritage Council of Oregon

Douglas County Courthouse, Rm. 111
PO Box 579
Roseburg, OR 97470

Oregon Genealogical Society

PO Box 10306
Eugene, OR 97440-2306
Phone: (503)746-7924
Nancy Hodgkinson, President

Staff: All volunteer. **Description:** To promote interest in genealogy, to maintain & staff genealogical research library, to publish genealogical & historical information in a quarterly periodical & other appropriate publications. Meets monthly, except December. Maintains a reference library which is open to public. Library holds books, periodicals, clippings, and A/V materials. Some coverage of all groups, African Americans, Hispanic Americans; extensive coverage of Native Americans; and little coverage of Asian Americans. National and regional scope. **Founded:** 1962. **Members:** 365. **Computerized services:** Some. **Telecommunications services:** Some. **Remarks:** Offers genealogical assistance, research programs, and education programs. Has large Oregon collection, and issues Oregon Pioneer Certificates. **Publications:** *OGS Quarterly,* 4 times per year (Jan., April, July, Oct.), included in dues; *OGS Newsletter,* 6 times per year; also publishes several Oregon census sources and other miscellaneous documents. List available from the Society.

Pennsylvania

African American Genealogy Group (AAGG)

PO Box 1798
Philadelphia, PA 19107
Phone: (215)572-6063
Fax: (215)885-7244
John Logan, President

Staff: 5. **Description:** Supports genealogy research in the African American community of Philadelphia and the Delaware Valley, with slight coverage of Hispanic and Native Americans. Programs with guest speakers, teaching sessions, seminars for beginners, field trips and conferences. Maintains a reference library open to public consisting of book and periodicals. **Founded:** 1989. **Members:** 130. **Local groups:** 1. **Remarks:** Speakers bureau, genealogical assistance, and educational programs. **Publications:** *Newsletter* quarterly to members.

Genealogical Society of Pennsylvania (GSP)

1300 Locust St.
Philadelphia, PA 19107
Phone: (215)545-0391
Antoinette J. Segraves, Executive Director

Description: Genealogical researchers in Pennsylvania and the Delaware Valley area of Delaware and New Jersey. Collects and preserves genealogical records. Conducts abstracting, indexing, and microfiliming of newspapers and records. **Founded:** 1892. **Members:** 2000. **Remarks:** Maintains library. **Publications:** *Journal,* periodic; *PENN In Hand,* quarterly newsletter; *Pennsylvania Genealogical Magazine,* periodic; special publications.

Rhode Island

Rhode Island Genealogical Society

13 Countryside Dr.
Cumberland, RI 02864-2601

South Carolina

South Carolina Genealogical Society (SCGS)

PO Box 20266
Charleston, SC 29413-0266
Phone: (803)766-1667
Kay Manning, Vice President

Description: Persons interested in genealogy. Maintains library. **Founded:** 1972. **Members:** 1,800. **Local groups:** 16. **Publications:** *Carolina Herald,* biennial; *Newsletter,* 4/year.

South Dakota

Augustana College Center for Western Studies

Box 727
Sioux Falls, SD 57197
Phone: (605)336-4007
Arthur R. Huseboe, Executive Director

Description: Publishes historical and cultural nonfiction dealing with the Midwest. Offers a bi-annual publication *CWS Newsletter.* Accepts unsolicited manuscripts. Distributes for *Nordland Heritage Foundation* and *University of Nebraska Press.* Reaches market through direct mail and trade sales. Subjects include immigration, settlement of the west, Sioux (Dakota) Indian culture. Cheyenne Indian history, Crow Indian history, Blackfoot Indian history. **Publications:** *Tomahawk and Cross: Lutheran Missionaries among the Northern Plains Tribes, 1858-1866* by Gerhard M. Schmutterer; *The Last Contrary: The Story of Wesley Whiteman (Black Bear)* by Warren G. Schwartz; *Natural History of the Black Hills and Badlands* by Sven G. Froiland.

Catholic Chancellery of Sioux Falls

Box 5033
Sioux Falls, SD 57117

Catholic Diocese of Rapid City

Box 678
Rapid City, SD 57709

South Dakota Genealogical Society (SDGS)

PO Box 1101
Pierre, SD 57501
Marilyn Heesch, President

Staff: Volunteers. **Description:** Purpose is to promote an interest in genealogy; encourage, educate, and instruct members in the art and practice of genealogical research; maintain and elevate genealogical standards; stress the importance of accuracy through careful documentation; locate, preserve, and index public and private genealogical records and make such records available to members and the general public; raise funds for any of the foregoing purposes and to accept donations, gifts, legacies, and bequests. Collection of genealogical materials housed at the Alexander Mitchell Library in Aberdeen. **Remarks:** Genealogical assistance. **Publications:** *The South Dakota Genealogical Quarterly,* $15.00 (included with membership), circulation: 150; *No Year Index* (consists of alpha name index of 10 yrs. of quarterlies), $35.00.

Tennessee

Tennessee Genealogical Society

PO Box 111249
Memphis, TN 38111-1249
Phone: (901)327-3273
Lincoln Johnson, President

Staff: 15. **Description:** Purpose is to preserve and publish genealogical records important to Tennessee and Tennesseans. Focus is regional. Minor coverage of Native Americans. Maintain library for members only consisting of books, periodicals, clippings, and material. Supports the genealogical collection at the Memphis-Shelby County Public Library and Information Center. **Founded:** 1953. **Members:** 1,600. **Remarks:** Genealogical assistance, educational programs. **Publications:** *''Ansearchin'' News,* quarterly, $20.00, circulation: 1,600.

Texas

Texas State Genealogical Society

Rte. 4, Box 56
Sulphur Springs, TX 75482
Phone: (903)885-3523

Description: Individuals interested in the genealogy of Texas. Conducts annual lecture series. Issues Texas Pioneer certificates. **Founded:** 1960. **Members:** 800. **Publications:** *Stirpes,* quarterly journal; *TSGS Newsletter,* periodic.

Utah-Pan America University

1201 University
Edinburg, TX 78539

Utah

Genealogical Society of Utah

35 NW Temple
Salt Lake City, UT 84150
Phone: (801)240-2331

Utah Genealogical Association (UGA)

PO Box 1144
Salt Lake City, UT 84110
George Jordan, Vice-Pres/ Chmn. Publication Committee

Description: Promote active interest in genealogy; compilation of accurate, complete pedigrees; preservation of genealogical records; foster genealogical education and training; conduct seminars, conferences, workshops, and chapter meetings; locate genealogical source materials and records and make them available to genealogists and historians; actively disseminate information on research techniques and procedures; provide research assistance to aid people with their pedigree searches. International, national, and regional coverage. Direct access to holdings of the Family History Library in Salt Lake City. **Founded:** 1971. **State groups:** 3. **Local groups:** 4. **Remarks:** Speakers bureau, genealogical assistance, research and educational programs. **Publications:** *U.G.A. Journal,* quarterly (included with membership), $25.00/year, circulation: approximately 750, available on microform from University Microfilms, 300 North Zeeb Road, Ann Arbor, MI 48106; *U.G.A. Newsletter,* quarterly, included with membership.

Vermont

Genealogical Society of Vermont

46 Chestnut St. Joann H. Nichols, President
Brattleboro, VT 05301

Description: Individuals interested in their Vermont ancestors and in promoting genealogical activity. Assembles, preserves and makes available genealogical records. **Founded:** 1971. **Members:** 1300. **Remarks:** Offers research assistance. **Publications:** *Branches and Twigs,* quarterly.

Vermont Genealogical Society

PO Box 422 Phone: (802)483-2957
Pittsford, VT 05763

Virginia

Genealogical Research Institute of Virginia

PO Box 29178 Peter Broadbent, President
Richmond, VA 23242-0178

Staff: All volunteer. **Description:** Promotes, fosters and encourages serious and accurate genealogical and historical research by all means possible, including instruction, seminars, workshops and fieldtrips. No library. Some regional coverage. **Founded:** 1981. **Members:** 350. **Remarks:** Answers queries. **Publications:** *News 'n Notes* 10/year; $10/yr; 450.

Washington

SearchMasters Genealogical Research Group

PO Box 308 Phone: (509)535-6821
Veradale, WA 99037 Kathie MacGregor, Researcher

Description: Genealogical research services to individuals searching Native Indian lines in the U.S. and Canada. **Computerized services:** Research and histories are computer generated. **Remarks:** Speakers bureau, genealogical assistance.

Washington State Genealogical Society

PO Box 1422 Phone: (206)352-0595
Olympia, WA 98507

West Virginia

West Virginia Genealogy Society Inc.

PO Box 249
Elkview, WV 25071

Wisconsin

Menominee Indian Tribe of Wisconsin

PO Box 397 Phone: (715)799-5100
Keshena, WI 54135 Fax: (715)799-3802
Ben Miller, Chairman

Remarks: Tribal records back to early treaties of 1848.

Wisconsin Genealogical Council, Inc.

Rte. 3, Box 253 Phone: (608)378-4388
Black River Falls, WI 54615-9405 Fax: (608)378-3006
Carolyn Habelman, President

Description: Sponsors annual state educational conference; ''Beginners Handbook.'' Largely regional focus. **Founded:** 1986. **Members:** 120. **State groups:** 9. **Remarks:** Speakers bureau, genealogical assistance, and educational programs. **Publications:** Newsletter, quarterly, included with membership.

Wisconsin State Genealogical Society

2109 20th Ave. Phone: (608)325-2609
Monroe, WI 53566

Wyoming

Arapaho Cultural Museum

PO Box 127
Ethete, WY 82520

Print Resources

National and Regional

Africans and Creeks: From the Colonial Period to the Civil War

Greenwood Press
88 Post Rd. W
PO Box 5007
Westport, CT 06881

Phone: (203)226-3571
Fax: (203)226-1502
Daniel F. Littlefield Jr., Author

Pages: 286. **Publication date:** 1979. **Also includes:** Bibliography, index, maps.

Africans and Seminoles: From Removal to Emancipation

Greenwood Press
88 Post Rd. W
PO Box 5007
Westport, CT 06881

Phone: (203)226-3571
Fax: (203)226-1502
Daniel F. Littlefield Jr., Author

Pages: 278. **Publication date:** 1977. **Also includes:** Bibliography, index, lists.

A.K.A. (Also Known As)

Cherokee Woman Publishing
PO Box 48
Spavinaw, OK 74366

Phone: (918)589-2236
Sandi Garrett, Author

Description: Provides an alphabetical listing of both the English and Indian names for those researching Cherokee ancestry. Information is included on the Dawes Commission; the Guion Miller Rolls; the reservations; the Treaty of May 6, 1828; the Cherokee Census Records of 1835, 1893, and 1896; the Old Settler payrolls of 1851 and 1895; the Drennan and Chapman Rolls of 1851; and Cherokee population statistics from 1650 to 1937. **Indexes:** By name (Indian and English). **Pages:** 35. **Publication date:** 1993. **Price:** $15.00, postpaid.

American Family Records Association—Member Directory and Ancestral Surname Registry

American Family Records Association
PO Box 15505
Kansas City, MO 64106

Phone: (816)373-6570

Covers: Nearly 300 member family historians and genealogists; 4,300 surnames. **Entries include:** Name, address, member number, ancestral surnames with geographic locations and approximate time period. **Arrangement:** Alphabetical. **Frequency:** Annual. **Remarks:** To be available on CD-ROM only, starting late 1993.

American Genealogist

American Genealogist
PO Box 398
Demorest, GA 30535-0398

Phone: (706)865-6440
David L. Greene, Editor and Publisher

Description: Scholarly genealogical journal. **First published:** 1922. **Frequency:** Quarterly. **Circulation** 1,600. **Subscription:** $20.00; $39.00, two years; $58.00, three years. **ISSN:** 0002-8592.

American Indian and Alaska Native Newspapers and Periodicals, 1826-1924

Greenwood Press
88 Post Road West
PO Box 5007
Westport, CT 06881-5007

Phone: (203)226-3571
Fax: (203)222-1502
Daniel F. Littlefield Jr.
James W. Parins

Pages: 482. **Publication date:** 1984. **Price:** $105.00. **ISBN:** 0-313-23426-4.

American Indian and Alaska Native Newspapers and Periodicals, 1925-1970

Greenwood Press
88 Post Road West
PO Box 5007
Westport, CT 06881-5007

Phone: (203)226-3571
Fax: (203)222-1502
Daniel F. Littlefield Jr.
James W. Parins

Pages: 577. **Publication date:** 1986. **Price:** $105.00. **ISBN:** 0-313-23427-2.

American Indian and Alaska Native Newspapers and Periodicals, 1971-1985

Greenwood Press
88 Post Road West
PO Box 5007
Westport, CT 06881-5007
Phone: (203)226-3571
Fax: (203)222-1502
Daniel F. Littlefield Jr.
James W. Parins

Pages: 629. **Publication date:** 1986. **Price:** $105.00. **ISBN:** 0-313-24834-6.

American Indian Archival Material: A Guide to Holdings in the Southeast

Greenwood Press
88 Post Rd. W
PO Box 5007
Westport, CT 06881
Phone: (203)226-3571
Fax: (203)226-1502

Covers: Manuscript repositories with significant collections on Native Americans; coverage limited to Alabama, Florida, Georgia, Kentucky, Louisiana, Mississippi, North and South Carolina, Tennessee, Virginia, and West Virginia. **Entries include:** Respository name, location, and description of holdings. **Pages:** 325. **Frequency:** Published 1982. **Price:** $49.95.

American Indian Archival Material: Guide to the Holdings in the Southwest

Greenwood Press
88 Post Rd. W
PO Box 5007
Westport, CT 06881
Phone: (203)226-3571
Fax: (203)222-1502
Chepesium Ron, Author
Arnold Shankman, Author

Publication date: 1982.

American Indians: A Select Catalog of National Archives Microfilm Publications

Publications Staff
National Archives
PO Box 2580
Alexandria, VA 22301

Description: Lists available federal records along with microfilm numbers. **Pages:** 91. **Publication date:** 1984. **Price:** $2.00 (paper). **ISBN:** 0-911333-09-6.

American Newspapers, 1821-1936: A Union List of Files Available in the United States and Canada

Kraus Reprints
Rte. 100
Millwood, NY 10546
Phone: (914)762-2200
Toll-Free: 800-223-8323
Winifred Gregory

Publication date: 1937. **Price:** $198.00.

Ancestry's Red Book: American State, County & Town Sources

Ancestry
PO Box 476
Salt Lake City, UT 84110-0476
Phone: (801)531-1790
Toll-Free: 800-531-1790
Fax: (801)531-1798
Alice Eichholz, Editor

Covers: Genealogical resources in every state and the District of Columbia, including names and addresses for county seats and parent counties; definitive maps and map listings; vital records; census records; local history collections; land records and maps; probate, court, and tax records; cemetery and church records; military records; periodical, newspaper, and private manuscript collections; archival, library, and genealogical and historical society collections; ethnic collections with unique emphasis; immigration and naturalization resources; and bibliographic references. **Description:** Provides county and town listings within an overall state-by-state organization. **Type:** Book. **Arrangement:** Geographical. **Indexes:** General. **Pages:** 858. **Frequency:** Irregular; previous edition 1987; latest edition January 1992. **Price:** $39.95 (Members, $33.95). **ISBN:** 0-916489-47-7.

Archives: A Guide to the National Archives Field Branches

Ancestry
PO Box 476
Salt Lake City, UT 84110-0476
Toll-Free: 800-531-1790
Fax: (801)531-1798
Loretto Dennis Szucs, Author
Sandra Hargreaves Luebking, Author

Covers: American Expeditionary Forces; World War I; U.S. Attorneys and Marshals; Bureau of Census; Continental and Confederation Congresses and the Constitutional Convention; U.S. Courts of Appeals; Farmers Home Administration; Federal Housing Administration; Foreign Service Posts of the Department of State; U.S. Housing Corporation; Immigration and Naturalization Service; Bureau of Indian Affairs; Office of the Judge Advocate General; Naturalization Records; Bureau of Refugees, Freedmen, and Abandoned Lands; Selective Service System; Office of the Surgeon General; War Department Collection of Revolutionary War Records; and Work Projects Administration. **Publication includes:** Descriptions of the individual field branches, listings of microfilm copies held by all branches, printed descriptions and inventories, histories of the agencies and their records, cross-references to microfilm holdings, suggestions for research topics, etc. **Description:** Discusses the holdings of the National Archives. **Pages:** 340. **Publication date:** 1988. **Price:** $35.95; (Members $30.50). **ISBN:** 0-916489-23-X.

Campbell's Abstract of Creek Freedman Census Cards and Index

Phoenix Job Printing Co.
John Bert Campbell

Pages: 223. **Publication date:** 1915.

Catalog to Manuscripts at the National Anthropological Archives

Smithsonian Institution
470 L'Enfant Plaza, No. 1700
Washington, DC 20560
Phone: (202)287-3738
Toll-Free: 800-782-4612
Fax: (202)287-3184

Cherokee Blood

Shirley Hoskins
Chattanooga, TN
Shirley Hoskins, Author

Cherokee by Blood

Heritage Books
1540-E Pointer Ridge Pl.
Bowie, MD 20716
Phone: 800-398-7709
Toll-Free: 800-398-7153
Fax: (301)390-7153
Jerry Wright Jorden

Subtitled: Records of Eastern Cherokee Ancestry in the U.S. Court of Claims, 1906-1910. **Covers:** In 1904 the Eastern Cherokees won a million dollar judgment against the U.S. because of its violations of the treaties of 1835-36 and 1845. The payments were to go to all living persons who had been members of the Cherokee tribe at the time of the treaties, or to their descendants if they were deceased. Over 46,000 people filed claims. This series presents detailed abstracts of those applications. **Description:** Applications. Eight volumes. Vol. 1: 1-1550; Vol. 2: 1551-4200; Vol. 3: 4201-7250; Vol. 4: 7251-10170; Vol. 5: 10171-13260; Vol. 6: 13261-16745; Vol. 7: 16746-20100; Vol. 8: 20101-23800. **Type:** Book. **Indexes:** General. **Pages:** 482 (Vol. 1); 485 (2); 485 (3); 490 (4); 489 (5); 505 (6); 490 (7); 489 (8). **Publication date:** 1987 (Vol. 1); 1988 (2,3); 1989 (4); 1990 (5,6); 1991 (7); 1992 (8). **Price:** $25.00 each (paper).

Cherokee Emigration Rolls, 1817-1835

Baker Publishing Co.
1102 Marlboro Ln.
Oklahoma City, OK 73116
Phone: (405)840-1377
Jack D. Baker, Compiler

Publication includes: Notes from the Bureau of Indian Affairs in the National Archives. **Publication date:** 1977.

Cherokee Family Researcher

Legacy Plus
516 N 38th St.
Mesa, AZ 85205
Phone: (602)832-1467
Donna J. Williams, Editor

Description: Newsletter for Cherokee Family Ties. Offers assistance on general genealogy with a strong emphasis on Cherokee ancestry. **Type:** Newsletter. **Pages:** 25. **Frequency:** Biennial. **Circulation** 300. **Price:** Included in membership ($10.00, plus $2.50 P&H). **Remarks:** All back issues are available.

The Cherokee Freedmen: From Emancipation to American Citizenship

Greenwood Press
88 Post Rd. W
PO Box 5007
Westport, CT 06881
Phone: (203)226-3571
Fax: (203)226-1502
Daniel F. Littlefield Jr., Author

Publication date: 1978. **Also includes:** Bibliography, index.

Cherokee Nation Marriages, 1884-1901

Cooke and McDowell Publications
Owensboro, KY
Dixie Bogle, Author

Cherokee Old Timers

James Carselowey
Adair, OK
James Carselowey, Author

Cherokee Pioneers

James Carselowey
Adair, OK
James Carselowey, Author

Cherokee Reserves

Baker Publishing Co.
1102 Marlboro Ln.
Oklahoma City, OK 73116
Phone: (405)840-1377
David Keith Hampton, Author

Cherokee Roots

Heritage Books
1540-E Pointer Ridge Pl.
Bowie, MD 20716
Toll-Free: 800-398-7709
Fax: (301)390-7153
Bob Blankenship

Description: Volume I: *Eastern Cherokee Rolls* consists of eleven different rolls, 1817-1924, containing background material and rosters of tribal members with identifying file numbers. Volume II: *Western Cherokee Rolls* consists of four rolls, 1851-1914. **Type:** Book. **Pages:** 164, 306. **Publication date:** Second edition was published in 1992. **Price:** $10.00 (vol. I), $18.00 (vol. II), $25.00 (set). **ISBN:** 0-9633774-1-8 (vol. I), 0-9633774-2-6 (vol. II), 0-9633774-0-X (set). **Remarks:** Paper.

The Chickasaw Freedmen: A People Without a Country

Greenwood Press
88 Post Rd. W
PO Box 5007
Westport, CT 06881
Phone: (203)226-3571
Fax: (203)226-1502
Daniel F. Littlefield Jr., Author

Pages: 248. **Publication date:** 1980. **Also includes:** Bibliography, index, photographs.

Choctaw Claimants and Their Heirs

Oldbuck Press
PO Box 1623
Conway, AR 72032-1623
Phone: (501)336-8184
Joe R. Goss, Author

Pages: 193. **Publication date:** 1992. **Price:** $34.00 (hardcover); $26.00 (softcover). **ISBN:** 1-56869-00X-X.

Computer Genealogy: A Guide to Research through High Technology

Ancestry
PO Box 476
Salt Lake City, UT 84110
Phone: (801)531-1790
Toll-Free: 800-531-1790
Paul Andereck
Richard Pence

Description: Illustrated. **Pages:** 280. **Publication date:** 1991. **Price:** $12.95 (paper). **ISBN:** 0-916489-02-7.

Confederate Cherokees: John Drew's Regiment of Mounted Rifles

Louisiana State University Press
PO Box 25053
Baton Rouge, LA 70894-5053
Phone: (504)388-6666
Fax: (504)388-6461
W. Craig Gaines, Author

Pages: 200. **Price:** $19.95. **ISBN:** 0-8071-1488-X.

County Courthouse Book

Genealogical Publishing Co.
1001 N Calvert St.
Baltimore, MD 21202-3897
Phone: (410)837-8271
Toll-Free: 800-296-6687
Elizabeth Petty Bentley

Description: Furnishes the names, addresses, phone numbers, and dates of organization for over 3,300 U.S. county courthouses. Over fifty percent of the courthouses provide further information on record holdings, personnel, and services. **Type:** Book. **Arrangement:** Geographical. **Pages:** 386. **Publication date:** 1990. **Price:** $29.95 (paper).

Delaware and Shawnee Admitted to Cherokee Citizenship and the Related Wyandotte and Moravian Delaware

Heritage Books
1540-E Pointer Ridge Pl., Ste. 300
Bowie, MD 20716
Toll-Free: 800-398-7709
Fax: (301)390-7153
Toni Jollay Prevost, Author

Publication includes: Information on migration patterns of the Delaware, Shawnee and Wyandotte; names of ancestors who were listed in the treaty signed in Ohio in 1816; missionary school data; Indians in the 1860 and 1870 Wyandotte County, Kansas federal censuses; biographical material about the Indians who migrated to Kansas and those who served in the Civil War from Wyandotte Co.; register of names of Delaware Indians who were admitted to Cherokee citizenship; data from the census of 1900; and information about the Moravian Delaware of Middlesex and Kent Counties, Ontario, Canada. **Description:** Collection of records for the Delaware, Shawnee, and Wyandotte Indians. **Type:** Book. **Pages:** 129. **Publication date:** 1992. **Price:** $21.50.

Directory of Family Associations

Genealogical Publishing Co., Inc.
1001 N. Calvert St.
Baltimore, MD 21202
Phone: (410)837-8271
Toll-Free: 800-296-6687
Fax: (410)752-8492

Covers: Over 4,000 organizations, each devoted to the study of a family name. **Type:** Directory. **Entries include:** Family name, related family names, organization name, address, phone, contact name, publications. **Arrangement:** Alphabetical. **Pages:** 318. **Frequency:** Biennial, odd years. **Publication date:** 1993. **Price:** $29.95 (paper). **ISBN:** 0-8063-1319-6.

Eastern Band of Cherokees, 1819-1900

University of Tennessee Press
293 Communications Bldg.
Knoxville, TN 37996-0325
Phone: (615)974-3321
Toll-Free: 800-621-2736
Fax: (615)974-3724
John R. Finger

Pages: 268. **ISBN:** 0-87049-409-0 (cloth); 0-87049-410-4 (paper).

Eastern Cherokees

Polyanthos
New Orleans, LA
David W. Siler, Compiler
Fred B. Kniffen, Editor

Subtitled: A Census of Cherokee Nation in North Carolina, Tennessee, Alabama, and Georgia in 1851. **Pages:** 38. **Publication date:** 1972.

Ethnic Periodicals in Contemporary America

Greenwood Press
88 Post Road West
PO Box 5007
Westport, CT 06881-5007
Phone: (203)226-3571
Fax: (203)222-1502
Sandra Jones Ireland, Compiler

Subtitled: An annotated guide. **Publication includes:** Comprehensive listing of ethnic periodicals in the United States. **Description:** Provides information targeting ethnic-interest periodicals and groups. **Type:** Guide. **Pages:** 256. **Publication date:** 1990. **Price:** $49.95. **ISBN:** 0-313-26817-7.

Everton's Genealogical Helper

The Everton Publishers, Inc.
PO Box 368
Logan, UT 84323-0368
Phone: (801)752-6022
Fax: (801)752-0425
George B. Everton Jr., Publisher

Description: Genealogy magazine. **First published:** 1947. **Frequency:** 6 times/year. **Circulation** 48,000. **Subscription:** $21.00/year. **Former titles:** The Genealogical Helper (1992).

Everton's Genealogical Helper—Genealogy & the Public Library Issue

Everton Publishers, Inc.
3223 S. Main St.
Logan, UT 84321
Phone: (801)752-6022
Toll-Free: 800-443-6325
Fax: (801)752-0425

Covers: More than 200 public libraries nationwide which have separate genealogical collections or a special interest in such materials. **Entries include:** Library name, address. **Arrangement:** Geographical. **Frequency:** Annual. **Price:** $4.50, postpaid, payment with order.

Exploring Your Cherokee Ancestry

Cherokee National Historical Society
PO Box 515
Tahlequah, OK 74465
Thomas G. Mooney, Author

Publication date: 1987; reprinted 1988. **Price:** $12.00

Family Associations, Societies and Reunions

Ye Olde Genealogie Shoppe
PO Box 39128
Indianapolis, IN 46239-0128
Phone: (317)862-3330
Toll-Free: 800-419-0200
J. Konrad, Editor

Covers: About 2,000 family associations, societies, and regularly scheduled reunions; includes Scottish clan associations; coverage includes Canada. **Entries include:** Group name, address of contact, variant names. **Arrangement:** Alphabetical by surname. **Pages:** 100. **Frequency:** Annual. **Price:** $8.00, plus $3.00 shipping. **Remarks:** Formerly published by Summit Publications.

Family Tree Digest

Family Tree Genealogical Society
450 Potter St.
Wauseon, OH 43567
Phone: (419)335-6485
Howard V. Fausey, Editor

Description: Features genealogical information and responses to queries on a national basis. **First published:** 1978. **Audience:** Genealogical societies in approximately 40 states. **Frequency:** Monthly. **Price:** $7.50/year for individuals; free for institutions. **ISSN:** 0742-9045.

First Families of the Southwest

Fred Harvey
Kansas City, MO
Fred Harvey, Author

Genealogical & Biographical Research

National Archives Trust Fund
NEDC Dept. 735
PO Box 100793
Atlanta, GA
Toll-Free: 800-788-6282
Fax: (301)763-6025

Subtitled: A select catalog of National Archives microfilm publications. **Publication includes:** Detailed descriptions of the records and roll-by-roll content listings for each publication. **Type:** Catalog. **Pages:** 77. **Publication date:** 1983. **Price:** $2.00 (paper). **ISBN:** 0-911333-06-1.

Genealogical and Local History Books in Print

Genealogical Books in Print
PO Box 394
Maine, NY 13802-0394
Phone: (607)786-0769

Publication includes: List of over 3,600 suppliers of genealogical books, microform, and computer software. **Entries include:** Organization or personal name, address, name and title of contact, product. **Arrangement:** Alphabetical, by publisher name. **Pages:** 1,700. **Frequency:** Every 10 years, with two interedition supplements; latest base edition 1985; first supplement February 1990; second supplement January 1993; new edition expected 1995. **Price:** $37.50, for base edition; $21.95, first supplement; $21.60, second supplement; $75.00, set. **Remarks:** Principal content is a description of genealogical and local history books, reprints, microform collections, and specific surname publications.

Genealogical Periodical Annual Index

Heritage Books, Inc.
1540 E. Pointer Ridge Pl.
Bowie, MD 20716
Phone: (301)390-7708
Toll-Free: 800-398-7709
Fax: (301)390-7153

Publication includes: List of about 260 periodicals published by genealogical societies and genealogists and used in indexing surnames, place names, and related topics for this book. **Entries include:** Name of publication, name of publisher, address, issues indexed, title abbreviation used in book. **Arrangement:** Alphabetical by title abbreviation. **Frequency:** Annual, August. **Price:** $22.50. **Remarks:** Publication mainly consists of a list of 14,000 genealogical citations (surnames, place names, etc.).

Genealogical Research and Resources: A Guide for Library Use

American Library Association (ALA)
50 E. Huron St.
Chicago, IL 60611
Phone: (312)944-6780
Toll-Free: 800-545-2433
Fax: (312)440-9374

Publication includes: List of genealogical organizations and societies. **Arrangement:** Alphabetical. **Frequency:** Latest edition 1988. **Price:** $15.00. **Remarks:** Principal content of publication is information on genealogical research publications.

Genealogical Research in the National Archives

Ancestry
PO Box 476
Salt Lake City, UT 84110-0476
Toll-Free: 800-531-1790
Fax: (801)531-1798

Covers: Principal genealogical record groups within the National Archives including population, military, ethnic, land, court, and civilian records. **Description:** A resource that explains the research potential of genealogical materials in the National Archives of the United States. **Type:** Book. **Pages:** 299. **Price:** $35.00; (Members, $29.95). **ISBN:** 0-911333-00-2.

Genealogical Societies and Historical Societies in the United States

Ye Olde Genealogie Shoppe
PO Box 39128
Indianapolis, IN 46239
Phone: (317)862-3330
Toll-Free: 800-419-0200

Covers: About 3,000 groups in the United States. **Entries include:** Society name, address. **Arrangement:** Geographical. **Pages:** 80. **Frequency:** Annual. **Price:** $8.00, plus $3.00 shipping. **Remarks:** Formerly published by Summit Publications.

Genealogist's Handbook for New England Research

NEHGS Sales Dept.
101 Newbury St.
Boston, MA 02116
Marcie Wiswall Lindberg, Compiler

Description: For each of the six New England states, lists towns, sections on vital, census, probate, land, church, military, and immigration records, plus libraries with significant or unique genealogical holdings; genealogical societies; journals; and a bibliography of how-to guides and surveys of state-wide records. Covers over 90% of the genealogical repositories and sources in New England, with many revisions and more coverage of ethnic genealogical societies. Also lists all Mormon New England libraries with Family Search on CD-ROM. **Pages:** 178. **Publication date:** 1993. **Price:** Soft: $15.00, plus $2.50 P&H; Hard: $20.00, plus $3.50 P&H. **Send orders to:** Publisher. **Remarks:** Third edition.

Genealogy & Computers for the Complete Beginner

Clearfield Company
200 E Eager St.
Baltimore, MD 21202
Phone: (410)625-9004
Karen Clifford

Subtitled: A Step-by-step Guide to the PAF Computer Program, Automated Databases, Family History Centers & Local Sources. **Pages:** 269. **Publication date:** 1992. **Price:** $29.95 (paper). **ISBN:** 0-685-60307-5.

Genealogy of Old and New Cherokee Indian Families

George Bell
Bartlesville, OK
George Bell, Author

Going to Salt Lake City to Do Family History Research

Marietta Publishing Co.
2115 N Denair Ave.
Turlock, CA 95380
J. Carlyle Parker, Author

Description: Designed to prepare researchers for a visit to the world's largest genealogical library, the Family History Library at Salt Lake City. The three parts of the book address preparation for the trip, making the most of your time while you are there, and reviewing your research once you return home. **Indexes:** Subject. **Pages:** Over 200. **Frequency:** First ed., 1989; latest ed., 1993. **Price:** $12.95 (paper), plus $1.50 P&H. **Send orders to:** Publisher. **Also includes:** Maps, information on transportation and lodging, floor plans, a discussion of finding aids, and an appendix which lists Family History Centers. **Remarks:** Second edition.

Guide to American Indian Documents in the Congressional Serial Set, 1817-1899

University Publications of America
4520 East-West Hwy.
Bethesda, MD 20814
Toll-Free: 800-692-6300
Steven Johnson, Author

Guide to Catholic Indian Mission and School Records in Midwest Repositories

Marquette University Libraries
Department of Special Collections and University Archives
Milwaukee, WI 53233
Phone: (414)288-7256
Mark G. Thiel, Assistant Archivist
Philip C. Bantin, Editor

Description: Identifies 277 collection of unpublished sources pertaining to the history of Catholic Indian missions and schools in the United States. **Type:** Directory. **Entries include:** Institution name, address, phone, hours, access information, copying facilities, history of institution, description of holdings. **Arrangement:** Geographical, then alphabetical. **Indexes:** Institution name, Indian Nations, individual name, organizations, archival repositories, periodicals and newspapers. **Pages:** 446. **Publication date:** 1984. **Price:** $15.00, postpaid.

Guide to Cherokee Documents in the Northwestern United States

Scarecrow Press
52 Liberty St.
Metuchen, NJ 08840
Phone: (908)548-8600
Toll-Free: 800-537-7107
Fax: (908)548-5767
Paul Kutsche, Author

Description: Seventh volume of Native American bibliography series. **Pages:** 531. **Publication date:** 1986.

Guide to Genealogical Research in the National Archives

National Archives Trust Fund
NEPS Dept. 630
PO Box 100793
Atlanta, GA 30384
Toll-Free: 800-788-6282
Fax: (404)501-5239

Publication includes: Information about individuals whose names appear in census records, military service and pension files, ship passenger arrival lists, land records, and many other types of documents. **Description:** Revised. Explains what types of records are preserved in the National Archives and what specific information about individuals is included in each type of record. **Type:** Guide. **First published:** 1982. **Pages:** 304. **Publication date:** 1985. **Price:** $35.00; $25.00 (paper). **ISBN:** 0-911333-00-2, 0-911333-01-0 (paper).

Guide to Multicultural Resources

Praxis Publications, Inc.
2215 Atwood Ave.
PO Box 9869
Madison, WI 53715
Phone: (608)244-5633
Toll-Free: 800-558-2110
Fax: (414)563-7395
Charles Taylor, Editor

Description: Over 4,000 minority and multicultural organizations, including libraries, media, fraternities and sororities, historical societies, and religious and women's organizations, all involved with the Asian, Hispanic, African, and Native American communities. **Type:** Directory. **Entries include:** Organization name, address, phone, fax, year founded, purpose, services and service area, funding, budget, staff, and publications. **Arrangement:** Classified by racial/minority group. **Indexes:** Subject, geographical. **Pages:** 500. **Frequency:** Biennial, January of odd years. **Price:** $49.00. **Remarks:** Published jointly with Highsmith Press.

Guide to Records in the National Archives Relating to American Indians

National Archives Trust Fund
NEPS Dept. 630
PO Box 100793
Atlanta, GA 30384
Toll-Free: 800-788-6282
Fax: (404)501-6025
Edward E. Hill, Compiler

Publication includes: Concise information about records that trace the evolution of federal Indian policy, the effects of national policies on traditional Indian culture, Indian wars and their results, and the role of Native Americans in the development of U.S. society. **Description:** Enables the researcher to review descriptions of records that are available in the National Archives and in its regional archives. **Type:** Guide. **First published:** 1981. **Pages:** 467. **Publication date:** 1984. **Price:** $25.00. **ISBN:** 0-911333-13-4.

Guide to the National Archives of the United States

National Archives Trust Fund
NEPS Dept. 630
PO Box 100793
Atlanta, GA 30384
Toll-Free: 800-788-6282
Fax: (404)501-5239

Description: Provides a general description of the basic records of the three branches of the federal government of the U.S. from the first Continental Congress within the context of the government agencies that created them or received them in the course of official business. **Type:** Guide. **First published:** 1974. **Pages:** 928. **Publication date:** 1987. **Price:** $25.00. **ISBN:** 0-911333-23-1. **Also includes:** Appendix containing additional record group descriptions.

Handbook for Genealogical Correspondence

The Everton Publishers, Inc.
PO Box 368
Logan, UT 84323-0368
Toll-Free: 800-443-6325
Fax: (801)752-0425

Covers: The problems and procedures involved in genealogical correspondence including essentials of letters, postmaster and mails, geography, relatives, libraries, church record keepers, public officials, advertising, filing, opportunities. **Pages:** 274. **Price:** $20.00. **Remarks:** Prepared by Cache Genealogical Library. Reprint.

Handy Book for Genealogists

Everton Publishers
PO Box 368
Logan, UT 84323-0368
Toll-Free: 800-443-6325
Fax: (801)752-0425

Publication includes: A chapter on each of the fifty states in the U.S. In each chapter is an alphabetically arranged table of counties which is keyed to a corresponding state map found at the back of the volume. **Description:** New Eighth Edition. Provides researcher with at-a-glance genealogical guidance for every county in the U.S. **Type:** Book. **Entries include:** For each county, a table furnishes a map index number, the date of the county's creation, the parent county (counties) or territory (territories) from which it was created, and the address and phone number for the appropriate county court. **Arrangement:** Arranged alphabetically by state. **Pages:** 382. **Publication date:** 1991. **Price:** $31.95. **Also includes:** Special section, with maps, pertaining to migration routes throughout the eastern half of the U.S. Fold-out map of the U.S.

Heritage Quest

Heritage Quest
PO Box 392
Bountiful, UT 84011-0329
Phone: (801)298-5446
Fax: (801)298-5468
Bradley W. Steuart, Publisher

Description: Contains how-to articles on locating genealogical information. **First published:** 1985. **Frequency:** 6 times/year. **Circulation** 10,000. **Subscription:** $28.00, U.S.; $40.00, other countries. **ISSN:** 0886-0262.

How to Locate Anyone Who Is or Has Been in the Military

Military Information Enterprises
PO Box 340081
Fort Sam Houston, TX 78234
Phone: (512)828-4054
Richard S. Johnson

Subtitled: Armed Forces Locater Directory. **Description:** 4th, rev. ed.; illustrated. **Pages:** 176. **Publication date:** 1991. **Price:** $12.95 (paper). **ISBN:** 1-877639-07-9.

Immigration History Newsletter

Immigration History Society
c/o Balch Institute
18 S 7th St.
Philadelphia, PA 19106
Phone: (215)853-1363
M. Mark Stolarik, Editor

Description: Concerned with the field of immigration-ethnic history. Promotes study concerning the U.S. and Canada and the history of emigration from all parts of the world. Includes study of regional groups in the U.S., Native Americans, and forced immigrants. Aims to promote understanding of the processes of acculturation and of conflict. Recurring features include information on research, organizations, and publications in the field of immigration history. **First published:** 1968. **Pages:** 24. **Frequency:** Semiannually. **Circulation** 600. **Price:** Included in membership. **ISSN:** 0579-4374.

Indian Rights Association: Annual Reports, 1883-1929

Indian Rights Association
1801 Market St.
Philadelphia, PA 19103-1675
Phone: (215)665-4523

Journal of American Ethnic History

Transaction Periodicals Consortium
Rutgers—The State University of New Jersey
Dept. 3092
New Brunswick, NJ 08903
Phone: (908)932-2280
Fax: (908)932-3138
Ronald H. Baylor, Editor

Description: Journal addressing various aspects of American immigration and ethnic history including background of emigration, ethnic and racial groups, native Americans, and immigration policies. **First published:** 1981. **Frequency:** Quarterly. **Circulation** 1,200. **Subscription:** $30.00; $60.00 institutions; $100.00 other countries (airmail). **ISSN:** 0278-5927.

Journal of American Indian Family Research

Histree
23011 Multon Pkwy., No. C-8
Laguna Hills, CA 92653
Phone: (714)859-1659

First published: 1980. **Frequency:** Quarterly.

The Library: A Guide to the LDS Family History Library

Genealogy Unlimited, Inc.
PO Box 537
Orem, UT 84059-0537
Phone: (801)226-8971
Toll-Free: 800-666-4363
Johni Cerny, Editor
Wendy Elliott, Editor

Covers: Holdings of the Family History Library, the time periods they cover, and how they can be accessed. **Description:** The largest single collection of genealogical information and sources in the world is described. **Pages:** 746. **Price:** $40.00.

Library of Congress: A Guide to Genealogical & Historical Research

Ancestry
PO Box 476
Salt Lake City, UT 84110-0476
Toll-Free: 800-531-1790
Fax: (801)531-1798
James C. Neagles, Author

Pages: 382. **Publication date:** 1990. **Price:** $35.95. **ISBN:** 0-916489-48-5.

List of 96 Ethnic and Religious Genealogical and Historical Societies and Archives

Summit Publications
Box 222
Munroe Falls, OH 44262

Frequency: Irregular; latest edition March 1989. **Price:** $4.00, postpaid.

List of Publications of the Bureau of American Ethnology with Index to Authors and Titles

Government Public Office
N Capitol and H St. NW
Washington, DC 20401

Publication date: 1962.

Managing a Genealogical Project

Genealogical Publishing Co., Inc.
1001 N. Calvert St.
Baltimore, MD 21202-3897
Phone: (410)837-8271
Toll-Free: 800-296-6687
William Dollarhide

Publication includes: Set of master forms: relationship chart, reference family data sheet, compiled family data sheet, master data sheet, research log, ancestor table, pedigree ancestor index, research journal, and correspondence log. **Description:** Focuses on a particular method of organizing research materials, starting with the preliminary note-gathering stage and ending with the final presentation of all research in the form of a book or report. **First published:** 1988. **Pages:** 96. **Publication date:** 1991, includes a revised and expanded chapter on genealogical software. **Price:** $14.95 (paper). **ISBN:** 0-8063-1222-X.

Midwest Research

Carlberg Press
1782 Beacon Ave.
Anaheim, CA 92804
Phone: (714)772-2849
Nancy E. Carlberg

Description: Illustrated. **Pages:** 110. **Publication date:** 1991. **Price:** $10.00 (paper). **ISBN:** 0-944878-11-3.

Minority Organizations: A National Directory

Garrett Park Press
PO Box 190B
Garrett Park, MD 20896
Phone: (301)946-2553
Robert Calvert Jr., Editor

Description: Over 9,700 groups composed of or intending to serve members of minority groups, including Asian, Hispanic, African, and Native Americans; coverage includes cultural & historical museums, professional associations, minority newspapers and periodicals, professional associations, religious organizations, etc. **Type:** Directory. **Entries include:** Organization name, address, description of activities, purpose, publications, etc. **Arrangement:** Alphabetical. **Indexes:** Organizational name, geographical, program, defunct organizations. **Pages:** 514. **Frequency:** Irregular: Previous edition 1987; latest edition 1992. **Price:** $50.00. **ISBN:** 0-912048-30-1.

National Archives and Records Administration Staff Guide to Genealogical Research in the National Archives

National Archives and Records Administration
Publications Division
NECR Room G9
7th St. & Pennsylvania Ave. NW
Washington, DC 20408
Phone: (202)501-5235
Toll-Free: 800-788-6282

Description: Illustrated. **Pages:** 304. **Publication date:** 1985. **Price:** $35.00 (casebound); $25.00 (paper). **ISBN:** 0-911333-00-2 (casebound); 0-911333-01-0 (paper).

National Archives Microfilm Resources for Research

National Archives Trust Fund
NEDC Dept. 735
PO Box 100793
Atlanta, GA 30384
Toll-Free: 800-788-6282
Fax: (301)763-6025

Subtitled: A comprehensive catalog. **Covers:** Over 2,000 series of federal records which have been microfilmed. **Type:** Catalog. **First published:** 1986. **Arrangement:** By record group. **Pages:** 126. **Publication date:** 1990, revised. **Price:** $5.00 (paper). **ISBN:** 0-911333-34-7.

National Genealogical Society Newsletter

National Genealogical Society (NGS)
4527 17th St. N
Arlington, VA 22207-2399
Phone: (703)525-0050
Ann Crowley, Editor

Description: Features news of the Society and the genealogical community, articles on genealogical methods, sources, repositories, and NGS's library acquisitions; and members' queries. Recurring features include a calendar of events. **First published:** 1975. **Frequency:** Bimonthly. **Indexed:** Annually. **Circulation** 11,000. **Price:** Included in membership. **ISSN:** 0887-1353. **Former titles:** National Genealogical Society Newsletter.

National Genealogical Society Quarterly (NGSQ)

National Genealogical Society
4527 17th Street N
Arlington, VA 22207-2399
Phone: (703)525-0050
Fax: (703)525-0052
Elizabeth S. Mills, Editor

Description: Genealogy journal. **First published:** 1912. **Frequency:** Quarterly. **Circulation** 13,000. **Subscription:** $25.00/year. **ISSN:** 0027-934X.

Native American Archives: An Introduction

Society for American Archivists
600 S. Federal, Ste. 504
Chicago, IL 60605
Phone: (312)922-0140
John A. Fleckner, Author

Pages: 72. **Publication date:** 1985. **Price:** $7.00. **ISBN:** 0-931828-66-X.

Native American Periodicals and Newspapers, 1828-1982

Greenwood Press
88 Post Rd. W
PO Box 5007
Westport, CT 06881
Phone: (203)226-3571
Fax: (203)222-1502
James Phillip Danky, Author

Pages: 532. **Price:** $75.00. **ISBN:** 0-313-23773-5.

New England Historical and Genealogical Register

New England Historic Genealogical Society
101 Newbury St.
Boston, MA 02116
Phone: (617)536-5740
Fax: (617)536-7307
Jane F. Fiske, Editor

Description: Focuses on history and genealogy. **First published:** 1847. **Frequency:** Quarterly. **Circulation** 14,000. **Subscription:** Free to qualified subscribers; $45.00. **ISSN:** 0028-4785. **Remarks:** Subscription rate includes NEXUS newsletter.

Newspaper Genealogical Column Directory

Heritage Books, Inc.
1540 E. Pointer Ridge Pl.
Bowie, MD 20716
Phone: (301)390-7709
Toll-Free: 800-398-7709
Anita Cheek Milner, Editor

Covers: About 150 columnists appearing in over 250 newspapers and periodicals, offering help to researchers in nearly 250 counties and 30 states. **Entries include:** Columnist name, publications carrying column, mailing address, counties covered, frequency, fees, whether columns are compiled or indexed. **Arrangement:** Geographical. **Pages:** 112. **Frequency:** Irregular; previous edition June 1989; latest edition November 1992. **Price:** $14.00. **Also includes:** Notes on discontinued columns. **Former titles:** Newspaper Genealogy Columns: A Preliminary Checklist (1979).

Newspapers in Microform, United States, 1948-1983

Library of Congress
101 Independence Avenue SE
Washington, DC 20540
Phone: (202)707-5000

Description: Two volumes. **Publication date:** 1983.

Only the Names Remain: Flint District

Cherokee Woman Publishing
PO Box 48
Spavinaw, OK 74366
Phone: (918)589-2236
Sandi Garrett, Author

Publication includes: The Drennen Roll of 1851, and the Guion Miller Application Roll of 1910. **Description:** Identifies Cherokee emigrants who were forced to move from the Old Flint District of the Cherokee Nation. Cross-referenced by both English and Indian names. **Type:** Book. **Pages:** 116. **Price:** $15.00.

Our Native Americans: Their Records of Genealogical Value

Everton Publishers
PO Box 368
Logan, UT 84323-0368
Toll-Free: 800-443-6325
Fax: (801)752-0425
E. Kay Kirkham, Author

Publication includes: Vol. 1 includes records from the federal government, Oklahoma Society records, and the Genealogical Society of Utah listings. Vol. 2 includes records from the same three organizations along with the 1900 Federal Census of Native Americans on Indian reservations, religious denominations, and Canadian bands. **Pages:** 235 (Vol. 1), 262 (Vol. 2). **Price:** $17.75 (Vol. 1), $19.95 (Vol.2). **Also includes:** Examples of the various records have also been included.

Pan-American Indian Association News

Pan-American Indian
Association and Adopted
Tribal Peoples
c/o Chief Piercing Eyes
Box 244
Nocatee, FL 33864-0244
Phone: (813)494-6930

Description: Provides genealogy aid for people with Native American heritage. **First published:** 1984. **Frequency:** Irregular. **Former titles:** *Tribal Advisor.*

Passports of Southeastern Pioneers, 1770-1823

Genealogical Publishing Co.
1001 N. Calvert St.
Baltimore, MD 21202-3897
Phone: (410)837-8271
Toll-Free: 800-296-6687
Dorothy Williams Potter, Author

Subtitled: Indian, Spanish and Other Land Passports for Tennessee, Kentucky, Georgia, Mississippi, Virginia, North and South Carolina. **Publication includes:** Names of over 5,000 people who either traveled through or settled in the Spanish and Indian lands. **Description:** Collection of the passports and travel documents which were issued to individuals and families traveling or migrating into the Mississippi Valley area from Tennessee, Kentucky, Georgia, Mississippi, Virginia, North Carolina, and South Carolina. **Pages:** 461. **Publication date:** 1982; reprinted 1994. **Price:** $32.50. **ISBN:** 0-8063-1272-6.

Pocahontas Trails Quarterly

Pocahontas Trails
Genealogical Society
6015 Robin Hill Dr.
Lakeport, CA 95453

Description: Focuses on the pursuit and study of the genealogy of Pocahontas and Powhatan. **First published:** October 1983. **Frequency:** Quarterly. **Price:** Included in membership.

Prologue: Quarterly of the National Archives

National Archives and
Records Administration
7th St. and Pennsylvania Ave.
NW
Washington, DC 20408
Phone: (202)501-5235

Description: Includes information about the National Archives, its holdings, using its resources and copies of documents relating to American Indians. **Price:** $12.00/year.

Records of Genealogical Value for [Country]

Family History Library of The
Church of Jesus Christ of
Latter-Day Saints
35 NW Temple
Salt Lake City, UT 84150
Phone: (801)240-2331

Description: The Family History Library (formerly known as "The Genealogical Library" and "The Genealogical Society") is perhaps the world's leading genealogical research library, with over 240,000 volumes, 1,800,000 rolls of microfilm, and 300,000 microfiche that can be loaned to over 1,800 Family History Centers. The library publishes a series of research outlines for numerous countries, provinces, and states. Each research outline describes the types of records available, time period these records cover, contents of the records, and how to obtain them. Outlines emphasize records available at the Family History Library, and include addresses and descriptions of records at other archives and repositories. The outlines are available from the library and at the family history centers. **Pages:** 8-50. **Frequency:** Irregular. **Price:** $.25 to $3.50.

Searching on Location: Planning a Research Trip

Ancestry
PO Box 476
Salt Lake City, UT 84110
Anne Ross Balhuizen, Author

Description: Offers tips and advice designed to maximize the efforts of a research trip. **Indexes:** General. **Pages:** 102. **Publication date:** 1992.

Soundex Reference Guide

Precision Indexing
PO Box 303
Bountiful, UT 84011
Phone: (801)298-5468
Bradley W. Steuart, Editor

Pages: 253. **Publication date:** 1990. **Price:** $29.95 (lib. bdg.); $19.96 (paper). **ISBN:** 1-877677-12-4 (lib. bdg.); 1-877677-09-4 (paper).

The Source: A Guidebook of American Genealogy

Ancestry Publishing
440 S. 400 W., Bldg. D
PO Box 476
Salt Lake City, UT 84101
Phone: (801)531-1790
Arlene Eakle, Co-Editor
Johni Cerny, Co-Editor

Description: Comprehensive guide to U.S. genealogical records. Part one covers cemetery, church, census, and legal records. Part two identifies published sources with indexes, newspapers, and biographies. Part three focuses on ethnic resources and includes a chapter on computer databases. Sample records are included throughout. **Pages:** 786. **Publication date:** 1984. **Price:** $39.95. **ISBN:** 0-916489-00-0. **Also includes:** Glossary of genealogy terms, bibliographical index, subject index.

State Census Records

Genealogical Publishing Co.
1001 N. Calvert St.
Baltimore, MD 21202-3897
Phone: (410)837-8271
Toll-Free: 800-296-6687
Ann S. Lainhart, Author

Publication includes: List of what is available in state census records, where the records can be found, and what data is enumerated. **Description:** Comprehensive list of state census records. **First published:** 1992. **Arrangement:** State by state, year by year, and, often, county by county or district by district. **Pages:** 116. **Publication date:** 1993, reprint. **Price:** $17.95.

Survey of American Church Records: Major Denominations before 1860

The Everton Publishers
PO Box 368
Logan, UT 84323-0368
Phone: (801)752-6022
E. Kay Kirkham

Description: Fourth edition. **Publication date:** 1978.

United States Census Compendium

The Everton Publishers, Inc.
PO Box 368
Logan, UT 84323-0368
Toll-Free: 800-443-6325
Fax: (801)752-0425
Jack Stemmons, Author

Covers: Published census records in addition to any type of document that can be used as a census such as tax lists, petitions, oaths of allegiance, directories, poll lists. **Publication includes:** An abbreviated reference to the publisher or compiler of each record within each entry as well as a complete listing of these references. **Arrangement:** Geographic, by state. **Pages:** 143. **Price:** $12.50.

Using the Family History Library Computer System: Including the Library Catalog, Ancestral File, International Genealogical Index.

Carlberg Press
1782 Beacon Ave.
Anaheim, CA 92804
Phone: (714)772-2849
Nancy E. Carlberg

Pages: 120. **Publication date:** 1994. **Price:** $15.00 (paper). **ISBN:** 0-944878-08-3.

Where to Write for Vital Records: Births, Deaths, Marriages and Divorces

National Center for Health Statistics
6525 Belcrest Rd., Rm. 1064
Hyattsville, MD 20782
Phone: (301)436-8500

Covers: Vital statistics offices in each state. **Entries include:** Name and address of office, cost of full copy, cost of short form, any special requirements, dates of records held. **Arrangement:** Geographical. **Pages:** 20. **Frequency:** Irregular; previous edition April 1991; latest edition 1993. **Price:** $2.25 (S/N 017-022-01109-3). **Send orders to:** Superintendent of Documents, U.S. Government Printing Office, Washington, DC 20402-9371 (202-783-3238). **Former titles:** Where to Write for Vital Statistics.

WyMonDak Messenger

Tri-State Genealogical Society
c/o Public Library
905 5th Ave.
Belle Fourche, SD 57717
Phone: (605)892-4019
Pat Engebretson, Editor

Description: Contains genealogical material of interest to those searching for ancestors from Crook County, Wyoming; Carter County, Montana; Butte and Harding Counties in South Dakota, and parts of Perkins, Meade, and Lawrence Counties. **Audience:** Genealogical researchers. **Price:** $3.00/year. **Remarks:** Accepts articles of significance for the tri-state area for publication.

Alabama

Indian Place Names in Alabama

University of Alabama Press
Box 870380
Tuscaloosa, AL 35487-0380
Phone: (205)348-9534
William A. Read

Publication date: 1984. **Price:** $9.95 (paper). **ISBN:** 0-8173-0231-X. **Remarks:** Part of the Library of Alabama Classics Series.

Alaska

Documenting Alaskan History: Guide to Federal Archives Relating to Alaska

National Archives Trust Fund
NEPS Dept. 630
PO Box 100793
Atlanta, GA 30384
Toll-Free: 800-788-6282
Fax: (404)501-5239
George S. Ulibarri, Editor

Publication includes: Documents, maps, photographs, motion picture film, and sound recordings since 1867. **Description:** Guide is an aid to locating the more then 1 million cubic feet of records relating to Alaskan history in the National Archives. **Type:** Guide. **Pages:** 296. **Publication date:** 1982. **Price:** $10.00. **ISBN:** 0-912006-06-04. **Remarks:** Distributed for University of Alaska Press.

Arkansas

Arkansas Family Historians

Arkansas Genealogical Society, Inc.
PO Box 908
Hot Springs, AR 71902-0908
Phone: (501)262-4513
Margaret Harrison Hubbard, Editor

Description: Offers genealogical information on citizens of Arkansas. Contains primary and secondary source materials and family data. Recurring features include news of research. **Frequency:** Quarterly. **Price:** Included in membership.

Historical and Genealogical Source Materials

Arkansas History Commission
One Capitol Mall
Little Rock, AR 72201

Remarks: Write to the Arkansas History Commission for this brochure.

Researching Arkansas History

Rose Publishing Co.
2723 Foxcroft Rd., Ste. 208
Little Rock, AR 72207
Phone: (501)227-8104
Tom W. Dillard, Editor
Valeria Thwing, Editor

Publication includes: List of archives, libraries, government offices, and other repositories which hold materials significant in the study of Arkansas history and genealogy; includes sources for Black history and genealogy. **Entries include:** Institution or department name, address. **Arrangement:** Classified by type of source. **Frequency:** Published 1979. **Price:** $5.00, postpaid.

California

Guide to American Historical Manuscripts in the Huntington Library

Huntington Library
1151 Oxford Road
San Marino, CA 91108
Phone: (818)405-2172
Fax: (818)405-0225
Mary Robertson, Author
Jean F. Preston, Author

Publication date: 1979.

Connecticut

Connecticut Sources for Family Historians and Genealogists

Everton Publishers, Inc.
PO Box 368
Logan, UT 84321
Phone: (801)752-6022
Toll-Free: 800-443-6325
Fax: (801)752-0425
Kip Sperry, Author

Publication includes: Lists of manuscript collections, genealogical and historical libraries and societies, public libraries, and other sources. **Entries include:** Library or collection name, address, holdings. **Arrangement:** Geographical. **Pages:** 112. **Frequency:** Irregular; latest edition 1980. **Price:** $9.95, plus $1.50 shipping, payment with order. **Also includes:** Bibliographies, indexes, finding aids, etc., concerned with Connecticut history and genealogy.

District of Columbia

Lest We Forget: A Guide to Genealogical Research in the Nation's Capital District of Columbia

Annandale Stake
Church of Jesus Christ of Latter-day Saints
Box 89
Annandale, VA 22003
Phone: (703)780-1290
H. Byron Hall, Editor

Covers: Facilities available for genealogical research in Washington, D.C., primarily at various units of the National Archives (including information on regional archive offices) and the Library of Congress, and the libraries of the Daughters of the American Revolution and the National Genealogical Society. **Type:** Directory. **Entries include:** Facility or unit name, address, phone, hours, types of material available, and, in separate sections, detailed information on what materials are available, where and how to secure access, and notes on scope, content, limitations of the materials. **Indexes:** General subject-collection name-locality index. **Pages:** 154. **Frequency:** Irregular; previous edition December 1986; latest edition (eighth) 1992. **Price:** $12.60 National Genealogical Society members, $14.00 nonmembers, plus $3.00 shipping. **Send orders to:** NGS Special Publications, 4527 17th Street North, Arlington, VA 22207-2399.

Florida

Searching in Florida

ISC Publications
Independent Search Consultants, Inc.
PO Box 10857
Costa Mesa, CA 92627
Diane C. Robie, Author

Subtitled: A reference guide to public & private records. **Publication date:** 1982. **Price:** $10.95. **ISBN:** 0-942916-01-8.

Georgia

Georgia Genealogical Research

Ancestry
PO Box 476
Salt Lake City, UT 84110-0476
Toll-Free: 800-531-1790
Fax: (801)531-1798
George K. Schweitzer, Author

Description: Presents information about most of the principal sources used by anyone begining to search for an ancestor who lived in Georgia. **Type:** Book. **Pages:** 238. **Price:** $12.00; (Members, $10.50). **ISBN:** 0-913857-10-6.

Research in Georgia

Reprint Company Publishers
601 Hillcrest Offices
PO Box 5401
Spartanburg, SC 29304
Phone: (803)582-0732
Robert Scott Davis Jr., Author

Subtitled: With special emphasis on the Georgia Department of Archives and History. **Covers:** Sources in Georgia, especially the Georgia Department of Archives and History. **Publication includes:** Chapters dealing with: preparing for research, central research library, microfilm library, other sources, publishers and periodicals, reference maps of Georgia, basic data on Georgia counties and county records on microfilm, census records, colonial books of record and state tax digests on microfilm, land lottery records, county histories, etc. **First published:** 1981. **Pages:** 269. **Publication date:** 1991 (reprint). **Price:** $30.00 plus $3.00 P&H (paper).

Illinois

Genealogical Index of the Newberry Library (Chicago)

GK Hall & Co.
70 Lincoln St.
Boston, MA 02111
Phone: (617)423-3990
Toll-Free: 800-343-2806

Description: 4 vols. **Publication date:** 1970. **Price:** $380.00 (Set, lib. bdg.). **ISBN:** 0-8161-0498-0.

Guide to Local and Family History at the Newberry Library

Ancestry
PO Box 476
Salt Lake City, UT 84110-0476
Toll-Free: 800-531-1790
Fax: (801)531-1798
Peggy Tuck Sinko, Author

Description: A user-oriented guide to the Newberry Library's books, maps, atlases, journals, orginal sources, finding aids, etc. **Type:** Book. **Pages:** 202. **Publication date:** 1987. **Price:** $16.95; (Members, $14.00). **ISBN:** 0-916489-24-8.

Searching in Illinois

ISC Publications
Independent Search Consultants, Inc.
PO Box 10857
Costa Mesa, CA 92627
Gayle Beckstead, Author
Mary L. Kozub, Author

Subtitled: A reference guide to public & private records. **Pages:** 210. **Publication date:** 1984. **Price:** $12.95. **ISBN:** 0-942916-05-0.

Indiana

Genealogist's Guide to the Allen County Public Library

Watermill Publications
2238 Cimarron Pass
Fort Wayne, IN 46815
Phone: (219)493-1735
Karen B. Cavanaugh

Pages: 100. **Publication date:** 1989. **Price:** $16.95 (paper). **ISBN:** 0-3184-3234-X.

Manual for Indiana Genealogical Research

Genealogy Unlimited, Inc.
PO Box 537
Orem, UT 84059-0537
Phone: (801)226-8971
Toll-Free: 800-666-4363
Pat Gooldy
Ray Gooldy

Covers: History, federal, and state sources; land, military, church, and vital records; published county histories; newspapers; libraries; societies; colleges and universities; Black history. **Pages:** 94. **Price:** $15.00.

Searching in Indiana

ISC Publications
Independent Search Consultants, Inc.
PO Box 10857
Costa Mesa, CA 92627
Mickey D. Carty, Author

Subtitled: A reference guide to public & private records. **Pages:** 278. **Publication date:** 1985. **Price:** $14.95. **ISBN:** 0-94916-06-9.

Kentucky

Blue Grass Roots

Kentucky Genealogical Society, Inc.
PO Box 153
Frankfort, KY 40602
Landon Wills, Editor
Ilene Wills, Editor

Description: Publishes transcriptions, abstractions, and annotations of Kentucky public records of genealogical research value, as well as information on research sources, tips, and techniques. **First published:** 1973. **Audience:** Society members, libraries, and other societies. **Frequency:** 4/yr. **Indexed:** Annually. **Circulation** 2,150. **Price:** Included in membership. **Remarks:** Also available in microform. Cumulative index (1973-1984) is available for $15. Original issues (1973-1984) available on a roll of microfilm for $15.

Kentucky Ancestors

Kentucky Historical Society
Old State House
PO Box H
Frankfort, KY 40602-2108
Phone: (502)564-3016
Fax: (502)564-4701

Description: Features Kentucky family history. **Type:** Journal. **First published:** 1965. **Frequency:** Quarterly. **Subscription:**

$25.00 members of Kentucky Historical Society; $30.00 nonmembers.

Kentucky Ancestry

Ancestry
PO Box 476
Salt Lake City, UT 84110
Roseann Reinemuth Hogan, Author

Subtitled: A guide to genealogical and historical research. **Covers:** Kentucky. **Description:** Outlines resources in Kentucky libraries and archives, special subjects (vital records, county tax records, women's records, African-American records, secondary sources). **Indexes:** General. **Pages:** 388. **Publication date:** 1992. **Price:** $19.95 plus $2.50 shipping and handling. **Send orders to:** Publisher. **Also includes:** Maps; bibliographies; Kentucky journals; an inventory of microfilmed county records available at the Kentucky Department of Libraries and Archives, the Kentucky Historical Society, and the University of Kentucky Library; and a county-by-county survey of existing records types, including categories of records destroyed by fire, flood, etc.

Kentucky Genealogical Research

Ancestry
PO Box 476
Salt Lake City, UT 84110-0476
Toll-Free: 800-531-1790
Fax: (801)531-1798
George K. Schweitzer, Author

Description: Presents information about most of the principal sources used by anyone beginning to search for an ancestor who lived in Kentucky. **Type:** Book. **Pages:** 156. **Price:** $12.00 (Members, $10.50). **ISBN:** 0-913857-02-5.

Maryland

Genealogical Research in Maryland: A Guide

Maryland Historical Society Genealogical Committee
201 W. Monument Street
Baltimore, MD 21201
Phone: (301)685-3750
Mary K. Meyer, Author

Covers: Describes vital records, tax lists, military records, and various libraries and archives Maryland and their holdings. **Publication includes:** All the addresses of genealogical and historical societies in the state and a bibliography of Maryland genealogical source records. **Pages:** 117. **Publication date:** 1992, fourth edition. **Price:** $12.50. **Remarks:** Also available from Pipe Creek Publications, 5179 Perry Road, Mount Airy, MD 21771, (410)875-2824.

Maryland Genealogical Society Newsletter

Maryland Genealogical Society
201 N Monument St.
Baltimore, MD 21201
Phone: (301)685-3750
Ella Rowe, Editor

Description: Publishes news of the Society, its members, and its activities. Contains information on the location and availability of genealogical research resources such as tombstone inscriptions, wills, marriage records, and materials available in specific collections or regions of the U.S. Recurring features include news of other genealogical societies. **First published:** January 1974. **Frequency:** 4/yr. **Circulation** 1,400. **Price:** Included in membership.

Massachusetts

Massachusetts Genealogical Research

Ancestry
PO Box 476
Salt Lake City, UT 84110-0476
Toll-Free: 800-531-1790
Fax: (801)531-1798
George K. Schweitzer, Author

Description: Presents information about most of the principal sources used by anyone beginning to search for an ancestor who lived in Massachusetts. **Type:** Book. **Pages:** 281. **Price:** $12.00 (Members, $10.50). **ISBN:** 0-913857-12-2.

Michigan

1870 Annuity Payrolls of the Ottawas and Chippewas of Michigan

National Archives and Records Administration
Publications Division
7th St. & Pennsylvania Ave.
Washington, DC 20408
Phone: (202)501-5240
Fax: (202)501-5239

1908 Census of the Chippewa Indians in Michigan

National Archives and Records Administration
Publications Division
7th St. & Pennsylvania Ave., NW
Washington, DC 20408
Phone: (202)501-5240
Fax: (202)501-5239
Horace B. Durant, Compiler

1910 Annuity Roll of Ottawas and Chippewas in Michigan

U.S. Bureau of Indian Affairs, Group 75
Charles K. Dickson, Compiler

Detroit Society for Genealogical Research Magazine

Detroit Society for Genealogical Research Inc.
The Burton Historical Collection
Detroit Public Library
5201 Woodward Ave. & Kirby
Detroit, MI 48202
Ruth S. Kennedy, Editor

Type: Magazine. **First published:** 1936. **Frequency:** Quarterly. **Circulation** 1,100. **Subscription:** $15.00. **ISSN:** 0011-9687.

Genealogical Guide to the Burton Historical Collection, Detroit Public Library

Ancestry
PO Box 476
Salt Lake City, UT 84110
Phone: (801)531-1790
Toll-Free: 800-531-1790
Joseph Oldenburg, Author

Pages: 128. **Publication date:** 1988. **Price:** $7.95.

Methodist Indian Ministries in Michigan, 1830-1990

Michigan Area United Methodist Historical Society
Learning Resource Center
PO Box 6247
Grand Rapids, MI 49516-6247
Dorothy Reuter, Author
Ronald A. Brunger, Contributor

Description: Describes the history of the engagements between early Methodists and the Indians of Michigan. **Pages:** 434. **Publication date:** 1993. **Price:** $13.00, plus $2.50 S&H.

Michigan Ethnic Directory

Michigan Ethnic Heritage Studies Center
60 Farnsworth/Rackham Bldg., Ste. 120
Detroit, MI 48202
Phone: (313)832-7400
Fax: (313)831-5633
Otto Feinstein, Editor-in-Chief

Description: About 2,000 ethnic organizations and institutions in Michigan, including churches, clubs, consulates, fraternal and political organizations, and media. **Type:** Directory. **Entries include:** Organization name, address, phone, name and title of contact, description of activities and purpose. **Arrangement:** Classified by ethnic group. **Indexes:** Organization name. **Pages:** 118. **Frequency:** Irregular; previous edition October 1991; latest edition 1994. **Price:** $15.00. **Remarks:** Supersedes *Peoples of Michigan: A Two Volume Guide to Ethnic Michigan.*

Michigan Genealogy Sources and Resources

Genealogical Publishing
1001 N. Calvert St.
Baltimore, MD 21202
Phone: (301)837-8271
Toll-Free: 800-296-6687
Fax: (410)752-8492
Carol McGinnis, Author

Frequency: Irregular; latest edition fall 1989 (now out of print); new edition expected 1994. **Price:** $18.00 (1989 edition), postpaid.

Ottawa and Chippewa Indians of Michigan, 1855-1868

Heritage Books
1540-E Pointer Ridge Pl.
Bowie, MD 20716
Toll-Free: 800-398-7709
Fax: (301)390-7153
Raymond C. Lantz, Author

Subtitled: Including Some Swan Creek and Black River of the Sac and Fox Agency for the Years 1857, 1858, and 1865. **Covers:** The 1855 Ottawa and Chippewa Annuity Rolls, the Sault Ste. Marie Chippewa Annuity Roll, per capita rolls, and the goods and supplies lists. The annuity and per capita rolls were taken to determine eligibility of persons of Indian descent to receive money, as a result of congressional legislation and treaties signed between Indian tribes and the U.S. government. **Type:** Book. **Arrangement:** By band. **Pages:** 116. **Publication date:** 1992. **Price:** $14.00 (paper). **Remarks:** Information from the records of the Department of the Interior, Bureau of Indian Affairs, part of the holdings of the National Archives in Washington, DC.

Ottawa and Chippewa Indians of Michigan, 1870-1909

Heritage Books
1540-E Pointer Ridge Pl.
Bowie, MD 20716
Toll-Free: 800-398-7709
Fax: (301)390-7153
Raymond C. Lantz

Covers: Three censuses taken by the Bureau of Indian Affairs: 1870 census and annuity payment records of the Grand River, Mackinac, Sault Ste. Marie, and Traverse Bands of Ottawa and Chippewa Indians of MI; persons in the 1870 enumeration, and all their known descendants, found living on a special enumeration made 4 March 1907; children born after 4 March 1907, but before 1 August 1909 with name, date of birth, parents, etc. **Type:** Book. **Pages:** 288. **Publication date:** 1991. **Price:** $21.00.

Potawatomi Indians of Michigan, 1843-1904, Including some Ottawa and Chippewa, 1843-1866, and Potawatomi of Indiana, 1869 and 1885

Heritage Books
1540-E Pointer Ridge Pl.
Bowie, MD 20716
Toll-Free: 800-398-7709
Fax: (301)390-7153
Raymond C. Lantz

Covers: Annuity rolls on the Ottawa, Chippewa, and Potawatomi of Michigan, 1843-1866; the Potawatomi of Huron annuity rolls for 1861 (4th quarter), 1874-1880, and 1882-1889; Potawatomi of Indiana and Michigan annuity roll (3rd quarter) 1869; the Potawatomi of Indiana and Michigan 1895 census; and the Potawatomi of Michigan 1904 census. **Type:** Book. **Entries include:** Some or all of the following: name; number of men, women, and children in the household; annuity amount; relationships; age; and sex. Roll numbers are given. **Pages:** 92. **Publication date:** 1992. **Price:** $14.00 (paper).

Minnesota

Chippewa and Dakota Indians: A Subject Catalog of Books, Pamphlets, Periodical Articles, and Manuscripts in the Minnesota Historical Society

Minnesota Historical Society
345 Kellogg Blvd. W.
St. Paul, MN 55102-7436
Phone: (612)296-2264
Fax: (612)297-7436

Missouri

Missouri Genealogical Records & Abstracts

Heritage Books
1540-E Pointer Ridge Pl.
Bowie, MD 20716
Toll-Free: 800-398-7709
Fax: (301)390-7153
Sherida K. Eddlemon

Publication includes: Information on specific counties, and the state as a whole, i.e., marriage records, Spanish censuses, tax lists, estrays, letters at the post office, wills and bonds, jury lists, indictments, Indian trade records, cemetery listings, petitioners, animal marks and brands, slave bills of sale, French and Spanish land grants, military records, disaster victims. **Description:** Vol. 1: 1766-1839, 34 counties; Vol. 3: 1787-1839, 43 counties; Vol. 4: 1741-1839, 49 counties; Vol. 5: 1755-1839, 52 counties. **Type:** Book. **Indexes:** General. **Pages:** 336 (Vol. 1); 253 (3); 272 (4); 275 (5). **Publication date:** 1990 (Vol 1); 1991 (3); 1992 (4); 1993 (5). **Price:** $23.00 (Vol. 1); $20.00 (3); $21.00 (4); $23.00 (5); all paper.

Montana

New Race

Phillip Heritage House
605 Benton
Missoula, MT 59801
Phone: (406)543-3495
Ruth Phillip, Editor

Description: Contains genealogical information and family stories relating to the editor's ancestors and quest for her American Indian (Cherokee) heritage. Recurring features include letters to the editor, interviews, book reviews, and notices of publications available. **First published:** 1983. **Pages:** 10-20 pages. **Audience:** Individuals of East Coastal Native American descent. **Frequency:** Annual. **Circulation** 25. **Price:** $10.00/year.

Nebraska

Nebraska Local History and Genealogy Reference Guide

Sylvia Nimmo, Publisher
6201 Kentucky Rd.
Omaha, NE 68133
Phone: (402)331-2384
Sylvia Nimmo, Editor
Mary Cutter, Editor

Publication includes: Lists of about 450 genealogical archives and societies, libraries, and museums for genealogists in Nebraska. **Entries include:** Name, address or location. **Arrangement:** Geographical by county. **Frequency:** Published December 1986. **Price:** $35.00, postpaid. **Also includes:** Maps of Nebraska counties. **Former titles:** Guide to Nebraska Research. **Remarks:** Principal content includes citations to vital records, directories, historical publications, and other sources useful to Nebraska genealogists.

New Hampshire

Directory of Repositories of Family History in New Hampshire

Clearfield Co.
200 E Eager St.
Baltimore, MD 21202
Phone: (410)625-9004
Scott E. Green

Description: Provides a list of the major genealogy and local history collections throughout the state of New Hampshire. **Type:** Book. **Entries include:** For each of New Hampshire's ten counties, the addresses and phone numbers of the Register of Deeds and Registrar of Probate are given. Information listed under the towns and cities consists of the community date of foundation, mailing address and phone number of the clerk, prior names for that community, and a succinct listing of the prinicipal genealogy repositories. **Arrangement:** By county and immediately thereunder by municipality. **Indexes:** General. **Pages:** 61. **Publication date:** 1993. **Price:** $10.95 (paper).

New Hampshire Genealogical Research Guide

Heritage Books
1540-E Pointer Ridge Pl.
Bowie, MD 20716
Toll-Free: 800-398-7709
Fax: (301)390-7153
Laird C. Towle
Ann N. Brown

Publication includes: Several appendices which provide data on depositories within the state, a listing of manuscript sources, and the contents of several major series and periodicals published on the state. **Description:** Contains instructions on how to pursue research on New Hampshire families using sources both inside and outside the state. **Type:** Book. **Indexes:** General. **Pages:** 98. **Publication date:** 1983. **Price:** $20.50 (paper). **Also includes:** Maps.

New Jersey

Complete Public Records Guide: Central and Northern New Jersey Region

REyn, Inc.
Publishing Division
140 Huguenot St.
New Rochelle, NY
10801-5208
Fred D. Knapp

Description: Covers Bergen, Essex, Hudson, Hunterdon, Mercer, Middlesex, Monmouth, Morris, Passaic, Somerset, Sussex, Union, and Warren Counties. Begins with a basic description of types of records/indexes available throughout the state (land, court, corporate, election, etc.) and then explains where and how they are filed in each county. Contains detailed floor plans of each repository and explains computer systems where applicable. **Pages:** Over 178. **Publication date:** 1993. **Price:** $39.95. **Also includes:** Illustrations. **Remarks:** Also contains information on accessing motor vehicle/license information from all states.

Genealogical Resources in Southern New Jersey

Gloucester County Historical Society
17 Hunter St.
PO Box 409
Woodbury, NJ 08096
Phone: (609)845-4771
Edith Hoelle, Editor

Covers: Historical societies, public libraries, colleges, and other sources of records and information for genealogical research. **Entries include:** Name, address, phone, description of collection/records available, contact name, hours and days open, whether fee is charged, whether copier is available. **Arrangement:** Geographical by county. **Pages:** 30. **Frequency:** Irregular; previous edition 1989; latest edition 1993; new edition expected 1994. **Price:** $6.00, postpaid.

General Index to the New Jersey Archives

Genealogical Publishing Co.
1001 N. Calvert St.
Baltimore, MD 21202-3897
Phone: (410)837-8271
Toll-Free: 800-296-6687
Frederick W. Ricord, Compiler

Covers: References to about 7,500 individuals and to hundreds of special subjects relating to the founding and settlement of colonial New Jersey. **Description:** Index to the first ten volumes of New Jersey Archives; key to the historically important colonial documents published within. **Pages:** 198. **Publication date:** 1888; reprinted 1994. **Price:** $22.50. **ISBN:** 0-8063-1445-1.

New Jersey: Digging for Ancestors in the Garden State Genealogy

Detroit Society for Genealogical Research, Inc.
c/o Burton Historical Collection
Detroit Public Library
5201 N. Woodward Ave.
Detroit, MI 48202
Phone: (313)833-1480
Dr. Kenn Stryker-Rodda, Author

Pages: 40. **Frequency:** Latest edition 1984. **Price:** $5.00.

Personal Names of Indians of New Jersey

Patterson History Club
Patterson, NJ
William Nelson, Compiler

New York

Genealogical Resources in the New York Metropolitan Area

Ancestry
PO Box 476
Salt Lake City, UT 84110-0476
Toll-Free: 800-531-1790
Fax: (801)531-1798
Estelle M. Guzik, Editor

Covers: More than 100 facilities, including fifty-two government agencies and courts, thirty-two libraries, and twenty archives. **Description:** Discusses the records available for New York City's five counties, Long Island, Westchester, northern New Jersey counties, and the state capitals of Albany and Trenton. **Type:** Book. **Entries include:** Address, telephone number, and hours of operation; travel directions; geographic scope and time span of records; finding aids and access. **Pages:** 648. **Price:** $24.95 (Members, $21.00). **ISBN:** 0-9621863-0-9.

Guide to Records in the New York State Archives, 2nd ed.

New York State Archives and Records Administration
10D45 CEC
Albany, NY 12230

Description: Lists 3,200 records series, from colonial times to the present including land, military, probate, and state office records. Some records can be accessed on film, but many are only available at Albany. Appendix B lists all microfilm copies of local government records available at Archives. **Pages:** Over 500. **Frequency:** Previous edition 1981. **Publication date:** 1993. **Price:** $12.95, plus $3.00 P&H. Make check payable to SARA publications.

New York Atlas of Historical County Boundaries

Simon & Schuster
Academic Reference Division
15 Columbus Cir. 26th Fl.
New York, NY 10023
John H. Long, Editor
Kathryn Ford Thorne, Compiler

Description: The second volume of the Newberry Library's project to produce a 40-volume series of more than 3,000 U.S. counties. Introduction explains laws which have shaped county boundaries. Maps show changes and counties which are no longer in New York. No town boundaries are covered. Particularly valuable for northern, central, and western New York. **Pages:** 242. **Publication date:** 1993. **Price:** $50.00. **Also includes:** Bibliography; maps.

New York Genealogical and Biographical Record

122 E 58th St.
New York, NY 10022-1939
Phone: (212)755-8532
Henry B. Hoff, Editor

Description: Focus on New York state. **Type:** Magazine. **First published:** December 1869. **Frequency:** Quarterly. **Circulation** 1,950. **Subscription:** $25.00. **ISSN:** 0028-7237.

New York Genealogical Research

Ancestry
PO Box 476
Salt Lake City, UT 84110-0476
Toll-Free: 800-531-1790
Fax: (801)531-1798
George K. Schweitzer, Author

Description: Presents information about most of the principal sources used by anyone beginning to search for an ancestor who lived in New York. **Type:** Book. **Pages:** 254. **Price:** $12.00 (Members, $10.50). **ISBN:** 0-913857-11-4

Searching in New York

ISC Publications
Independent Search Consultants, Inc.
PO Box 10857
Costa Mesa, CA 92627
Kate Burke, Author

Subtitled: A reference guide to public & private records. **Covers:** Approximately 1,000 repositories of public and private records in the state of New York. **Entries include:** Record source name and address. **Arrangement:** Geographical. **Pages:** 270. **Publication date:** 1987. **Price:** $15.95, postpaid. **ISBN:** 0-942916-10-7.

North Carolina

North Carolina Genealogical Research

Ancestry
PO Box 476
Salt Lake City, UT 84110-0476
Toll-Free: 800-531-1790
Fax: (801)531-1798
George K. Schweitzer, Author

Description: Presents information about most of the principal sources used by anyone beginning to search for an ancestor who lived in North Carolina. **Type:** Book. **Pages:** 192. **Price:** $12.00 (Members, $10.50). **ISBN:** 0-913857-03-3.

Ohio

Cleveland Ethnic Directory

Nationalities Services Center of Cleveland
1715 Euclid Ave., Ste. 200
Cleveland, OH 44115
Phone: (216)781-4560

Description: Several thousand ethnic organizations, societies, cultural and political organizations, and performing groups in the Cleveland, Ohio area. **Entries include:** Organization name, address, phone, names, and titles of key personnel, subsidiary and branch names and location. **Arrangement:** Classified by nationality. **Indexes:** Subject. **Frequency:** Irregular; latest edition 1989.

Native Tribes of Old Ohio

Heritage Books
1540-E Pointer Ridge Pl.
Bowie, MD 20716
Toll-Free: 800-398-7709
Fax: (301)390-7153
Helen Cox Tregillis

Publication includes: Names drawn from treaties and old county histories dating before the turn of the century. Brief biographies of individuals. **Description:** The story of the Eries, who early inhabited the territory, to the later tribes before their removal west of the Mississippi. Specific Native American names are included. **Type:** Book. **Indexes:** Alphabetical. **Pages:** 129. **Publication date:** 1993. **Price:** $15.50 (paper). **Also includes:** Maps, illustrations from early records, county histories, and international expositions before 1900 and a list of resources consulted.

Ohio Genealogical Guide

Carol Willsey Bell, C.G.
4649 Yarmouth Ln.
Youngstown, OH 44512
Phone: (216)782-8380
Carol Willsey Bell, Editor

Covers: Location, content, etc., of land, tax, census, church, military, and other records in Ohio; includes lists of libraries, periodicals, etc. **Entries include:** Name of source, address, description of holdings. **Arrangement:** Classified by type of source or record. **Pages:** 120. **Frequency:** Irregular, latest edition 1990. **Price:** $16.25, postpaid.

Ohio Genealogical Periodical Index: A County Guide

4659 Yarmouth Lane
Youngstown, OH 44512
Phone: (216)782-8380
Carol Willsey Bell

Publication includes: List of publishers of about 110 genealogical periodicals. **Type:** Index. **Entries include:** Title of publication, publisher name, address, rates, and dates covered. **Arrangement:** Geographical by county. **Indexes:** Subject. **Frequency:** Biennial, spring of odd years. **Price:** $12.75, postpaid. **Remarks:** Primary content is a cumulative index of articles published on Ohio's counties and Bible and family records.

Ohio Genealogical Society Newsletter

Ohio Genealogical Society
PO Box 2625
Mansfield, OH 44906
Phone: (419)522-9077
Sunda Anderson Peters, Editor

Description: Fosters interest in people who helped to establish and perpetuate the state of Ohio. Connects the Society's 6,300 members and 100 chapters. Acts as a clearinghouse for genealogical information on Ohio families. Recurring features include news of research, a calendar of events, reports of meetings, news of educational opportunities, and notices of publications available. Also includes financial reports, listings of library acquisitions, computer genealogy articles, chapter addresses, and queries. **First published:** 1970. **Audience:** Genealogists and historians with Ohio interests. **Frequency:** Monthly. **Indexed:** Annually. **Circulation** 6,000. **Price:** $25.00/yr., U.S.; $33.00 elsewhere. **ISSN:** 1052-858X. **Remarks:** Only accepts member queries.

Ohio Guide to Genealogical Sources

Genealogical Publishing Co.
1001 N. Calvert St.
Baltimore, MD 21202-3897
Phone: (410)837-8271
Toll-Free: 800-296-6687
Carol Willsey Bell, Author

Publication includes: Records of the State Auditor, Clerks of Court, Court of Common Pleas, Children's Homes, Coroner, County Homes, County Commissioners, Probate Court, Recorder, Sheriff, Soldier's Relief Commission, and Treasurer; census records available for each county, a listing of the county's records on microfilm in the State Library, manuscript collections, newspapers, tax records, articles from periodicals, and published sources for that county. **Description:** Comprehensive guide to the genealogical records and sources in Ohio. **Entries include:** County creation date and the name(s) of the parent county; the county seat; the name and address of the county courthouse, library, historical society, genealogical society, archival district, and health department; a list of relevent land surveys (for land and deed research); the surrounding counties; and the names of all townships in the county. **Pages:** 372. **Publication date:** 1988; reprinted 1993. **Price:** $30.00.

Wyandot Tracers

Ohio Genealogical Society
PO Box 414
Upper Sandusky, OH 43351-0414
Nira Beaschler, Editor

Description: Provides historical and genealogical information on individuals who lived in Wyandot County, Ohio. Recurring features include news of research, a calendar of events, and notices of publications available. **First published:** March 1983. **Audience:** Genealogical societies and libraries. **Frequency:** Bimonthly. **Circulation** 350. **Price:** Included in membership.

Oklahoma

American Indian Resource Materials in the Western History Collections, University of Oklahoma

University of Oklahoma Press
660 Parrington Oval
Norman, OK 73019
Phone: (405)325-0311
Donald L. DeWitt, Editor

Bryan County Heritage—Quarterly

Bryan County Heritage Association
PO Box 153
Calera, OK 74730

Description: Gives genealogical information on individuals, including Indians who resided in Bryan County, Oklahoma. **Frequency:** Quarterly. **Circulation** 230. **Price:** $12.50/yr.

Forgotten Oklahoma Records

Gregath Publishig Co.
PO Box 505
Wyandotte, OK 74370
Phone: (918)542-4148
Toll-Free: 800-955-5232
Fax: (918)542-4148
Fredea Marlyn Hermann Cook, Author

Subtitled: Cherokee Land Allotment Book. **Description:** Contains microfilm information of records of the Cherokee Nation in Ottawa county, Oklahoma. Includes the roll number, name, post office, age, sex, blood quotient, acreage, land desription, and remarks. **Indexes:** Name. **Publication date:** 1992.

Guide to the Historical Records of Oklahoma

Heritage Books
1540-E Pointer Ridge Pl.
Bowie, MD 20716
Toll-Free: 800-398-7709
Fax: (301)390-7153
Bradford Koplowitz

Covers: Oklahoma's earliest white settlement and Native American records from the state's eastern counties. Commissioners' minutes, land records, probate records, civil records, divorces, marriages, criminal records, adoptions, elections, tax rolls, school records, oil and gas leases. **Description:** Identifies and describes public records which span the 1880s through 1920 for all county governments, all municipal governments for cities over 5,000 people, and for smaller cities of historical significance. **Type:** Book. **Pages:** 189. **Publication date:** 1989. **Price:** $20.00 (paper).

Index to Marriages, First United States Court, Northern District, Muskogee Indian Territory, 1890-1907

Oklahoma Genealogical Society
PO Box 12986
Oklahoma City, OK 73157
Phone: (405)348-0293

Oklahoma Imprints, 1835-1907: A History of Printing in Oklahoma before Statehood

University of Oklahoma Press
1005 Asp Ave.
Norman, OK 73019-0445
Phone: (405)325-5111
Toll-Free: 800-627-7377
Fax: (405)325-4000
Carolyn Thomas Foreman, Author

Oklahoma Indian Territory

American Reference Publishers
Ft. Worth, TX
Ted Byron Hall, Author

Publication date: 1971.

Smoke Signals

Ottawa County Genealogical Society
PO Box 1383
Miami, OK 74354

Pennsylvania

A Genealogist's Guide to Pennsylvania Records

Genealogical Society of Pennsylvania
1300 Locust St.
Philadelphia, PA 19107-5661
Phone: (215)732-6201
Helen Hutchison Woodroofe, Compiler

Description: Originally published over 17 issues of the *Pennsylvania Genealogical Magazine.* Arranged alphabetically by county. **Pages:** 464. **Publication date:** 1995. **Price:** $39.95, plus $4.00 S&H. **Also includes:** Appendix of county information (date organized, county seat, etc.).

Guide to Genealogical Sources at the Pennsylvania State Archives

Genealogy Unlimited, Inc.
PO Box 537
Orem, UT 84059-0537
Phone: (801)226-8971
Toll-Free: 800-666-4363
R.M. Dructor

Pages: 129. **Price:** $9.00.

Guide to the Manuscript Collections of the Historical Society of Pennsylvania

Historical Society of Pennsylvania
1300 Locust St.
Philadelphia, PA 19107
Phone: (215)732-6201

Description: Second edition. **Publication date:** 1949.

Guide to the Record Groups in the Pennsylvania State Archives

Pennsylvania Historical and Museum Commission
Box 126
Harrisburg, PA 17108
Phone: (717)787-2891
Frank M. Suran, Author

Pages: 84. **Publication date:** 1980.

Pennsylvania Genealogical Research

Ancestry
PO Box 476
Salt Lake City, UT 84110-0476
Toll-Free: 800-531-1790
Fax: (801)531-1798
George K. Schweitzer, Author

Description: Presents information about most of the principal sources used by anyone beginning to search for an ancestor who lived in Pennsylvania. **Type:** Book. **Pages:** 227. **Price:** $12.00 (Members, $10.50). **ISBN:** 0-913857-09-2.

Rhode Island

Rhode Island Sources for Family Historians and Genealogists

The Everton Publishers, Inc.
PO Box 368
Logan, UT 84323-0368
Toll-Free: 800-443-6325
Fax: (801)752-0425
Kip Sperry, Author

Covers: Getting started; historical chronology; evolution of Rhode Island; counties and major towns; sources of information. **Arrangement:** Alphabetical. **Pages:** 146. **Price:** $9.95. **Also includes:** Appendices.

South Carolina

Guide to South Carolina Genealogical Research and Records

Brent Howard Holcomb
Box 21766
Columbia, SC 29221
Phone: (803)772-6919
Brent Howard Holcomb, Author

Pages: 65. **Frequency:** Latest edition 1991. **Price:** $15.00, postpaid. **Also includes:** Maps of South Carolina counties, parishes, and district boundaries.

South Carolina Genealogical Research

Ancestry
PO Box 476
Salt Lake City, UT 84110-0476
Toll-Free: 800-531-1790
Fax: (801)531-1798
George K. Schweitzer, Author

Description: Presents information about most of the principal sources used by anyone beginning to search for an ancestor who lived in South Carolina. **Type:** Book. **Pages:** 192. **Price:** $12.00 (Members, $10.50). **ISBN:** 0-913857-08-4.

Tennessee

Cwy Ye: Cherokee Blood Newsletter

PO Box 2261
Chattanooga, TN 37422
Shirley Coats Hoskins, Editor

First published: 1983.

Guide to County Records and Genealogical Resources in Tennessee

Genealogical Publishing
1001 N. Calvert Street
Baltimore, MD 21202
Phone: (301)837-8271
Toll-Free: 800-296-6687
Fax: (410)752-8492
Richard Carlton Fulcher, Editor

Covers: Archives and libraries in Tennessee with genealogical records and statewide reference materials. **Entries include:** County seat, names and addresses of libraries and genealogical societies, public records, manuscripts, church records, etc. **Arrangement:** Geographical. **Pages:** 200. **Frequency:** Irregular; latest edition fall 1989. **Price:** $23.00, postpaid.

"Research in Tennessee"

National Genealogical Society Quarterly
National Genealogical Society
4527 17th St. N
Arlington, VA 22207-2309
Phone: (703)525-0050
Fax: (703)525-0052
Gale Williams Bamman, Author

Covers: Emphasizes the genealogical holdings of the Tennessee State Library and Archives and lists a variety of sources available elsewhere in Tennessee and the United States. **First published:** Volume 81:2, June 1993, issue of *National Genealogical Society Quarterly*. **Pages:** 99-125.

Tennessee Genealogical Records

Genealogical Publishing Co.
1001 North Calvert St.
Baltimore, MD 21202-3897
Phone: (410)837-8271
Toll-Free: 800-296-6687
Edythe Rucker Whitley, Author

Subtitled: Records of Early Settlers from State and County Archives. **Description:** Information abstracted from Tennessee records covering over 18,000 settlers. **Type:** Book. **First published:** 1985. **Indexes:** General. **Pages:** 393. **Publication date:** 1989, reprint. **Price:** $25.00.

Tennessee Genealogical Research

Ancestry
PO Box 476
Salt Lake City, UT 84110-0476
Toll-Free: 800-531-1790
Fax: (801)531-1798
George K. Schweitzer, Author

Description: Presents information about most of the principal sources used by anyone beginning to search for an ancestor who lived in Tennessee. **Type:** Book. **Pages:** 138. **Price:** $12.00 (Members, $10.50).

Texas

Genealogical Records in Texas

Genealogical Publishing Co.
1001 N Calvert St.
Baltimore, MD 21202-3897
Phone: (410)837-8271
Toll-Free: 800-296-6687
Fax: (410)752-8492
Imogene Kennedy
Leon Kennedy

Description: Covers nearly 200 years of genealogical records in Texas; describes what the records are and where they are located. **Type:** Book. **First published:** 1987. **Pages:** 248. **Publication date:** 1992, reprint. **Price:** $35.00.

Livingston's Directory of Texas Historical and Genealogical Organizations

Bee Tree Press
Box 135
Lake Jackson, TX 77566
Phone: (409)265-6342

Covers: Nearly 300 active historical and heritage societies, preservation, archeological, religious, ethnic, and genealogical groups within the state. **Entries include:** Organization name, mailing address, membership fees, titles of periodicals and other publications or transcriptions, projects completed or underway; listings may also include phone, hours for museum (if any). **Arrangement:** Alphabetical. **Indexes:** Geographical (including references to locations covered by an organization in addition to its own location). **Pages:** 60. **Frequency:** Irregular; first edition November 1984; new edition expected late 1989. **Price:** $12.50, plus $.69 shipping, payment with order. **Also includes:** County and town name cross-reference.

Virginia

Virginia Cemeteries: A Guide to Resources

University Press of Virginia
Box 3608, University Sta.
Charlottesville, VA
22903-0608
Phone: (804)924-6064
Fax: (804)982-2655
Anne M. Hogg, Editor
Dennis A. Tosh, Editor

Covers: About 1,300 cemeteries, cemetery recording projects in progress, and published and unpublished records in Virginia. **Entries include:** For cemeteries—Name, location, name of record keeper. For recording projects—Organization or researcher name, address. For published records—Title, publisher, location, bibliographic details. For unpublished records—Type of record, location. **Arrangement:** Geographical. **Indexes:** Geographical, cemetery name. **Pages:** 319. **Frequency:** Irregular. **Price:** $12.95.

Virginia Genealogical Research

Ancestry
PO Box 476
Salt Lake City, UT
84110-0476
Toll-Free: 800-531-1790
Fax: (801)531-1798
George K. Schweitzer, Author

Description: Presents information about most of the principal sources used by anyone beginning to search for an ancestor who lived in Virginia. **Type:** Book. **Pages:** 196. **Price:** $12.00 (Members, $10.50). **ISBN:** 0-913857-06-8

Virginia Genealogical Resources

Detroit Society for
Genealogical Research, Inc.
c/o Burton Historical
Collection
Detroit Public Library
5201 N. Woodward Ave.
Detroit, MI 48202
Phone: (313)833-1480
Robert Young Clay, Author

Publication includes: Lists of libraries, court houses, etc., that are of use in genealogical research in Virginia. **Frequency:** Published 1980. **Price:** $5.00, postpaid, payment with order.

Virginia Genealogical Society Newsletter

Virginia Genealogical Society
5001 W. Broad St., Ste. 115
Richmond, VA 23230-3023
Phone: (804)285-8954
Chris Hooper, Editor
JoAnn Nance, Editor

Description: Includes news of research, a calendar of events, news of educational opportunities, book reviews, notices of publications available, queries, and a column titled "Acquisitions at the Virginia State Archives." **Audience:** Historians, genealogists, and interested individuals. **Frequency:** Bimonthly. **Indexed:** Annually. **Circulation** 2,700. **Price:** Included in membership.

Virginia Genealogist

PO Box 5860
Falmouth, VA 22405
Phone: (703)371-9115
John F. Dorman, Editor and Publisher

Type: Magazine. **First published:** January 1957. **Frequency:** Quarterly. **Circulation** 1,000. **Subscription:** $20.00. **ISSN:** 0300-645X

Virginia Genealogy: Sources & Resources

Genealogical Publishing Co.
1001 N Calvert St.
Baltimore, MD 21202-3897
Phone: (410)837-8271
Toll-Free: 800-296-6687
Carol McGinnis, Author

Description: Describes the types of resources available, where they are found, and what information they provide for Virginia as a whole, for the 95 counties, and for 41 independent cities. **Indexes:** General. **Pages:** 505. **Publication date:** 1993. **Price:** $35.00. **ISBN:** 0-8063-1379-X.

West Virginia

West Virginia Genealogy: Sources and Resources

Genealogical Publishing Co.
1001 North Calvert St.
Baltimore, MD 21202-3897
Phone: (410)837-8271
Toll-Free: 800-296-6687
Carol McGinnis, Author

Description: Describes which West Virginia records are available and how they can be located. **Type:** Book. **Indexes:** General. **Pages:** 135. **Publication date:** 1988. **Price:** $18.50.

Wisconsin

"Research at the State Historical Society of Wisconsin"

Minnesota Genealogical Society
PO Box 16069
Saint Paul, MN 55116-0069
Phone: (612)645-3671
Paula Stuart Warren

Description: In-depth guide to the library of the State Historical Society of Wisconsin. **First published:** September 1993 in *Minnesota Genealogist,* volume 24:3.

Searching for Your Wisconsin Ancestors in the Wisconsin Libraries

Genealogy Unlimited, Inc.
PO Box 537
Orem, UT 84059-0537
Phone: (801)226-8971
Toll-Free: 800-666-4363
Carol W. Ryan

Pages: 100. **Publication date:** Second edition, 1988. **Price:** $8.50.

Outside the U.S.

Canada Research Outline

Family History Library-Salt Lake Distribution Center
1999 West 1700 South
Salt Lake City, UT 84104-4233

Covers: Canadian records available through LDS, and other archives. **Description:** Provides description of sources of Canadian records and strategies for Canadian searching through cemetery listings, census, family biographies, church records, court records, directories, land records, military records, periodicals and probates. **Languages:** English. **Type:** Outline. **Pages:** 48. **Publication date:** 1993. **Price:** $.75, plus $2.00 for phone orders (U.S.). **Send orders to:** Publisher. **Remarks:** Contains some information on Native Americans and slave records/underground railroad.

Canadian Genealogical Handbook: A Comprehensive Guide to Finding Your Ancestors in Canada

Wheatfield Press
506 King Edward St.
Winnipeg, MB, Canada R3J 1L8
Phone: (204)885-5731
Eric Jonnsson, Author

Publication includes: Illustrations, facsimiles, and maps. **Description:** Revised 2nd edition. **Pages:** 352. **Publication date:** 1978.

Everton's Genealogical Helper—Directory of Genealogical Societies, Libraries, and Periodicals Issue

Everton Publishers, Inc.
3223 S. Main St.
Logan, UT 84321
Phone: (801)752-6022
Toll-Free: 800-443-6325
Fax: (801)752-0452

Publication includes: Lists of genealogical societies, libraries, and periodicals throughout the world. **Entries include:** All entries include organization or individual name and address; periodical listings include frequency and price. **Frequency:** Annual, July-August issue. **Price:** $4.50, postpaid, payment with order.

Everton's Genealogical Helper—Directory of Professional Researchers Issue

Everton Publishers, Inc.
3223 S. Main St.
Logan, UT 84321
Phone: (801)752-6022
Toll-Free: 800-443-6325
Fax: (801)752-0425

Publication includes: List of professional genealogical researchers, worldwide; a listing fee is charged. **Entries include:** Researcher name, address, specialties; some listings may include additional detail. **Frequency:** Annual, September/October. **Price:** $4.50, postpaid, payment with order. **Remarks:** Researchers were formerly listed in ''Genealogical Helper—Directory of Genealogical Societies and Professionals Issue,'' now split into this issue and ''. . . Societies, Libraries, and Periodicals Issue,'' (see separate entry).

Genealogical Computing

Ancestry, Inc.
440 South 400 West, Bldg. D.
Salt Lake City, UT 84101
Phone: (801)531-1790
Toll-Free: 800-531-1790
Fax: (801)531-1798

Covers: Genealogical computer databases, bulletin boards, and interest groups in the United States, Australia, and Great Britain. **Entries include:** Company name, address, phone, requirements for membership, and description of service. **Arrangement:** Geographical. **Pages:** 48. **Frequency:** Quarterly. **Price:** $8.50 per issue; $25.00 per year. **Also includes:** Articles and information on using computers and genealogy.

Genealogy in Ontario: Searching the Records

Ontario Genealogical Society
40 Orchard View Blvd., Ste. 102
Toronto, ON, Canada M4R 1B9
Phone: (416)489-0734
Brenda Merriman, Author

Publication includes: Maps. **Pages:** 168. **Publication date:** 1988.

Indian Voice

Canadian Indian Voice Inc.
Vancouver, BC, Canada

International Vital Records Handbook

Genealogical Publishing Co., Inc.
1001 N Calvert St.
Baltimore, MD 21202-3897
Phone: (410)837-8271
Toll-Free: 800-296-6687
Fax: (410)752-8492
Thomas Jay Kemp, Author

Covers: Vital records offices for 67 countries and territories in North America, the British Isles and other English-speaking countries, and Europe. **Entries include:** Office name, address, phone, application fees, method of payment, description of holdings, actual application forms to use in obtaining copies of birth, marriage, divorce, and death records, and alternative record locations. **Arrangement:** Alphabetical by country. **Pages:** 430. **Publication date:** 1994, third edition. **Price:** $29.95 (paper). **ISBN:** 0-8063-1424-9. **Also includes:** List of national and provincial records repositories or key addresses of other instiutions which may be helpful for non-English-speaking nations as well as details about records created prior to statewide vital records administration. **Former titles:** Vital Records Handbook.

Inventory of Ontario Newspapers, 1793-1986

Micromedia Ltd.
20 Victoria St.
Toronto, ON, Canada M5C 2N8

Phone: (416)362-5211
J. Brian Gilchrist, Editor

Pages: 74. **Publication date:** 1987.

Other Media

This chapter provides the names and producers of other media sources of information, including on-line databases, CD-ROM products, and microfiche, which provide guidance or records of value to researchers whether interested in genealogy in general or in a specific ethnic group. Listings are arranged alphabetically by product name.

American Indian: A Multimedia Encyclopedia

Facts of File, Inc.
460 Park Ave. S
New York, NY 10016
Phone: (212)683-2244
Toll-Free: 800-322-8755
Fax: (212)213-4578

Description: Contains maps, treaties, and other documents from the National Archives covering more than 150 tribes of North America. Includes complete text of *Encyclopedia of Native American Tribes, Voices of the Winds, Atlas of the North American Indian,* and *Who Was Who in Native American History.* Also 1,100 illustrations, ''sound bites'' from Native-American songs and stories, and legends from over 60 tribes. **Type:** CD-ROM.

American Indian Periodicals from the Princeton University Library

University Publications of America
4520 East-West Highway
Bethesda, MD 20814-3389
Phone: (301)657-3200
Toll-Free: 800-692-6300
Fax: (301)657-3203

Description: Over one hundred periodicals each of which are also sold separately. **Type:** Microfilm in two parts. **Timespan:** 1839-1982. **Remarks:** Part 1: $7525, Part II $1515.

American Indian Periodicals from the State Historical Society of Wisconsin

University Publications of America
4520 East-West Highway
Bethesda, MD 20814-3389
Phone: (301)657-3200
Toll-Free: 800-692-6300
Fax: (301)657-3203

Type: Microfilm. **Timespan:** 1884-1981. **Remarks:** $895.00.

Ancestral File

The Church of Jesus Christ of Latter-day Saints
Family History Library
35 N West Temple St.
Salt Lake City, UT 84150
Phone: (801)240-2331
Jay Roberts, Ancestral File Specialist

Description: Directory contains genealogical information on 15 million individuals throughout the world, linking individuals into pedigrees indicating ancestors and descendants. Enables the user to search by similar last name spelling, exact last name spelling, and Ancestral File number. Includes the names and addresses of people who have contributed information. Comprises six individual compact disks. Typical record items: name, gender, birth date, christening date, death date, burial date, parents, spouse. Can show in one entry several events, unlike IGI which shows single events. The information in Ancestral File is GEDCOM compatible. Users can print in several different formats or download information onto diskette from Ancestral File for their own family records. The names and addresses of submitters are also available for records in Ancestral File so that research efforts may be coordinated and shared between genealogists. Users are encouraged to contribute their own efforts and findings so that they may be included in future updates. **Languages:** English. **Type:** CD-ROM. **Subjects:** Genealogy. **Updating:** Regularly. **Online availability:** Producer. Available as part of *FamilySearch,* which is made publicly available through the Family History Library and family history centers operated by the LDS.

City Directories of the United States

Research Publications International
12 Lunar Drive
Woodbridge, CT 06525-9957
Phone: (203)397-2600
Toll-Free: 800-444-0799
Fax: (203)397-3893

Description: Comprehensive retrospective collection of information on U.S. urban dwellers found in city directories. **Type:** Microfiche (directories through 1860) and microfilm (directories from 1861 to 1935). **Subjects:** City residents with their occupations and street addresses; churches, schools, and benevolent and literary organizations, along with the names of their leaders; local government officers; street guides; business listings and advertisements. **Geographic coverage:** U.S. (includes Washington D.C.). **Timespan:** Early nineteenth century through 1901. **Updating:** Filming continues from 1902 forward. **Remarks:** The guide *City Directories of the United States, 1860-1901: Reel Guide to the Microfilm Collection,* 487p., arranged alphabetically by city and chronologically within each city, with an index of cities and regions grouped by state, is provided with each order. For directories from 1902-1935, a temporary reel guide is provided. Film and fiche for specific states can be purchased separately.

Duke Indian Oral History Collection

Kraus Microform
358 Saw Mill River Rd.
Millwood, NY 10546-1035
Phone: (914)762-2200
Toll-Free: 800-223-8323
Fax: (914)762-1195

Description: 310 fiches.

Family History Library Catalog

The Church of Jesus Christ of Latter-day Saints
Family History Library
35 N West Temple St.
Salt Lake City, UT 84150
Phone: (801)240-2331
Jay Roberts, Ancestral File Specialist

Description: Contains descriptions of records, books, microforms, and microfiche held in the Family History Library. Features information on census records, birth records, family histories, church registers, immigration, military, probate and vital records. Typical Record Items: Author; title; publication date; publication year; publisher; notes; content. CD version allows searching by key words and spelling variations, locality, family name, or film number. 1992 list included 235,000 books; 1.75 million microfilms and 325,000 microfiche; maps, and other materials. **Languages:** English. **Subjects:** Genealogy. **Online availability:** CD-ROM: Producer. Rates/Conditions: Available as part of *FamilySearch*, which is made publicly available through the Family History Library and family history centers operated by the LDS. **Alternate electronic formats:** Microform: Family History Library Catalog.

FamilySearch

The Church of Jesus Christ of Latter-day Saints
Family History Library
35 N West Temple St.
Salt Lake City, UT 84150
Phone: (801)240-2331

Description: Contains five CD-ROM packages: Ancestral File, International Genealogical Index, Family History Library Catalog, Social Security Death Index, Military Index. Information on millions of names from around the world, since the Middle Ages. **Languages:** English. **Type:** CD-ROM packages. **Subjects:** Genealogy. **Price:** Approximately $2,000.00. **Updating:** Regularly. **Remarks:** See separate entries on: Ancestral File, International Genealogical Index, Family History Library Catalog, Social Security Death Index, and Military Index.

Genealogical Collection

Library Preservation Systems
4209 Woodcliff Rd.
Sherman Oaks, CA 91403
Phone: (213)538-2662

Description: Early California records. **Price:** $75.00 (three rolls of 16 mm microfilm). Individual records are available.

Genealogical Index of the Newberry Library (Chicago)

GK Hall & Co.
70 Lincoln St.
Boston, MA 02111
Phone: (617)423-3990
Toll-Free: 800-343-2806
Fax: (617)423-3999

Description: 8 reels of records or 109 microfiche, available in 35 mm film (ISBN: 0-8161-1317-3) or 4 x 6 microfiche (ISBN: 0-8161-1771-3). **Price:** $345.00 ($415.00 export).

Genealogy Forum

CompuServe Information Service
5000 Arlington Centre Blvd.
PO Box 20212
Columbus, OH 43220
Phone: (614)457-8600
Toll-Free: 800-848-8199
Fax: (614)457-0348
Dick Eastman, Forum Administrator

Description: Provides text files equipped with appropriate information on starting or continuing a family history search. Includes shareware programs to help trace birthdates, baptismal records, and marriages. Contains a message board, forum libraries, a surname exchange, and a member directory. **Languages:** English. **Type:** Bulletin board. **Subjects:** Genealogy. **Online availability:** CompuServe Information Service (ROOTS: $12.80/connect hour (1200 and 2400 baud); $22.80/connect hour (9600 baud)).

Genealogy RoundTable

GE Information Service (GEIS)
GEnie (General Electric Network for Information Exchange)
401 N Washington Blvd.
Rockville, MD 20850
Phone: (301)340-4000
Toll-Free: 800-638-9636

Description: Provides a forum enabling participants to share genealogical information and family anecdotes. Includes the Genealogy KnowledgeBase, which contains descriptive items on where to write for further information on a particular genealogical topic. **Languages:** English. **Subjects:** Genealogical and historical societies, family or surname associations, family or surname newsletters, books and magazines, publishers, professional researchers, sources of vital records and other information, computer interest groups, software, and research libraries. **Online availability:** GEnie (General Electric Network for Information Exchange) (GENEALOGY: prime-time rates: $18.00/connect hour; non-prime-time: $5.00/connect hour (300 baud), $6.00/connect hour (1200 baud), $10.00/connect hour (2400 baud)).

Guide to the Holdings of the Archives of Ontario

Ontario Ministry of Culture and Communications
77 Bloor St., W., 3rd Fl.
Toronto, ON, Canada M7A 2R9
Phone: (416)314-7611
Fax: (416)314-7635
Barbara L. Craig, Co-editor
Richard W. Ramsey, Co-editor

Description: 9 microfiches. **Publication date:** 1985.

Indian Census Rolls, 1885-1940

Scholarly Resources Inc.
104 Greenhill Ave.
Wilmington, DE 19805-1897
Toll-Free: 800-772-8937
Fax: (302)654-3871

Description: National Archives, Bureau of Indian Affairs, Record Group 75. **Type:** Microfilm. **Subjects:** Annual census rolls submitted by agents or superintendents in charge of Indian reservations. Informations reported varies but usually given are the English and/or Indian name, age or date of birth, sex, and relationship to the head of the family arranged alphabetically by name of Indian agency, then by name of tribe, and then by year (after 1916 most agents alphabetized the names). **Price:** $23.00 per roll (692 rolls). **Remarks:** Distributed for the National Archives.

International Genealogical Index (IGI)

The Church of Jesus Christ of Latter-day Saints
Family History Library
35 N West Temple St.
Salt Lake City, UT 84150
Phone: (801)240-2331
Jay Roberts, Ancestral File Specialist

Description: Provides more than 200 million names of deceased persons with the majority of names dating from the early 1500s to 1875. Comprises a parent index, marriage and birth index, and a similar and exact surname section. Typical Record Items: Name, event type, event year, event place, relative name, parent's name, child's name, birth/christening year and place, source information, description, batch and sheet numbers, and printout call number. Individual entries can be printed or downloaded. **Geographic coverage:** Over 30 individual disks containing information from every region of the world. **Online availability:** CD-ROM: Producer. Rates/Conditions: Available as part of *FamilySearch,* which is made publicly available through the Family History Library and family history centers operated by the LDS as well as through the genealogical and history sections of public libraries.

Military Index

The Church of Jesus Christ of Latter-day Saints
Family History Library
35 N West Temple St.
Salt Lake City, UT 84150
Phone: (801)240-2331
Jay Roberts, Ancestral File Specialist

Description: List of almost 110,000 servicemen and women who died while serving in the United States Armed Forces in Korea (1950-1957) and Vietnam (1957-1975). Birth and death dates, residence, place of death, rank and service number, and, in the case of those who served in Vietnam, religion, marital status, and race are provided. This index is on the fourth disk of the Social Security Death Index.

Native Americans and the New Deal

University Publications of America
4520 East-West Highway
Bethesda, MD 20814-3389
Phone: (301)657-3200
Toll-Free: 800-692-6300
Fax: (301)657-3203

Description: Key documents highlighting John Collier's work as Commissioner of Indian Affairs in designing and implementing the Indian New Deal. **Type:** Microfilm, 18 reels. **Subjects:** Files of the American Indian Association, the American Association of Indian Affairs, the California Indian Rights Association, interest groups, claims cases, the War Relocation Authority's internment of Japanese-Americans on Indian reservations, etc. **Remarks:** Subtitle is ''The office files of John Collier, 1933-1945.'' Accompaning the collection is a printed reel guide that lists all the files, their dates, pagination, and major correspondents. It includes a subject index as well. $2,140. ISBN: 1-55655-491-5.

Periodicals By and About Native Americans

University Publications of America
4520 East-West Highway
Bethesda, MD 20814-3389
Phone: (301)657-3200
Toll-Free: 800-692-6300
Fax: (301)657-3203

Type: Microfilm. **Timespan:** 1923-1981. **Remarks:** $4855.00.

Records of the U.S. Indian Claims Commission

University Publications of America
4520 East-West Highway
Bethesda, MD 20814-3389
Phone: (301)657-3200
Toll-Free: 800-692-6300
Fax: (301)657-3203

Description: Includes individual films of documents of decisions, expert testimony, transcripts of oral expert testimony, briefs, GAO reports, a legislative history of the ICC Act, docket books, and a journal as well as films arranged by ethnographical region. **Type:** Microfilm. **Remarks:** $18975 for collection; although films can be purchased separately.

Searching U.S. Census Records: An Invaluable Aid for Locating and Tracking Families

Family History Unlimited
3507 N University Ave, Suite 350 B
Provo, UT 84604
Phone: (801)375-2841
Jimmy B. Parker, Presenter

Description: Genealogical course presented on four audiocassettes. Includes workbook containing dozens of illustrations extracted from historical documents. **Subjects:** Content and availability of censuses, search strategies, and sources of additional information. **Price:** $75.00.

Social Security Death Index (SSDI)

The Church of Jesus Christ of Latter-day Saints
Family History Library
35 N West Temple St.
Salt Lake City, UT 84150
Phone: (801)240-2331
Jay Roberts, Ancestral File Specialist

Description: Contains the names of 39.5 million deceased people who had social security numbers and whose deaths were reported to the U.S. Social Security Administration (and whose families collected death benefits) primarily from between 1962 and 1988; some records date from 1937 to 1989. Comprises four individual compact disks. Typical Record Items: name, birth date, Social Security number, state of issuance of Social Security number, death date, state of residence at death and zip code, state where death benefit was sent and zip code. The Social Security Number will allow the researcher to obtain additional information from the Social Security Administration. On-line the researcher will find information on how to order a civil death certificate from the appropriate state. **Languages:** English. **Subjects:** Genealogy. **Updating:** Regularly. **Online availability:** CD-ROM: Producer. Rates/Conditions: Available as part of *FamilySearch,* which is made publicly available through the Family History Library and family history centers operated by the LDS.

Using U.S. Military Records: A Rich Source of Information for Genealogists and Family Historians

Family History Unlimited
3507 N University Avenue,
Suite 350 B
Provo, UT 84604

Phone: (801)375-2841
Jimmy B. Parker, Presenter

Description: Genealogical course consisting of four audiocassettes. Includes a workbook containing several illustrations extracted from historical documents. **Subjects:** History of conflicts in North America; discussion of the probability that an ancestor served in the military; content and availability of colonial, state, and national military records; and search strategies. **Price:** $75.00.

Part III
Indexes

Author Index

This index provides an alphabetical, letter-by-letter arrangement of all authors, editors, and producers listed in Part II.

N

O

P

R

S

T

U

W

Title and Organization Index

This index provides an alphabetical, word-by-word arrangement of all titles, products, organizations, archives, and libraries listed in Part II.

A

B

C

G

H

M

N

U

Y

Subject Index

This index provides an alphabetical arrangement of organizations, publications, subjects, and other entities that are discussed in Part I.

A

B

C

D

S

T

U

V

W

Y

Z